THE
SIERRA CLUB
GUIDE TO
THE
NATURAL AREAS
OF NEW MEXICO,
ARIZONA,
AND NEVADA

OTHER NATURAL AREAS GUIDES

Guide to the Natural Areas of the Eastern United States

Guide to the Natural Areas of California

Guide to the Natural Areas of Oregon and Washington

Guide to the Natural Areas of Colorado and Utah

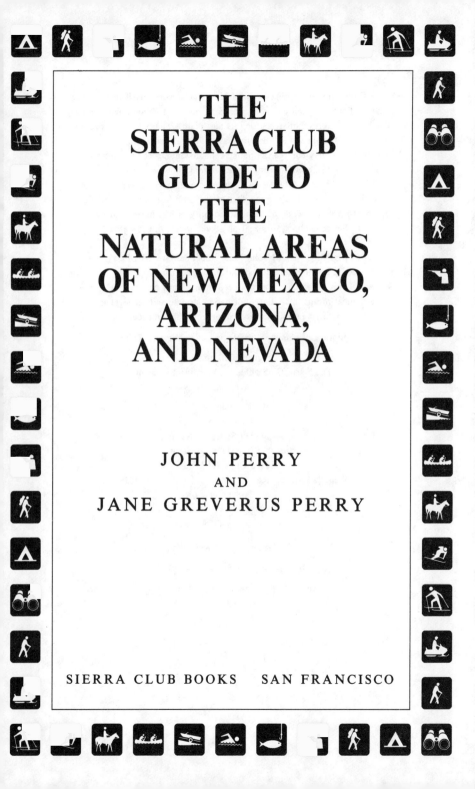

THE SIERRA CLUB GUIDE TO THE NATURAL AREAS OF NEW MEXICO, ARIZONA, AND NEVADA

JOHN PERRY
AND
JANE GREVERUS PERRY

SIERRA CLUB BOOKS   SAN FRANCISCO

The Sierra Club, founded in 1892 by John Muir, has devoted itself to the study and protection of the earth's scenic and ecological resources—mountains, wetlands, woodlands, wild shores and rivers, deserts and plains. The publishing program of the Sierra Club offers books to the public as a nonprofit educational service in the hope that they may enlarge the public's understanding of the Club's basic concerns. The point of view expressed in each book, however, does not necessarily represent that of the Club. The Sierra Club has some sixty chapters coast to coast, in Canada, Hawaii, and Alaska. For information about how you may participate in its programs to preserve wilderness and the quality of life, please address inquiries to Sierra Club, 730 Polk Street, San Francisco, CA 94109.

Library of Congress Cataloging in Publication Data

Perry, John, 1914-
The Sierra Club guide to the natural areas of
New Mexico, Arizona, and Nevada.

Bibliography: p.
Includes index.
1. Outdoor recreation—Sunbelt States. 2. Natural areas—Sunbelt
States. I. Perry, Jane Greverus.
II. Sierra Club. III. Title.
GV191.42.S89P47   1986   790'.0979   85-18481
ISBN 0-87156-753-9

Cover design by Gael Towey

Book design by Lilly Langotsky

Illustrations by Nancy Warner

Printed in the United States of America
10 9 8 7 6 5 4 3 2 1

TO THE RANGERS,
FORESTERS, NATURALISTS,
WILDLIFE BIOLOGISTS,
AND OTHER MEN AND WOMEN
WHO CARE FOR OUR FORESTS,
PARKS, AND PRESERVES

CONTENTS

INTRODUCTION

This is a guide to the quiet places, where plants grow, birds sing, and the signs of man are few. It includes some of the least-known places in the United States, visited by less than a dozen people in a year, if any. Some of these little-known places are within sites known to everyone, such as Grand Canyon National Park.

All three states are within the fast-growing Sun Belt. Although they have many differences, all three contain arid and semiarid regions, high plains, mountain ranges, canyons, forests, grasslands, and wetlands.

Travelers who drive on main highways through the region don't see its diversity. Highway planners choose the flattest routes they can find, avoiding mountains and canyons. The deserts where many pioneers died are just fine for interstates.

Almost all Nevada is within the Great Basin Desert; its southern tip is in the Mohave Desert. Southwestern Arizona, about a third of the state, is within the Sonoran Desert; a strip on the Nevada border is within the Mohave; fingers of the Great Basin Desert project into Arizona from Utah. New Mexico has a small portion of the Chihuahuan Desert in its S central region, a tiny fragment of the Great Basin Desert at its NW corner.

All three states have fast-growing populations and ineffective growth management. All three have outdoor recreation areas that are crowded in season, but they also have many spectacular wild areas that are little known and seldom visited.

People congregate. In summer, residents gather at lake and mountain resorts, while tourists overtax facilities at Grand Canyon National Park. In winter, visitors from northern states find the deserts a refuge from snow and ice. In 15,000 miles of travel, we saw these crowds but never had difficulty avoiding them. Almost every evening, when we parked our motor home, we were in a delightful natural place and usually alone.

Is it harmful to publicize places that now have few visitors? The managers of parks and forests urge us to do so. Popular campgrounds, trails, lake shores, and canyons are suffering heavy damage from overuse. Dispersal may be the best hope for saving them.

We are sometimes asked not to publicize priceless places so small and fragile that more visitors would destroy them, and we honor such requests.

CHANGES

We are conservationists, environmentalists, politically active. What we see in our travels is horrifying. The Reagan Administration's purposeful ravaging of our public lands proceeds on an immense scale. Much of the damage to our National Parks, National Forests, National Wildlife Refuges, and the public domain is irreversible, a permanent depletion of our nation's wealth. On every field trip, we talk with the men and women responsible for land management. These people who have dedicated their lives to caring for these places are now required to aid in their exploitation and alienation. We share their feelings of rage, sorrow, and determination.

Some of the damage is sheer vandalism: roads slashed through pristine areas solely to prevent their designation as wildernesses. Some of it is "privatizing," transferring the nation's wealth to the already wealthy. Some is removal of effective controls over ranchers, miners, loggers, and others who use public lands for private profit.

Many of the sites described in our entries are under threat: a lovely canyon likely to be submerged by a dam, a waterfowl refuge deprived of water, a prospective wilderness handed over to coal mining. Should each entry describe the sources and strategies of such threats? Combining guidebook and polemic would serve neither purpose well. We write about the threats, but not here.

One threat *must* be mentioned: the large-scale theft of artifacts from archeological sites on government land. A BLM archeologist said his District alone has at least 10,000 such sites, only about 1,000 of them cataloged. More than half of those he finds have been rifled, not by casual hikers but by professional thieves, often operating with bulldozers and other equipment. Dealers, museums, and private collectors pay well for this stolen government property. Little effort is made to apprehend or prosecute.

Readers must also be told that the Reagan Administration is dismantling the nation's outdoor recreation resources. More and more we find the following changes:

- Trail maintenance funds cut off; trails deteriorating; some impassable
- Campgrounds closed or open for shorter seasons; plumbing unrepaired; trash uncollected
- No more campfire programs, guided walks, other naturalist activities
- Nature trails abandoned
- No printing funds for leaflets, trail maps, pamphlets, and other visitor information
- Recreation personnel assigned to other duties
- Public information offices abolished

The services and publications we list in each entry were offered when we made our site visits. They may not be there when you arrive.

An incidental effect is our greater difficulty in gathering data for these guides. Always, before Reagan, we received warm and generous help wherever we went. Now the responses are still warm, but the pressures are noticeable. Answers are often delayed and sometimes say, "Sorry, we don't have manpower to assemble this information for you." When we visit field offices, people try to help, but under handicaps. Many are working overtime without compensation. In a few offices, employees have been forbidden to respond to inquiries such as ours.

Our practice is to send each entry to the appropriate office, asking that it be checked for accuracy. In the past, the response rate was near 100 percent. Now it's about half that. Telephone calls bring in more, but some never come.

HOW WE SELECT SITES

We use the term *natural area* broadly, generically. We look for places where a visitor can enjoy nature. Many of these areas are roadless, some of them truly pristine, but we do not reject an area that has been logged, grazed, mined, or otherwise disturbed if the healing processes of nature are at work. Nor do we reject a wildlife refuge because its impoundments are man-made and feed crops are planted. When thousands of waterfowl and shorebirds endorse such a refuge, that's good enough for us.

Large National Forests, National Parks, and some National Monuments are automatic selections, as are National Wildlife Refuges. Most State Parks are designed for intensive use; we include one if it has a significant natural area. We mention a State Park briefly if it adjoins a natural area.

All three of the states covered in this guide have state wildlife management areas. They were not planned for public use, except by hunters and fishermen, but other visitors are seldom excluded and increasingly welcomed. We selected those outdoorsmen will enjoy.

THE PUBLIC DOMAIN

By far the largest areas of public lands are what remains of the undivided public domain: more than 12 1/2 million acres in Arizona, almost 49 million acres in Nevada, 13 million in New Mexico. These lands, administered by the Bureau of Land Management, are not subdivided into named units, like National Parks or Forests. They include some of the finest natural areas of these three states.

No previous guidebook describes them. No posted signs identify them. BLM has published maps for only a few areas, and some of those are out of print.

The Wilderness Act required BLM and other land-managing agencies to identify all roadless areas of 5,000 or more acres and to determine their suitability for formal Wilderness designation, which would close them to logging, mining, motor vehicles, and other disruption. These studies helped us identify the most interesting natural areas. We also recorded hours of interviews with BLM staff members who have hiked these areas. Then we went to see for ourselves, not every site but a good sampling.

These BLM entries have been named for mountains and other prominent features. Visitors will find no signed entrances or other identification and, except at a few recreation sites, no facilities. The sites have no resident personnel.

Most of these sites border on some kind of public road, usually unpaved. Most are fair-weather roads, suitable for ordinary cars in dry weather, but some require a high-clearance or 4-wheel drive vehicle. Of the three states, only Nevada publishes maps useful for backcountry pathfinding. Inquire at the BLM office or locally; you'll learn about current road conditions.

These millions of acres are yours to enjoy. Here you can drive, hike, backpack, ride horseback, hunt, fish, camp almost anywhere. In most places, it's unlikely that you'll see other visitors.

Much of this land has been leased for grazing, mining, and other purposes. Ranchers often fence the land they lease. Where public land has been fenced and gated, you have the right to enter, closing the gate behind you. (A proposal recently aired in Washington would give leaseholders the right to shut you out.)

How do you know you're on public land? In some areas, public and private holdings are intermixed. Indeed, we had to omit some fine sites because they are surrounded by private land, and BLM has no legal access. We've chosen sites with few if any private inholdings.

If a rancher orders you off, go quietly, even if you're sure you're on public land.

OTHER PUBLIC LANDS

All three states have large military reservations. A few of our entries are for sites administered by other federal agencies on military land. Some parts of some reservations are sometimes open to public use for some purposes; we don't include them. A noteworthy exception is Fort Huachuca in Arizona, where birders are welcome to seek the rare species frequenting its canyons.

In previous guides, for reasons that seemed compelling, we did not include municipal and county parks. We had to change policy in Arizona. Maricopa County's park system is far larger than all Arizona State Parks combined, and with far more extensive natural areas. Mohave and Pima counties also have large natural areas in their park systems.

WILDERNESS AREAS

The Wilderness Act required federal land-managing agencies to identify all roadless tracts of 5,000 or more acres and study their suitability for Wilderness designation. The Administration is supposed to recommend qualifying sites to Congress. If Congress approves a Wilderness Area, it is then legally protected. Logging and mining are prohibited; no roads may be built; motor vehicles are excluded.

Timber, mining, and other commercial interests oppose wilderness protection, and environmentalists have accused the Forest Service and BLM of foot-dragging. Each year some Wilderness Areas are added to the system. When we mention a Wilderness or Wilderness Area, thus capitalized, it is one designated by Congress. Many areas not legally designated have wilderness qualities. Mention of a *wilderness area,* uncapitalized, refers to one of the latter.

INDIAN RESERVATIONS

All three states have Indian Reservations. Strangers to the West often suppose these Reservations are federal land. They are not. Reservations are Indian lands governed by tribal councils. Visitors are subject to tribal laws and regulations.

Tribes differ greatly in their tourism policies. Some invite visitors to centers where they can witness dances and buy jewelry and other handicraft products. Some tribes sell hunting and fishing licenses.

We looked for Reservations where visitors can, without undue difficulty, enjoy some of the splendid natural areas these Reservations include. If a tribal council did not respond to our inquiry, we wrote no entry.

This is not a comprehensive guide to the Reservations. A resident with time, interest, and courtesy can become familiar with a Reservation, and, by understanding the prevailing policies, broaden his area of exploration.

HOW WE GATHER INFORMATION

Roughly a third of the information assembled here is available somewhere in print: technical reports, species checklists, leaflets, maps, books, pamphlets, reprints, hearing transcripts, and so on. Materials collected for this book occupy 16 feet of our shelf space.

Another third is in the files of state and federal agencies, chiefly in local and district offices. When our friends imagined we were hiking in the mountains, we were often combing through dozens of file drawers.

The final third we obtain by questionnaire, interview, and observation. In the past our 9-page questionnaire was completed for more than 80 percent of the sites. In the Reagan years, the yield has dropped below 35 percent. We rely increasingly on interviews and site visits.

We are often asked if we visit every site we describe. We have visited all the major sites and a good sampling of others. But the data we require couldn't be assembled at first hand in one or several lifetimes. We depend on the men and women who know them best, and we're indebted to them.

The task would have been impossible were we strangers here. We've visited these states frequently, over several decades, working on books and films, camping in the desert, hiking in the mountains.

HOW TO USE THIS BOOK

We have divided each state into zones. A zone map precedes each state chapter. At the beginning of each zone section is a map on which sites are spotted with key numbers, with a list of sites in numerical order. Entries are arranged alphabetically within zones. Once you have a destination in mind, the map will show what other sites are nearby or on your way.

Information in entries is presented in the following standard sequence.

SITE NAME

Parks are for people. Most parks have formal entrances. National Parks are closed to hunting and logging. Parks have more facilities, more supervision, more rules, and more visitors than forests or refuges. National Parks and Monuments were established "to conserve the scenery and the natural and historic objects and the wild life therein and to provide for the enjoyment of same."

National Forests are managed for wood, water, wildlife, and recreation, although critics charge imbalance. Campgrounds are less elaborate than those in National Parks and often less congested. Further, one can camp almost anywhere in a National Forest. Fishing and hunting are regulated by state laws.

National Recreation Areas give more emphasis to recreation, less to strict preservation.

National Wildlife Refuges are for birds and beasts. Some have visitor facilities, such as auto tour routes. Hunting is usually permitted, often in a part of a refuge and with special rules.

Public lands administered by BLM have many uses, including grazing, mining, forestry, and geothermal development. Most areas are open to public use.

ADMINISTERING AGENCY

Entries name responsible agencies, not parent departments. Addresses appear in state prefaces.

ACREAGE

Many National Forests and some other sites have "inholdings," land owned by others, within their boundaries. Entries note this when significant.

Acreages given for BLM sites do not measure the limits of public ownership. They refer to selected areas, often surrounded by other public land.

HOW TO GET THERE

Routings begin from points easily found on highway maps. For large sites, entries describe main access routes.

Don't rely on our directions. Only in Nevada can you get good backcountry road maps. If the routing leaves paved roads, inquire locally.

OPEN HOURS
Most, not all, National Parks are open 24 hours.
Some State Parks close their gates at night.
National Forests have no gates.
Most National Wildlife Refuges are closed at sundown.

SYMBOLS
Symbols designate the principal activities available. Most have obvious meanings; for example:

 Without the pack, day hiking. With it, backpacking opportunities.

 Whitewater rafting. May also include kayaking.

DESCRIPTION
Each site is briefly characterized: landform, principal physical features, vegetation. Beyond this, data resources varied. For some sites we could obtain weather data; others are far from any weather station. Some have detailed accounts of their flora and fauna; most areas have never been studied.

Such blanks can be filled deductively: one can infer the presence of species from studies of similar sites. We chose not to do this, inviting readers to do it for themselves. We provide rather full accounts of flora and fauna for the sites which could supply them. If Douglas-fir grows on a N-facing slope at 8,500 ft. elevation in one location, one can expect to find it on a similar slope not far away. The reader who studies entries will soon recognize common patterns and associations.

Many entries mention or describe plant communities. An interested visitor soon realizes that the plants of the Sonoran Desert differ from those of the Mohave Desert, and that patterns of vegetation change as one ascends a mountain. Common patterns are named in several ways: life zones, such as the Transition and Canadian life zones, and associations such as palo verde-saguaro and creosote-bursage. These are useful and valuable concepts. One soon learns that above a certain elevation one is likely to find ponderosa pine forest. Many entries, using data from site sources, state the elevations at which certain patterns occur.

Useful and valid as these concepts are, they cannot be applied mechanically. Patterns on N-facing slopes differ from those on S-facing slopes. Soils, microclimates, and past activities such as grazing and logging cause variations. Seldom are patterns sharply divided; they merge, and one should not be surprised to find a saguaro growing beside an oak tree.

Some of the species checklists we received seemed unreliable. A few listed species long since exterminated from those places. A few bird species were obvious misidentifications. Some species labeled "common" aren't common anywhere. Use of obsolete Latin and common names dated a few lists. On the whole, however, patterns were consistent and illuminating. We deleted only the most improbable items.

We use currently accepted common names for birds and mammals. Thus "myrtle warbler" and "Audubon's warbler" are now lumped together as "yellow-rumped warbler." The "black-tailed jackrabbit" is now "blacktail jackrabbit." And so on.

FEATURES

Noted first are Wilderness Areas and other large, natural portions of sites, followed by mentions of such outstanding features as canyons, waterfalls, and lakes.

Major recreation centers are noted, chiefly to tell readers where the crowds are.

Because our concern is with natural areas, we give little or no attention to historical sites.

INTERPRETATION

Visitor centers, campfire talks, guided walks, and other naturalist programs for visitors are conspicuously on the decline. Entries report the status in 1984, but further cuts are in prospect.

ACTIVITIES

Camping: Camping in parks is generally limited to campgrounds. One can camp almost anywhere in a National Forest or on the public domain. Entries note campgrounds and the number of sites. For details, see a standard campground guide.

Hiking, backpacking: Before undertaking anything more ambitious than a day hike on marked trails, we strongly recommend visiting the appropriate Forest, Park, or BLM office. They can recommend routes and destinations. Trail conditions can change overnight. Once, not taking our own advice, we hiked for half a day, found a landslide across the route, and had to turn back.

Horse riding: Some ranches and outfitters offer pack trips, with and without guides. Lists are usually available from state tourist offices, chambers of commerce, National Forest headquarters, etc.

Hunting: Prohibited in National Parks. Regulated in wildlife areas. Always subject to state laws.

Fishing: Subject to state laws. Endangered fish species occur in some waters; taking such a fish subjects the fisherman to a heavy fine.

Boating: The largest boating waters are Lake Mead and Lake Powell. The largest natural lake is Nevada's Pyramid Lake, but there are large impoundments such as Lake Havasu and Roosevelt Lake in Arizona, Elephant Butte

Lake in New Mexico, and many smaller ones. Boating is popular in all three states, and the more accessible lakes are often crowded in season.

Rafting: Float trips through canyons are spectacular experiences. On most, the rafting season is short, during spring runoff.

HAZARDS

Many site managers urged us to warn you about dangers lurking in the backcountry for the inexperienced. A hiker lost in the woods of the Northwest or Northeast can survive for days even if he carries no food or water. In the desert, a waterless day is life-threatening. For a solo hiker, even an ankle sprain can be. Several of the managers included rattlesnakes in their warnings.

Desert hiking isn't dangerous; ignorance and carelessness are. Each of the following books has vital information about desert hiking.

Ganci, Dave. *Hiking the Southwest.* San Francisco: Sierra Club Books, 1983.

Ganci, Dave. *Hiking the Desert.* Chicago: Contemporary Books, 1979.

Larson, Peggy. *A Sierra Club Naturalist's Guide to the Deserts of the Southwest.* San Francisco: Sierra Club Books, 1977.

RULES AND REGULATIONS

All sites have them. Parks have the most.

Pets are banned by only a few sites. In National and State parks dogs must be leashed; they are usually banned from swimming and picnic areas; often they are banned from hiking trails. Wildlife areas require that pets be leashed, except for dogs when used in legal hunting.

PUBLICATIONS

Entries list leaflets, maps, and other publications issued by sites. There was a time when you could write for such publications and expect to receive them. Fewer and fewer sites can respond. Your chances are best if you send a stamped, self-addressed envelope of suitable size. Many of the publications listed won't be reprinted when present supplies are gone.

REFERENCES

These are books and other publications offered by commercial publishers or natural history associations. Site-specific references are listed in entries. Those pertaining to a state or region within a state appear in state prefaces. Those pertaining to all three states follow:

General

Frome, Michael. *Rand McNally National Park Guide.* Chicago, New York, San Francisco: Rand McNally. Annual editions.

Hilts, Len. *Rand McNally National Forest Guide.* Chicago, New York, San Francisco: Rand McNally, 1976.

Riley, Laura and William. *Guide to the National Wildlife Refuges.* New York: Doubleday, 1979.

Tilden, Freeman. *The National Parks.* New York: Knopf, 1976.

Trimble, Stephen. *The Bright Edge.* Flagstaff: Museum of Northern Arizona Press, 1979.

Larson, Peggy. *Deserts of the Southwest.* San Francisco: Sierra Club Books, 1977.

Nelson, Dick and Sharon. *Desert Survival.* Glenwood, NM: Tecolote Press, 1977.

Plants

Lamb, Samuel H. *Woody Plants of the Southwest.* Santa Fe, NM: Sunstone Press, 1975.

Benson, Lyman D. and Robert A. Darrow. *Trees and Shrubs of the Southwestern Deserts.* Tucson: University of Arizona Press, 1981.

Elmore, Francis H. *Shrubs and Trees of the Southwest Uplands.* Globe, AZ: Southwest Parks and Monuments Association, 1976.

Dodge, Natt N. *100 Roadside Wildflowers of Southwest Uplands.* Globe, AZ: Southwestern Monuments Association, 1967.

Arnberger, Leslie P. *Flowers of the Southwest Mountains.* Globe, AZ: Southwest Parks and Monuments Association, 1974.

Patraw, Pauline M. *Flowers of the Southwest Mesas.* Globe, AZ: Southwest Parks and Monuments Association, 1977.

Dodge, Natt N. *Flowers of the Southwest Deserts.* Globe, AZ: Southwest Parks and Monuments Association, 1976.

Mammals

Olin, George. *Mammals of the Southwest Deserts.* Globe, AZ: Southwest Parks and Monuments Association, 1975.

Camping

Rand McNally Campground and Trailer Park Guide. New York, Chicago, San Francisco: Rand McNally. Annual editions.

THE
SIERRA CLUB
GUIDE TO
THE
NATURAL AREAS
OF NEW MEXICO,
ARIZONA,
AND NEVADA

NEW MEXICO

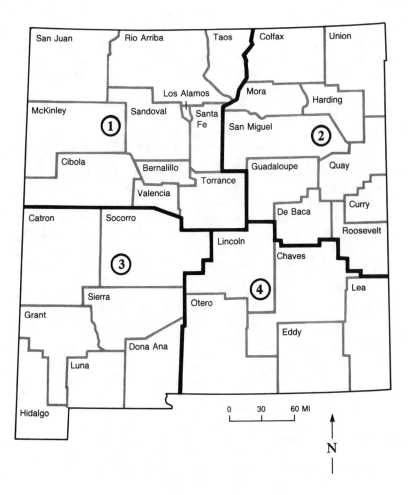

San Juan   Rio Arriba   Taos   Colfax   Union

McKinley   Sandoval   Los Alamos   Mora   Harding

①   Santa Fe   San Miguel   ②

Cibola   Bernalillo   Guadaloupe   Quay

Torrance   Valencia

Catron   Socorro   De Baca   Curry

③   Lincoln   Roosevelt

Chaves

④   Lea

Sierra   Otero

Grant

Eddy

Dona Ana

Luna

Hidalgo

0   30   60 MI

N

NEW MEXICO

The New England resident is likely to think of Arizona and New Mexico as alike, both of them hot and dry. They look much alike on maps, about the same size, both in the Sun Belt. In fact, they differ, and the differences are reflected in their growth rates.

As recently as 1940, New Mexico had more people. The Sun Belt boom began in the 1950s, and Arizona got most of it. From 1940 to 1980, New Mexico added 770,000 residents to its population, Arizona three times as many. Arizona's population is now more than double New Mexico's.

Arizona is significantly drier. Almost half of Arizona is in one of three deserts: the Sonoran, the Mohave, and the Great Basin. New Mexico has only the N tip of the Chihuahuan Desert and a small bit of the Great Basin Desert.

The southern Rocky Mountains enter central and western New Mexico from the N, forming two major ranges, the San Juan and Sangre de Cristo, continuing S in a series of ranges, oriented roughly N–S, diminishing in altitude. The highest country is in the Sangre de Cristos, several peaks over 13,000 ft. elevation. Although the southern ridges are lower than those of the N, they don't look that way, because they rise from lower bases.

More than half of the state is mountainous. In summer the forests of the high country are pleasantly cool, with splendid opportunities for camping, hiking, and backpacking. In winter, the lower mountains and valleys are inviting.

The eastern third of the state is gently sloping rangeland, much of it pancake-flat, descending from 6,000 ft. in the W to 4,000 ft. at the E border.

New Mexico has 155 sq. mi. of permanent water surface, and such rivers as the Colorado, San Juan, Rio Grande, Pecos, Canadian, Cimarron, and Gila. The Gila flows about 100 mi. through New Mexico, and into Arizona. Several of these rivers have exciting whitewater.

New Mexico's climate is mild, arid or semiarid, continental: abundant sunshine, low humidities, relatively large daily and seasonal temperature ranges. In summer, temperatures often exceed 100°F at elevations below 5,000 ft. In the hottest month, July, average monthly maximums range from a little over 90° at low elevations to the upper 70s in the mountains. Jan. average daytime temperatures range from the middle 50s in the southern and central valleys, to the middle 30s in the higher elevations of the N.

Average annual precipitation ranges from less than 10 in. in the southern desert and river valleys to more than 40 in. on high slopes in the N. Snow remains on the highest peaks through the summer, although the snowfields dwindle to mere patches.

About one-third of New Mexico is federal land, most of this in the western and central area. The largest acreage is public domain, administered by the Bureau of Land Management. Much of this is a checkerboard, alternate mile-square blocks of public and private land. We had to omit a number of attractive sites because they are hemmed in by private land; citizens have no legal land access to these public lands.

By far the largest solid blocks of federal land are in the National Forests, a total of more than 9 million acres. State lands make up 12% of the total area, but most of this acreage is in scattered mile-square blocks.

We found some large, roadless, relatively undisturbed areas of BLM-administered land, attractive for hiking, birding, and other outdoor activity. New Mexico has one National Park, Carlsbad Caverns. There are 9 National Monuments, White Sands being the largest. Five National Forests are wholly within the state, two others shared with Arizona. It has 4 National Wildlife Refuges, plus 2 others not open to the public.

New Mexico has 43 State Parks, most of them planned for intensive use, not to preserve natural areas. We have entries for 19. There are no State Forests. The New Mexico Department of Game and Fish owns 160,000 acres, most of it big-game habitat in the N part of the state, about 12,000 acres in 12 waterfowl areas. We have entries for 12 Game and Fish sites that offer opportunities for the nonconsumptive user as well as sportsmen.

GOVERNMENT OFFICE AND PUBLICATIONS

U.S. Bureau of Land Management
P.O. Box 1449
Santa Fe, NM 87107
(505) 988-6227

PUBLICATION:

New Mexico Public Land Recreation Map (shows the distribution of public lands, not much more; at the side are local maps of 6 BLM recreation sites).

U.S. Forest Service
Southwestern Region
517 Gold Ave. SW
Albuquerque, NM 87102
(505) 766-2401

PUBLICATION:

Recreation Sites in Southwestern National Forests (campground information for each Forest).

National Park Service
Southwest Regional Office
P.O. Box 728
Santa Fe, NM 87501
(505) 988-6375

New Mexico Park and Recreation Division
P.O. Box 1147
Santa Fe, NM 87503
(505) 827-2726

New Mexico Game and Fish Department
Villagra Building
Santa Fe, NM 87503
(505) 827-2923

PUBLICATION:
New Mexico Wildlife, Special Department Lands Issue, Aug. 1981.

REFERENCES

GENERAL

Ungnade, Herbert Ernst. *Guide to the New Mexico Mountains.* Albuquerque: University of New Mexico Press, 1971.
Armstrong, Ruth W. *New Mexico Magazine's Enchanted Trails.* Santa Fe: New Mexico Magazine, 1980.
Christiansen, Paige W., and Frank E. Kottlowski. *Mosaic of New Mexico's Scenery, Rocks, and History.* Socorro: New Mexico Bureau of Mines and Mineral Resources.
Young, John A. *The State Parks of New Mexico.* Albuquerque: University of New Mexico Press, 1984.
Nichols, John. *If Mountains Die.* New York: Knopf, 1979.

PLANTS

Nelson, D. and S. *Easy Field Guide to the Common Trees of New Mexico.* Glenwood, NM: Tecolote Press, 1976.
Fox, Eugene J., and Mary J. Sublette. *Roadside Wildflowers of New Mexico.* Portales: Natural Sciences Research Institute, Eastern New Mexico University, 1978.

BIRDS

Hubbard, Dr. John. *Birds of New Mexico, Checklist.* Albuquerque: New Mexico Ornithological Society, 1978.
Hubbard, John P. and Claudia. *Birds of New Mexico Parklands.* Glenwood, NM: Tecolote Press, 1979.

5 🐿 NEW MEXICO

MAMMALS

Findley, James S., Arthur H. Harris, and others. *Mammals of New Mexico*. Albuquerque: University of New Mexico Press, 1975.

Halloran, Arthur F. *The Mammals of Navajoland*. Window Rock, AZ: Navajo Tribal Museum, 1964.

Nelson, Dick and Sharon. *Easy Field Guide to the Common Mammals of New Mexico*. Glenwood, NM: Tecolote Press, 1978.

HIKING

Santa Fe Group, Sierra Club. *Day Hikes in the Santa Fe Area*. Santa Fe, NM: National Education Association Press, 1981.

BOATING

New Mexico Whitewater. Santa Fe: New Mexico State Park Division, 1983.

SKI TOURING

Beard, Sam. *Ski Touring in Northern New Mexico*. Albuquerque: Sam Beard, 1980.

ZONE 1

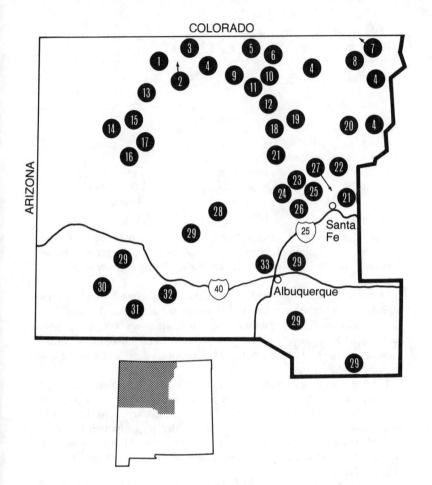

ZONE 1

Includes these counties:

San Juan	Rio Arriba	Taos
McKinley	Sandoval	Los Alamos
Santa Fe	Valencia	Bernalillo
Torrance	Cibola	

Zone 1 is the NW quarter of New Mexico. It includes Santa Fe, Albuquerque, and Gallup and two of the state's most heavily traveled routes: I-40 and I-25. Here we found more sites for entries than in any of the other 3 zones.

The zone includes the Northern Mountains and Central Highlands, the highest terrain in the state. On the mountains are three great National Forests, the Carson, Cibola, and Santa Fe. The mountains are high enough to catch up to 40 in. of precipitation per year, supplying numerous lakes and streams, including whitewater rivers. The Continental Divide crosses the zone from NE to SW.

The National Forests include a range of life zones from desert to alpine, with impressive canyons, gorges, cliffs, pinnacles, and mesas. Other sites offer other distinctive features. El Malpais is a dark expanse of lava flows, with cinder cones, lava tubes, and ice caves, bounded by sculptured sandstone formations including the state's largest natural arch. At Angel Peak, one comes unexpectedly to an edge where sagebrush flats stop and colorful badlands lie below.

Bandelier National Monument is best known for its 13th- to 16th-century cliff houses, but it has its own Wilderness and miles of backcountry trails. Hiking trails follow the Rio Chama from Heron Lake to its confluence with the Rio Grande, through State Parks and Wildlife Areas, National Forest land, and public domain. Rafting through the Rio Chama Gorge is sometimes possible. The Rio Grande is floatable for much of its length, with rapids to Class VI and beyond.

Navajo Lake is the largest body of water in the zone. The only developed areas are near the dam. From there to the Colorado border are miles of uncluttered shore, where one can camp, picnic, or hike.

Almost every road in the zone offers visual delights, with surprisingly rapid changes of scene, geologically and botanically. The road tops a rise, and the landscape ahead is unlike the one just left behind.

Some of the most attractive sites, especially those on lakes or streams, are seasonally crowded, and some have been degraded by excessive use. But one can still find splendid quiet places where nature has not yet been compromised.

ABIQUIU LAKE
U.S. Army Corps of Engineers
3,368 acres.

30 mi. NW of Espanola on US 84, then 2 mi. W on SR 96.

A flood control project on the Rio Chama. The permanent lake surface is 4,150 acres, third-largest body of water in NM. Elevation at the lake is 6,368 ft. The area is in the foothills of the Jemez Mountains, rocky, with arroyos, canyons, and bluffs. Low hills around the lake have a sparse vegetation of pinyon, juniper, cacti, and grasses.

Recreational use is chiefly water-based. This was the busiest site we saw on a Labor Day weekend. The lake is over 2 mi. long with several arms. The longest, Canones Creek, is a no-wake area.

Checklists of flora and fauna are not available. The response to our inquiry noted, "The area is rich in paleontology. The sedimentary formations in the vicinity of the project are full of fossils. Fossiliferous rocks in the surrounding mesas give evidence of amphibians and reptiles of the Mesozoic Era. . . . Several archeological sites have been located on the project. . . ."

ACTIVITIES
Camping: 36 sites. All year.
Fishing: Brown and rainbow trout, channel catfish, bass, crappie.
Boating: No hp limit. Ramp.
Swimming: Season May–Sept.

INTERPRETATION: *Nature trail.* Scenic, 1 mi.

PUBLICATION: Leaflet with map.

HEADQUARTERS: Drawer D, Abiquiu, NM 87510; (505) 685-4371.

AH-SHI-SLE-PAH
U.S. Bureau of Land Management
6,563 acres.

From US 64 at Bloomfield, 36 mi. S on SR 44, then SW on SR 57. Site is about 3 mi. N of Chaco Culture National Historical Park.

See entries for Bisti Badlands and De-Na-Zin. These three areas have similar geologic formations and scenic qualities. After study, BLM recommended the others for wilderness status. Ah-Shi-Sle-Pah was not recommended, because of anticipated future developments.

Anyone planning more than a brief, casual look at these areas should stop first at the Farmington BLM office for advice on which of the three to visit, considering road conditions and other factors.

HEADQUARTERS: BLM, Farmington Resource Area, 900 La Plata Highway, Farmington, NM 87401; (505) 325-3581.

ANGEL PEAK
U.S. Bureau of Land Management
275 acres.

From Bloomfield on SR 44, S 21 mi. Left on access road.

To say this site is 275 acres is misleading; almost all the surrounding land is public domain. This small area has been designated for recreation, but there are no barriers.

The introduction is dramatic. US 44 crosses extensive sagebrush flats, as does the entrance road for about 1/4 mi., with no break in the visual monotony. The road turns right abruptly at an overlook. The flats disappear. Standing at the edge of a precipice, the visitor looks out and down at colorful badlands extending as far as one can see. The scene changes from hour to hour with the angle of the sunlight.

The layers in shades of red, brown, yellow, lavender, tan, and gray were laid down under the sea eons ago, capped by a layer of sand that turned to stone. Wind, rain, and freezing have eroded the landscape into fanciful shapes, with multicolored fan-shaped slopes below the caprock. From the first overlook, one sees in the distance a flat-topped mesa. Nearby is Angel Peak, a castlelike formation on the horizon. In years past, the formation appeared to be in the form of an angel. Changes in the formation have altered it to that of a single-winged angel.

This is desert country: sparse grass, scattered shrubs, a few gnarled trees; in season, many wildflowers.

The road's condition beyond the first turn depends on how recently it was bladed. It was a dusty washboard when we visited, but not difficult. The Sage Picnic Area is near the overlook. The road then follows the rim, passing other overlooks and a picnic area, before arriving at the Angel Peak campground.

One can also drive to the bottom, where the view is only slightly marred by gas wellheads and their service roads. Hiking and hunting are not confined to the 275 acres.

Continuing S, SR 44 comes closer to the badlands. S of Nageezi, the road enters the badlands area, with colorful formations on both sides.

ACTIVITIES
Camping: 16 sites. No water.
Hunting: Small game.

PUBLICATION: Leaflet with map.

HEADQUARTERS: BLM, Farmington Resource Area, 900 La Plata Highway, Farmington, NM 87401; (505) 325-3581.

BANDELIER NATIONAL MONUMENT
National Park Service
32,737 acres.

From Santa Fe, N on US 285 to Pojoaque, then W on SR 4 to 10 mi. beyond White Rock.

Most visitors come to see the 13th- to 16th-century cliff houses of the Pueblo Indians, on the slopes of Pajarito Plateau. The main ruins can be seen in an hour's easy walk. Some visitors take the more strenuous Falls Trail that drops 300 ft. in 1 1/2 mi. Only a few venture into the scenic backcountry, 23,267 acres of roadless wilderness.

The Monument lies between two portions of the Jemez Division of the Santa Fe National Forest (see entry). SR 4 is its N boundary. Its SE boundary is White Rock Canyon, through which the Rio Grande flows into Cochiti Lake (see entry). Just to the NW are the Jemez Mountains, rim of a giant volcanic caldera. The Monument's geology is largely volcanic, steep-walled canyons cut 600 to 800 ft. deep through tuff and basaltic lava draining toward the Rio Grande. Elevations within the Monument range from 5,300 to 10,200 ft.

From the vehicle entrance on the NE boundary, roads lead to the campground and visitor center. Beyond, all travel is on foot or horseback. The most accessible area is Frijoles Canyon, extending NW. Cliff ruins extend for about 2 mi. along the base of the N wall. Indians chose this site because the canyon was then, as it is now, a channel of green in the desert. Average annual precipitation is about 16 in., but runoff is quick, as is evaporation. Summer days are usually hot, nights cool. Early summer is dry. Afternoon thunderstorms are common in Aug.–Sept. Fall is one of the best times to visit: moderate daytime temperatures, clear skies, little rain. Winters are unpredictable rather than severe. Snow seldom lasts long in the canyons, but at times it's deep enough for ski touring on the mesas, and significant snowfalls can occur as late as Apr. Spring comes late, with days likely to be windy and chilly until May, nights often below freezing.

Plants: Checklists of trees, shrubs, and flowering plants available. Pinyon-juniper and ponderosa pine forests predominate on the mesas, with mixed conifers on the mountain slopes to the NW. Canyon bottoms have tall cotton-woods, boxelder, Gambel oak, with shrubs including desert olive, choke-cherry, Mormon tea, sagebrush, gooseberry, wax currant, squawbush.

In 1977 a fire originating outside the W boundary of the Monument burned 15,000 acres of mesa forest in the N portion of the Monument. Vegetation in the burned area is slowly regenerating, illustrating the process of postfire succession.

Flowering plants of the *Upper Sonoran zone* include banana and narrowleaf yuccas, sacred datura, claret cup cactus, yellow pricklypear, cane cholla, New Mexico thistle. *Transition zone:* common mullein, lupine, Rocky Mountain beeplant, Apache plume, globemallow, evening primrose, red penstemon, goldenrod, gaillardia, salsify, Indian paintbrush. *Canadian zone:* Rocky Mountain iris, clematis, skunk cabbage, Canada violet, wild rose, blue aster.

Birds: Checklist of 185 species available. Seasonally common species include turkey vulture, red-tailed hawk, American kestrel, mourning dove, common nighthawk, white-throated swift, broad-tailed hummingbird, northern flicker, hairy woodpecker, Hammond's and western flycatchers, western wood-pewee, violet-green swallow, Steller's and scrub jays, common raven, mountain chickadee, plain titmouse, white-breasted nuthatch; house, canyon, and rock wrens; American robin, hermit thrush, western bluebird, Townsend's solitaire, ruby-crowned kinglet, solitary and warbling vireos. Warblers: Virginia's, yellow-rumped, Grace's. Western tanager, black-headed grosbeak, lesser goldfinch, rufous-sided and brown towhees, gray-headed junco, chipping sparrow.

Mammals: Checklist of 54 species available. Common: vagrant shrew; Yuma, long-eared, and long-legged myotis; silver-haired and hoary bats, desert cottontail, blacktail jackrabbit, least and Colorado chipmunks; rock, Abert, and red squirrels; golden-mantled squirrel, valley and northern pocket gophers, silky pocket mouse; deer, white-footed, brush, pinyon, and rock mice; mountain, longtail, and boreal redback voles; muskrat, coyote, raccoon, striped skunk, elk, mule deer.

Reptiles and amphibians: Checklist of 37 species available. Common: tiger salamander, Woodhouse's and red-spotted toads, bullfrog, leopard frog, painted turtle, spiny softshell. Lizards: collared, eastern fence, tree, short-horned; many-lined skink, plateau and Chihuahua whiptails. Snakes: striped whipsnake, bullsnake, western terrestrial and black-necked garter snakes, western diamondback rattlesnake.

FEATURES

Bandelier backcountry. 90% of the Monument is virtually undisturbed wild land. Most of it is a designated Wilderness Area. This rugged, scenic land has 70 mi. of trails. Features include the gorges of Alamo Canyon, Stone Lions Shrine, Painted Cave, pueblo ruins, and the White Rock Canyon of the Rio Grande. Longest round trip is 20 mi., a route that includes trails into and out of deep, steep-walled canyons. Permits are required to enter the backcountry. Water must be carried.

Open to hiking and backpacking in winter, but visitors should understand the hazards and requirements of wilderness winter travel.

Frijoles Canyon extends from White Rock Canyon to the base of the Jemez Mountains. Most visitor activity is from the visitor center NW up the canyon. The principal ruin area is within an easy walk of the center. Ceremonial Cave is a mile up-canyon. Most visitors go no farther. Beyond the cave, the canyon narrows. The trail continues beside the stream about 6 mi. to the Monument's N boundary.

Lower Frijoles Canyon, Falls Trail. Upper Falls is 1.3 mi. down Frijoles Creek from the Visitor Center, Lower Falls 1.6 mi. downstream, the Rio Grande River 2.4 mi. The trail is narrow, rough in places, with some sheer dropoffs. This is a nature trail, with numbered stakes keyed to a guide. Interesting rock formations, plants, sometimes birds.

INTERPRETATION

Visitor Center has exhibits, films, talks, literature. Open daily except Christmas; 8 A.M.–5 P.M. Labor Day–Memorial Day, until 7 P.M. in summer.

Campfire programs nightly in summer.

Guided walks, several each day in summer.

Self-guiding trail to the ruins in Frijoles Canyon.

Nature trail to Upper and Lower Falls.

ACTIVITIES

Camping: 72 sites, Mar.–Nov.

Hiking, backpacking: Trails to ruins and other features in Frijoles Canyon. 70 mi. of backcountry trails.

Horse riding: Horses are permitted in the backcountry, subject to special rules. No grazing is permitted; feed must be carried.

Boating, rafting: On the Rio Grande, here a whitewater stream. Outside the Monument boundary, but Frijoles Canyon is a take-out point for rafts. Overnight camping in the Monument requires a wilderness permit. *Ski touring:* Routes in the high country. Not every year. *Pets are prohibited on trails and in buildings.*

PUBLICATIONS

Leaflet with map.

Bandelier Backcountry trail map and information.

Information pages:

Welcome to Bandelier National Monument.

Campground information.

Interpretive services.

Use of Private Saddle and Pack Stock.

Creatures to Watch For.

Species checklists:

Trees and shrubs.

Flowering plants.

Birds.

Mammals.

Reptiles and amphibians.

The Trail to Frijoles Ruins, guidebook, $1.

Falls Trail Geology Guide.

REFERENCES

Dorothy Hoard's guide is one of the best we've seen anywhere, and a delight to read. Don't go without it!

Hoard, Dorothy. *A Guide to Bandelier National Monument.* Los Alamos, NM: Los Alamos Historical Society, 1983.

Evans, Harry. *50 Hikes in New Mexico.* Pico Rivera, CA: Gem Guides Book Co., 1984, pp. 66–75.

Ganci, Dave. *Hiking the Southwest.* San Francisco: Sierra Club Books, 1983, pp. 330–332.

New Mexico Whitewater, a Guide to River Trips. Santa Fe: New Mexico State Park Division, 1983, pp. 53–54.

HEADQUARTERS: Los Alamos, NM 87544; (505) 672-3861.

BISTI BADLANDS
U.S. Bureau of Land Management
3,968 acres.

About 30 mi. S of Farmington. SR 371 skirts the W boundary. A primitive road goes to the boundary of the restricted area; no vehicles are permitted inside. Pickup or 4-wheel drive recommended. Inaccessible in winter because of snow or mud. Inaccessible or nearly so for 3 or 4 days after summer rains. BLM says, "Inquire locally." (A paved road to the boundary is planned.)

Upland rolling topography and badlands terrain. Elevation is about 5,850 ft. Despite its remoteness and harshness, visitation to this designated Wilderness is increasing. It's fascinating: colorful and unusual rock and soil formations created by thousands of years of wind erosion. From a vantage point, one looks out over a sea of billowy mounds formed by rapidly eroding silt and clay. On the horizon and closer are many mushroom-shaped formations, their stems made of eroding sandstone, caps of more resistant shale.

The harsh environment supports little plant or animal life. Scattered vegetation includes greasewood, saltbush, cactus, sparse grasses. Animals include rodents and their predators: ferruginous hawk, golden eagle, coyote, various snakes. Petrified logs and dinosaur fossils record a more productive era. The area was once a rich swampland, populated by reptilian creatures, near the edge of an inland sea.

Summers are hot and dry. Sudden thunderstorms in July and Aug. provide most of the 8 in. annual precipitation. Winters are cold. Spring and fall are the best seasons for a visit. A hikeable wash runs SW from near the entrance through the most scenic area. Inlets entering the wash are worth exploring.

No water, campground, or other facilities.

NEARBY: De-Na-Zin; Ah-Shi-Sle-Pah (see entries).

PUBLICATION: Leaflet with map.

HEADQUARTERS: BLM, Farmington Resource Area, 900 La Plata Highway; Farmington, NM 87401; (505) 325-3581.

CARSON NATIONAL FOREST
U.S. Forest Service
1,491,121 acres; 1,590,594 acres within boundaries.

Four blocks. The three principal blocks are W, NE, and SE of Taos. (1) The W block, the largest, is crossed by US 64. (2) The SE block is closest to Taos. US 64 crosses near its N boundary. (3) The NE block is crossed by SR 3 and SR 38. In 1982, the Pennzoil Corporation donated 100,000 acres of its 492,560-acre Vermejo Ranch to the people of the United States. This tract adjoins Block 3 on the NE and is administered by the Forest. (See below, Valle Vidal Unit.) (4) Smallest is the Jicarilla block, 100 air mi. W of Taos, also crossed by US 64.

The Carson includes some of New Mexico's finest high country, a land of lakes, streams, and coniferous forests. The large block W of Taos is high plateau land with ridges, canyons, and mesas, elevations from 8,000 to almost 11,000 ft. The Cruces Basin Wilderness is in the N portion of this block, near the Colorado border. A small portion of the Chama River Canyon Wilderness is located on the SW edge of the block. The remainder of this wilderness is managed by the Santa Fe National Forest (see entry). Principal rivers in this block are the Rio Nutritas, Rio Tusas, Rio Vallecitos, and El Rito. Many private land inholdings are on the roads that follow these streams. The block has many small lakes and numerous streams.

Blocks 2 and 3 are to the E of Block 1, across the Rio Grande Gorge, in the spectacular Sangre de Cristo Mountains. US 64 follows the Rio Fernando de Taos across the N of Block 2. Much of this route is scenic, but most roadside land is privately owned. Fewer inholdings are along SR 3, which runs beside the Rio Grande del Rancho S from Taos, then SE near the Rio Pueblo, bisecting the block. The N half is crossed by several unpaved Forest roads that follow streams flowing from the W side of the Sangre de Cristos. Cerro Vista Peak is 11,939 ft. elevation; several others are above 10,000 ft. The Pecos Wilderness is in the extreme S of the block.

Wheeler Peak in Block 3 is the highest point in New Mexico: 13,161 ft. The Wheeler Peak Wilderness includes 19,289 acres in the SE corner of the block. The Latir Peak Wilderness encompasses about 20,000 acres in the N portion of the block. All-weather roads within the block follow Cabresto Creek, Red River, and Rio Hondo. There are many hiking trails between the Red River and Rio Hondo and within both Wildernesses. The W boundary of the block follows the Rio Grande Wild and Scenic River (see entry).

The Jicarilla Ranger District is a series of mesas, 33 mi. N–S, 6 to 10 mi. E–W. Elevations are mostly between 7,000 and 7,500 ft. Dominant plant species are sagebrush, pinyon pine, ponderosa pine, and juniper. The Jicarilla Apache Indian Reservation bounds it on the E and S. This district produces a substantial amount of oil and gas. Chief recreational uses are hunting and ORV travel.

With elevations from 6,000 to over 13,000 ft., the Forest has a wide range of climates. Annual precipitation varies from 12 in. to more than 40 in., annual snowfall from occasional dustings to 200 in. July and Aug. are usually the wettest months, June the driest.

Plants: No lists available. Almost two-thirds of the area is forested. Pinyon-juniper predominates at lower elevations, ponderosa pine and mixed conifers on the mesas and mountain slopes, with spruce in the zone just below timberline where snow remains into June. Wheeler Peak has interesting tundra vegetation. Much of the ponderosa forest is open, with grasses as the chief understory. Meadows, often fringed by aspen, are interspersed.

Birds: Checklist for species recorded in Sangre de Cristo Mountains, noting seasonality and abundance, is no longer available for distribution. The copy we saw showed "Common, as residents or migrants": turkey vulture, red-tailed hawk, northern harrier, American kestrel, blue grouse, killdeer, band-tailed pigeon, rock and mourning doves, great horned owl, common nighthawk, white-throated swift; black-chinned, broad-tailed, and rufous hummingbirds; belted kingfisher, northern flicker, yellow-bellied sapsucker; ash-throated, dusky, and olive-sided flycatchers; western wood-pewee, horned lark; violet-green, barn, and cliff swallows. Gray, Steller's, scrub, and pinyon jays. Black-billed magpie, common raven, American crow, Clark's nutcracker, black-capped and mountain chickadees, plain titmouse, white-breasted and pygmy nuthatches, dipper; house, canyon, and rock wrens; mockingbird, sage thrasher, American robin, hermit and Swainson's thrushes, western and mountain bluebirds, Townsend's solitaire, golden-crowned and ruby-crowned kinglets, northern and loggerhead shrikes, European starling, solitary and warbling vireos. Warblers: orange-crowned, Virginia's, yellow-rumped, Wilson's. House sparrow, western meadowlark, red-winged and Brewer's blackbirds, northern oriole, common cowbird, black-headed grosbeak, pine siskin, lesser goldfinch, green-tailed towhee, gray-headed junco. Sparrows: chipping, Brewer's, white-crowned, song.

Mammals: No checklist available for distribution. We saw an extensive list of wildlife species arranged by habitats. Mammals include badger, beaver, black bear, bobcat, coyote, mule deer, blackfooted ferret, several bat species, gray fox, mountain lion, yellowbelly marmot, marten, mouse species, muskrat, pika, porcupine, prairie dog, blacktail and whitetail jackrabbits, desert and Nuttall's cottontails, raccoon, mountain sheep, striped skunk; Abert, red, and golden-mantled squirrels; thirteen-lined ground squirrel, voles, weasels.

FEATURES

Pecos Wilderness: 24,736 acres, plus 198,597 acres in the Santa Fe National Forest. The Wilderness boundary is about 24 mi. S of Taos. The Visitor's Guide lists 34 points of entry on the perimeter, all shown on a good 1 in. per mile map. The Wilderness has about 15,000 visitor-days of use per year.

Established in 1955, the area includes Truchas Peak, 13,103 ft., second highest in NM. Within the area are 15 fishing lakes, 150 mi. of streams, many springs. Overnight camping is restricted on most lake shores because of past trampling. Camping quotas are applied at some popular destinations.

Average annual precipitation is 35 to 40 in., about half in summer showers, half as snow. May and June are generally dry. Afternoon thundershowers occur almost daily in July and Aug. Snows usually begin in Nov., but skis or snowshoes may be needed as early as Oct. Access to northern trailheads is often blocked by snow until the end of May. Daytime summer temperatures are often in the 70s, but some nights are subfreezing.

Permits are required for overnight trips.

Wheeler Peak Wilderness: 19,829 acres. Attractive, small, and accessible. Portions are heavily used; the Wilderness receives over 8,000 visitor-days of use annually. Trail access is from the N. The 13,161-ft. peak and its tundra vegetation are the chief attraction, but area also has three small lakes in glacial cirques, several streams, broad alpine meadows, and dense forest. Tundra plant species include Indian paintbrush, moss campion, bluebell, stonecrop. Ptarmigan are sometimes seen near timberline. Mammals occurring at high elevations include pika and marmot. Other mammals include mountain lion, black bear, elk, mule deer.

Climate is similar to that of the high country in the Pecos Wilderness.

Latir Peak Wilderness: 20,000 acres. At the N end of Block 3. Forest Road 134 follows the S boundary of the area. A spur, 34A, extends N to Cabresto Lake; here is a campground and wilderness trailhead. The Wilderness includes a portion of the Sangre de Cristo Range, with 3 peaks over 12,000 ft. elevation. The area attained Wilderness status in 1980 and has yet to be discovered by many visitors. Most species of wildlife indigenous to the Hudsonian zone of the southern Rocky Mountains are to be found in this remote and spectacular area.

Cruces Basin Wilderness: 18,000 acres. In the NW corner of Block 1, N of Forest Road 87. Trailheads on 87 and a spur, Forest Road 572. A rolling mountain plateau, elevations to 10,000 ft. Ridge tops have aspen and spruce-fir. Bottoms are open grassland used for grazing. Summer range for elk. Most of the area is drained by Beaver Creek, flowing NE. Lightly visited.

Valle Vidal Unit: In 1982 the Pennzoil Corporation donated approximately 100,000 acres adjoining Block 3 to the U.S. people. This unit is now managed as part of the Carson National Forest, subject to outstanding mineral rights. Protection and enhancement of wildlife habitat is the primary management goal, with other resource production secondary.

The Unit includes E slopes of the Sangre de Cristo Range. Much of the area is forested with stands of mixed conifers, aspen, and ponderosa pine. The wide Valle Vidal is located in the S central part of the Unit. Elevations range from 7,700 ft. to 12,584 ft. at Little Costilla Peak. Major fishing streams include Costilla Creek, Comanche Creek, and Middle Ponil Creek.

Questa Ranger District: The most popular hiking area in the Forest. It includes the Wheeler Peak and Latir Peak Wildernesses. The central portion, between SR 38 and SR 150, is crossed by many trails, ranging in difficulty from moderate to strenuous. Most are lightly used. Hiking season is generally June–Oct.

Hopewell Lake is on US 64, 19 mi. W of Tres Piedras. The Department of Game and Fish dammed Placer Creek, creating this pond and maintaining it for all-year trout fishing. Primitive camping. Difficult to reach in winter except by snowmobile.

Scenic Drives: Two popular routes are (1) from Taos E on US 64, N on SR 38 to Red River and Questa, S on SR 3 back to Taos, and (2) US 64 from Tres Piedras to Tierra Amarilla (closed in winter). These are well-traveled highways. Blocks 1 and 2 have miles of lightly traveled all-weather and dirt roads, shown on the Forest map. Ask about road conditions.

We made special note of SR 3 along the Rio Pueblo NW of Mora: handsome forest, campgrounds, trailheads; fine hiking country. Also on US 84 NW of Abiquiu: cliffs with sculptured turrets, fins, and other formations, in bands of red, brown, cream, and purple.

Ghost Ranch Living Museum on US 84 NW of Abiquiu has many exhibits including living plants and animals and imaginative interpretation. It provides a delightful introduction to desert geology and ecology, appealing to all ages (see entry).

INTERPRETATION

Ghost Ranch Living Museum serves as interpretive center.

Nature trail at El Nogal campground.

No campfire programs, guided walks, other naturalist programs.

ACTIVITIES

Camping: 9 campgrounds in Block 1, 14 in Block 2, 13 in Block 3. One open all year at the Ghost Ranch Museum. Most open in May, a few earlier or later; most close in Oct. Informal camping almost anywhere, unless posted.

Hiking, backpacking: 274 mi. of trail on the Forest, available for hiking and horse riding. Some of the trails in Blocks 2 and 3 are also available for motorcycles and other ATV's. Check at the District Offices for detailed information. Three National Recreation Trails are in Blocks 2 and 3: the Columbia Twining, the South Boundary, and the Jicarta Peak NRT's. The entire Forest is suitable for off-trail hiking by experienced outdoorsmen.

We received conflicting information about trail maintenance. The HQ staff member who reviewed this entry inserted the sentence "All trails are maintained." Hikers said otherwise, and every other National Forest we know about has had its trail maintenance budget deeply cut.

Horse riding: On any suitable trail. Outfitters located near town of Red River.

Hunting: Chiefly deer, elk, turkey.

Fishing: Trout in mountain lakes and streams.

Rafting: On the Red River; Apr.–May when snowmelt is sufficient. Also on sections of the Rio Grande, usually May through July. Some sections are dangerous; get detailed information.

Ski touring: On many trails and unplowed forest roads.

Skiing: Three ski areas. Season generally Nov.–Apr.

PUBLICATIONS
Forest map. $1.
Other maps, $1 each:
Visitor's Guide to the Pecos Wilderness.
Wheeler Peak Wilderness.
Latir Peak Wilderness.
Cruces Basin Wilderness.
Valle Vidal Unit.
Information pages:
General information.
Backcountry Ethics.
Recreation Sites in Southwestern National Forests.
El Nogal Nature Trail.
National Forest Ski Areas, Southwestern Region.
Ghost Ranch Living Museum folder.

REFERENCES
Ganci, Dave. Hiking the Southwest; Arizona, New Mexico, and West Texas. San Francisco: Sierra Club Books, 1983, pp. 209–216.
Evans, Harry. 50 Hikes in New Mexico. Pico Rivera, CA: Gem Guides Book Co., 1984, pp. 98–116.
Overhage, Carl. Six One-Day Walks in the Pecos Wilderness. Santa Fe: Sunstone Press, 1980.
New Mexico Whitewater. Santa Fe: New Mexico State Park Division, 1983.

HEADQUARTERS: P.O. Box 558, 112 Cruz Alta Road, Taos, NM 87571; (505) 758-6200.

RANGER DISTRICTS: Canjilon R.D., P.O. Box 488, Canjilon, NM 87515; (505) 684-2486. El Rito R.D., P.O. Box 56, El Rito, NM 87530; (505) 581-4554. Jicarilla R.D., Gobernador Route, Blanco, NM 87412; (505) 325-0508. Taos R.D., P.O. Box 558, 302 Armory St., Taos, NM 87571: (505) 758-2911. Tres Piedras R.D., P.O. Box 728, Tres Piedras, NM 87577; (505) 758-8678. Questa R.D., P.O. Box 110, Questa, NM 87556; (505) 586-0520. Penasco R.D., P.O. Box 68, Penasco, NM; (505) 587-2255.

CHACO CULTURE NATIONAL HISTORICAL PARK
National Park Service
34,000 acres.

From Bloomfield on US 64, SE 38 mi. on SR 44 to Nageezi Trading Post, then SW 20 mi. on County Road A35. County road is slick or impassable when wet. Call Park for current weather and road conditions.

Our definition of "natural areas" excludes historical sites, but we could not omit this one.
Much has been written about Chaco Canyon. The recurrent word is "mystery." Archeological research began in the 1890s, but only recently has remote sensing, including satellite imagery and sophisticated aerial photography, discovered a network of "roads" extending far beyond the present Park boundaries—long, straight roads, often 30 ft. wide, linking outlying pueblos. An aspect of the mystery is that the Chacoans had neither the wheel nor any beasts of burden. More than 4,000 ruins, including one of the largest single prehistoric structures in the Southwest, enclosed plazas, Great Kivas, irrigation systems, 4-story construction, earthworks, etc.

The Chaco Canyon is wide and shallow, in the Colorado Plateau desert. Elevations from 6,050 to 6,860 ft. The setting is sagebrush desert, with greasewood, four-wing saltbush, and interspersed grasses. Birds such as turkey vulture, common raven, and canyon and rock wrens are often seen; occasional golden eagle, prairie falcon, red-tailed hawk. Mammals include coyote, mule deer, bobcat, antelope ground squirrel, kangaroo rat, prairie dog, cottontail, jackrabbit, bobcat.

The Park protects what is believed to have been the center of the Chaco civilization; the surrounding area also is rich with archeological sites, far more than have yet been studied, cataloged, or even discovered. Since the basin is rich with uranium and strippable coal, commercial exploitation may obliterate many of these sites before they are documented. It seems unlikely that those on private land can be saved, and the Park itself may be adversely affected by exploitation nearby.

INTERPRETATION
Visitor center has exhibits, films, literature. Open 8 A.M.–4:30 P.M. in winter, to 5 P.M. in summer.
Self-guiding trails, each about 1/4 mi. long.
4 backcountry trails, each 3 to 6 mi. long, highlight vegetation, paleontology, geology, and cultural resources.
Campfire programs and *guided walks* mid-May to mid-Sept.

Permit is required for hiking in the backcountry. Some backcountry sites are off limits.

PUBLICATIONS
Leaflet with map.
Backcountry trail guide. $.50.
Self-guiding trail guides. $.40 each.

REFERENCES

Anderson, Douglas and Barbara. *Chaco Canyon.* Globe, AZ: Southwest Parks and Monuments Association, 1981.

Lister, R. H., and F. C. Lister. *Chaco Canyon Archaeology and Archaeologists.* Albuquerque: University of New Mexico Press, 1981.

Nobel, D. G., editor. *New Light on Chaco Canyon.* Santa Fe: School of American Research Press, 1984.

HEADQUARTERS: Star Rt. 4, Box 6500, Bloomfield, NM 87413 (mail). In Chaco Canyon: (505) 786-5384.

CIBOLA NATIONAL FOREST

U.S. Forest Service

1,653,301 acres; 2,120,635 acres within boundaries.

Four Ranger Districts include nine scattered units in central and western NM. (1) Mt. Taylor R.D. has two units, E and W of Grants. Access from roads off I-40. (2) Sandia R.D. is just E of Albuquerque, crossed by I-40. (3) Mountainair R.D. has two units: the Manzano Division, SE of Albuquerque, N of US 60; and the Gallinas Division, just W of Corona; access from roads off US 54. (4) Magdalena R.D. Four units. Two are N of US 60, W of Magdalena, two S of Magdalena.

The nine units straddle mountain ranges. Most of the area between them is desert at about 5,000 ft. elevation. Mountain ridge elevations are generally above 8,000 ft. Mount Taylor, 11,301 ft., is the highest peak. Sandia Crest is 10,678. Several others are also over 10,000 ft.

The Cibola also includes 4 National Grasslands. Only one of these, the Kiowa, is in NM, the others in Texas and Oklahoma. An entry for the Kiowa National Grassland is in Zone 2.

Sandia, smallest of the four R.D.'s, has by far the most visitors, chiefly because it adjoins Albuquerque and is easily accessible. Most of the publications describing Forest features, flora, fauna, and trails concern the Sandia. Forest managers hope to relieve pressure on the Sandia by encouraging use of the other R.D.'s, which are no less attractive.

The ecology of these mountain regions is much alike. They have the same life zones at comparable elevations, and almost all the same flora and fauna occur. The species checklists for the Sandia are applicable Forest-wide, with minor exceptions.

The Forest can be enjoyed at any season. At lower elevations, summer days are hot but nights cool. Above 8,000 ft., nights can be cold. Winters at high elevation are cold, but heavy snow seldom falls until Dec., and trails are usually snow-free by May. Hiking is possible all year at middle elevations. Annual precipitation ranges from 10 in. at lower elevations to 24 in. up high. Heavy showers are common in July and Aug.

Like all public lands, the Cibola has been adversely affected by the Reagan Administration's budget slashing. "Nearly all sites are operating at a reduced service level which results in a shorter season of use and limited clean-up and maintenance," a Forest report says. "At many sites the quality of the visitors' experience has deteriorated considerably. Water quality, visitor control and general resource protection continue to decline." Trail maintenance has virtually ceased except for the activity of volunteers. In the Sandia R.D., the Adopt-a-Trail program has been helpful.

The Forest has about 1,700 mi. of roads in its system, roads that would be maintained at a higher level if funds were available. A few US and county paved roads cross the Forest, but system roads are dirt or gravel. In dry weather, most can be negotiated by ordinary autos. Roads at high elevations may require a pickup truck or 4-wheel drive. Rain makes some sections impassable. Local inquiry is always wise; a washout or damaged bridge may not be quickly repaired.

The Forest also has 2,500 mi. of "ways," routes created by repeated passage of vehicles. More are created each year by hunters, firewood gatherers, and other off-road drivers. These unplanned, unmaintained ways cause erosion and siltation, a serious concern to Forest managers, who estimate that soil loss from all causes averages 3 tons per acre per year Forest-wide. At least 1,500 mi. of these ways would be closed if the Forest had funds to do it, but without field personnel to enforce closures the problem is likely to worsen.

Roads and ways do offer opportunities for hikers. In the Zuni Mountains of the Mt. Taylor R.D., for example, there are only a few short trails. Some ways, rarely used by vehicles, serve just as well.

"But you don't need trails in much of the Forest," we were told. "You can walk the ridge down the Continental Divide without difficulty."

The Forest's chief deficiency is water. The only fishing is in a small pond in the Mt. Taylor R.D. Most streams are intermittent, and most springs have only seasonal flow.

Plants: Life zones are typical of New Mexican mountains. The Upper Sonoran life zone extends from the desert floor to about 7,000 ft.; predominant flora are grasses, pinyon pine, and juniper. A transition zone extends to about 9,500 ft., with ponderosa pine, Douglas-fir, oak, maple, manzanita. Still higher are Engelmann spruce, white fir, aspen.

The pattern has many variations. White fir isn't found on Mt. Taylor, for example. Ponderosa pine forest is sometimes found at 10,000 ft.; we often saw it at 8,000. Small stands of ocotillo occur in the Magdalena R.D., unusually far N for this species.

A Forest pamphlet says that 884 types of plants, including 5 species of orchids, live on the Sandias, but no list is available. We obtained a one-page list of common species, not keyed to life zones. Trees, in addition to those mentioned, include limber pine, corkbark fir, boxelder. Common shrubs include locust, Gambel oak, snowberry, mountain spray, gooseberry, currant, ninebark, baneberry, raspberry, thimbleberry, mountain-mahogany.

Flowering species include fairy slipper, golden banner, Rocky Mountain iris, buttercup, Canada violet, harebell, purple vetch, red-and-yellow columbine; purple, scarlet, and dusky penstemons; wild rose, wild geranium, Jacob's ladder, golden draba, western wallflower, Indian paintbrush, cinquefoil, false solomonseal, sandwort, Franciscan bluebells, larkspur, rock jasmine, clematis, sunflower, fireweed, death camas, daisy, aster. In the Manzano Mountain Wilderness, we saw skyrocket, scarlet sage, Hooker's evening primrose, curlycup gumweed, coralroot orchid.

Birds: Forest HQ supplied a 112-page document listing the birds and other animals found in each type of habitat; it did not report abundance, and many of those listed are uncommon or rare. A checklist, *Birds of the Sandia Mountains,* notes abundance for each species but not the habitats where it occurs. The checklist seems more useful to a visitor and is generally applicable to the other mountains.

Seasonally common or abundant species include turkey vulture, scaled quail, band-tailed pigeon, mourning dove, great horned owl, common nighthawk, white-throated swift; black-chinned, broadtailed, and rufous hummingbirds; northern flicker, yellow-bellied and Williamson's sapsuckers; hairy, downy, and ladder-backed woodpeckers; Cassin's kingbird; ashthroated, western, and olive-sided flycatchers; Say's phoebe, western woodpewee, horned lark, violet-green and barn swallows; Steller's, scrub, and pinyon jays; common raven, American crow, mountain chickadee, plain titmouse, bushtit; white-breasted, red-breasted, and pygmy nuthatches; house, Bewick's, canyon, and rock wrens; mockingbird, American robin, hermit thrush, western and mountain bluebirds, Townsend's solitaire, blue-gray gnatcatcher, ruby-crowned kinglet, loggerhead shrike, solitary and warbling vireos. Warblers: orange-crowned, Virginia's, yellow-rumped, MacGillivray's, Wilson's. House sparrow, brown-headed cowbird, western tanager, black-headed and evening grosbeak, Cassin's and house finches, pine siskin, lesser goldfinch; green-tailed, rufous-sided, and brown towhees; blackthroated, chipping, and white-crowned sparrows; dark-eyed and gray-headed juncos.

Mammals: No checklist is available. *A Guide to the Mammals of the Sandia Mountains,* 24 pp., describes the principal species and where they occur. Included are 3 species of shrews, 11 bats, black bear, raccoon, ringtail, longtail weasel, spotted and striped skunks, badger, coyote, gray fox, bobcat, whitetail prairie dog, whitetail antelope squirrel, spotted ground squirrel, rock squirrel, Colorado chipmunk, red and tassel-eared squirrels, valley and Mexican pocket gophers, western harvest mouse; deer, brush, and pinyon mice, whitethroat and Mexican woodrats, longtail vole, porcupine, blacktail jackrabbit, desert and eastern cottontails, mule deer, Rocky Mountain bighorn sheep.

Reptiles and amphibians: Checklist for the Sandia Mountains includes tiger salamander, western spadefoot, Woodhouse's and red-spotted toads, leopard and chorus frogs, desert box turtle. Great Plains and variable skinks; spotted, little striped, New Mexican, checkered, and plateau striped whiptails. Lizards: western collared, speckled earless, mountain short-horned, round-tailed horned, southern prairie, desert side-blotched, tree. Snakes: New Mexico blind, western black-necked garter, wandering garter, plains hognose, prairie ringneck, western coachwhip, desert striped whipsnake, mountain patch-nosed, Great Plains rat, glossy, Sonora gopher, New Mexico milk, Texas long-nosed, western hook-nosed, Texas night, plains black-headed; western diamondback, northern black-tailed, and prairie rattlesnakes.

RANGER DISTRICTS

Mount Taylor R. D.: Includes two mountain ranges. The San Mateo Mountains lie NE of Grants. Highest point is Mt. Taylor, 11,301 ft. All-weather SR 547 runs NE from Grants into the heart of this unit, which has a network of dirt and primitive Forest roads. We were told one can drive "almost to the top" of Mt. Taylor in an ordinary car in dry weather, on dirt road for the last 4 mi. The highest country is SE of SR 547. Other parts of this unit are high mesas. A 3-mi. trail leads from Forest Road 501 to the summit of Mt. Taylor. A few hundred hikers per year may take this route. Some campers use the two small campgrounds off SR 547. Most other visitors to this unit are hunters.

Both ranges have ponderosa pine forests between 7,000 and 8,500 ft., mixed conifers above. The crest of Mt. Taylor is blanketed by Engelmann spruce.

The Zuni Mountain unit has a maximum elevation of 9,200 ft. SR 400 penetrates its NW corner to a summer home area on small McGaffey Lake. SR 53, running S from Grants, turns W across the unit's SE corner, at El Malpais (see entry). An all-weather road S from Thoreau on I-40 passes Bluewater Lake and enters the Forest as Forest 178, connecting with several dirt and primitive Forest roads. The Continental Divide crosses the S part of the unit along the Oso Ridge of the Zunis. Few visitors venture far from the campgrounds and all-weather roads. The unit has no trails, but one can hike along the ridge and the beds of abandoned logging railroads, as well as on roads. "Why come here?" we asked, seeing no distinguishing features on the map. "It's one of the prettiest parts of the Forest," we were told. Campgrounds are located at McGaffey Lake, on SR 400 on the way to the lake, and near the end of SR 178.

Sandia R.D.: The Sandias, occupying 400 sq. mi., are a tilted fault block, 22 mi. long, moderate slopes on the E, rising so steeply on the W that hang-glider enthusiasts leap from the crest. One of the attractions of NM mountains is that they are cool at the top when it's hot down below. Here one can make the transition quickly. Sandia Crest, 10,678 ft., is the most accessible mountain in NM. A paved road goes to the top. From 5 mi. N of Albuquerque, one can ride up by aerial tram. At the top are a visitor center, picnic sites, three nature trails, a ski area, restaurants, an observation tower, radio and TV towers, and—remarkably—a Wilderness.

We saw several estimates of visitors using this District, the highest estimate being 1.5 million per year and rising. Whatever the number, it's too many for anyone wanting solitude. Other parts of the Forest, including the other Wildernesses, offer that. Fewer than 1,000 people per year visit the Apache Kid Wilderness.

The 36,977-acre Sandia Mountain Wilderness is just W of the crest. Within it are 70 mi. of the best-maintained and most heavily used trails in the Forest. Most of them intersect the Crest Trail, which extends the length of the Sandias. The longest trail is 28 mi. Portions of the area above 10,000 ft. are predominantly spruce-fir forest, with mixed conifers just below.

The District is divided by I-40 and a strip of privately owned land. Sandia Crest and the Wilderness are in the larger N portion. SR 14 S from Tijeras crosses the S portion, with a dirt-road spur to Cedro Peak. The map shows no trails.

The Sandia Ranger District has no campgrounds.

Mountainair R.D.: The Manzano Division of this R.D. includes about 112,000 acres of the Manzano Mountains, a long, narrow N–S range. It lies N of US 60, W of SR 14. Most access roads enter from SR 14. The mountain slopes are gentle from the Estancia Valley on the E to about 8,000 ft., then steepen to the crest. Manzano Peak is at 10,098 ft. The W side drops sharply toward the Rio Grande Valley.

The Manzano Mountain Wilderness occupies 36,875 acres along the crest and W slope, which has several steep, rugged canyons. The Wilderness has 64 mi. of trails, several of them originating at campgrounds outside the boundary on the E. We parked our motor home at Fourth of July Campground, on Forest Road 55, W from Tajique. The Wilderness boundary is at the edge of the campground, and the trail to the crest is only 1 1/2 mi. long, through a handsome ponderosa forest. From here the Crest Trail extends 22 mi. S to Manzano Peak. On a Friday night, we had the campground to ourselves. Most sites were filled Saturday, but only two other couples took the trail, and they stopped short of the ridge. Campgrounds and trails farther S have even less traffic.

The second Division of the R.D., W of Corona on US 54, includes the Gallinas Mountains, a small isolated range. Gallinas Peak is 8,637 ft. Chief access is by a dirt Forest road about 3 mi. S of Corona, which leads to this Division's only campground.

Magdalena R.D.: The four units of this R.D. are on the Magdalena, San Mateo, Bear, Gallinas, Datil, Crosby, and Sawtooth Mountains. (We blinked, too, and checked several maps. *These* Gallinas Mountains are a hundred mi. from the Gallinas Mountains of the Mountainair R.D., separated by desert and the Rio Grande Valley. Each has a "Gallinas Peak." The U.S. Geological Survey, in its 1:500,000 map, sidesteps this redundancy by showing only "Gallinas Mountains" in the W, only "Gallinas Peak" in the E.)

The Magdalenas, S of the town of Magdalena, rise to 10,700 ft. at Baldy Peak. This unit, with 92,000 acres, has 63 mi. of attractive but relatively short trails, better suited to day hikes than overnights. They offer several routes to Baldy Peak. A paved road from US 60 leads to the only campground, at Water Canyon.

Further S and W is the largest unit, including the San Mateo Mountains, a 32-mi.-long range paralleling the Rio Grande Valley. Forest land begins on the high benches W of the river and slopes steeply to the crestline. On the W, the land drops rapidly to the high benchlands sloping toward the San Agustin Plains and Alamosa Creek. Elevations range from 5,000 ft. to 10,336-ft. West Blue Mountain and 10,139-ft. San Mateo Peak in the S portion of the unit, and to 10,119-ft. Mount Withington in the N. Drainages are generally to the SW and SE. Canyon bottoms often have strips of ponderosa pine that merge at higher altitudes into pine forest. Mixed conifers predominate at the highest elevations. Small stands of ocotillo occur at low elevations on the E and S.

The only all-weather road is Forest Road 478, penetrating to the center of the unit from SR 52 on the W through West Red Canyon, with a branch up Hudson Canyon.

The two southern peaks are surrounded by the 45,000-acre Apache Kid Wilderness. A 13-mi. crest trail has 68 mi. of connecting side trails. The Springtime campground, at the end of a dirt road, is the most popular trailhead. Trails offer many splendid vistas. Terrain makes off-trail hiking difficult and limits choice of campsites. Public use is less than 1,000 visitor-days per year.

The 19,000-acre Withington Wilderness in the N receives even fewer visits, but has only 11 mi. of trails. Mount Withington is on the W edge of the Wilderness. The Bear Trap campground is about a mi. from the Wilderness boundary; it could be a base for pleasant day hikes.

The unit N of Magdalena includes the Bear Mountains and the S end of the Gallinas Mountains. Neither is high enough to have stands of ponderosa pine. SR 52 crosses the unit through Dry Lake Canyon. The map shows no trails. This unit has no campground.

Farthest W, N of the town of Datil on US 60, is the unit including the Datil, Crosby, and Sawtooth Mountains. Highest elevation is 9,585-ft. Madre Mountain, near the unit's center. Some ridges are high enough to have ponderosa pine forest. US 60 crosses the unit through White House Canyon, usually bordered by privately owned land. No trails or campground.

INTERPRETATION

Wilderness skills trail, on Sandia Crest. Manned by uniformed Forest Service Personnel, the trail has 18 stations, each designed to teach some aspect of wilderness travel.

Nature trails on Sandia Crest include one for handicapped visitors.

ACTIVITIES

Camping: 17 campgrounds, 238 sites. Most camping from vehicles is informal, along Forest roads and ways.

Hiking, backpacking: Most trails and heaviest use are in the Sandia R.D. Many other areas are no less attractive, with few visitors. Where trails are lacking, consider little-used dirt roads and ways or abandoned railbeds. Off-trail crestline hiking is feasible in some areas. Carry water.

Hunting: Deer, elk, pronghorn, turkey.

Fishing: Only at McGaffey Lake.

Horse riding: We met a few horsemen on our hikes and saw tracks on other trails. Forest information handouts make no mention of horsepacking, special rules, or outfitters. Anyone not familiar with the area should write or call an R.D.

Skiing: Ski area with lifts, served by aerial tram, on Sandia Crest. Usual season: Dec.–Mar.

Ski touring: Increasingly popular. Most present activity is on the E slopes of the Sandia and Manzano Mountains, chiefly on unplowed road and trails. However, similar opportunities exist on other R.D.'s, wherever elevations catch sufficient snow.

PUBLICATIONS

Forest maps, for each R.D. $1 each.
Off Road Vehicles Travel Guide and Map.
Wilderness maps. (These are merely portions of the R.D. maps with solid green blocks showing Wilderness areas. No added information.)
General information pages.
Natural History of the Sandia Mountains. Pamphlet, 12 pp.
Motor Trip Guide to the Sandia Mountains. Pamphlet, 12 pp.
Bird checklist, Sandia Mountains.
Reptile and amphibian checklist, Sandia Mountains.
A Guide to the Mammals of the Sandia Mountains. Mimeo, 18 pp.
Soaring the Sandia Mountains; A Basic Guide for Hang Glider Pilots. Mimeo, 8 pp.

REFERENCES

Ganci, Dave. *Hiking the Southwest; Arizona, New Mexico, and West Texas.* San Francisco: Sierra Club Books, 1983, pp. 239–264.
Evans, Harry. *50 Hikes in New Mexico.* Pico Rivera, CA: Gem Guides Book Co., 1984, pp. 76–97.

Ungnade, Herbert E. *Guide to the New Mexico Mountains.* Albuquerque: University of New Mexico Press, 1972.

HEADQUARTERS: 10308 Candelaria NE, Albuquerque, NM 87112; (505) 766-2185.

RANGER DISTRICTS: Mt. Taylor R.D., 201 Roosevelt, Grants, NM 87020; (505) 287-8833. Magdalena R.D., Box 45, Magdalena, NM 87825; (505) 854-2381. Mountainair R.D., P.O. Box E, Mountainair, NM 87036; (505) 847-2990. Sandia R.D., Star Rt. Box 174, Tijeras, NM 87059; (505) 281-3304.

COCHITI LAKE
U.S. Army Corps of Engineers
Lake area: 1,200 acres.

From Albuquerque, 36 mi. NE on I-25, then 15 mi. NW on SR 22.

The lake was formed in the late 1970s by constructing a 5-mi.-long earth dam across the Rio Grande River. The lake is narrow, about 10 mi. long, at the foot of the Jemez Mountains. Elevation is about 5,300 ft. Average annual precipitation is 14–16 in.

Close to both Albuquerque and Santa Fe, the lake quickly attracted recreationists. A resort community developed near the dam, on land leased from the Cochiti Pueblo. The Pueblo operates the campground and other recreation facilities.

Development is confined to the S end of the lake. The N end of the lake is within White Rock Canyon, where much of the W shore is the boundary of Bandelier National Monument (see entry). This area is shallow, interesting to explore by canoe. Birding is reasonably good, especially at the upper end.

ACTIVITIES
Camping: 33 sites. All year.
Hiking: 3/4-mi. nature trail at visitor center. Easy to rough off-trail hiking in the lakeside hills. A Bandelier National Monument trail follows the W shore; this is within the Monument's Wilderness Area, where a permit is required.
Fishing: Walleye, catfish, crappie, large- and smallmouth bass.
Boating: Ramps. Boats restricted to no-wake speed. Lake is often frozen Dec.–Feb.
Rafting, kayaking: From Otowi Bridge on SR 4. 24 mi. to boat ramp area,

or exit at Frijoles Canyon in the Monument to avoid long slackwater paddle. (This exit requires a 2 1/2 mi. uphill hike.) Rapids are Class III and IV.

PUBLICATIONS
  Brochure.
  Coyote Nature Trail guide.
  White Rock Canyon Boaters Map.

REFERENCE: *New Mexico Whitewater, a Guide to River Trips.* Santa Fe: New Mexico State Park Division, 1983, pp. 53–54.

HEADQUARTERS: P.O. Box 1238, Pena Blanca, NM 87041; (505) 242-8302.

DE-NA-ZIN
U.S. Bureau of Land Management
19,922 acres.

From Farmington, about 35 mi. S on SR 371. Then NE on C15. The state highway map shows the road, but no route number, at "Bisti Badlands." From Bloomfield, 30 mi. S on SR 44, to El Huerfano Trading Post, then 7 mi. SW on C15.

Route C15 is the SE boundary. Three scenic overlooks are on or near the road. No vehicles are permitted within the unit. While there are no marked trails or formal entrance, foot travel is not difficult along the principal washes and tributaries. De-Na-Zin Wash parallels C15, generally about 1/2 mi. from the road. The most striking scenery and the best opportunities for hiking and horse riding are in the southern two-thirds of the unit.

The road and overlooks are in rolling uplands. Below are colorful rough badlands. In the middle distance are mesa tops, intricately wind-carved bluffs, spires, and mushroom formations. The area is cut by several washes and their tributaries. Colors of the formations range from cream and tan to maroon and purple. The colors are most striking when the sun is low.

Elevation is about 6,300 ft. Annual precipitation is about 8 in., much of it in July–Aug. thundershowers. Summers are hot, winters cold.

The site has greater natural diversity than nearby Bisti Badlands (see entry). Although plant and animal life are scarce in the badlands, the unit also includes rolling grasslands and slopes with good stands of pinyon-juniper. On the E edge is a pinyon-juniper community with yucca, Mormon tea, snake-weed, sagebrush, cacti, and grasses. Birds of the area include pinyon jay, common raven, scaled quail, mourning dove, red-tailed and ferruginous hawks, prairie falcon, golden eagle. Mammals include desert cottontail, prairie dog, coyote, badger.

Petrified wood and fossils are abundant (federal law prohibits collecting). The site contains the geological transition from formations of the age of dinosaurs to those formed as mammals became dominant. It is among the few places where the final extinction of the dinosaurs is recorded.

The site, which has few visitors, is a designated Wilderness. It has three inholdings, parcels of Navajo land totaling 1,120 acres.

We suggest calling at the BLM office in Farmington before a visit.

NEARBY: Bisti Badlands; Ah-Shi-Sle-Pah (see entries).

PUBLICATION: Leaflet with map.

HEADQUARTERS: BLM, Farmington Resource Area, 900 La Plata Highway, Farmington, NM 87401; (505) 325-3581.

EDWARD SARGENT FISH AND WILDLIFE MANAGEMENT AREA
New Mexico Department of Game and Fish
20,400 acres.

From Chama on SR 17 just N of US 84, near the Colorado border, N on Pine St.

Schedule and weather kept us from exploring this site, to our regret. We were urged to try again, preferably in late Sept.–early Oct. when the oak and aspen are colorful in the high mountains and the elk are bugling. The Nature Conservancy bought the site and held it until the state assembled purchase money. The property extends from Chama and SR 17 to the CO border. Elevation is about 8,000 ft. The rolling land includes high aspen meadows, forested slopes, alder-lined streams, a small lake. Fishing for cutthroat and rainbow trout.

Only the road NW from Chama is open to vehicles. All other travel in this 32-sq.-mi. area is on foot or horseback. The entire area is closed for a period just prior to the elk-hunting season.

Hunting is chiefly for elk, though some deer and a few bear are taken each year. The management objective is enhancing the area as a spring, summer, and fall range for elk. At Game and Fish HQ in Santa Fe, we were told that hikers and sightseers outnumber hunters: "It's a beautiful area!"

Camping is limited to primitive sites near the entrance. We were told backpacking is permissible except in hunting season.

Snowmobiles are restricted to 200 acres in the S end.

HEADQUARTERS: Department of Game and Fish, Villagra Building, Santa Fe, NM 87503; (505) 827-7899.

EL MALPAIS
U.S. Bureau of Land Management
98,369 acres.

From Grants, S on SR 117, the E boundary.

Four lava flows spread into this valley within the past 3,000 years, the latest less than 1,000 years ago. Indian legends describe the river of fire. The dramatic landscape includes cinder and spatter cones, ice caves, pressure ridges, and some of the largest and longest lava tubes on the continent. On the E are high sandstone bluffs sculptured in a variety of formations, including balancing stones. Many roadside wildflowers.

BLM spokesmen are understandably reluctant to call attention to some of the outstanding features not visible from the highway. A few years ago, annual visitation was negligible. Even then, two interpretive exhibits were destroyed by vandals. Archeological sites have been rifled; fires have melted crystals in ice caves; trees have been cut for fuelwood; and ORV drivers ignore protective regulations. Traffic has increased since SR 117 was paved. BLM has no budget for on-site personnel, and matters can only become worse during the Reagan years.

BLM's recreation specialists are quick to share their enthusiasm for El Malpais with visitors who seem understanding and responsible. They can steer you to features not noted on signs or maps.

The lava fields are black, rugged, abrasive. We were surprised by the abundance of vegetation growing in crevices: grasses, cacti, aspen, and other plants. We were told that the lava fields create a microclimate moister than the surroundings. Some isolated ponderosa pines are stunted and twisted. Islandlike depressions have accumulated wind-blown soil, where trees such as pinyon, juniper, ponderosa pine, and Douglas-fir have rooted. Most of these depressions are small, but one, called Hole-in-the-Wall, covers 6,000 acres.

Elevations in El Malpais range from 6,700 ft. to 7,700 ft. atop the bluffs. Annual precipitation is about 10 in., much of it falling in July–Sept. The water percolates quickly, rather than running off or accumulating. We saw no surface water except in potholelike hollows in sandstone.

There is much to be seen along SR 117, which runs at the edge of the lava field, at the foot of the sandstone bluffs. The following are milepoints from I-40, traveling S:

0.1   Lava fields on the right.

7.4   On the left is a tree-covered highland, Cebolita Mesa, in the Acoma Indian Reservation.

10.0   Sandstone Bluffs Overlook. Plan to spend some time here. The views are spectacular. The sandstone formations invite rock scrambling. We saw standing water in smooth hollows, one of them about 12 ft. across. The ORV tracks below were made illegally, but it's not illegal to hike along the bluffs. Camping is permitted.

15.1   The formation on the right is called La Vieja, "Old Woman."

17.6   A track on the left leads to a parking area from which to explore La Ventana, the largest natural arch in New Mexico, in a picturesque setting.

17.9   The Narrows, where the lava field is closest to the foot of the cliffs. Look for golden eagle, red-tailed hawk, and prairie falcon on the cliffs or soaring nearby.

21.1   End of tour route. A track on the left leads to a picnic site.

FEATURES

Ice Caves Resort is on SR 53, on the W side of El Malpais, about 26 mi. S of I-40. We seldom mention private commercial sites, but this one is described in BLM's literature and is warmly recommended by BLM staff members. We saw it, met the owners, and concur. The 4,800 acres include Bandera Crater, largest cinder cone in El Malpais, a fine ice cave, and other features, including lava tubes and interesting wildlife. Most visitors stay within a relatively small area, and the owners say that one can see in this small area the principal features that are spread all over El Malpais. The main ice cave is remarkable in that it has an open mouth; the outer ice, in daylight, has patches of green algae.

Open all year, 8 A.M. to 30 min. before sundown.

At various times the National Park Service, BLM, and State Park and Recreation Division have expressed interest in buying the site, but the owners are not eager to sell.

Chain of Craters is a series of large, symmetrical cinder cones extending SW from Bandera Crater. This scenic area is crossed by a dirt road, SR 109, linking SR 53 and SR 117 across the W side of El Malpais. When we visited, the road was in poor condition, suitable only for 4-wheel-drive vehicles. Inquire at the Ice Caves Resort or BLM office.

ACTIVITIES

Camping: No designated site or facilities, but several opportunities for informal camping.

Hiking, backpacking: A trail crosses the NE sector. The route has long historical associations. Supposedly it is marked by white concrete pillars. However, an exhibit at the trailhead was vandalized, and BLM is not now publicizing the route. Ask about it. Short trails lead to features near SR 117, and jeep tracks offer hiking routes to the interior. Hikers considering more than short strolls should know the requirements of desert travel.

NEARBY: Rimrock (see entry).

PUBLICATION: Leaflet with schematic map.

HEADQUARTERS: BLM, Rio Puerco Resource Area, 3550 Pan American Freeway, Albuquerque, NM 87107; (505) 766-3114.

EL MORRO NATIONAL MONUMENT
National Park Service
1,278 acres.

From Grants on I-40, S and W 43 mi. on SR 53. From Gallup, S and E 58 mi. on SR 32.

This small Monument is in high plateau country about 18 mi. W of the Continental Divide, surrounded by the Ramah Navajo Indian Reservation. Central feature is El Morro, also called Inscription Rock, a mesa rising on a gradual slope from the SW to a point 200 ft. above the base. The point was a landmark for early travelers, many of whom cut inscriptions in the soft sandstone. At the foot of the mesa is a perennial pool fed by runoff from rain and snow.

Visitors can hike a 2-mi. trail to the mesa top, visiting Indian ruins and enjoying a sweeping vista. A 1/2-mi. trail leads to the inscriptions carved into the rock and to the pool.

Elevation at the Visitor Center is 7,219 ft. Average annual precipitation is 18 in., average snowfall 42 in. Much of the rain falls in July–Aug. thunderstorms. Most visitors come in summer.

Plants: Checklist available. The site is about 75% forested, chiefly with pinyon-juniper, some ponderosa pine extending from higher ground. Understory includes snakebush, rabbitbrush, scrub oak. Flowering plants include pricklypear, evening primrose, blue gilia, skyrocket, blue and red penstemons, Indian paintbrush, yarrow, copper mallow, Colorado-four o'clock.

Birds: Checklist available. Seasonally common or abundant species include turkey vulture, Cooper's hawk, American kestrel, great horned owl, common nighthawk, white-throated swift, broad-tailed and rufous hummingbirds, northern flicker, Lewis' woodpecker, Cassin's kingbird, ash-throated flycatcher, Say's phoebe, violet-green and cliff swallows, scrub jay, common raven, mountain chickadee, plain titmouse, Bewick's and rock wrens, sage thrasher, western and mountain bluebirds, Townsend's solitaire, blue-gray gnatcatcher, ruby-crowned kinglet, yellow-rumped and Wilson's warblers, house finch, lesser goldfinch, green-tailed towhee; vesper, lark, and chipping sparrows; gray-headed junco.

Mammals: Checklist available, not indicating abundance. Includes coyote, red fox, whitetail and mule deer, badger, whitetail jackrabbit, mountain cottontail, cliff chipmunk, spruce and rock squirrels, porcupine, northern pocket gopher, whitetail prairie dog, bushytail woodrat, deer mouse.

Reptiles and amphibians: Partial checklist available, includes tiger salamander. Toads: western spadefoot, plains spadefoot, Woodhouse's. Lizards: eastern fence, tree, short-horned, plateau striped whiptail. Snakes: wandering garter snake, bull snake, western rattlesnake.

INTERPRETATION
Visitor center has exhibits, literature. Open 8 A.M.–5 P.M. Oct.–May, to 8 P.M. June–Sept.
Campfire programs and *guided hikes,* June–Sept. (Budget cuts may curtail these programs.)

ACTIVITIES
Camping: All year unless closed by snow. 9 sites.
Hiking: 2 1/2-mi. trail to ruins, mesa top.

NEARBY: Ice Caves Resort (see entry, El Malpais).

PUBLICATIONS
El Morro trail guide.
Leaflet with map.
Species checklists.

HEADQUARTERS: Ramah, NM 87321; (505) 783-4226.

EL VADO LAKE STATE PARK
New Mexico State Park and Recreation Division
1,728 acres.

From US 84 at Tierra Amarilla, 14 mi. SW on SR 112.

We didn't like this site. It is included because of the trail to Heron Lake (see entry). The lake covers 3,380 acres at full pool but averages only 550 acres.

Heron Lake was full; on the same day El Vado was far down, the shoreline raw. Our opinion was shared: the Heron Lake facilities were crowded; few people were at El Vado. We saw only six campers, one boat on the lake. At 6,902 ft. elevation, El Vado is only 284 ft. lower than Heron, but the contrast is extreme. Heron is surrounded by a ponderosa pine forest; the setting at El Vado is sagebrush meadows near the shoreline, low hills with pinyon-juniper above. The campground is exposed, unshaded.

Perhaps we came at the wrong season (early Sept.). Others have described El Vado as a popular water-based recreation area.

ACTIVITIES
Camping: 67 sites. All year.

Hiking, backpacking: Near the entrance is the trailhead for the 5.5-mi. trail along the canyon of the Rio Chama to the dam at Heron Lake. Below the dam is a trail extending through the Rio Chama Canyon to Abiquiu Reservoir, 33 mi. downstream, with links to the Rio Chama Canyon Wilderness Area in Santa Fe National Forest.

Rafting: The Rio Chama can be floated above and below El Vado. Downstream is a 33-mi. whitewater trip to Abiquiu Reservoir. See entries, Rio Chama and Santa Fe National Forest.

ADJACENT: Rio Chama Wildlife and Fishing Area; Rio Chama (BLM section) (see entries).

REFERENCE: *New Mexico Whitewater, a Guide to River Trips.* Santa Fe: State Park Division, 1983, pp. 18–20.

HEADQUARTERS: P.O. Box 29, Tierra Amarilla, NM 87575; no telephone.

GHOST RANCH LIVING MUSEUM
Carson National Forest
About 10 acres.

On US 84, N of Abiquiu.

The Museum is a feature of the Carson National Forest (see entry), but it merits an entry of its own.

If you have visited the Arizona-Sonora Desert Museum, the Ghost Ranch may seem familiar. It should. The same men, Arthur Pack and Bill Carr, were responsible for concept, planning, and design.

The Museum offers a splendid introduction to the geology, fauna, and flora of the region. Here one can study an exhibit explaining the principal rock formations, then look out to the hills and recognize the geologic "staircase."

Most of the Museum is outdoors, and most of the exhibits are living plants and animals. Exhibits include a trout stream, beaver pond, prairie dog colony.

Mammals include mountain lion, bobcat, pronghorn, mule deer, Abert squirrel, raccoon, badger.

The Museum receives over 100,000 visitors a year. Allow two hours for your visit.

PUBLICATION: Brochure.

HEADQUARTERS: Abiquiu, NM 87510; (505) 685-4312.

HERON LAKE STATE PARK
New Mexico State Park and Recreation Division
4,107 acres.

From US 84 at Tierra Amarilla, 11 mi. W on SR 95.

This seemed to us the most attractive man-made lake in New Mexico. It was at full pool, with a surface of 5,905 acres. The design permits drawdown to less than half that size, but we were told the lake level is usually high. Altitude at the dam is 7,186 ft.

It looks like a natural lake, ponderosa pine forest down to the water's edge, an irregular shoreline with many coves and arms, some rock outcrops. Thus far the state has resisted the pressures of the water-ski and high-decibel lobbies, designating this a "quiet lake," power boats restricted to trolling speed. Sailing is popular.

The Park has no controlling entrance. SR 95 follows the S shore at a decent distance, finally crossing the dam. Spurs lead to lakeside campgrounds and boat ramps. Along the road are overlooks and a visitor center.

The canyon of the Rio Chama below the dam is scenic. A spur road E of the dam leads to a trailhead. The trail follows the canyon through the Rio Chama Wildlife and Fishing area to El Vado Lake (see entries).

We passed a few sagebrush meadows, but the low, rolling hills around the lake are mostly covered with mature trees. The forest is open, parklike, yet it conceals the developed areas. Several hundred campers and boaters were present when we visited, but away from the campgrounds we weren't aware of them.

The state has problems here. It owns only part of the lake shore, and the beginnings of a resort are evident on the other side. Access to the Park is uncontrolled, and campers aren't restricted to campgrounds. People camp wherever they please, creating an unwanted network of vehicle tracks. The forest is so open that any auto, not just an ORV, can be driven through the woods to the shore. Hiking around the lake, we saw many tracks and considerable litter.

Evidence of insufficient budget is unmistakable. The state built a handsome visitor center in 1972, but it stands bare, lacking interpretive exhibits. The two Park employees at the information counter when we visited were courteous but untrained. They told us there is no hiking trail along the Rio Chama to El Vado Lake, but there is a fine trail. No information was to be had about the Park's flora, fauna, or geology.

This could remain one of the state's most attractive parks, but not unless the legislature provides for management.

ACTIVITIES

Camping: Officially, 60 campsites. Many more campers were present when we visited.

Hiking: Rio Chama trail, 5.5 mi. to El Vado Lake. We hiked for several miles around the lake shore through open forest.

Fishing: Trout, kokanee salmon.

Boating: Ramp. Trolling speed. Sailing.

Rafting: The Rio Chama is floatable above and below the lake. Upstream is private land, limited access, no camping. Downstream is the Game and Fish Rio Chama Wildlife and Fishing Area, to El Vado Lake.

REFERENCE: *New Mexico Whitewater, a Guide to River Trips.* Santa Fe: State Park Division, 1983, pp. 15–18.

HEADQUARTERS: P.O. Box 31, Rutheron, NM 87563; (505) 588-7470.

HYDE MEMORIAL PARK
New Mexico State Park and Recreation Division
350 acres.

From Santa Fe, 12 mi. NE on SR 475.

We camped here once in the 1950s and thought it delightful. A short drive took us from the hot city up into the cool ponderosa pine forest of the Sangre de Cristo Mountains. The campground was lightly used then. The Park is surrounded by the Santa Fe National Forest (see entry) and serves as a trailhead.

The city has grown rapidly and Forest visitation even more. SR 475 now leads to several Forest campgrounds and ends at the Santa Fe Ski Basin. Many Forest visitors use this Park as a base. It is still attractive but often crowded on weekends, sometimes mid-week.

Camping: 127 sites. All year.

HEADQUARTERS: P.O. Box 1147, Santa Fe, NM 87504; (505) 983-7175.

IGNACIO CHAVEZ, CHAMISA
U.S. Bureau of Land Management
90,500 acres.

From SR 44 about 20 mi. N of San Ysidro, SW on SR 279 (not shown on highway map) about 20 mi. 279 passes between the Ignacio Chavez and Chamisa units.

A scenic area with many opportunities for camping, backpacking, horse riding, and wildlife observation. Visitation is light, and the terrain offers excellent opportunities for solitude.

From the vicinity of San Ysidro, a large area of public land extends about 40 mi. W, 20 mi. N. Within this block are numerous inholdings of private and state land. BLM identified four roadless tracts to be screened for wilderness characteristics. The acreage within these tracts was sharply reduced pending the outcome of a legal dispute, but that does not now inhibit public enjoyment of the area.

The only good map of the area we found is at the BLM office. We recommend consulting there before a visit. Staff members can recommend the most attractive destinations and how to get there.

(The area adjoins a portion of the Cibola National Forest NE of San Mateo, and Forest Road 239 crosses into the area. This is a long and not especially interesting route.)

BLM's evaluation of the N portion of the area was that it offers "opportunities for recreation, but no single recreation opportunity may be characterized as outstanding." In the S portion, the Ignacio Chavez-Chamisa roadless units include the N tip of the Cebolleta Mountains. These units have superior scenic qualities and a greater diversity of land forms and plant communities.

The *Ignacio Chavez* area, in the SW, was given a high rating for scenic values. BLM's description cites "tremendous variation in terrain, environmental transition zones, and vegetation." It includes mesas, cuestas (ridges with steep faces on one side, gentle slopes on the other), rock terraces, retreating escarpments, canyons, and arroyos; its S portion has volcanic features: cinder cones, basalt plains, plugs, dikes, and extensive talus slopes. The area rises 2,000 ft. from desert floor to 7,731 ft. elevation on Bear's Mouth, at the N point of Mesa Chivato.

The level terrain of the mesas provides fine opportunities for camping, backpacking, and day hiking. The proposed Continental Divide National Scenic Trail would cross the area. The mesa rims offer fine views. The site is rich in historical, geological, botanical, and archeological features.

The area is in the watershed of the Rio Puerco. Annual precipitation is about 11 in., half of this falling in July–Sept. Summer storms cause rapid runoff on open slopes and flash floods in valleys and arroyos. Average snowfall is about 37 in., falling any time between Oct. 1 and Apr. 30. Summers are usually pleasant, although temperatures above 100°F have been recorded. Winters are relatively mild.

Plants: Cacti, saltbush, tamarisk, and assorted grasses are at lower elevations, surrounding the mesas. Slopes have a thick cover of pinyon-juniper. Mesa tops have a cover of pinyon pine, ponderosa pine, and Gambel oak, with scattered Douglas-fir and numerous grassy meadows. No information is available on wildflowers, other than "abundant in season."

Birds: 146 bird species are thought to occur. Species collected or sighted include turkey vulture, golden eagle, red-tailed and sharp-shinned hawks, American kestrel, great horned owl, wild turkey, hairy woodpecker, mountain and western bluebirds, mountain chickadee, common raven, common crow, mourning dove, Clark's nutcracker, pinyon and Steller's jays, purple finch, northern flicker; ash-throated, dusky, gray, and western flycatchers; black-headed grosbeak, broad-tailed hummingbird, gray-headed and Oregon juncos; pygmy, red-breasted, and white-breasted nuthatches; horned lark, roadrunner, American robin, loggerhead shrike, Townsend's solitaire, violet-green and cliff swallows, solitary vireo, plain titmouse, rufous-sided towhee, Grace's warbler, chipping and vesper sparrows.

Mammals: 71 mammal species are thought to occur. Species collected or sighted include badger, black bear, bobcat, coyote, porcupine; cliff, Colorado, and least chipmunks; cottontail, Gunnison prairie dog, whitetail antelope squirrel, Abert and rock squirrels, bannertail kangaroo rat; Mexican, Stephens, and whitethroat woodrats; deer and pinyon mice, silky pocket mouse.

Numerous prairie dog towns on the mesa tops.

Reptiles and amphibians: 40 species are thought to occur. Only 4 are recorded as collected or sighted: lesser earless lizard, gopher snake, western and western diamond-backed rattlesnakes.

The *Chamisa* area is immediately E of Ignacio Chavez. From a mesa top on the W the land slopes gradually downward about 1,800 ft. Principal features are Guadalupe Canyon and Canyon Chamisa. Ponderosa pine and pinyon-juniper are at the higher elevations, changing to shortgrass, bunchgrass, cacti, and shrubs below. Hiking opportunities are good, routes ascending to the higher ground of Ignacio Chavez.

The cliffs of SE Chamisa have large colonies of cliff swallows.

The *Ojito* area is closest to San Ysidro, extending about 12 mi. W from SR 44. The area has a maintained county road on its S edge, another on part of its E edge.

Bernalillito Mesa is in the S. The unit has an interesting mix of badlands and sandstone formations. Terrain is generally steep and rocky, with several steep canyons. Two arroyos have intermittent streams. Elevations are generally about 6,000 to 6,500 ft.

Vegetation is primarily pinyon-juniper, shrubs, and grasses. Illegal woodcutting has been one of BLM's management problems.

The Ojito area is only about 40 mi. from Albuquerque. BLM recreation specialists say it is popular with nearby residents for picnicking and day hiking.

The *Cabezon* area lies between and slightly to the N of the Ojito and Chamisa areas. SR 279 is on its NW border. A roadless tract of 7,236 acres qualified for preliminary wilderness study. Its principal feature is Cabezon Peak, a 7,775-ft. volcanic plug rising almost vertically from rolling hills cut by a network of arroyos. Rock climbers scale the peak. There is a rough, unmarked trail to the top, to be used with caution.

ACTIVITIES

Camping: The area has no designated campgrounds, but there are many suitable sites along the gravel and dirt roads.

Hiking, backpacking: No marked trails, but many possible routes, along little-used roads or cross-country. For anything more than a short day hike, one should have a USGS topo map.

Hunting: Big game. Opportunities rated "medium."

The area has no potable water.

Motorized vehicles are restricted to existing roads.

PUBLICATIONS

Ignacio Chavez/Chamisa leaflet with map.
Cabezon leaflet with map.

HEADQUARTERS: BLM, Rio Puerco Resource Area, 3550 Pan American Freeway, Albuquerque, NM 87107; (505) 766-3114.

NAVAJO DAM AND LAKE

Multiple agencies, federal and state
Land, about 40,000 acres; lake, 15,610 acres when full.

To the dam: From US 64 E of Bloomfield, NE on SR 511.

The dam on the San Juan River, built and operated by the U.S. Bureau of Reclamation, was completed in 1962. It backs up a long reservoir into Colorado and a narrower arm on Los Pinos River also extending into Colorado. Elevation at the dam is about 6,000 ft.

The New Mexico State Park and Recreation Division manages recreation on the lake, at Navajo Lake State Park (see entry), and on 3 1/2 mi. of the San Juan River below the dam, a section designated a quality fishing stream. The New Mexico Department of Game and Fish has responsibility for fish and wildlife management. It manages the Miller Mesa Waterfowl Area on the Colorado border.

The 34,000 acres of high mesa land between the two arms of the lake is a mixture of federal, state, and private ownerships. Filling of the lake cut off access to this area except from Colorado. The U.S. Bureau of Land Management and the New Mexico Department of Game and Fish joined in a cooperative effort to improve range conditions for grazing and compensate for the inundation of wildlife habitat.

Much of the public and private land around the lake has natural gas wells, served by a network of unpaved roads. Those on public land are open to use, but maintenance is up to the well operators, and drivers should ask about road conditions or proceed with caution.

Except for these service roads and limited access at Miller Mesa, there is no road access to the lake shore between the State Park units at the S end and Colorado's State Parks at the N end. Even when boat traffic on the lake is heavy, it concentrates near these developments. The midsection of the lake is uncrowded and the shore undeveloped. Boaters can easily find solitude and many suitable sites for picnicking, boat camping, or hiking.

Plants: The lake is bordered by low hills with sparse vegetation: grasses, pinyon pine, juniper, oak, sagebrush, cacti, yucca. Along the shore: cottonwood, willow, tamarisk.

Wildlife: No lists available. Mentioned or observed: waterfowl, deer, rabbit, raccoon, fox, coyote, bobcat. Lizards are common, snakes in rocky and brushy areas; rattlesnakes present but seldom seen.

INCLUDES: *Miller Mesa Waterfowl Area,* 3,060 acres. Access from Colorado route 151, by a dirt road S from Allison or a parallel road 2 mi. E. On a fork of the San Juan arm of Navajo Lake. Dotted with ponds, the area has acres of wheat and other feed crops for waterfowl. Most of it is closed to hunting. Lake access, but no developed ramp. Good birding in season.

ACTIVITIES

Camping: At the State Park (see entry). In NM, camp anywhere along the shore, in Colorado at designated sites only.

Hiking: The uplands offer open-country hiking. This could be pleasant during the season of spring flowers.

Fishing: The lake has brown and rainbow trout, kokanee salmon, largemouth bass, crappie, bluegill, catfish. Below the dam, brown and cutthroat trout; special regulations on the 3 1/2 mi. just below the dam.

Hunting: Mule deer. Some waterfowl below the dam.

Boating: Facilities at the State Park.

PUBLICATION: Leaflet.

HEADQUARTERS: See State Park entry.

NAVAJO LAKE STATE PARK
New Mexico State Park and Recreation Division
16,500 acres.

(1) Pine area: Near Navajo Dam. 25 mi. E of Bloomfield via US 64 and SR 511. (2) Sims area, by unimproved road off SR 539, E of SR 511.

See the entry for Navajo Dam and Lake. The Pine (or "Pine River") site is the principal recreation area, including a busy campground and the only marina on the NM part of the lake. The campground is well above the lake, many of the sites offering good views. On the last day of the Labor Day weekend, a quarter of the campsites were vacant. A day earlier we would have had less choice but would not have been turned away.

Access to the Sims site, across the lake, is by 17 mi. of dirt road, which was in poor condition when we visited and might be impassable after rain. Sims has a campground and boat ramp but no marina. It attracts fewer visitors.

We were told most visitors come for water-based recreation, but less than a third of those we saw camping had brought boats. Apparently the others were there just to camp. Except for hunters, few use the uplands. The acreages reported by HQ (16,000 for Pine, 500 for Sims) don't correspond to land-ownership maps, but it doesn't matter—most of the surrounding land is open to public use.

Below the dam, the San Juan River meanders across its flood plain. SR 511 is on the S side. The Parks and Recreation Division administers 3 1/2 mi. of the river as a fishing area.

ACTIVITIES
Camping: Pine: 137 sites. Sims: 65 sites. All year.
Hiking: No trails, but none are needed. See Navajo Lake entry.
Fishing: Brown and rainbow trout, kokanee salmon, largemouth bass, crappie, bluegill, catfish.
Boating: At Pine, marina with ramp, slips, moorings, rentals. At Sims, ramp. Houseboating is popular.
Swimming: No beach. We saw swimmers on several sections of shoreline.

INTERPRETATION: *Visitor center* at the entrance to the Pine site.

NEARBY: Simon Canyon. See entry.

HEADQUARTERS: Pine: 1448 NM 511, #1, Navajo Dam, NM 87419; (505) 632-2278. Sims: 1448 NM 511, #5, Navajo Dam, NM 87419; no telephone.

RIMROCK
U.S. Bureau of Land Management
60,450 acres.

From I-40 E of Grants, S about 13 mi. on SR 117. Site is on the E, between the road and the Acoma Indian Reservation.

Most visitors who travel S on SR 117 have come to see El Malpais, W of the road, an area of lava fields, cinder and spatter cones, lava tubes, and ice caves (see entry). Immediately E of the road are sculptured sandstone bluffs. The land rises to Cebollita Mesa, where the Acoma Indian Reservation begins.

The area between the road and the boundary of the reservation is a strip from about 2 to 6 mi. wide, continuing about 5 mi. E along the S boundary of the reservation. Although not as scenically dramatic as El Malpais, it is less forbidding, offering visitors greater opportunities for foot and horse travel, with interesting diversity of land forms, flora, and fauna. In studying this area for wilderness classification, BLM had to divide it into four tracts because of primitive roads in Cebolla Canyon, Sand Canyon, and Armijo Canyon. We judged these roads required 4-wheel-drive vehicles, but they serve as trails for foot or horse travel.

Elevations range from 6,900 ft. at the highway to 8,300 ft. The area includes open grasslands, parklike valleys, large sandstone cliffs, sandstone mesas cut by canyons and draws. The terrain is generally rugged, but wide canyon bottoms and flat mesa tops provide travel routes and campsites.

Annual precipitation is about 10 in., much of it falling in summer showers. No perennial streams. Surface water limited to tanks constructed for cattle.

Plants: Grasses, chiefly blue grama, extensive enough to support cattle grazing. Scattered pinyon-juniper, with some harvestable stands. Areas with ponderosa pine, Douglas-fir.

Wildlife: No checklists. Bird species typical of pinyon-juniper and ponderosa pine communities. The cliffs are nesting sites for golden eagle, red-tailed hawk, prairie falcon, and other species. Merriam's turkey. Mammals are not abundant. Small resident mule deer population. Coyote, tassel-eared squirrel. Occasional pronghorn, elk, black bear, mountain lion.

The Acoma Indians have opposed wilderness designation for this area, claiming it as ancestral land. Visitors should have an adequate map and avoid straying into the Reservation or disturbing archeological sites.

FEATURE: *La Ventana,* largest natural bridge in NM. Look for dirt road off SR 117, 17.6 mi. from I-40. Attractive area for short hikes.

HEADQUARTERS: BLM, Rio Puerco Resource Area, 3550 Pan American Freeway, Albuquerque, NM 87107; (505) 766-3114.

RIO CHAMA
U.S. Bureau of Land Management
11,985 acres.

From Cebolla, 2 mi. S on US 84, then W on BLM road 1023; branch roads to E side of canyon. For W side, through the Santa Fe National Forest from SR 112. Inquire at BLM or NF offices, or locally, before trying either route.

Entries for Heron Lake State Park and El Vado State Park describe a trail between them in the canyon of the Rio Chama. The next 30 mi. of the Rio Chama, from El Vado Reservoir to Abiquiu Reservoir, flow through a spectacular gorge. The river is designated a New Mexico State "Scenic and Pastoral River." The upper 10 mi. of the gorge is in a BLM wilderness study area. The lower 20 mi. is in the Chama River Canyon Wilderness of the Santa Fe National Forest (see entry).

The canyon can be hiked from Heron Lake to Abiquiu. The river is floatable. The upland area is undistinguished, mostly open range with private inholdings, used chiefly for grazing. Hunting is the only significant recreational use of this upland.

The canyon, however, has a unique diversity of vegetation types and abundant wildlife. About 900 ft. deep, it follows a meandering course. As seen from El Vado Reservoir, the canyon bottom is 50 to 100 yds. wide, with moderate slopes rising to rimrock. Some other segments are narrower, with steep rocky walls. Some side canyons are boulder-strewn. The canyon is colorful, green shades of vegetation contrasting with the brilliant red, brown, and orange of the rock walls.

Annual precipitation ranges from 14 to 16 in. Average temperatures range from 84°F in summer to 4°F in winter. July is the hottest month, Jan. the coldest.

Plants: Ponderosa pine predominates along the rim, with an understory of oakbrush, serviceberry, currant, and mountain-mahogany. Sloping canyon walls are dotted with pinyon-juniper. Riparian vegetation includes cottonwoods, willows, ponderosa pine, and various deciduous shrubs. A survey of the site's vegetation is filed at HQ.

Birds: No checklist. Cliffs provide nesting sites for wintering bald eagle, golden eagle, red-tailed and Cooper's hawks, American kestrel, prairie falcon. Riparian areas attract waterfowl and passerines. Wild turkey on rangeland. *Mammals:* No checklist. Species mentioned include mule deer, elk, mountain lion, bobcat, beaver, raccoon. Black bear and coyote occur, usually above the canyon.

ACTIVITIES

Camping: No designated sites. From autos at various points on canyon rim.
Hiking, backpacking: Through the canyon. Access by dirt roads to various points on the rim. Many hikers enter from Santa Fe NF or at El Vado.
Fishing: Brown and rainbow trout.
Rafting: About 2,000 people floated the river in 1984. These are usually 2-day trips, El Vado to takeouts near Abiquiu. Class I, II, and III water. Most rapids are downstream from the BLM section. Dam control makes flow unpredictable, but usual season is late Apr.–early July.

(Rio Chama is floatable, with portages, from the Colorado border to its confluence with the Rio Grande. Segments are described in the following reference.)

REFERENCE: *New Mexico Whitewater, a Guide to River Trips.* Santa Fe: State Park Division, 1983, pp. 19–20.

HEADQUARTERS: BLM, Taos Resource Area, Montevideo Plaza, Taos, NM 87571; (505) 758-8851.

RIO CHAMA WILDLIFE AND FISHING AREA
New Mexico Department of Game and Fish
13,000 acres.

From US 84 at Tierra Amarilla, SW on SR 112.

One long side of this triangular site extends for about 9 mi. along SR 112 to El Vado Lake. Along the road are 3 openings in the fence, with dirt roads. At 14 mi. comes the access road to El Vado Lake State Park (see entry). The lake is the triangle's base. The State Park and Recreation Division manages the park facilities. The Wildlife and Fishing Area has 4.5 mi. of lake shore as well as 12 mi. of the Rio Chama above and below El Vado Lake. Between Heron Lake (see entry) and El Vado, the river flows through a handsome canyon.

The site includes a tract below the El Vado dam that includes about 3 mi. of the Rio Chama and 2 mi. of its tributary, the Rio Nutrias.

Most of the site appears to be rolling hills with sagebrush meadows, pinyon-juniper slopes, scattered ponderosa pine. The several roads that crisscross the site are rutted. We saw small truck campers lurching carefully along them in dry weather.

The site was acquired to provide additional hunting and fishing in a part of the state where most land is privately owned. It is open to campers, hikers, and other visitors. Except in hunting season, few are present.

A 5.5-mi. trail extends through the site, along the Rio Chama canyon, from El Vado State Park to Heron Lake dam.

HEADQUARTERS: Department of Game and Fish, Villagra Building, Santa Fe, NM 87503; (505) 827-7899.

RIO GRANDE GORGE STATE PARK
New Mexico State Park and Recreation Division
1,341 acres.

16 mi. SW of Taos on SR 68. Access, on W side, is signed, not conspicuously.

From the Colorado border S to the Taos Junction Bridge on SR 96, the Rio Grande River, flowing across public land managed by BLM, is protected as a Wild and Scenic River. For much of this 48 mi., the river is at the bottom of a 1,000-ft. gorge, inaccessible from above. (See entry, Rio Grande Wild and Scenic River.) The State Park is downstream from the bridge. Here the gorge broadens into a canyon. A paved road offers a scenic 5-mi. drive beside the river. Clusters of campsites, some with ramadas (open shelters with slat roofs), are spaced along the road. On the Friday afternoon of a Labor Day weekend, only 10% of the sites were occupied.

The canyon walls are moderately steep, sparsely vegetated, littered with brown and red-brown volcanic rocks, in size from pebbles to boulders. One could scramble up. There is some riparian vegetation.

This section of the river has riffles rather than rapids, and people float it in canoes, kayaks, and small rafts.

We saw no riverside trail, but the road has little traffic. If one is driving between Taos and Santa Fe, the park offers a pleasant interlude: the motorist's closest look at the Rio Grande, or a quiet walk. Birding is moderately good.

ACTIVITIES
Camping: 46 sites. All year.
Rafting: The river can be floated S of the bridge when flow is too low for

floating the whitewater section above. Several hundred people floated it on a late Aug. weekend.

NEARBY: Continuing S, SR 68 gradually descends and enters the gorge. For several miles, this route is pleasantly scenic, with numerous pullouts.

HEADQUARTERS: P.O. Box 215, Penasco, NM 87553; (505) 587-2765.

RIO GRANDE NATURE CENTER STATE PARK
New Mexico State Park and Recreation Division
170 acres.

In Albuquerque, W end of Candelaria Rd.

An attractive simulation of a natural area, skillfully isolated from its urban surroundings. The park is a small wildlife refuge on the Rio Grande River, much of it in natural "bosque," the dense riparian vegetation occurring along much of this river's course. As in larger refuges, cereal crops were planted, and waterfowl have endorsed the project by their presence. The visitor center, with exhibits, overlooks a marshy pond. Visitors can look through glass under water. Riverside trails.

HEADQUARTERS: 2901 NW Candelaria Rd., Albuquerque, NM 87107; (505) 344-7240.

RIO GRANDE RIVER: WHITE ROCK CANYON
U.S. Bureau of Land Management
24 river miles.

From Otowi Bridge on SR 4, 1 mi. E of SR 30, W of Pojoaque.

Below the bridge is 17 mi. of whitewater, designated Class III. Most of this distance is on land managed by BLM, with the Santa Fe National Forest on the E. After entering White Rock Canyon, the river flows between the National Forest and Bandelier National Monument (see entry).

The first takeout is at the end of the Monument's Falls Trail, in Frijoles Canyon. Exiting here requires a 2 1/2 mi. hike up a rough, narrow trail. At about this point, the river enters Cochiti Lake (see entry), and boaters have a 7-mi. paddle on flat water to the boat ramp at Cochiti Dam.

Camping in the Monument requires a wilderness permit.

PUBLICATION: Leaflet with map.

REFERENCE: *New Mexico Whitewater, a Guide to River Trips.* Santa Fe: New Mexico State Park Division, 1983, pp. 53–54.

HEADQUARTERS: BLM, P.O. Box 1045, Taos, NM 87571; (505) 758-8851.

RIO GRANDE WILD AND SCENIC RIVER
U.S. Bureau of Land Management
1,200 acres; 48 river miles.
From SR 3, 3 mi. N of Questa, W and S on SR 378.

This was among the first areas to be protected under the Wild and Scenic Rivers Act. The special status includes 48 mi. of the Rio Grande S from the Colorado border and the lower 4 mi. of its tributary, the Red River. Efforts to include the adjacent section of the gorge in Colorado have been frustrated by political roadblocks.

The river has cut a gorge into the Taos Plateau through alternating layers of gravel rubble and basaltic lava. The gorge is 200 ft. deep at the CO border, up to 800 ft. near the confluence of the Rio Grande and Red rivers. It can be seen by floating the river, by hiking a riverside trail, or from one of the overlooks on the rim.

The access road parallels the E rim of the gorge for about 7 mi., passing several campgrounds and overlooks. Trailheads are at camping areas near the Rio Grande-Red confluence. Maps show no access to the Gorge from the W rim.

Plants: The plateau back of the canyon rim is relatively dry, sparsely vegetated by grasses and sagebrush. The pinyon-juniper community occurs on slopes and in scattered clusters back of the rim. At the bottom of the canyon is a riparian ecosystem with cottonwood, ponderosa pine, boxelder, willow, sedges, horsetail, poison ivy, Apache plume, mountain-mahogany. On slopes and benches: oak, cottonwood, chamisa, purple aster, Indian paintbrush, yucca, pricklypear, cholla, hedgehog cactus.

Birds: No inventory of species has been made. The river attracts many birds, including ducks and geese. Songbirds nest in the cottonwoods and pines. The vertical cliffs are habitat for golden and bald eagles, prairie falcon, red-tailed hawk, great horned owl, and other raptors.

Mammals: No inventory has been made. Species observed include mule deer, elk, black bear, mountain lion, pronghorn, coyote, beaver, muskrat, raccoon, bobcat, porcupine, other small mammals.

INTERPRETATION
Visitor center has exhibits, information, publications.
Nature hikes and *campfire programs.* Ask about schedules at the visitor center.

ACTIVITIES

Camping: 5 campgrounds, 47 developed sites. Informal camping permitted elsewhere.

Hiking, backpacking: The Rio Grande Wild River Recreation Area is now included in the National Recreation Trails System. It offers 12 mi. of developed and maintained trails. Trailheads are located near each campground area. 2-mi. trail from Big Arsenic Springs campground down to the river. 8 mi. of riverside trail to the confluence, with other access trails.

Fishing: Rainbow and German brown trout, northern pike. Fishing is said to be excellent.

Rafting: Popular whitewater river. Usual season: May–July. Permits required for private and commercial boating, issued only on showing of proper equipment and experience. The Upper Box run begins at Lobatos Bridge in CO. Rafters must get full information, because some downstream sections cannot be run. The most popular section, Lower Box, begins at John Dunn Bridge Recreation Site and extends 16 mi. to Taos Junction Bridge, with Class I–IV rapids. The bridge marks the boundary of the Rio Grande Gorge State Park (see entry).

PUBLICATION: *Rio Grande Wild and Scenic River,* brochure with map.

REFERENCES

Evans, Harry. *50 Hikes in New Mexico.* Pico Rivera, CA: Gem Guides Book Co., 1984, pp. 105–107.

New Mexico Whitewater: A Guide to River Trips. Santa Fe: New Mexico State Park Division, Natural Resources Department, 1983, pp. 46–50.

River Information Digest. Interagency Whitewater Committee: U.S. Forest Service and Bureau of Land Management, 1982, p. 47.

HEADQUARTERS: BLM, Taos Resource Area, P.O. Box 1045, Taos, NM 87571; (505) 758-8851.

SANTA CRUZ LAKE

U.S. Bureau of Land Management
7,768 acres.

From US 84/285, 24 mi. N of Santa Fe, right on SR 4.

An irrigation lake set among high desert hills. The lake surface is 121 acres at full pool. Elevation at the lake is 6,285 ft. BLM manages the land above the high-water line, a boat-launching area, and an overlook, both with campgrounds. The lake is surrounded—at some distance—by SR's 4, 76, and 520. The road to the launching area is the only paved access to the shore.

Visit the overlook first. High above the lake, it offers a 360° view of the desert landscape, hills colorful with bands of dark brown, cream, and red rock and patches of green vegetation. The campsites here share the view. They are sometimes windswept. Most have ramadas.

Several foot trails lead from the overlook to the lake shore. The shortest is 0.8 mi. Other trails wander among the hills, which are also marked by the tracks of ORVs.

The launching and mooring area has more campsites. On Labor Day weekend, this area was congested. Most campsites were occupied, and RVs were parked close together around the large parking area. Unless one has a boat, the uncrowded and scenic hilltop camp would seem more attractive.

ACTIVITIES

Camping: About 40 primitive campsites at the launching area, 18 at the overlook.

Fishing: Brown and rainbow trout.

Boating: Ramp, moorings. Rentals may be available.

PUBLICATION: Leaflet.

HEADQUARTERS: BLM, Taos Resource Area, Montevideo Plaza, Taos, NM 87571; (505) 758-8851.

SANTA FE NATIONAL FOREST
U.S. Forest Service
1,589,184 acres; 1,734,801 acres within boundaries.

Two divisions, W and E of the city of Santa Fe. W division is crossed by SR 4, SR 96, US 84, SR 126. I-25 runs between N and S portions of E half; SR 63 penetrates to the center of its N portion.

This splendidly scenic Forest offers a full spectrum of outdoor recreation opportunities, from sightseeing and picnicking to wilderness backpacking and ski touring. Its diversity of natural communities ranges from arid to humid, desert to alpine tundra, grassland to deep forest. It has some of NM's highest ridges, good fishing in clear mountain lakes and rushing streams, abundant wildlife, a network of backcountry roads and trails, almost 300,000 acres of roadless wilderness.

The Forest lies on both sides of the Rio Grande Valley. To the W is the *Jemez Division,* including the Jemez Mountains and other ranges, rising to nearly 12,000 ft. at Chicoma Peak. This huge block of Forest land is broken by several Indian reservations, Bandelier National Monument, the Los

Alamos atomic site, and numerous private holdings. It is drained by the Rio Chama, Rio Puerco, Rio Cebolla, Rio Gallina, Rio de las Vacas, Jemez River, and Rio Grande.

On the E side of the valley, the *Pecos Division* is dominated by the Sangre de Cristo Mountains, the most southern extension of the Rocky Mountains, highest and largest range in NM. The Sangre de Cristos extend for 200 mi. from Ponchas Pass near Salida, Colorado to between Santa Fe and Pecos. Highest point in the range is 13,160-ft. Wheeler Peak in the Carson National Forest (see entry). In the N portion of the Pecos Division is the 223,000-acre Pecos Wilderness. Principal rivers are the Pecos, Santa Fe, and Mora. Many high mountain lakes are in the N portion.

Terrain is generally mountainous, ranges rising from bases at about 6,000 ft. elevation, with numerous river valleys, mesas, and plateaus. The Jemez Division is characterized by steep, narrow, V-shaped canyons separating gentle to moderately steep mesas. The Pecos Division is more rugged, secondary ranges branching from the Sangre de Cristos, with many deep canyons and steep sidehills.

A remarkable aspect of the Forest is its moisture. Upper elevations receive up to 40 in. of precipitation per year. Many perennial streams rush down hillsides or wander across wet meadows, supporting a rich riparian vegetation.

Such attractions close to cities bring people. Population of the Albuquerque-Santa Fe area is growing rapidly. Forest visitation increases at an even faster rate. Facilities and operating funds have fallen behind. The most accessible areas are overused and undermaintained. The Forest's Environmental Impact Statement commented that no major addition to recreation facilities has been made since 1969:

> The result has been the overuse of many sites located in the high attractor areas, especially those offering water-based opportunities. In several instances, overuse has caused heavy degradation of the existing quality of these sites.

The EIS said there are growing problems in the backcountry as well:

> Conflicts occur among cross-country skiers, snowmobilers, and four-wheel-drive vehicles; among hikers, horseback riders, and trail bikers; essentially between those who choose quiet, self-propelled means of travel and enjoyment and those who choose motorized and generally noisesome [sic] means of travel and enjoyment.

On our first visit to the Forest some twenty years ago, we camped beside a mountain stream in a cool ponderosa forest just a short drive up SR 475 from Santa Fe. We had no neighbors. This road, only 18 mi. long, now carries traffic to three Forest campgrounds, two Forest picnic grounds, a large state park, the Santa Fe Ski Basin, and a wilderness trailhead. The area is heavily impacted.

Not far away is another busy corridor, SR 63, extending N from Pecos to the Pecos Wilderness boundary. Although this road penetrates to the heart of the Forest's largest block of land, much of the strip beside it is privately owned and subject to development. It, too, has several camp and picnic grounds.

In the Jemez Division, SR 4 carries the heaviest recreational traffic, much of it originating in Albuquerque as well as in Santa Fe. It also runs through a corridor of privately owned land, along the Jemez River.

Still, those who wish to do so can avoid the crowds and find quiet places. People tend to congregate, to choose the popular places, the best-known trails, the publicized Wilderness. Many roads into the Forest are not shown on highway maps but are easily seen on the Forest map. Some are spurs approaching a mountain range and ending in a canyon. Some are all-weather routes connecting with a network of dirt and primitive roads.

The Forest has about 3,200 mi. of roads, all but a few unpaved. Many miles of roads were built to facilitate logging and were not maintained afterward. The Forest budget permits maintenance work on only about 400 mi. per year. Many miles have deteriorated, and the Forest Supervisor has recommended that 1,000 mi. be obliterated. Roads shown on the Forest map as "all-weather" are now sometimes impassable after summer rain. Snow plowing is limited to a few roads. Visitors planning to travel off main routes are advised to check road conditions at an R.D. office.

An unmaintained or abandoned road is often a good hiking route, supplementing the Forest's 834 mi. of trails.

Plants:

Elevation	Principal plant communities
5,000–7,000 ft.	Grama-galleta grassland
4,500–7,500 ft.	Grasses, pinyon-juniper
6,500–7,500 ft.	Pinyon-juniper woodlands, grasses, gambel oak
7,500–8,500 ft.	Pinyon-juniper, ponderosa pine, with kinnikinnick, snowberry
8,000–9,500 ft.	Ponderosa pine forest with Douglas-fir, white fir, grouse whorlberry
8,500–10,000 ft.	Mixed conifers: ponderosa pine, Douglas-fir, white fir, corkbark fir, Engelmann spruce
9,000–12,000 ft.	Engelmann spruce-corkbark fir forest
11,500–13,160 ft.	Alpine tundra

Pinyon-juniper woodlands cover about 30% of the Forest area, ponderosa pine, mixed conifers, and spruce-fir about 50%.

No wildflower list is available.

Birds: No checklist available. We obtained a copy of a list recording 260 species. It lacked information on abundance and doubtless includes accidentals and rarities. However, 260 species is an extraordinarily high count for a New Mexico site, and it reflects the great diversity of habitats in this Forest. Hubbard's *Birds of New Mexico, Checklist* (see State Preface) would be more useful than the Forest list.

Mammals: No checklist available. HQ has a list of 84 species recorded. As in the case of birds, this reflects the great diversity of habitats. One of the mammal guides listed in the Preface, such as Cockrum's, would be more useful than the unannotated Forest list.

Reptiles and amphibians: 44 species recorded. Same general comment.

FEATURES

Pecos Wilderness, 198,597 acres, plus 24,736 acres in the Carson NF. Astride the Sangre de Cristo Mountains, the wilderness occupies much of the N portion of the Pecos Division. Most visitors enter from the ends of SR's 63 or 475 (Forest Road 101). The wilderness map lists 34 entry points, 22 of them from other roads.

This is by far the Forest's most-used Wilderness, with 372,000 visitor-days recorded in 1984. Because of this heavy use, a permit is required to enter, even for day hiking. Nine areas have camping restrictions; camping is prohibited at two, rationed by special permits at the others.

Heaviest use is near lakes and streams, and on the main trails to them. Weekends are busy from May to Oct. Maximum use is June–Aug. The deep backcountry is uncrowded.

Elevations range from 8,400 ft. to 13,103 ft. on South Truchas Peak, second highest in NM. Average annual precipitation is 35 to 40 in., about half from summer rains, half from winter snows. May and June are usually dry, July and Aug. wet. Snowfall usually begins in Nov. Winter access is by ski or snowshoe, since snowmobiles are prohibited. Entry from the N is often difficult before the end of May because of snow on access roads.

The area includes 15 mountain lakes and 30 perennial streams. Fishing is said to be excellent. Shores of popular destination lakes have been damaged by trampling, so camping is prohibited during revegetation. Visitors are asked to camp at least 300 ft. from any stream, lake, or main trail.

Much of the wilderness is forested; principal species are Engelmann spruce, corkbark fir, ponderosa pine, Douglas-fir, white fir, limber pine, bristlecone pine, and aspen.

Principal game animals are elk, mule deer, bighorn sheep, black bear, Abert and red squirrels, blue grouse, wild turkey.

San Pedro Parks Wilderness, 41,132 acres, is in the W central sector of the Jemez Division, on the San Pedro Mountains. Principal access routes are from SR 96, which crosses the Forest about 3 mi. N of the Wilderness.

The area averages 10,000 ft. above sea level. These mountains have no dramatic cliffs or peaks, but gentle, rolling topography. Large grassy parks and wet meadows are separated by dense stands of spruce and mixed conifers interspersed with stands of aspen. Clear streams meander through the meadows.

Annual precipitation is about 35 in., more as snow than rain. May and June are usually dry. Afternoon showers are common in July and Aug. Significant snowfall usually begins in Nov.

A calculation of visitor-days per acre gives this Wilderness a higher ratio than the Pecos, but this is because of its most heavily impacted area—San Gregorio Reservoir, near the S border of the area. It may be excluded from the Wilderness because it is artificial, not natural, and because it attracts crowds inconsistent with a wilderness experience.

A permit is required to enter the Wilderness, even for day hiking. Commercial outfitter-guide operations have been restricted because horses have had damaging impact on some areas.

Chama River Canyon Wilderness, 46,360 acres in the Coyote Ranger District, plus 2,900 acres in the Carson NF. The Canyon can be hiked from Heron Lake to El Vado Lake and on to Abiquiu Reservoir, with a section in this Wilderness. The river, a whitewater stream, can be floated, with portages, from the Colorado border to its confluence with the Rio Grande. Neither the Carson nor the Santa Fe National Forests could supply maps of this Wilderness, nor have they any printed information for prospective visitors. Established in 1978, it is not shown on the Forest map, dated 1975, but a Ranger can point out the area and access routes.

Dome Wilderness, 5,200 acres, is the smallest and newest, established in 1980. In the Tesuque R.D. No information is in print.

ACTIVITIES

Camping: 33 campgrounds, 517 sites. Season generally May–Oct.

Hiking, backpacking: The Forest has 834 mi. of recognized trails, more than half of this mileage in the 4 Wildernesses. Trails are deteriorating for lack of maintenance. Budgeted funds are insufficient to provide for more than clearing downed timber. Washouts and soil erosion are unchecked. No funds have been available to build or improve trails that would encourage dispersion, lightening the impact on stressed areas. Inquire at an R.D. office before undertaking more than a limited day hike.

Hunting: Chiefly big game.

Fishing: Trout, said to be excellent in lakes and many streams.

Horsepacking: Outfitters serve both Divisions, but horse travel is restricted in the Jemez Division. Special rules are in effect to limit damage in popular areas.

Rafting: Rio Chama Canyon.

Skiing: Santa Fe Ski Basin has full facilities.

Ski touring: Chiefly on trails and unplowed roads.

PUBLICATIONS
Forest map. $1.
Wilderness maps: Pecos; San Pedro Parks. Each $1.
General information; mimeo pages.

REFERENCES
Ganci, Dave. *Hiking the Southwest.* San Francisco: Sierra Club Books,
1983, pp. 216–265.
Overhage, Carl. *Six One-Day Walks in the Pecos Wilderness.* Santa Fe,
NM: Sunstone Press, 1980.
New Mexico Whitewater, a Guide to River Trips. Santa Fe: New Mexico
State Park Division, 1983, pp. 19–20.

HEADQUARTERS: 1220 St. Francis Dr., Santa Fe, NM 87504; (505) 988-6940.

RANGER DISTRICTS: Coyote R.D., Coyote, NM 87012; (505) 638-5547. Cuba
R.D., Cuba, NM 87013; (505) 289-3265. Jemez R.D., Jemez Springs, NM
87025; (505) 829-3535. Las Vegas R.D., 1926 N. 7th St., Las Vegas, NM
87701; (505) 425-3534. Pecos R.D., P.O. Drawer 3, Pecos, NM 87552;
(505) 757-6121. Tesuque R.D., 1220 St. Francis Dr., Santa Fe, NM 87504;
(505) 988-6935. Espanola R.D., P.O. Box R, Espanola, NM 87532; (505)
753-7331. Los Alamos Office, 528 35th St., Los Alamos, NM 87544; (505)
667-5120.

SIMON CANYON
U.S. Bureau of Land Management
3,811 acres.

From US 550 at Aztec, 23 mi. E on SR 173 and 2 mi. on unpaved access
road.

Simon Canyon drains into the San Juan River about 2 3/4 mi. below Navajo
Dam (see entry) and extends about 6 mi. N. The canyon bottom is relatively
flat, sloping gently upward along the stream, making for easy hiking and—
unfortunately—ORV driving. Canyon walls are steep, broken by numerous
side canyons. Elevations from 5,800 to 6,275 ft. at the rim. Topography of the
site includes terraces, mesas, plateaus, breaks, upland hills.
Streams flowing from the side canyons are ephemeral, with considerable
flows for short periods in spring melt and summer thunderstorms. The main
stream flows intermittently during the year. The site has about 1 mi. of
frontage on the San Juan River, a stream with 3 3/4 mi. of quality fishing
waters (see entry, Navajo Dam and Lake).

Vegetation is typical of the Upper and Lower Sonoran life zones. Cottonwood along the canyon bottom, pinyon-juniper on slopes, scattered patches of ponderosa pine and Douglas-fir along the rims. Grasses include blue grama, western wheatgrass, galleta, ring muhly, three-awn. Various cacti occur, chiefly in the canyon bottom.

No bird or mammal inventories have been made. Bird species noted include bald and golden eagles, prairie falcon, great horned owl, scrub jay, quail, wrens. Mammals: spotted ground squirrel, mountain cottontail, skunk, beaver, gray fox, porcupine, coyote.

The canyon was designated an Area of Critical Environmental Concern in 1980, because of recreational, wildlife, and cultural resources. A Navajo refugee pueblito, a single-room structure atop a boulder, is in reasonably good condition. BLM stabilized the site in 1975 by reinforcing and patching.

However, both the cultural site and the lower canyon have been damaged by neglect, abuse, and vandalism. Although the canyon is officially closed to ORVs, admonitory signs and barriers have been torn down, and ORV activity continues. Because of soil conditions, poor drainage, and heavy vehicle use, an area used for camping area adjacent to the canyon mouth is a maze of deep vehicle ruts, destroying native vegetation. A barrier of welded steel pipes set in concrete at the canyon mouth was erected to exclude vehicles from the canyon; it was destroyed. Funds are not available to station personnel at the canyon. BLM staff is working to develop cooperative agreements to use state personnel in the area.

Plans call for restoration of vegetation, upgrading the access road, constructing parking areas, and limiting the canyon and most of the recreation area to foot traffic. The New Mexico Department of Game and Fish would patrol and issue citations for ORV violations. The State Park and Recreation Division would enforce tent camping regulations in the recreation area. Vehicle camping would be available at the adjacent Cottonwoods site. Limited funds were provided for the first phase of the plan.

An off-season visit to the Canyon can be rewarding. On the Tuesday following Labor Day, only 3 RVs were in the camping area, and these seemed to belong to fishermen working the river. No hikers were in the canyon.

The site is surrounded by public lands, federal and state.

NEARBY: Navajo Lake State Park (see entry).

HEADQUARTERS: BLM, Farmington Resource Area, Farmington, NM 87401; (505) 325-3581.

TENT ROCKS
U.S. Bureau of Land Management
About 4,200 acres.

Access route best seen on Santa Fe National Forest map, which shows "Tent Rocks" NW of Cochiti Lake (see entry). From SR 22 near Cochiti Pueblo, NW about 5 mi. on well-maintained Forest Road 266.

Although within an hour's drive of Santa Fe or Albuquerque, this attractive site isn't shown on highway maps. It is known to and enjoyed by relatively few people, most of them living nearby, chiefly for day hiking and picnicking.

Badlands topography has made this a movie location. The "tent rocks" are formations resembling giant tepees. Elevations from about 5,600 to 6,750 ft.

Plants: Mostly pinyon-juniper woodland, with small ponderosa stands in canyons and at higher elevations, where Gambel oak is also common. Apache plume dominates canyon bottoms at lower elevations. A large population of pointleaf manzanita grows on the Tent Rocks slopes, the northernmost population of this shrub.

Birds: Abundant. Common species include northern flicker, Townsend's solitaire, plain titmouse, American robin, western and mountain bluebirds, Oregon and gray-headed juncos, violet-green swallow, western meadowlark, canyon wren, red-breasted nuthatch; pinyon, Steller's, and scrub jays; rufous-sided towhee, American kestrel, red-tailed hawk, common raven.

HEADQUARTERS: BLM, Rio Puerco Resource Area, 3540 Pan American Freeway, Albuquerque, NM 87107; (505) 766-3114.

URRACA WILDLIFE AREA
New Mexico Department of Game and Fish
13,870 acres.

Dirt access road, E from SR 3, 12 1/2 mi. N of Questa.

Few people come here, almost none outside hunting season. Most of the land between the Carson NF and the Colorado border is privately owned. Game and Fish acquired this site in 1966 to provide winter feeding grounds for deer and elk.

On the W slopes of the Sangre de Cristo Mountains. The access road goes to HQ, 2 mi. in, then turns S toward Urraca Canyon. The higher country can be reached only on foot or horseback. It's a steep climb, up from sagebrush flats to pinyon-juniper ridges, then through aspen parks into spruce-fir stands at about 11,000 ft. elevation.

Game animals include black bear, wild turkey, and grouse, in addition to deer and elk.

Camping: Designated primitive sites.

HEADQUARTERS: Villagra Bldg., Santa Fe, NM 87503; (505) 827-7899.

W. A. (BILL) HUMPHRIES WILDLIFE AREA
New Mexico Department of Game and Fish
10,868 acres.

S of US 64 where it separates from US 84 W of Chama.

The site straddles the Continental Divide at an elevation of about 7,500 ft. Some day there may be a Continental Divide National Trail. Those who wish to hike the route now can make this one of the segments. They will enjoy fine scenery and, except in hunting season, solitude. The area is open to foot and horse travel only; no vehicles.

The site was acquired in increments, beginning in 1966, to develop an elk herd. Reconditioning overgrazed slopes and providing water has helped the population to increase from an initial 20 or 30 to ten times that number.

Lower elevations are rolling hills with pinyon-juniper. Higher are mountain meadows and mixed conifers. The site includes part of Amargo Canyon.

HEADQUARTERS: Department of Game and Fish, Villagra Building, Santa Fe, NM 87503; (505) 827-7899.

ZONE 2

1 Cimarron Canyon State Park; Colin Neblett Wildlife Area
2 Elliott S. Barker Wildlife Area
3 Maxwell National Wildlife Refuge
4 Capulin Mountain National Monument
5 Clayton Lake State Park
6 Kiowa National Grassland
7 Chicosa Lake State Park
8 Coyote Creek State Park
9 Charette Lakes Fishing and Waterfowl Area
10 Morphy Lake State Park
11 Santa Fe National Forest
12 Las Vegas National Wildlife Refuge; McAllister Lake Fishing and Wildlife Area
13 Villanueva State Park
14 Santa Rosa Lake State Park

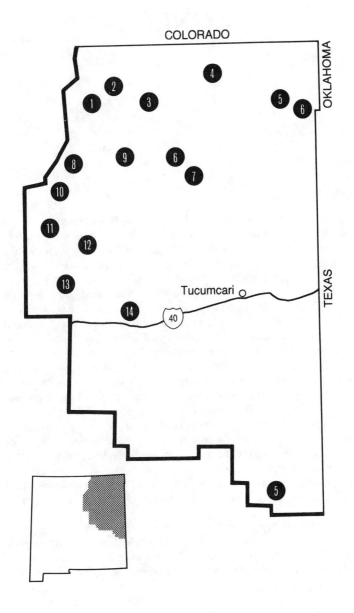

ZONE 2

Includes these counties:

Colfax	Union	Quay
Harding	San Miguel	Curry
Guadalupe	De Baca	
Roosevelt	Mora	

A good introduction to Zone 2 is entering from Texas and driving W on US 64. From the border to Clayton the road crosses the Kiowa National Grassland (see entry), but no sign marks it. The landscape is almost flat, seemingly featureless grazing land. Rabbit Ear Mountain, only 5,940 ft., seems almost impressive against the skyline.

It's a good road carrying little traffic. We became fascinated by the wildflowers. The cattle fences on either side are set about 20 ft. from the shoulder. These 20-ft. strips on either side are mowed occasionally but not grazed, and each has a swale to accommodate drainage. The swales are microhabitats, moister than the land beside them, producing fine crops of blossoms. In the season when we last passed this way, the predominant color was yellow.

These are the eastern plains, sloping gradually upward to the W, punctuated here and there by Capulin Mountain (see entry) and other volcanic cinder cones. To the N, the land is a bit higher and more rolling. Ahead, as one drives W, are the magnificent heights of the Sangre de Cristo Mountains.

The largest and best natural areas in this zone are a large block of the Santa Fe National Forest and the recent 100,000-acre Valle Vidal addition to the Carson National Forest; both Forests are entries in Zone 1. The Elliot S. Barker Wildlife Area (see entry) adjoins the Valle Vidal. One could hike there by bushwhacking along a creek, with near-zero likelihood of meeting other hikers.

Several other state and federal wildlife areas offer interesting hiking opportunities outside hunting season. The 7 State Parks included were all marginal selections. Each is pleasant, attractive, but not an exceptional natural area. In each case, there seemed to be sufficient reason for inclusion.

CAPULIN MOUNTAIN NATIONAL MONUMENT
National Park Service
775 acres.

From US 87 at Capulin, 3 mi. N on SR 325 to turnoff.

A well-preserved volcanic cinder cone rising over 1,000 ft. above the surrounding plain. Spectacular views from the top, extending into four states, the snow-capped Sangre de Cristo Mountains to the W, a volcanic landscape below. Highest point is 8,182 ft. The crater is 415 ft. deep.

From the visitor center at the foot, a road spirals up to a parking area at the edge of the crater. From here a 1-mi. trail circles the rim. The entire hillside is open to off-trail hiking.

Plants: List of flora available. Average annual precipitation is about 16 in., supporting a good plant cover. About 40% of the site is forested: pinyon pine, junipers, and ponderosa pine on the lower slopes, mountain-mahogany, chokecherry, Gambel oak, and squawbush higher up. Flowering species include mariposa tulip, false solomonseal, four-o'clock, virgin's bower, pasqueflower, prickly poppy, wallflower, lupine, clovers, globemallow, blazing star, evening primrose, gentian, morning glory, bluebell, forget-me-not, Indian paintbrush, asters, yarrow, chicory, coneflower, gilia, skyrocket, sunflower. Displays in late spring and summer depend on rainfall.

Birds: Checklist of 115 species available. Seasonally common or abundant species include: turkey vulture, mourning dove, black-chinned and broad-tailed hummingbirds, western kingbird, western wood-pewee, common raven, house wren, American robin, mountain bluebird, blue-gray gnatcatcher, western meadowlark, black-headed grosbeak, red crossbill, brown towhee, lark sparrow, Oregon junco, chipping sparrow.

Mammals: Checklist of 27 species available. Often or occasionally seen are mule deer, desert cottontail, least chipmunk, rock squirrel. Recorded but seldom seen: coyote, porcupine, badger, black bear, longtail weasel.

Reptiles and amphibians: Checklist available. Lizards: red-lipped prairie, lesser earless, short-horned. Barred tiger salamander, Great Plains skink. Bullsnake, western coachwhip, desert massasauga, prairie rattlesnake, common and wandering garter snakes, plains hognose snake. Boreal chorus and leopard frogs. Plains spadefoot. Musk turtle.

Other fauna: Large numbers of ladybugs sometimes swarm in summer, covering portions of trees and shrubs near the crater rim.

INTERPRETATION

Visitor center has exhibits, film, publications. Open 8:00 A.M.–4:30 P.M., possibly longer in summer. Exhibits at rim parking lot and on Rim Trail.

Nature trail behind the visitor center. The *Rim Trail* has numbered posts keyed to a booklet.

Campfire programs are presented by a Park interpreter on Friday and

Saturday evenings in summer at a commercial campground in the village of Capulin.

The road to the summit is occasionally closed by snow for a few days in winter.

Visitors should seek shelter in their vehicles or in buildings during summer thunderstorms.

PUBLICATIONS
Park leaflet.
General information page.
Crater Rim Trail Guide. $.50.
Checklists: flora, birds, reptiles and amphibians, and mammals.

HEADQUARTERS: Capulin, NM 88414; (505) 278-2201.

CHARETTE LAKES FISHING AND WATERFOWL AREA
New Mexico Department of Game and Fish
1,840 acres.

From I-25, 9 mi. S of Springer, 14 mi. W and S on SR 569.

The site was acquired to provide fishing and a resting area for waterfowl in a part of the state with little publicly owned land. On a mesa top at 6,500-ft. elevation, it includes two lakes, 300 acres and 110 acres. The S boundary is on the deep canyon of Ocate Creek.

The setting is extensive grama grass prairie. The Sangre de Cristo Mountains are visible on the W horizon.

Fishing is said to be good: yellow perch, rainbow trout. The lower lake is a refuge, attracting geese and ducks in migration. The smaller upper lake has limited waterfowl hunting.

Pronghorn and bald eagle are often seen, deer occasionally.

While not an exciting place, it offers quiet primitive camping and a bit of birding in an area where opportunities are limited.

HEADQUARTERS: P.O. Box 1145, Raton, NM 87740; (505) 445-2311.

CHICOSA LAKE STATE PARK
See entry, Kiowa National Grassland.

CIMARRON CANYON STATE PARK
See entry, Colin Neblett Wildlife Area.

CLAYTON LAKE STATE PARK
New Mexico State Park and Recreation Division; New Mexico Department of Game and Fish
417 acres of land; 170-acre lake.

From US 87 on W side of Clayton, 12 mi. N.

A man-made lake used for water-based recreation. Our first reaction was "not an entry." Looking further, we saw natural attractions. So do the waterfowl that winter here. The Department of Game and Fish manages the lake; the State Park came later.

About 1 mi. high. The surrounding country is moderately rugged: mesas, rimrock, juniper on slopes below, grasslands. Nearby is Rabbit Ear Mountain, 5,940 ft., source of the old lava flows. In late Aug., sunflowers were everywhere.

The lake, about 1/2 mi. long, is irregular in shape, with some rock bluffs along the shore. Campsites are attractively scattered along the S shore, not jammed together. Boats are limited to trolling speed. It's possible to hike around the lake, though few visitors do.

The lake is stocked with crappie, rainbow trout, and other species. Hunters often camp here. The Kiowa National Grassland (see entry) is about 3 mi. E.

The nearest large city, Amarillo, is 122 mi. away, so the site is seldom crowded.

Camping: 78 sites. All year.

HEADQUARTERS: Star Route, Seneca, NM 88437; (505) 374-9045.

COLIN NEBLETT WILDLIFE AREA; CIMARRON CANYON STATE PARK
New Mexico Department of Game and Fish; New Mexico State Park and Recreation Division
33,116 acres.

Both sides of US 64, between Cimarron and Eagle Nest.

This is New Mexico's largest wildlife area. Most visitors see only the scenic canyon of the Cimarron River, traversed by the highway for 9 mi. within the site. Informal camping became too popular, severely damaging vegetation between road and river. The .Department of Game and Fish closed and revegetated the informal campsites. Camping along the highway is now permitted only in designated areas. The camp areas are managed and maintained by the Park and Recreation Division. An unusual provision is that campers must have valid New Mexico hunting or fishing licenses. All available campsites are filled on many weekends.

One campground is beside the small Gravel Pit Lakes, formed by excavating for road-building materials. This campground was crowded when others we passed were almost empty, but we were told all campsites are filled early on popular weekends.

Except for hunters, few people visit the backcountry. All backcountry roads and tracks have been closed to vehicles. The terrain is mountainous; the canyon was cut through the Cimarron Range. Baldy Mountain, to the N, is 12,441 ft., Agua Fria Peak, to the S, 11,086 ft. Both appear to be on private land outside the site. Highest point within the site, Touch-Me-Not Mountain, is 12,045 ft. Elevation at the river is 7,400 ft.

The canyon is relatively narrow. Several sections have vertical cliffs with sculptured formations that attract both photographers and climbers. The river has two main tributaries, Tolby Creek and Clear Creek. The upper portion of Clear Creek has three 8-ft. waterfalls.

About 75% of the site is forested. Cottonwood and aspen are prominent on the bottomland, ponderosa pine and juniper on sloping canyon walls. Fir at higher elevations.

ACTIVITIES

Camping: 80 sites, all year. Hunting or fishing license required, one per car.

Hiking, backpacking: We saw several marked trailheads. The small map published by Game and Fish shows trails on both sides of the highway, three of them extending beyond the site boundaries. Topo maps are needed for backcountry travel.

Hunting: Deer, elk, bear, mountain lion, turkey, grouse.

Fishing: Rainbow and brown trout stocked.

Horse riding: Horses are used mostly by elk hunters, but horse travel is generally permitted.

Ski touring: Small but increasing use. Usual season: Jan.–Feb.

HEADQUARTERS: *Wildlife Area:* P.O. Box 136, Cimarron, NM 87714; (505) 376-2682. *State Park:* P.O. Box 147, Ute Park, NM 87749; (505) 377-6271.

COYOTE CREEK STATE PARK
New Mexico State Park and Recreation Division
80 acres.

From SR 3 at Mora, 14 mi. N on SR 38.

The park is small and surrounded by private land, but it seems spacious. The private land is as yet undeveloped, and park boundaries aren't conspicuous. The site, in the foothills of the Sangre de Cristos, is in a bowl or amphitheater formed by low hills around the creek's flood plain. Slopes are forested with ponderosa pine and pinyon-juniper. Cottonwood, willow, and tamarisk on the flood plain, as well as abundant wildflowers. The meandering creek is shallow and 5 to 15 ft. wide. We found an active beaver dam. The park manager told us he hears coyotes and has seen signs of bear.

Camping is informal. A few sites have shelters, but people camp wherever they find a level spot. A 1-mi. trail begins at the group campsite, ascends to the ridge, and returns.

The road from Mora is paved to the park and a short distance beyond. There, according to the manager, it becomes an unpaved fair-weather road.

HEADQUARTERS: P.O. Box 428, Guadalupita, NM 87722; (505) 387-2328.

ELLIOTT S. BARKER WILDLIFE AREA
New Mexico Department of Game and Fish
5,415 acres.

From US 64 just E of Cimarron (23 mi. E of Eagle Nest), NW 14 mi. on SR 204 (not shown on state highway map).

The unpaved road begins decently but deteriorates sharply after passing through a part of Philmont, the huge area owned by the Boy Scouts. In snow or after a rain it should be attempted only by 4-wheel-drive vehicles. Our motor home made it for 12 mi., but with storm clouds threatening we decided not to cross a ford.

Ponil Creek has cut a canyon through a long, high mesa extending from the Cimarron Mountain branch of the Sangre de Cristos. The road follows the creek. In places the canyon is narrow. Mud and boulders had been bladed off after a recent storm.

The Wildlife Area is bisected by the canyon and includes small side canyons, rock outcrops, timbered slopes, and meadows, some of which have been planted with feed crops for wildlife. Elevations from 7,300 to 8,700 ft. About 50% of the area is forested. Principal tree species are ponderosa pine and juniper, with cottonwood and Gambel oak along the stream.

This is good habitat for deer, elk, bear, and turkey. Indeed, five turkeys greeted us. Also present: dusky grouse, band-tailed pigeon, magpie, raven, hawks. Mammals include coyote, mountain lion, squirrel, raccoon, cottontail. Deer are here all year, elk in winter. The number of elk hunters is limited.

An attractive area with few visitors except in hunting season.

ADJACENT: The *Valle Vidal Unit of Carson National Forest* (see entry, Zone 1). This 100,000-acre area was given to the nation by the Pennzoil Corporation. It adjoins the Wildlife Area on the N. North and Middle Ponil Creeks arise in the area, joining to form Ponil Creek. Our Game and Fish informant described the area as "splendid." Access from the Wildlife Area would be by foot or horse, following Middle Ponil Creek.

Camping: Limited to the lower third of the canyon bottom. Primitive.

HEADQUARTERS: Donald Jones, P.O. Box 136, Cimarron, NM 87714; (505) 376-2682.

KIOWA NATIONAL GRASSLAND
Cibola National Forest
136,412 acres.

Two units: (1) between Clayton and the Oklahoma-Texas border, crossed by US 56/64 and US 87; (2) crossed by SR 39 S of Abbott on US 56.

Most people pass the Grassland without knowing it's there. No signs mark it. Two National Grasslands we studied in Colorado are major attractions for birders; they have auto tour routes, checklists, primitive campgrounds. Few people come here.

Has it less to offer? Someone at Forest HQ dismissed it as "typical Texas Panhandle country. Not much wildlife of any kind." The District Ranger disagreed: "This is heaven!" he declared.

Gentle to rolling terrain with shortgrass cover. Soils range from clays to deep sand. Vegetation ranges from buffalo and blue grama grass to a bluestem complex on the deeper sands. Elevation is about 5,000 ft., annual precipitation about 15 in. Most of the area shows signs of past overgrazing; range management is geared to improving the ecosystem of the entire area, not just that within the Grassland boundaries.

The Canadian River crosses the W side of the second unit. Not far to the N, this river is little more than a swale, but here it meanders in a splendid canyon, between 1/4 and 1 mi. from rimrock to rimrock, 700 to 800 ft. deep. The riparian environment is more productive than the upland and attracts more wildlife. A Forest Service contact showed us photographs of the canyon bottom and said he often camps there with his family. "Beautiful! It's a real paradise!"

About a hundred miles of the river, including the 13 mi. within the Grassland, have been studied for possible designation under the Wild and Scenic Rivers Act. The Grassland portion would merit Scenic designation.

Public use of the canyon is light: about 600 visitor-days per year. Developments are a primitive campground, the partially preserved ruins of a Butterfield Stage station, and a homestead.

Birds: Checklist indicates abundance and seasonality. Fairly common to common summer residents include turkey vulture, killdeer, long-billed curlew, mourning dove, burrowing owl, western kingbird, Say's phoebe; barn and cliff swallows; white-necked raven, mockingbird, northern oriole, lark sparrow. Fairly common to common species in migration include Canada goose, gadwall, green- and blue-winged teals, American wigeon, shoveler, redhead, lesser scaup, ruddy duck, Baird's sandpiper, Wilson's phalarope, northern harrier, sandhill crane, American coot, common nighthawk, alder flycatcher, western wood-pewee, rough-winged swallow, house wren, gray catbird, sage thrasher, American robin, hermit and Swainson's thrushes, mountain bluebird; yellow, yellow-rumped, McGillivray's, and Wilson's warblers; yellow-headed blackbird, lark bunting, vesper sparrow, Oregon junco; chipping, clay-colored, white-crowned, and Lincoln's sparrows; chestnut-collared longspur.

Mammals: Fairly abundant. Include blacktail jackrabbit, cottontail, coyote, fox, badger, prairie dog, mule deer, and the exotic Barbary sheep and Siberian ibex. Many smaller species. Pronghorn are abundant, providing most of the hunting.

Camping: no restrictions on camping in the Grassland. Developed campground in Mills Canyon area, 7 sites. Access road is primitive, not for ordinary cars in wet weather.

NEARBY: Chicosa Lake State Park, a 600-acre park with a 40-acre reservoir. A feature of the park is its herd of longhorn cattle. Also some bison. *Camping:* 46 sites. All year.

PUBLICATION: Map. $1. Order from Cibola National Forest (see entry).

HEADQUARTERS: *National Grassland,* 16 N. Second, Clayton NM 88415; (505)

374-9652. *National Forest,* 10308 Candelaria NE, Albuquerque, NM 87112; (505) 766-2185. *Chicosa Lake State Park,* Roy, NM 87743; (505) 485-2424.

LAS VEGAS NATIONAL WILDLIFE REFUGE
U.S. Fish and Wildlife Service
8,672 acres.

MCALLISTER LAKE FISH AND WATERFOWL AREA
New Mexico Department of Game and Fish
623 acres.

From Las Vegas, E 1.6 mi. on SR 104, then S on SR 281.

Most of the Game and Fish land is managed as part of the National Wildlife Refuge. The Department retains only the 100-acre lake and the land around it for fishing and camping.

Slightly rolling rangeland, mountains in the far distance, only low hills nearby. Large areas of native grasses. Also cropland, marsh, ponds, timbered canyons, streams. Elevation is 6,500 ft. Climate is generally mild, seldom over 90°F in summer or below freezing on winter days. Snow accumulation seldom exceeds 12 in. Summer showers provide most of the 15 in. annual precipitation. Ponds sometimes freeze, but the larger ones usually have some open water.

The Refuge is near the Continental Divide. Records of 170 species include birds common to both eastern and western United States, among them: bald and golden eagles, prairie falcon, sandhill crane, long-billed curlew, rough-legged hawk, many shorebirds, ducks, geese.

The auto tour route is a public road bisecting the area. All other roads are closed to visitors, whether driving or walking. Most of the impoundments are beyond the range of binoculars. In early Sept., there wasn't much to see. A leaflet was posted on the bulletin board, but no supply was provided, nor was there a bird checklist. The leaflet mentions a nature trail "available by special use permit only." The Manager told us that special auto tours are available on Sunday afternoons in Nov.

The Refuge ponds, wetlands, and irrigation depend on runoff from snowpack in distant mountains. In dry years, many migrants must seek other stopovers.

We do not recommend this area for a casual visit. Those interested should telephone to find out how good the birding is and to gain access to better vantage points than the road offers.

The McAllister Lake area is managed by Game and Fish. The access includes a short section of poorly maintained dirt road that could be a problem after heavy rains. Camping, boating, and fishing are available.

ACTIVITIES
Camping: Primitive. No fixed sites. All year.
Boating: Ramp. No posted limit, but anything more than a small motor would be inappropriate.
Fishing: Trout.

HEADQUARTERS: (NWR) Route 1, Box 399; Las Vegas, NM 87701; (505) 425-3581.

MAXWELL NATIONAL WILDLIFE REFUGE
U.S. Fish and Wildlife Service
3,699 acres.

From I-25 at Maxwell, N on SR 85, then W on SR 505.

When conditions are favorable, here is some of the best birding in eastern New Mexico. In gently rolling terrain, the Refuge lies in a closed basin, surrounded by mountains and high mesas. Elevation is about 6,000 ft.

The Refuge was established in 1966 to provide a resting and feeding area for migratory waterfowl. It includes three irrigation reservoirs, the largest with 400 acres of surface, the other two with 100 each, as well as wetlands. The Refuge depends for water on the annual runoff from mountain watersheds, and it takes second place to other claimants. In dry years, most migrants must look elsewhere. We suggest telephoning before visiting.

Average annual precipitation is about 14.5 in. About 12 in. of snow falls in winter. Aug. is the wettest month. Jan.–Apr. are usually dry.

Viewing is good. About 10 mi. of roads cross the Refuge or mark its boundaries. Check with HQ about hiking in other areas; some are closed seasonally.

Birds: 153 species recorded; visitors are asked to report others. Species nesting include mallard, gadwall, pintail; green-winged, blue-winged, and cinnamon teals; northern harrier, American kestrel, scaled quail, ring-necked pheasant, killdeer, American avocet, mourning dove, roadrunner; barn, great horned, and burrowing owls; common nighthawk, rufous hummingbird, northern flicker, red-headed and Lewis' woodpeckers; eastern, western, and Cassin's kingbirds; Say's phoebe, horned lark; violet-green, barn, and cliff swallows; black-billed magpie, common raven, house wren, mockingbird, American robin, European starling, house sparrow, western meadowlark; yellow-headed, red-winged, and Brewer's blackbirds; Bullock's oriole, brown-headed cowbird, blue grosbeak, house finch, brown towhee, savannah sparrow. Seasonally common or abundant species include: eared and pied-billed grebes, double-crested cormorant, great blue heron, American wigeon, shoveler, redhead, lesser scaup, bufflehead, ruddy duck, common merganser, Swainson's and rough-legged hawks, golden and bald eagles, American coot, solitary sandpiper, greater and lesser yellowlegs, Wilson's phalarope, herring and ring-billed gulls, black tern, mountain bluebird, pine siskin, lark bunting, slate-colored and Oregon juncos, white-crowned and song sparrows. Other visitors include sandhill crane, Canada goose, snowy egret, hooded merganser.

ACTIVITIES
Fishing: Feb. 27–Oct. 17 in designated areas.
Boating: On the large lake, fishing season only. Boats limited to trolling speed.

Periodic winter storms Nov.–May can make driving hazardous. Check road conditions.

PUBLICATIONS
Leaflet with map.
Bird checklist.
Fishing and boating regulations.

HEADQUARTERS: P.O. Box 276, Maxwell, NM 87728; (505) 375-2331.

MCALLISTER LAKE FISH AND WATERFOWL AREA
See entry, Las Vegas National Wildlife Refuge.

MORPHY LAKE STATE PARK
New Mexico State Park and Recreation Division

MORPHY LAKE FISHING AREA
New Mexico Department of Game and Fish
238 acres; 30-acre lake.

From SR 3 at Mora, S 4 mi. on SR 94.

Various state documents say the lake, an irrigation reservoir, is 15, 30, and 50 acres; a posted sign says 25 acres at minimum pool. All agree it's a scenic gem, a small lake in high mountains surrounded by ponderosa pine forest in the Canadian River watershed. Elevation is 7,840 ft. Game and Fish stocks the lake; State Parks manages the primitive campground. The site is surrounded by private land, although the Santa Fe National Forest is just a few miles away.

SR 94 is steep, rough, and crooked. Four-wheel-drive vehicles are recommended, although there may be times when ordinary automobiles are adequate. There is conflict with locals, and on a couple of occasions visitors have been threatened.

Snow closes the road in winter.

ACTIVITIES
Camping: 20 primitive sites.
Fishing: Stocked with rainbow trout.
Boating: No motors.

HEADQUARTERS: (State Park) P.O. Box 428, Guadalupita, NM 87722; (505) 387-2328.

SANTA FE NATIONAL FOREST
See entry in Zone 1, which has a majority of the acreage.
One large block lies between Santa Fe and Las Vegas, and most of this is in Zone 2.

SANTA ROSA LAKE STATE PARK
New Mexico State Park and Recreation Division
13,640 acres.

From Santa Rosa on I-40, out 8th St. and 7 mi. N.

We first marked this one "not an entry," then reconsidered. The Corps of Engineers dammed the Pecos River here for irrigation and flood control, completing the main embankment in 1981. Drawdown is extreme. At full pool the reservoir has a surface area of 12,294 acres, but the Corps says, "There is no permanent pool." When there is sufficient water, the lake attracts many boaters and campers. No other public land is nearby.

We make it a marginal entry because of the natural setting: steep canyon sides along much of the W and SW boundary, gentle slopes on the E and SE. Desert vegetation: pricklypear, cholla, four-wing saltbush, Russian thistle, Apache plume, sunflower, loco. 62 bird species have been recorded, with waterfowl numbers increasing. Mammals seen include pronghorn, mule deer, coyote, striped skunk, porcupine, rock squirrel, cottontail, and blacktail jackrabbit.

The Park has a short "scenic trail." Hiking opportunities are greater when the water surface is low, exposing land along the old river channel and canyon.

ACTIVITIES
Camping: 48 sites, plus primitive sites. All year.
Hunting: Outside the Park boundaries. Dove, quail, waterfowl.
Boating: Ramp. No hp limit.

PUBLICATION: Leaflet available from Corps of Engineers.

HEADQUARTERS: *State Park,* P.O. Box 384, Santa Rosa, NM 88435; (505) 472-3110. *Corps,* Box 345, Santa Rosa, NM 88435; (505) 472-3115.

VILLANUEVA STATE PARK
New Mexico State Park and Recreation Division
1,015 acres.

From I-25 between Pecos and Las Vegas, S 12 mi. on SR 3.

An attractive small campground between sandstone bluffs on the Pecos River. The river here is about 30 ft. wide, shallow, moderately swift. The tan to reddish bluffs are 50 to over 150 ft. high. Cottonwoods grow near the river. Slopes are dotted with pinyon-juniper. Short trails follow the river and ascend the bluffs to a lookout. From a bridge over the river, a trail leads to an historic ruin.

The road from the Interstate is quiet, often close to the river, passing through old Spanish towns where adobe houses are being replaced by mobiles. The highway map suggests that the park might adjoin the Santa Fe National Forest. It does not, although a disjunct section of the Forest is less than 2 mi. away.

On a fine Labor Day weekend, most of the campsites with shelters were occupied, but there were vacancies.

Camping: 77 sites. All year.

HEADQUARTERS: Villanueva, NM 87583; (505) 421-9767.

ZONE 3

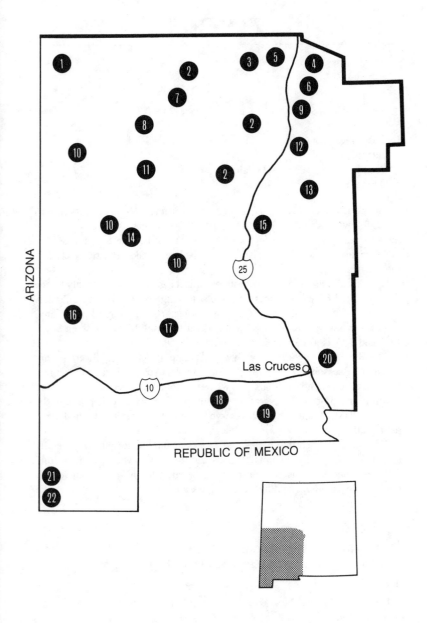

ARIZONA

ARIZONA

REPUBLIC OF MEXICO

Las Cruces

ZONE 3

Includes these counties:

Catron	Socorro	Luna
Grant	Hidalgo	
Dona Ana	Sierra	

The Zone is New Mexico's SW quarter. I-25 runs N–S through its eastern third, following the Rio Grande. I-10 runs W–E across its lower third. The terrain N and W of these highways is mountainous. The S and E sectors includes large areas of volcanism, desert, isolated peaks, and relatively low mountain ranges.

If we could choose only one destination in NM, it would probably be the Gila National Forest. Its mountains are not as high as the Sangre de Cristos, but they offer some of the best hiking and backpacking opportunities anywhere. We have yet to meet other hikers on the trail. SR 90 between Silver City and I-25 is a fine scenic drive.

The Rio Grande Valley is a flyway. Whooping and sandhill cranes are among the seasonal visitors at the Bosque del Apache National Wildlife Refuge. On our first visit, years ago, we were fascinated to see cormorants and bullfrogs in mid-desert. Several smaller but pleasant wildlife areas are in the valley. So is the Elephant Butte Reservoir, the state's largest water body, fine for aquatic sports but not, in our view, a natural area.

The many isolated mountains and ranges of modest height are generally lacking in springs and perennial streams, but they have a variety of interesting features. Their canyons, natural routes upward, often have riparian vegetation and considerable wildlife. Guadalupe Canyon (see entry) is well known for its unusual bird species.

BERNARDO WATERFOWL AREA
New Mexico Department of Game and Fish
1,573 acres.

From Bernardo on I-25, E on US 60 across tracks. Area is on both sides of the road.

This small site offers good birding, especially in winter. Several whooping cranes may be present, a number of sandhill cranes, and numerous snow geese and other waterfowl.

On Rio Grande bottomland, the site has a small marsh, pond, and 450 acres of feed crops. Hunting and camping are not permitted.

NEARBY: La Joya Waterfowl Area (see entry).

BOSQUE DEL APACHE NATIONAL WILDLIFE REFUGE
U.S. Fish and Wildlife Service
57,191 acres.

From US 380 at San Antonio, 8 mi. S on SR 1.

Open: 1/2 hr. before sunrise to 1/2 hr. after sunset.

Much of the natural waterfowl habitat of the Rio Grande Valley has been lost to agriculture and other developments. This refuge was established in 1939 to provide habitat for wintering waterfowl. It had an important role in saving the then-endangered sandhill crane.

In the late 1930s and early 1940s, construction of water impoundments began. When we first visited the Refuge in 1963, we were fascinated by the contrast between the surrounding desert and this green wetland with its cormorants and bullfrogs. Most of the water is taken through ditches from the Rio Grande. The Refuge is at the downstream end of a farming district that relies on irrigation. The Refuge irrigates 1,300 acres of cropland. In dry years there isn't enough water for all. More water is underground, 80 to 100 ft. down, but pumping is too costly for today's slender refuge budgets. In summer, most of the impoundments are drained to promote growth of vegetation for waterfowl, but some ponds are kept watered for the benefit of egrets, rails, and other marsh and shorebirds.

With the sandhill crane apparently safe, attention shifted to the endangered whooping crane. Rescue efforts at the nesting grounds have included placing whooping crane eggs in sandhill nests, with the expectation that whoopers successfully hatched would migrate with their foster parents. When we visited in 1984, it was expected that 38 migrant whoopers would arrive in New Mexico that winter, and about 20 would spend some time at the Refuge.

It's the best place to see the whooping cranes. This attracts birders from far and wide. They also come to see the fast-increasing flocks of snow geese, as many as 40,000 on the Refuge at one time.

Annual visitation was about 10,000 in the early 1960s. Now it's about 80,000, peaking in Dec.–Jan. Most visitors come in the period Nov.–Feb., but the Refuge leaflet says visits during other seasons are "just as rewarding." That's an overstatement. There's less to see when most impoundments are dry and most waterfowl are nesting up north. But summer visits are enjoyable, especially early and late in the day.

The main portion of the Refuge is on Rio Grande bottomland. On the W side of I-25, Refuge land includes rolling desert hills and Chupadera Peak. On the E, it includes the Little San Pascual Mountains. These uplands, as well as an area W of HQ, just E of I-25, have little direct role in the Refuge's mission. They are now declared Wilderness Areas, roadless and undeveloped. Visitors are free to hike in these areas, but few do so; New Mexico has many such areas of desert hills.

When we first visited, the salt cedar or tamarisk was a curiosity. In 1984 we were shocked to see how rapidly it has spread, crowding out cottonwoods. The species was brought to North America about 1900 as an ornamental bush and to control erosion. It has become a pest in much of the Southwest. A deep-rooted plant that takes up and transpires much water, wastefully, it has defeated all efforts to eliminate it.

Stop first at the visitor center in the HQ area, on the W side of the road. A 12-mi. auto tour route begins on the E side. Leaflets are available at the contact station. Bring binoculars or, better still, a spotting scope.

A sign at the beginning of the tour route advises visitors to remain in their cars. The birds are accustomed to vehicles but fly off if a person on foot appears. One individual stepping from his car can spoil things for others. The sign's message is not a rule but a request that matters most when others are present. But those who do walk are urged to walk only on Refuge trails.

Birds: Checklist of 295 species available. This is one of NM's birding hotspots. The checklist includes a fascinating supplement of "accidentals" observed at some time since 1940, including wood stork, surf scoter, long-tailed jaeger, black-legged kittiwake, groove-billed ani.

Seasonally common or abundant species include pied-billed grebe, double-crested and olivaceous cormorants, great blue heron, snowy egret, black-crowned night-heron, American bittern, Canada and snow geese, mallard, gadwall, pintail; green-winged, blue-winged, and cinnamon teals; American wigeon, northern shoveler, redhead, ring-necked duck, canvasback, bufflehead, ruddy duck, common merganser. Turkey vulture; sharp-shinned, Cooper's, and red-tailed hawks; northern harrier, American kestrel, Gambel's quail, whooping crane, sandhill crane, Virginia rail, sora, American coot, killdeer, common snipe, spotted sandpiper, greater yellowlegs, long-billed dowitcher, American avocet, black-necked stilt, Wilson's phalarope, ring-billed gull. Also mourning dove, roadrunner, lesser nighthawk, northern flicker, ladder-backed woodpecker, western kingbird, ash-throated and western flycatchers, black and Say's phoebes, horned lark. Swallows: violet-green, tree, bank, rough-winged, barn, cliff. Scrub jay, common raven, common crow, mountain chickadee. Wrens: cactus, marsh, canyon, rock. Mockingbird, American robin, hermit thrush, western bluebird, ruby-crowned kinglet, water pipit, loggerhead shrike, European starling. Warblers: Lucy's, yellow-rumped, common yellowthroat, yellow-breasted chat, Wilson's. Western meadowlark; yellow-headed, red-winged, and Brewer's blackbirds; northern oriole, great-tailed grackle, brown-headed cowbird, western tanager, black-headed and blue grosbeaks, house finch, pine siskin, American and lesser goldfinches, rufous-sided towhee. Sparrows: savannah, vesper, lark, black-throated, sage, chipping, Brewer's, white-crowned, song. Dark-eyed and gray-headed juncos.

Other wildlife: Checklists available for mammals (58 species), reptiles and amphibians (55 species), fishes (10 species).

FEATURES
Auto tour, 12 mi., passes 2 observation towers.
Bosque Trail, 1 3/4 mi., near N end of tour route.
Scenic walk, 3/4 mi., near mid-point of tour route.

INTERPRETATION
Visitor center has exhibits, literature.
Guided car tours are given occasionally, by reservation, Nov.–Feb., usually two per month.

ACTIVITIES
Hunting: In designated areas. Deer, dove, quail, rabbit. Snow goose by special permit.
Fishing: In designated waters only, during summer months. Chiefly catfish.

Pets are permitted, on leash.
Mosquitoes are thick in May and Aug.

PUBLICATIONS
Leaflet with map.
Bird checklist.
Checklists of mammals, reptiles and amphibians, fishes.
Hunting and fishing leaflet.

HEADQUARTERS: P.O. Box 1246, Socorro, NM 87801; (505) 835-1828.

CIBOLA NATIONAL FOREST
U.S. Forest Service
See entry in Zone 1. The Magdalena Ranger District of the Forest is in Zone 3.

CITY OF ROCKS STATE PARK
New Mexico State Park and Recreation Division
680 acres.

From Deming on I-10, 23 mi. NW on US 180, then NE on SR 61.

The central feature of this site is a 40-acre field of large boulders, volcanic rock eroded into fanciful shapes. The Park is at 5,000 ft. elevation in a desert environment. The attractive campground has a cultivated cactus garden.

Most surrounding land is privately owned. SR 61 continues N for 50 mi. to Lake Roberts in the Gila NF.

Camping: 56 sites. All year.

HEADQUARTERS: P.O. Box 54, Faywood, NM 88034; (505) 388-6026.

CONTINENTAL DIVIDE
U.S. Bureau of Land Management
68,761 acres.

No legal access in 1985. BLM hopes to establish legal access through Cottonwood Canyon on the W side by 1987. Inquire at HQ.

This irregularly shaped site is about 26 mi. W–E, 1 to 12 mi. N–S. It lies immediately to the S of the Plains of San Agustin, a closed desert basin. The site has two major landscapes: a vast expanse of rolling grasslands, and a more rugged forested environment. Elevations range from 6,785 ft. at the W edge to 9,212-ft. Pelona Mountain near the center. The forested area N and NW of the mountain has a diversity of landforms: steep canyons and broad ridges, with a variety of vegetation and color. The mountain geology is volcanic.

SR 78 runs along the E boundary of the site for about 5 mi., but the main features are in the W.

The Continental Divide runs from the W boundary across Pelona Mountain, then E and N, looping outside the N boundary for about 5 mi. before entering the site's NE corner. Each year a few hikers and horsemen attempt to follow the Divide from Canada to Mexico. BLM estimates that about 10 cross here yearly. If the Continental Divide National Scenic Trail Corridor becomes a reality, it will almost certainly cross this site.

Climate is mild, semiarid. This is a good summer area, with temperatures averaging in the 80s by day, dropping into the 40s at night. Winter temperatures average from the 40s by day to the teens at night, although lows of −28°F have been recorded. Annual precipitation averages 12 to 13 in. at low elevations, 16 in. above. Average snowfall is 2 to 3 ft., enough to limit access occasionally. The site has no perennial streams or ponds, no springs with potable water. Arroyos and canyons carry runoff after summer storms, but briefly.

Plants: About three-fourths of the site is rolling grassland, chiefly in the S and E sectors and on a large, high plateau extending NW and SW from Pelona Mountain. Blue grama predominates, with wolftail and, in lesser amounts, squirreltail, needle-and-thread, black grama. In swales and drainages: broom snakeweed, Apache plume, rubber rabbitbrush, four-wing saltbush, winterfat.

Pinyon-juniper predominates on southern and eastern slopes, intermingling with the ponderosa-pinyon association at higher elevations. Species include pinyon pine, alligator juniper, and one-seed juniper. Understory species include mountain-mahogany, oak, rubber rabbitbrush, globemallow, blue grama, western wheatgrass.

About 5,000 acres at the high elevations are dominated by ponderosa pine, with a few areas of Douglas-fir and scattered limber pine. This coniferous forest includes some pinyon-juniper, generally on S and E slopes. Understory includes gray and Gambel oaks, mountain-mahogany, snowberry, wax currant, buckbrush.

Birds: No checklist. HQ has a list of 175 species occurring in these habitats. Mentioned here: turkey vulture, golden eagle, red-tailed hawk, great horned owl, common raven, northern flicker.

Mammals: No checklist. HQ has a list of 75 species occurring in these habitats. Mentioned here: blacktail jackrabbit, desert cottontail, coyote, kit fox, porcupine, chipmunk, rock squirrel, bobcat, mountain lion, pronghorn, mule deer, elk.

The site has about 45 mi. of roads, including old and washed-out logging roads and roads used regularly by ranchers. Logging ceased in 1960, and some logging roads are returning to natural condition, possible hiking routes in the forested area. Some ORV use occurs, chiefly by hunters. If the site is declared a Wilderness Area, ORVs will be excluded, as will ranchers' vehicles, although grazing can continue.

ACTIVITIES

Hunting: Mostly deer, pronghorn.

Horse riding: Horse riding and packing occur, though rarely now outside hunting season. The site has 51 mi. of cattle fences.

HEADQUARTERS: BLM, Socorro Resource Area, Box 1219, Socorro, NM 87801; (505) 835-0412.

CORONADO NATIONAL FOREST
U.S. Forest Service

One block of this Forest extends from AZ into NM. On the Peloncillo Mountains, 3 mi. N of the Mexican border. See entry in AZ Zone 4.

DATIL WELL
U.S. Bureau of Land Management
640 acres.

Off US 60, 1 mi. NW of Datil.

BLM maintains a 10-acre wayside campground at the site of one of the wells spaced along an historic livestock trail. A 3-mi. hiking and nature trail passes through pinyon-juniper woodlands to three viewpoints overlooking the Plains of San Agustin.

Camping: 22 sites. All year.

PUBLICATION: Leaflet.

HEADQUARTERS: BLM, Socorro Resource Area, P.O. Box 1219, Socorro, NM 87801; (505) 835-0412.

EAGLE PEAK; MESITA BLANCA
U.S. Bureau of Land Management
49,177 acres.

From Quemado on U. S. 60, NW on SR 32, a dirt road, to Salt Lake. Then S on County Road A007, which runs between the two units.

These lightly visited areas offer pleasant desert hiking in a setting which, though low-key, has a variety of landforms. SR 32 from Quemado to Fence Lake is an attractive scenic drive. The dominant topographic feature of the area is a large cinder cone, Cerro Pomo, just S of the town of Salt Lake. At the bottom of the crater is Zuni Salt Lake, which has been a salt supply for many Indian tribes for more than a thousand years, a neutral ground with religious significance. The lava flow extends into the unit.

The Eagle Peak unit, E of the county road, includes smaller cinder cones, lava flows, gently rolling hills, and sandstone and basalt mesas and canyons. Elevations range from 6,400 to 7,550 ft., with the highest land in the E. Cottonwood Canyon is an especially scenic feature, in the W central part of the area.

Red Hill Cinder Cone is the principal feature of the Mesita Blanca unit, W of the county road. This cone, in the SW sector, has been likened to Sunset Crater in AZ, although it is smaller and less dramatic. The 2,000-acre lava flow is older than El Malpais (see entry in Zone 1) and has more mature vegetation. The N portion of Mesita Blanca is a flat to rolling grassland. In the central and S portions, this is broken by isolated sandstone and basalt mesas with vertical cliffs.

Climate of the area is mild, semiarid. Summer daytime temperatures average in the 80s but can exceed 100°F. Winter daytime temperatures average in the 40s. Annual precipitation is from 9 to 14 in., half of it falling in July–Sept. thunderstorms. There are no perennial streams or ponds. Flash floods occur in drainages after storms.

About half of the area is grassland, with scattered shrubs. About half, chiefly at higher elevations, is pinyon-juniper association.

Wildlife: No checklists are published, but HQ has lists of species believed to occur here. These indicate a considerable variety of species, although populations of most are small.

HEADQUARTERS: BLM, Socorro Resource Area, P.O. Box 1219, Socorro, NM 87801; (505) 835-0412.

ELEPHANT BUTTE STATE PARK
New Mexico State Park and Recreation Division
20,512 land acres; 36,558 water acres.

Off I-25, 7 mi. N of Truth or Consequences.

It's too big to ignore, but very little of this site meets our definition of "natural area." It's the largest water body in NM, almost 40 mi. long, and it attracts larger crowds than any other NM park, chiefly for water-based recreation. Shoreline development appears unplanned, uncontrolled, and—in our view—unattractive. The lake is surrounded by low desert hills with sparse vegetation. It lacks bays, coves, and other irregularities that might provide pockets of isolation. We were told a marsh at the N end attracts waterfowl.

Camping: 200 sites. All year.

HEADQUARTERS: P.O. Box 13, Elephant Butte, NM 87935; (505) 744-5421.

FLORIDA MOUNTAINS
U.S. Bureau of Land Management
22,336 acres.

From Deming on I-10, S 4 mi. on SR 11, then E on County Road B023.

It's the most prominent land feature for miles around, rising 2,800 ft. above the surrounding desert basins. The N–S range is about 10 mi. long, up to 5 mi. wide. Florida Peak is 7,295 ft. Also prominent are South and Gym peaks. Topography is rugged, with steep canyons and near-vertical cliffs. Alluvial fans slope toward the valley floors. BLM's evaluation gave the range top scenic rating.

The access road ends at the NE site boundary, about 2 mi. from Florida Peak. Ranch roads skirt the entire range, but some require 4-wheel drive. The upper slopes of the range have mixed shrub vegetation with patches of pinyon-juniper. Species include snakeweed, sumac, creosote, sotol, beargrass, mesquite, tarbush, pricklypear, feather peabush, and yucca, together with gramas, tobosa, and other grasses. Unlike most ranges of this desert area, the mountains are fairly well watered by springs and seeps, some of which support cattail, willow, grapevine, and other riparian vegetation. However, no streams are perennial.

Birds: No checklist. Species mentioned include prairie falcon; red-tailed, Swainson's, and ferruginous hawks; golden eagle, American kestrel, great horned owl, quail, dove, ladder-backed woodpecker, canyon wren, black-chinned sparrow.

Mammals: No checklist. Mentioned: mountain lion, deer, coyote, badger, ringtail, kit fox. Persian ibex were released here in the 1970s and multiplied. A 1983 census counted 647 in this area. The site has desert mule deer and a small javelina population.

Reptiles and amphibians: No checklist. Seven amphibian species known to occur, most abundant being western spadefoot and desert toad. Of 25 reptile species known here, most abundant are greater earless, collared, and Texas horned lizards; rock and black-tailed rattlesnakes.

No information is available on current recreational use, but it appears to be small, chiefly hunting. The site offers opportunities for day hiking, backpacking, and rockhounding.

NEARBY: *Rockhound State Park* is 2 mi. N, also reached by County Road B023. The Park is on the W slope of the Little Florida Mountains. Visitors are invited to collect and remove up to 15 lbs. of geodes, jasper, agate, carnelian, rhyolite, pitchstone, perlite, and other minerals. The

Park is a favorite meeting-place for rockhounds. When the collecting area has been picked over, it may be bladed to expose more specimens. Some collectors venture S into the BLM area.

Camping: 30 sites. All year.

HEADQUARTERS: BLM, Las Cruces District Office, 1800 Marquess St., Las Cruces, NM 88005; (505) 525-8228.

GILA CLIFF DWELLINGS NATIONAL MONUMENT
Gila National Forest
533 acres.

From Silver City on US 180, N on SR 15 to end. With trailer over 18 ft., take SR's 61 and 35 NW from San Lorenzo to Lake Roberts, then SR 15.

Administration of the Monument was transferred from the U.S. Forest Service to the National Park Service in 1933, back to the Gila National Forest in 1975. The visitor center serves both Forest and Monument. The Monument is within the Forest and at the edge of the Gila Wilderness.

A 1/2-mi. trail leads to the cliff dwellings occupied by the Pueblo people a thousand years ago. Ruins of other houses remain. Exhibits describe how these people lived and worked.

PUBLICATION: Leaflet.

HEADQUARTERS: Gila National Forest, 2610 N. Silver St., Silver City, NM 88061; (505) 388-1986.

GILA NATIONAL FOREST
U.S. Forest Service
3,320,135 acres; includes 614,202 contiguous acres of the Apache National Forest administered by the Gila.

Crossed by US 180, SR 12, SR 78, SR 90. The visitor center is at the end of SR 15, N from Silver City. (Cars with trailers over 18 ft. are advised to take SR's 61 and 35 NW from San Lorenzo to Lake Roberts, then continue on SR 15.)

Note: The Gila Cliff Dwellings National Monument, at the end of SR 15, is a unit of the National Park Service, administered jointly by the Park Service and the National Forest. It is described in the preceding entry.

By far the largest National Forest in New Mexico, and one of the largest in the United States, the Gila is all the more massive because 95% of it is in one huge block, occupying a large part of SW NM. It includes the vast Gila Wilderness, a roadless pristine area of 569,600 acres, the 211,300-acre Aldo Leopold Wilderness, and part of the Blue Range Wilderness. But while these Wildernesses are accessible only to hikers and horsemen, the Forest also has some of the state's most breathtaking scenic drives.

It's a hiker's forest, with few developed areas. Its 20 campgrounds have only 210 sites, very few for a National Forest of this size, although there is no lack of informal sites along both main routes and back roads. Most visitors come to hike, backpack, horsepack, hunt, fish, birdwatch—all dispersed activities. Total visitation is much less than in Forests closer to metropolitan centers.

The Forest has 1,220 mi. of trails. Trail maintenance is far short of need, but there is no lack of hiking opportunities. Many forested areas are sufficiently open for bushwhacking, and one can also hike abandoned or seldom-used primitive roads and canyon bottoms.

The Gila Wilderness was designated in 1924, first in any National Forest to be given this special protection. Because it is well known, most of the backpackers come here. "I wouldn't," one of our Forest informants said. "We have glorious areas outside this Wilderness where you're less likely to have company."

The Forest has a great diversity of topography and vegetation types, from semidesert grasslands at about 4,200 ft. elevation to steep mountain slopes with spruce-fir and aspen forests and rocky peaks almost 11,000 ft. high. Terrain includes deep and rugged canyons, flat mesas, and river flood plains.

On the E side, the Black Range and Mimbres Mountains, with peaks above 9,000 ft., are in N–S alignment. The Mogollon Mountains, second largest mountain mass, extend NW–SE in the W central sector, with several peaks over 10,000 ft. Three smaller ranges, the San Francisco, Saliz, and Kelly Mountains, are a parallel NE–SW series N of the Mogollons, the Tularosa Mountains continuing farther to the NE. The Gallo Mountains are a smaller W–E range in the far N. In the Big Burro Mountains, S of US 180 in the Silver City Ranger District, is an area called The Burros. The highest peak here is just over 8,000 ft.

This Forest has water: streams, rivers, man-made lakes, even some wet marshes. Perennial streams include the Gila, San Francisco, and Mimbres Rivers, Animas Creek, and their tributaries. The Gila and San Francisco are whitewater streams that can be run at certain seasons. Reservoirs include Lake Roberts, Quemado Lake, Snow Lake, and Wall Lake. Bill Evans Lake and Bear Canyon Reservoir are nearby.

Summer daytime temperatures are often in the 90°–100°F range at elevations below 6,000 ft., 70°–80° on the high slopes. Nights are cool, and frost occurs occasionally in some high canyons. From mid-July to mid-Sept., thunderstorms occur almost daily. Winter days are usually dry and sunny. Temperatures may rise to 70° on high slopes, but it is cold everywhere at night. Snow may fall from mid-Dec. through Feb. Sometimes enough snow accumulates for cross-country skiing and other snow play, but this is not dependable. Snow makes travel difficult. The Forest is at its best in spring and fall.

The Forest is so huge one could spend years exploring it. The occasional visitor must choose among many routes and destinations. The Forest map should be used with caution. Although there are 1,970 mi. of mapped roads in the Forest, only 15% of them are classed as "adequate." The highway map shows the paved routes. Most unpaved roads are fair-weather routes at best, and those shown on the Forest map as "primitive" usually require 4-wheel drive. Some of these roads were bulldozed for logging and then abandoned. Current management plans call for some to be reclaimed by nature.

The following are the principal access roads:

SR 15, N from Silver City, carries more visitor traffic than any other Forest road. It penetrates the Gila Wilderness and ends at the Gila Visitor Center and Gila Cliff Dwellings National Monument. Two campgrounds, trailheads, and a put-in for the Gila River are along the way.

SR's 61 and *35* run NW from San Lorenzo on SR 90, joining SR 15 near Lake Roberts, where there are two campgrounds. The upper portion follows Sapillo Creek; the lower, outside the Forest boundary, follows the Mimbres River.

SR 12, SW from US 60 at Datil, follows the Tularosa River to Apache Creek, continues SW to Reserve, turns W over the Saliz Mountains and the San Francisco River, ends at US 180. Although this is a main route through the Forest, much of it is a corridor of privately owned land, with a few small towns; none of the Forest recreation sites is on or close to this route.

US 180 cuts across the W side of the Forest. For about 15 mi. it follows the San Francisco River. Then, leaving the Forest, it turns SE, skirts The Burros, mentioned earlier, and continues E to Silver City. Several campgrounds, the Leopold Vista Historical Monument, and a put-in for the San Francisco River are on or near this route, which is also the W access to SR 78.

SR 78 crosses the heart of the Forest. Only the first few mi. E from US 180 are paved; the rest is gravel. Along this route are half a dozen campgrounds, The Catwalk, and trailheads for the Gila Wilderness.

SR 59, W from I-25, is paved for about 73 mi. to a junction point with several Forest roads that provide access to trailheads for the Gila and Aldo Leopold Wilderness Areas, Wall Lake.

SR 90, E from Silver City to I-25 at Caballo, is one of New Mexico's most scenic drives, once you've passed the clutter E of Silver City. It crosses the S end of the Black Range and the Mimbres Mountains. Campgrounds, overlooks, and trailheads, including trailheads for the Aldo Leopold Wilderness Area. This was our introduction to the Gila years ago, and we return whenever we can, each time sampling another of the many marked trails. At times the road twists its way among a maze of hills and canyons, then climbs steeply to a high viewpoint. Often there is sharp contrast of plant associations, pinyon-juniper on S-facing slopes, with ponderosa forest across the way.

RANGER DISTRICTS

Black Range, 552,615 acres. On the Black Range, including much of the Aldo Leopold Wilderness. Elevations from 4,200 to over 10,000 ft. 263 mi. of trails.

Mimbres, 464,112 acres. E boundary is on the W slopes of Black Range. Includes portions of Aldo Leopold and Gila Wildernesses. 260 mi. of trails.

Reserve, 573,300 acres, approximately 100 mi. N of Silver City. 50 mi. of trails. Four campgrounds are near trailheads of the Gila Wilderness.

Silver City, 404,375 acres. Includes the S portion of the Gila Wilderness, the visitor center, and The Burros. 110 mi. of trails.

Wilderness, 257,480 acres, includes most of the Gila Wilderness. About 330 mi. of trails.

Quemado, 321,000 acres in the N end of the Forest, near US 60. No Wilderness. Known for elk herds. Probably under 50 mi. of trails.

Glenwood, 426,672 acres. About 65 mi. NW of Silver City; Wilderness includes 126 mi. of trails.

Luna, 339,890 acres. Includes the Blue Range Wilderness. W of the Reserve R.D. on the state line. About 25 mi. of trails.

Plants: Most of the land on the Forest perimeter, at elevations of 4,000 to 7,000 ft., is woodland. Annual precipitation is 12 to 20 in. Trees include several juniper species, pinyon pine, several species of oak, with a varied understory of shrubs and grasses. This zone includes some open grasslands. Above 7,000 ft. are mixed conifers, chiefly ponderosa pine, with Douglas-fir, white fir, spruce, corkbark fir, southwestern white pine, and aspen, with shrubs and grasses in the understory. Moisture is a key factor as well as elevation; a ponderosa forest may be on a N-facing slope at 8,000 ft., with pinyon-juniper on a S-facing slope across the way. Riparian vegetation along streams includes cottonwoods, willows, boxelder.

Birds: Checklist available indicates "rare" but no other indication of abundance. (The list does indicate resident or transient, winter or summer resident.) Excluding those marked "rare," the list includes pied-billed and western grebes, double-crested cormorant, great blue heron, snowy egret, black-crowned night-heron, Canada and snow geese, mallard, gadwall, pintail; green-winged, blue-winged, and cinnamon teals; American wigeon, northern shoveler, wood duck, redhead, ring-necked duck, canvasback, lesser scaup, common goldeneye, bufflehead, ruddy duck, common merganser. Turkey vulture. Hawks: sharp-shinned, Cooper's, red-tailed, Swainson's, zone-tailed, black. Northern harrier, golden and bald eagles, prairie falcon, merlin, American kestrel, osprey. Also blue grouse; scaled, Gambel's, and Montezuma quail; ring-necked pheasant, chukar, wild turkey, sandhill crane, Virginia rail, sora, American coot, killdeer, common snipe; spotted, solitary, pectoral, and least sandpipers; willet, greater and lesser yellowlegs, long-billed dowitcher, ring-billed gull. Band-tailed pigeon; rock, mourning, and white-winged doves; yellow-billed cuckoo, roadrunner. Owls: barn, screech, great horned, pygmy, elf, burrowing, spotted, flammulated, long-eared, saw-whet. Whip-poor-will, poor-will, common and lesser nighthawks, white-throated swift. Hummingbirds: blackchinned, broad-tailed, rufous, calliope, Rivoli's. Belted kingfisher. Woodpeckers: northern flicker, Gila, acorn, Lewis', yellow-bellied sapsucker, hairy, ladder-backed, downy, Williamson's sapsucker. Western and Cassin's kingbirds. Flycatchers: Wied's crested, ash-throated, eastern phoebe, black phoebe, Say's phoebe, gray, willow, Hammond's, dusky, western, western wood-pewee, olive-sided, vermilion. Horned lark. Swallows: violet-green, rough-winged, barn, cliff, purple martin. Steller's, Mexican, scrub, and pinyon jays; common and white-necked ravens, common crow, Clark's nutcracker, Mexican and mountain chickadees, plain and bridled titmice, verdin, bushtit; white-breasted, red-breasted, and pygmy nuthatches; brown creeper, dipper. Wrens: house, Bewick's, cactus, canyon, rock. Mockingbird, curvebilled and crissal thrashers, American robin, hermit thrush, western and mountain bluebirds, Townsend's solitaire, blue-gray gnatcatcher, rubycrowned kinglet, water pipit, cedar waxwing, loggerhead shrike, European starling; Bell's, solitary, and warbling vireos. Warblers: orange-crowned, Virginia's, Lucy's, olive, yellow, yellow-rumped, black-throated gray, Townsend's, hermit, Grace's, northern waterthrush, MacGillivray's, common yellowthroat, yellow-breasted chat, red-faced, Wilson's, American and painted redstarts. Eastern and western meadowlarks; yellow-headed, redwinged, and Brewer's blackbirds; hooded, northern, and Scott's orioles; greattailed grackle, brown-headed and bronzed cowbirds; western, hepatic, and summer tanagers; cardinal, black-headed and blue grosbeaks, lazuli and indigo buntings, house and Cassin's finches, pine siskin, American and lesser goldfinches, red crossbill; green-tailed, rufous-sided, brown, and Abert's towhees; lark bunting, gray-headed and dark-eyed juncos. Sparrows: lark, rufouscrowned, black-throated, chipping, Brewer's, white-crowned, fox, Lincoln's, swamp, song, savannah, black-chinned, chestnut-colored.

Mammals: Checklist available. Includes Merriam, vagrant, and gray shrews. Myotis: Yuma, long-eared, fringed, long-legged, California, smallfooted, short-eared. Bats: big brown, red, hoary, spotted, western big-eared, Mexican big-eared, pallid, Mexican freetail, big freetail. Black bear, raccoon, coatimundi, ringtail, longtail weasel, badger; spotted, striped, hooded, and hognose skunks; coyote, kit fox, gray fox, mountain lion, bobcat, whitetail prairie dog, spotted ground squirrel, cliff and grayneck chipmunks; rock, golden-mantled, tassel-eared, Arizona gray, and red squirrels; valley and pygmy pocket gophers; silky, desert, and rock pocket mice; bannertail, Ord, and Merriam kangaroo rats. Mice: western harvest, cactus, deer, white-footed, brush, pinyon, rock, southern grasshopper. Woodrats: Mexican, southern plains, hispid cotton, least cotton. Longtail and Mexican voles, muskrat, porcupine, blacktail jackrabbit, eastern and desert cottontails, peccary, Rocky Mountain elk, mule deer, whitetail deer, pronghorn, bighorn sheep.

Reptiles and amphibians: Checklist available. Includes tiger salamander; Couch's, western, plains, and Great Basin spadefoots. Toads: Woodhouse's, southwestern, red-spotted, Great Plains, green. Chorus frog, canyon and Arizona treefrogs, leopard frog, bullfrog. Western box turtle, Sonora mud turtle, spiny softshell. Lizards: lesser and greater earless, collared, crevice and Clark's spiny, eastern fence, striped plateau, side-blotched, tree, short-horned. Great Plains and many-lined skinks. Whiptails: New Mexico, little striped, desert-grassland, Chihuahua, western. Arizona alligator lizard, Gila monster. Snakes: Texas blind, ringneck, coach and striped whipsnakes, western and mountain patch-nosed, common and Sonora mountain kingsnakes; narrow-headed, western terrestrial, black-necked, and checkered garter snakes; western ground, western and plains black-headed, and night snakes.

FEATURES

The three Wildernesses together get about 80,000 visitor-days of use per year. The Gila gets three-fourths of this, the Aldo Leopold about a fifth, and the Blue the rest.

Gila Wilderness, 558,065 acres. Oldest and one of the largest National Forest Wildernesses. Circling it by road requires a 235-mi. drive. On the Mogollon Mountains and Plateau. Streams, rivers, canyons, mesas. Wider variety of plant and animal life than in most SW Wildernesses. Many trails, the more popular ones entering from the Gila Visitor Center N of Silver City, for foot and horse travel. Heavy use season, mid-May through August. Moderate from Apr. to mid-May and Sept.–Oct. Light Nov.–Mar. Much of the use is concentrated in river bottoms.

Aldo Leopold Wilderness, formerly the Black Range Primitive Area, 202,-016 acres. Contains the most rugged and wild portion of the Black Range. Spectacular mountain country, with a network of deep canyons, rincons, timbered benches, and many high vista points. A section of what may become the Continental Divide National Scenic Trail runs S along the ridgeline of the Black Peak before heading W along the Divide. Moderate use May–Oct.; light Nov.–Apr. About half of the visits are along the crest.

Blue Range Wilderness, 29,304 acres, about 65 mi. NW of Silver City. Deep, rugged canyons; steep, timbered ridges, sweeping reaches of stark, broken country. The Mogollon Rim crosses the Wilderness W to E. Adjoins the Blue Range Primitive Area of the Apache-Sitgreaves NF on the W (see entry in AZ Zone 3). Not heavily used; moderate May–Nov. and light Dec.–Apr. About a fourth of the use is along the river bottom.

The *Gila River* rises in the Gila Wilderness. Three forks join near the visitor center. The river then flows generally SW, crossing US 180 near the town of Gila, crossing the NW corner of The Burros, then turns W into AZ. The river can be floated from the SR 15 bridge to the AZ line, with a variety of landscapes and conditions. From the bridge to Gila, most of the course is through spectacular canyons in the Gila Wilderness. Kayaks and canoes are recommended for the first 7 mi., to East Fork, because of narrow, dangerous passages, although there are no actual rapids. Next comes the 32-mi. float to Turkey Creek, a 4- to 5-day trip, Class II and III rapids, few calm spots. The floating season is short, usually in Mar.; some years have no season. This section of the river can be hiked; a 33-mi. trail follows the river, with frequent crossings. Cottonwood and sycamore grow on the flood plain, ponderosa pine on N-facing slopes, pinyon-juniper and grassy areas on S-facing slopes. Numerous side canyons.

The next section, to Forest Road 809 in the N end of the Burro Mountains unit, is through private and state land, seldom run because of slow flow and barbed-wire fences. Then comes Middle Box, through The Burros, an 18-mi. run with Class II and III rapids, usually runnable mid-Mar. to mid-Apr. Steep canyon walls limit campsites.

For the next section, see entry, Gila River, Lower Box.

No one should attempt a float trip without checking on current conditions and hazards. The river canyon has several long sections with no escape route other than downstream.

San Francisco River: This river enters NM from AZ near US 180, flows E and S past Reserve on SR 12, turns SW and W, crossing US 180, and returns to AZ. It's not a large river and its flow is seasonal, but it has much of interest. A 40-mi. section from San Francisco Plaza, 5 mi. S of Reserve, can usually be floated for a few days in Mar., occasionally after heavy summer rain. Most of the course is through a broad desert canyon. It's a 2- to 3-day trip, if the water level holds, with take-out at Pleasanton or Lower San Francisco Hot Springs. Raft or kayak; Class II or III rapids; rocky channel; possible logjams. The route can be hiked.

A 14-mi. section downstream, from the confluence with Dry Creek to the AZ border, has been considered for Wilderness status. This is also a 40-mi. float trip, usually run after summer rains. Here the canyon is narrower, as little as 200 ft., 500 on the average. The river meanders on a small flood plain. Benches of varied width at the base of the canyon walls support riparian vegetation, chiefly cottonwood, sycamore, boxelder, ash, soapberry, and walnut. Canyon walls are generally steep, 1,000 to 1,600 ft. high. Numerous side canyons.

The Forest Service estimates annual use to be 3,500 visitor-days: 1,300 by hunters, 900 by fishermen, 700 by ORV enthusiasts, the remaining 600 by backpackers and day visitors.

The original Wilderness proposal of about 60,000 acres included surrounding mesas and ridges. Conservationists urged that this be increased to join with the Blue Range Wilderness, a total of 360,000 acres. Instead, the proposal was reduced to a 6,700-acre strip along the canyon.

Conservationists and the Forest Service have disagreed strenuously on the need to exclude ORV's from the canyon, which has the largest remaining tract of Lower Sonoran riparian woodland. More than 200 bird species breed within a 50-mi. radius of the canyon, which is habitat for such raptors as bald eagle, peregrine falcon, Mexican black hawk, zone-tailed hawk, and osprey. A 1973 study commissioned by the Forest Service concluded that damage by ORV's was so severe that they should be banned immediately. Many visitors, including scientists, have reported damage, including disturbance to wildlife. The Forest Service has rejected such reports, insisting that floods erase ORV tracks.

The *Continental Divide National Scenic Trail* has not yet been constructed, but some people are hiking the route. Some existing trails follow the Divide. The Gila's proposed management plan would include a half-mile corridor for the Trail, protecting the portions of it outside Wilderness Areas.

The *Inner Loop* is a favorite scenic drive: N from Silver City on SR 15, returning by SR 35 at Lake Roberts to SR 90 at San Lorenzo, and back to Silver City. Along the way are several campgrounds, many informal campsites, numerous trailheads. From Lake Roberts N to the end, SR 15 is a "cherry stem," with the Gila Wilderness on both sides.

Lake Roberts has only 72 acres but is an active resort, with some private and commercial development. Two campgrounds, two nature trails. No swimming.

Willow Creek and *Snow Lake* are low-key recreation areas on SR 78. The road E from Reserve has easier grades and wider curves than the road W from Mogollon. Elevations are 8,000 and 7,400 ft. Easy access to the Gila Wilderness.

Quemado Lake has 131 acres. Reached by 19 mi. of unpaved Forest Road 13 from SR 32. Primitive campground, boat ramp.

The Catwalk is a metal walkway hanging on the cliffside of steep, boulder-choked Whitewater Canyon, about 6 mi. from Glenwood, in the rugged Mogollon Mountains. A 2 1/4-mi. spectacular hike. Nature trail. The Catwalk is also a trail into the Gila Wilderness.

Wood Haul Wagon Road is a scenic, interesting 11 1/2-mi. hike. Begins at the Fort Bayard State Hospital Complex, N of Central on SR 90. The road was used by wagons hauling timber to the fort; wheel ruts are still conspicuous. Meanders through lush timber stands, along streams. Elevations from 6,200 to 8,000 ft. Viewpoints. Sawmill Trail is an alternate return route.

ACTIVITIES

Camping: 20 campgrounds, 210 units. About half are open all year, others Apr.–Nov. or May–Oct.

Hiking, backpacking: Permits required for entry to Wilderness Areas. The most popular trails are in the Gila Wilderness, but not all are crowded. Rangers can suggest many lightly used trails elsewhere. All-year hiking at lower elevations, and even the high country is often open in winter.

Hunting: Mule and whitetail deer, elk, pronghorn, mountain lion, bear, wild turkey, quail, dove.

Fishing: Trout in principal streams and rivers, and in Lakes Roberts, Quemado, and Snow. Certain streams are closed to protect a rare native fish.

Horsepacking: Most trails are suitable for horse travel. Lists of outfitters and guides available.

INTERPRETATION

Visitor center, all year, 8 A.M.–5 P.M. Exhibits include artifacts used by primitive inhabitants, including Apache. Slide-tape presentation on ecology. Maps, pamphlets, books, posters, etc.

Self-guided *Trail to the Past* originates in Scorpion Campground. Petroglyphs. Small signs explaining natural phenomena. Terminates in a small cave dwelling.

Contact station, gateway to *Gila Cliff Dwellings National Monument (see entry).* Open 8 A.M.–5 P.M. in summer, 9 A.M. to 4 P.M. in winter. About 1/2 mi. W of Trail to the Past.

Occasional outdoor talks in small amphitheater outside the visitor center.

PUBLICATIONS

Forest map. $1.

Visitor Information. Folder.

A Brief History of the Gila Wilderness.

Checklist/Ecology. Pamphlet.

Information pages:

General information.

Gila Hot Springs, facilities and services.

Wilderness permit system.

List of outfitters-guides.

Floating the Gila River.

Species checklists:

Plants of the Gila River-Lake Roberts Recreation Area.

Edible plants.

Birds.

Mammals.

Reptiles and amphibians.

Trail descriptions:

Mimbres District (SE sector of the Forest).

Silver City District.

Gila Wilderness.

REFERENCES

Ganci, Dave. *Hiking the Southwest.* San Francisco: Sierra Club Books, 1983, pp. 283–326.

Ungnade, Herbert E. *Guide to the New Mexico Mountains.* Albuquerque: University of New Mexico Press, 1972.

New Mexico Whitewater. Santa Fe: New Mexico State Park Division, 1983.

HEADQUARTERS: 2610 N. Silver St., Silver City, NM 88061; (505) 388-1986.

RANGER DISTRICTS: Black Range R.D., 2601 S Broadway, P.O. Box 431, Truth or Consequences, NM 87901; (505) 894-6677. Glenwood R.D., Box 8, Glenwood, NM 88039; (505) 539-2481. Luna R.D., Box 91, Luna, NM 87824; (505) 547-2611. Mimbres R.D., Rt. 11, Box 50, Mimbres, NM 88049; (505) 534-2250. Quemado R.D., Box 158, Quemado, NM 87829; (505) 773-4678. Reserve R.D., Box 117, Reserve, NM 87830; (505) 533-6231. Silver City R.D., Route 8, Box 124-1, Hwy 180 E, Silver City, NM 88061; (505) 538-2771. Wilderness R.D., Route 11, Box 100, Silver City, NM 88061; (505) 534-9461.

GILA RIVER: LOWER BOX
U.S. Bureau of Land Management
8,555 acres.

River access at Red Rock Bridge, off SR 464 N of Lordsburg. Land access by county roads W of Red Rock to Fisherman's Point and Spring on the Bluff. Inquire locally.

The Gila River flows SW from the Gila National Forest, then W into AZ. See Gila NF entry for descriptions of upstream sections. The 97 mi. from the confluence of the river's East and West Forks to the AZ border has been identified as eligible for study for Wild, Scenic, or Recreational River status. Just upstream from Lower Box is Middle Box, most of it within the Burro unit of Gila NF.

The Lower Box, a lightly visited 6-mi. section between Red Rock and Virden, is a scenic corridor with exceptional natural qualities. The Gila extends from the Chihuahuan Desert into the Sonoran, forming a pathway for many wildlife species. By contrast with the surrounding deserts, this pathway has a verdant riparian vegetation, habitat for an abundant and varied wildlife population.

The Lower Box is composed of massive blocky outcrops that break into a steep-walled canyon over 600 ft. deep in places, with numerous short canyons joining. In the eastern, upstream half of the canyon, predominant rock colors are pinks and reds. In the W half, colors change to browns and black. Benches occur along parts of the river. Erosion has formed numerous hoodoos, rock columns in fanciful shapes. Below the canyon, the river flows into an area of rounded rolling hills.

Average annual precipitation here is about 12 in., with wide year-to-year variations. Usually about half falls in July–Sept. thunderstorms. July is the hottest month, daytime averages in the 90s, sometimes above 100°F. Winters are cold; spring is windy.

Plants: Vegetation in the canyon is dense beside the river. Species include cottonwood, Arizona sycamore, Arizona walnut, willow. Many seasonal wildflowers. Upland areas, above the canyon, have desert vegetation, prominently creosote and snakeweed.

Wildlife: Almost half of all vertebrate species found in NM occur along the lower Gila. 265 bird species have been recorded between the National Forest and the AZ border, 144 species during the summer. As many as 116 species may breed here. Breeding densities of riparian birds are among the highest in America. Breeding densities of raptors are also high. Some of the species recorded are at the northern or southern limits of their ranges.

67 mammal species, as well as 66 species of reptiles and amphibians, occur in or near the valley.

ACTIVITIES

Camping: No designated campground, but ample informal sites.

Hiking, backpacking: Foot access to the canyon is easy from several road access points. The canyon can be hiked, side canyons explored.

Swimming: The river water is not drinkable but has been judged safe for swimming. Occasional pools.

Boating, rafting: Water levels are best in Mar., periodically adequate after spring and summer rains. No real rapids: Class I and I+ at all water levels. Kayaks and canoes are recommended because of shallows and need to paddle. The run from Red Rock to Virden is about 20 mi.

REFERENCE: *New Mexico Whitewater.* Santa Fe: New Mexico State Park Division, 1983, pp. 33–34.

HEADQUARTERS: BLM, Las Cruces District Office, 1800 Marquess St., Las Cruces, NM 88005; (505) 525-8228.

GUADALUPE CANYON
U.S. Bureau of Land Management
3,692 acres in BLM's study area. The canyon extends into the NM section of the Coronado National Forest (see entry in AZ Zone 4).

From Douglas, AZ, 42 mi. E on county road to NM line, then 2 mi. up canyon on dirt road.

Most visitors to the canyon are birders. They come from all over, despite the remote location. The site is on the Mexican border, and some species are here at the northern limit of their ranges. BLM proclaimed it an Outstanding Natural Area to protect its special qualities.

These Guadalupe Mountains are a southern extension of the Peloncillos and are much smaller than the Guadalupe Range near Carlsbad. The site borders on AZ and Mexico, as well as a wilderness area of the Coronado National Forest and 454 acres of state land. Average elevation is 4,800 ft. The canyon is not especially deep; relief within the site is only 300 to 600 ft.

The canyon stream is intermittent, usually flowing from late summer into autumn. The site has no recorded springs. Annual precipitation is about 10 in., much of it coming in summer thundershowers, causing a flash flood hazard in the canyon.

Riparian vegetation includes Fremont cottonwood, Arizona sycamore, thickets of Arizona oak.

Birds: 159 species recorded. List available, with "positive breeding records," and indication of nonbreeders. Breeding species include Cooper's and zone-tailed hawks, American kestrel, Gambel's quail, ladder-backed woodpecker, rose-throated becard (single record); western, Cassin's, and thick-billed kingbirds; olivaceous, ash-throated, and Wied's crested flycatchers; black phoebe, white-winged and mourning doves, screech and elf owls; black-chinned, violet-crowned, and broad-billed hummingbirds; western wood-pewee, vermilion and beardless flycatchers, Mexican and scrub jays, bridled titmouse, verdin, Bewick's and cactus wrens, mockingbird, curve-billed thrasher, Gila and acorn woodpeckers, phainopepla, Bell's vireo, Lucy's warbler, brown towhee; rufous-crowned and black-throated sparrows, summer tanager, cardinal, hooded oriole, brown-headed and bronzed cowbirds, black-headed grosbeak, house finch.

Rarities sometimes seen in the canyon include buff-colored nightjar, thick-billed kingbird, fan-tailed warbler, and coppery-tailed trogon. When we asked birder friends in Arizona for a comparison, they ranked Guadalupe just below Madera Canyon, a better-known and more accessible birding hot spot.

Mammals: Wide variety of species, including Coue's whitetail deer, bobcat, mountain lion, possibly two endangered bat species, coatimundi.

ACTIVITIES

Camping: No campground, but many informal sites in and near the canyon. Bring water. Camp on high ground; flash floods are a hazard.

Hiking, backpacking: The road into the canyon ends in a trail to Bunk Robinson Peak in the Peloncillo Mountains in the NM portion of the Coronado National Forest (see entry in AZ, Zone 4).

HEADQUARTERS: BLM, Las Cruces District Office, 1800 Marquess Dr., Las Cruces, NM 88004; (505) 525-8228.

HORSE MOUNTAIN
U.S. Bureau of Land Management
5,032 acres.

From Datil on US 60, 26 mi. SW on SR 12. At Horse Springs, about 2 1/4 mi. E of the town of Old Horse Springs, N about 4 1/4 mi. on unpaved county road, then E on a primitive access road to site boundary, about 3/4 mi.

BLM acquired legal access to this little-known site in 1983. The county road N from SR 12 is a fair-weather route for passenger cars. The short access road requires 4-wheel drive but can easily be hiked.

Horse Mountain is an isolated peak, 9,490 ft. elevation, rising 2,500 ft. above the Plains of San Agustin, a closed-basin desert S of SR 12. The mountain has steep slopes on all sides, but routes to the top can be hiked in less than an hour, easy except for the last hundred yards or so. At the top one can enjoy a 360° view, at times for 100 mi.

Annual precipitation ranges from 12 in. at lower altitudes to 16 in. above. Average annual snowfall is 2 to 3 ft., enough to limit access at times. Brief, often heavy thunderstorms in July–Sept. This is a good area for summer hiking, with temperatures averaging 80°F by day, dropping into the 40s at night. Winter days in the 40s, nights in the low teens; subzero temperatures are not uncommon.

The site has no permanent stream or pond.

Plants: About 600 acres in the SW are open grassland, where broom snakeweed and blue grama predominate, with fringed sage, winterfat, and squirreltail. The mountain is forested with mature ponderosa pine at higher elevations, pinyon pines on drier slopes. Some Douglas-fir is mixed with the ponderosa, especially on N-facing slopes. Forest understory is chiefly mountain-mahogany, oak, rabbitbrush.

Birds: No checklist. HQ has a list of 175 resident and migratory species recorded for these habitats. Mentioned here: turkey vulture, great horned owl, golden eagle, red-tailed hawk, wild turkey.

Mammals: No checklist. HQ lists 71 species found in these habitats. Mentioned here: coyote, kit fox, gray fox, black bear, mountain lion, bobcat, striped skunk, jackrabbit, desert cottontail, prairie dog, pronghorn, elk, mule deer.

Some ORV use occurs, chiefly by hunters and holders of grazing allotments. This will be outlawed if the site achieves wilderness status.

Although the site is too small for extensive backpacking, it offers solitude in a scenic setting.

Hunting: Mostly deer, turkey.

HEADQUARTERS: BLM, Socorro Resource Area, Box 1219, Socorro, NM 87801; (505) 835-0412.

JORNADA DEL MUERTO
U.S. Bureau of Land Management
31,147 acres.

From US 380, E of San Antonio, S on County Roads 2268 and 2322.

Jornada del Muerto appears on the highway map E of I-25. This 31,147-acre Wilderness Study Area is only a part of the BLM-managed public land in the vicinity.

The name "journey of death" is apt. The site is a lava flow with a maximum relief of only 200 ft. It includes lava tubes and other volcanic features, but many have been silted in by wind-blown sand and clay. The surface is mostly deep sand on the fringes, jagged and fractured lava rock in the interior. Summer daytime temperatures sometimes reach 105°F. Vegetation is sparse, wildlife populations small.

Few people come here, but some find the rugged, open landscape challenging and attractive.

The site is entirely within a White Sands Missile Range Safety Evacuation Zone. Those within the Zone may be evacuated during test firings.

HEADQUARTERS: BLM, Socorro Resource Area, P.O. Box 1219, Socorro, NM 87801; (505) 835-0412.

LA JOYA WATERFOWL AREA
New Mexico Department of Game and Fish
3,550 acres.

From Bernardo on I-25, 7 mi. S. Site is E of the Interstate.

A good birding spot, between the highway and the Rio Grande River, with a small bit across the river. A series of ponds is connected by canals and ditches edged with cattails and bulrushes. Along the river are cottonwood, salt cedar, Russian olive, saltgrass. A marshy area is at the S end.

Whooping cranes stop here occasionally. More dependable are the sandhill crane, pintail, teals, mallard, shoveler, lesser scaup, canvasback, redhead, Canada and snow geese. Mammals seen occasionally include muskrat, raccoon, coyote, bobcat.

NEARBY: Bernardo Waterfowl Area (see entry).

ORGAN MOUNTAINS
U.S. Bureau of Land Management
35,000 acres.

E of Las Cruces. W side access road S from US 70 about 10 mi. E of I-25. E side access road from US 70 about 17 mi. E of I-25, not recommended for trailers over 23 ft. Several others from the W.

As one travels I-10 near Las Cruces, the jagged spires and needles of the Organ Mountains dominate the eastern skyline. Twenty peaks are aligned N–S, the highest (Organ Peak, 9,012 ft.) rising almost a mile above the surrounding desert floor. The public lands are a rough triangle, bounded by I-10 and I-25 on the W, US 70 on the N, and the Fort Bliss Military Reservation and White Sands Missile Range on the E. The entire area, 27,167 acres, has been designated the Organ Mountain Recreation Lands. Roads and other developments disqualified all but 7,144 acres for wilderness study area status, but BLM designated 8,847 acres as an Area of Critical Environmental Concern to protect its natural and scenic qualities.

The spires and needles, thought to resemble organ pipes, are of quartz monzonite, gray to light pinkish-gray. Cliffs attract technical climbers.

The W side access road runs close to the base of the mountains. Several roads and trails lead W into the desert; spurs and trails lead E into the mountains. The E side access road ends at Aguirre Spring campground. The Baylor Pass and Pine Tree developed hiking trails begin at this campground. The Baylor Pass Trail also has a trailhead on the W side access road. The campground and developed trails are often crowded in summer. BLM has set a limit; when it is reached, no more cars are allowed to enter. Other parts of the site are uncrowded, and one can hike on vehicle tracks or crosscountry. ORV's are barred from the developed trails and, within the protected area, restricted to vehicle routes. Special areas have been provided on the W side for intensive ORV action. Average annual precipitation for the area is 8 to 12 in., but at the higher elevation of Aguirre Spring campground the average is 24 to 26 in. July–Sept. is the rainy season, with occasional thunderstorms. In late winter and early spring, high winds may cause dust and sand storms. Except at the high elevations, summers are hot. Most visitors come in the Sept.–May period.

Plants: The area includes three life zones. The Lower Sonoran zone occupies the valley land and, on the W side, the middle slopes. It is characterized by creosote, mesquite, grama grasses, and cacti. Vegetation of the Upper Sonoran zone, up to 7,500 ft., is dominated by juniper, little-leaf mahogany, and oaks. Above is the transition zone, with ponderosa pine, oak, juniper, and mountain-mahogany. Douglas-fir occurs at higher elevations on E-facing slopes.

Birds: Checklist of 185 species available. Birding is best in early spring, late fall. Seasonally common or abundant species include western kingbird; ash-throated, dusky, and western flycatchers; cliff swallow, scrub jay, white-necked raven, verdin, chipping sparrow, mourning dove, great horned and long-eared owls, black-chinned and broad-tailed hummingbirds, northern flicker, acorn and hairy woodpeckers, yellow-bellied sapsucker, canyon and rock wrens, mockingbird, American robin, phainopepla, western bluebird, ruby-crowned kinglet; western, hepatic, and summer tanagers; indigo bunting, pine siskin, lark bunting, horned lark, Brewer's sparrow, dark-eyed junco, yellow-rumped warbler. Also western meadowlark, Scott's oriole, brown-headed cowbird; sharp-shinned, red-tailed, and Swainson's hawks; northern harrier, golden eagle, prairie falcon, Gambel's and scaled quail.

Mammals: No checklist. BLM reports 80 species occur.

ACTIVITIES

Camping: Aguirre Spring campground has 57 sites, no water. All year.

Hiking: Pine Tree Trail loop, 4 1/2 mi., begins at 5,700 ft. elevation, rises to 6,880 ft. Baylor Pass Trail, 6 mi., crosses the mountains from the campground to the W side access road. Both are part of the National Trails System.

Hunting: Upland birds only.

PUBLICATIONS

Organ Mountains Recreation Lands leaflet, with map.
Aguirre Spring Recreation Site leaflet, with map.
Self-guided Tour of Pine Tree Trail.
Bird checklist.

HEADQUARTERS: BLM, Las Cruces District Office, P.O. Box 1420, 1800 Marquess St., Las Cruces, NM 88005; (505) 525-8228.

SEVILLETA NATIONAL WILDLIFE REFUGE
U.S. Fish and Wildlife Service
228,134 acres.

On both sides of I-25 S of Bernardo.

We mention this site because it appears prominently on maps. Used for research, it is not open to the public. It is managed by the Bosque del Apache National Wildlife Refuge (see entry).

SIERRA DE LAS CANAS; PRESILLA
U.S. Bureau of Land Management
28,600 acres.

E of the Rio Grande at Socorro. From US 85 at Escondido, bridge across the river. Continue E to Quebradas Road, BLM-maintained, which runs S between the two units; rough, but OK when dry.

When the river is low, local residents often walk across, then up one of the several large arroyos cut into the rolling benchlands above the flood plain. The Presilla unit rises from 4,700 ft. to rugged white limestone and red sandstone hills, some forming parallel N–S ridges, with a maximum elevation of 5,450 ft. Landforms of this unit include scenic box canyons and sand dunes.

Further E, across Quebradas Road, the Sierra de las Canas is a rugged desert mountain range with multicolored sheer rock escarpments, deep narrow canyons, ridges, and mesa tops, rising to 6,200 ft. Three large drainages trend SW toward the river.

These two units are within a much larger area of public land. To the N of this area is the 229,000-acre Sevilleta National Wildlife Refuge, not open to the public. To the S is the Bosque del Apache National Wildlife Refuge (see entry). The entire area is within the Chihuahuan desert. Summer visits are inadvisable; temperatures often exceed 100°F. Other seasons are pleasantly sunny and mild, although spring is usually windy. Annual precipitation averages 10 in., more than half of it falling in summer thundershowers.

Vegetation is typical of the northern Chihuahuan desert. Creosote predominates in the area rising from the river, with fluffgrass, bush muhly, broom snakeweed, mesquite, mariola, Mormon tea. More areas of creosote occur on the higher ground beyond Quebradas Road, with roughly equal areas of pinyon-juniper, this association with an understory made up chiefly of grasses. Both units have scattered patches of desert shrub: creosote, cholla, datil yucca, pricklypear, desert willow, ocotillo, honey mesquite.

Wildlife: Checklists are not published but can be seen at HQ. BLM reports the area has 145 resident and migratory bird species, 52 mammal species, 53 species of reptiles and amphibians. Great horned owls roost in the canyon walls of Arroyo del Tajo. Also noted: red-tailed and Cooper's hawks, American kestrel, prairie falcon, dove, scaled quail, horned lark, pinyon jay, common raven. Mammals include whitethroat woodrat, blacktail jackrabbit, desert cottontail, rock squirrel, bobcat, coyote, gray fox, mule deer, pronghorn.

FEATURES

Arroyo del Tajo, extending E from just S of Socorro, has a notable array of Indian pictographs. For preservation, a 1,280-acre area surrounding the pictographs has been designated the Tinajas Natural Area of Critical Environmental Concern.

ACTIVITIES

The Presilla unit, only 2 mi. from Socorro and accessible by fording the river at low water, is a fairly popular day-use area for local residents: hunting, hiking, camping, rockhounding, rock climbing, ORV use in the arroyos and on vehicle tracks. (ORV use is prohibited in most of the area, but continues.)

Sierra de las Canas, although only a 45-minute drive from Socorro, has few visitors.

Hunting: Chiefly deer, quail.

HEADQUARTERS: BLM, Socorro Resource Area, Box 1219, Socorro, NM 87801; (505) 835-0412.

SIERRA LADRONES

U.S. Bureau of Land Management
42,688 acres.

From Bernardo on I-25, W on County Road 12. From Magdalena on US 60, N on County Road 67. County roads not shown on highway map.

From the Interstate at Bernardo, the mass of the Ladron Mountains dominates the western horizon. The mass is roughly circular, about 6 mi. in diameter, rising abruptly from the Rio Grande Valley on the E, mesa grasslands and pinyon-juniper woodlands on the N, W, and S. Base elevation is about 5,200 ft., Ladron Peak 9,176 ft. The unit described here is about 14 mi. N–S, 8 mi. W–E. The Gallinas Division of Cibola National Forest (see entry, Zone 1) is on the W, Sevilleta National Wildlife Refuge, closed to the public, on the E. The main peaks are extremely rugged. The N end terminates at abrupt escarpments, beyond which are several large canyons. The S end of the area slopes more gradually from the main peaks, a long narrow ridge tapering down to box canyons and arroyos. Our BLM advisor said ascending Ladron Peak is a challenge, not a casual hike.

Present recreational use of the site is moderate. Fall, winter, and spring are favored. Activities include day hiking, backpacking, horse riding, technical rock climbing, rockhounding, hunting. ORV action is chiefly along the Rio Salado and larger arroyos.

Maximum summer temperatures at the base range from 90°F to over 100°. On the upper slopes, the averages are 10 to 15° cooler. Average winter daytime temperatures are mild at lower elevations, 20 to 40° on the peaks. Annual precipitation is about 12 in. at the base, 16 to 20 in. on upper slopes. Over half of the moisture falls in July–Sept. It runs off quickly; the site has no perennial streams or ponds.

Plants: The pinyon-juniper association covers nine-tenths of the site, one-seed juniper and pinyon pine dominating the overstory. In relatively flat areas at lower elevations, understory species include mostly grasses, with scattered broom snakeweed, creosote, four-wing saltbush, feather peabush, cholla, pricklypear. On steep slopes at higher elevations, the proportion of shrubs is higher and they also include datil yucca, shrub live oak, hairy mountain-mahogany, skunkbush sumac, Apache plume, and beargrass. Vegetation along the Rio Salado is mainly bosque, dominated by salt cedar. Ponderosa pine is the principal species in the upper ends of the main canyons, with some Douglas-fir and aspen.

Wildlife: No published checklists, but HQ has lists of species presumed to occur here: 94 resident and migratory bird species, 56 mammal species, 51 species of reptiles and amphibians. Birds noted include Gambel's and scaled quail, pinyon jay, common raven, mourning dove, western bluebird, horned lark. Mammals noted: coyote, bobcat, gray fox, badger, desert cottontail, blacktail jackrabbit, whitethroat woodrat, deermouse, ground squirrel, various bats.

NEARBY: Bernardo Waterfowl Area. See entry.

HEADQUARTERS: BLM, Socorro Resource Area, P.O. Box 1219, Socorro, NM 87801; (505) 835-0412.

WEST POTRILLO MOUNTAINS; MOUNT RILEY; ADEN LAVA FLOW

U.S. Bureau of Land Management
180,000 acres.

SW of Las Cruces, in the triangle formed by the Luna-Dona Ana county line, the Mexican border, and the Southern Pacific Railroad. A local road, not shown on highway maps, parallels the railroad. Several links with SR 28 S of Las Cruces. Access from the S by the Columbus-Anapra road, not shown on map, paralleling the Mexican border. Inquire locally or at BLM office.

The volcanic cones of the West Potrillos, the Mt. Riley peaks, Indian Basin, the Aden Crater, and Kilbourne Hole are the outstanding features of the area. Over 48 volcanic cones are concentrated N–S in the center of the Potrillo area. These cones are from 1,000 to 3,000 ft. in diameter. The highest peaks reach 5,400 ft. from a base elevation of about 4,100 ft.

Mt. Riley and Mt. Cox are high, steep, intrusive peaks clustered together E of the West Potrillo Mountains. The highest is nearly 6,000 ft. Prominent talus slopes and alluvial fans surround them.

Indian Basin, a large depression in the SW part of the West Potrillo area, is rimmed with sand dunes. The bottom of the Basin, at 4,029 ft., is about 75 ft. below the surrounding desert floor. During the rainy season, the basin floods, and many ducks can be found on the temporary pond.

Aden Crater, in the NW sector, is nearly circular, about 1/4 mi. across. The Afton volcanoes are a cluster of 3 cones in the SE. The lava flow has numerous steep-walled holes, the largest 100 ft. across and 40–50 ft. deep. Most of the landscape is jagged basalt, with grasses and desert shrubs growing in pockets where soil has accumulated. A vehicle trail through the SE sector is used as a scenic drive, chiefly by residents of nearby towns. Some ORV activity occurs on vehicle trails on the E perimeter of the flow.

Kilbourne Hole, 2 mi. S of the Aden Lava Flow, is a designated National Natural Landmark. It is a maar: a crater caused by a volcanic explosion in which little volcanic material except gas is emitted. Maars are far less common than cinder cones. The crater is 1 to 2 mi. across, and 280–450 ft. deep. Most of the 5,760-acre site is public land; however, 320 acres in the bottom of the Hole are privately owned.

The area is of interest to rockhounds.

Climate is arid, with mild winters and pleasant to hot summers. Summer daytime temperatures are often over 100°F. The Jan. average minimum is in the middle 20s. Average annual precipitation is around 8 in., locally higher in upper elevations. More than half of the precipitation normally occurs July–Sept., often in brief, hard thunder showers. Occasional light snow.

Plants: Creosote is dominant over much of the area, with snakeweed, cacti, tarbush, mesquite, mariola, spicebush, zinnia, and various grasses.

Wildlife: No bird or mammal list. Rodents and rabbits are numerous, especially at the edges of lava flows. BLM notes that this abundant prey base results in high wintering raptor numbers. Golden eagle and great horned owl nest in the cinder cones, Swainson's hawk in the soaptree yucca. There are a few mule deer. Bats of several species find sheltered roosts in the formations.

Wildlife scientists have found this a good research setting. About 4,000 acres are protected as a Research Natural Area.

HEADQUARTERS: BLM, Las Cruces District Office, 1800 Marquess St., Las Cruces, NM 88005; (505) 525-8228.

ZONE 4

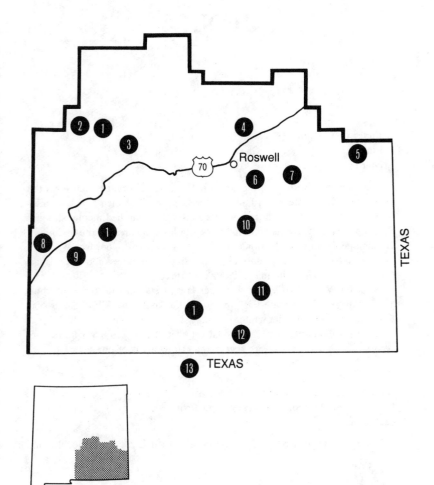

ZONE 4

Includes these counties:

Lincoln	Chaves	Lea
Otero	Eddy	

The dominant features of the zone are the mountain ranges that form the N–S spine of its western third, chiefly the Capitan, Sacramento, and Guadalupe Mountains. Most of the mountain country is within the Lincoln National Forest. Carlsbad Caverns National Park adjoins the Forest in the S. So does Guadalupe Mountains National Park, below the Texas border. We have included it because of its geological relationship to the Forest and to Carlsbad Caverns, and because hiking trails link all three.

In the far W of the zone, a flow of black lava meets a moving desert of white sand. Valley of Fires State Park overlooks the lava flow. White Sands National Monument has the white dunes.

E of the mountains, the land is relatively flat. The Pecos River flows N–S across this plain. Along it are several waterfowl areas of interest.

ARTESIA WATERFOWL AREA
New Mexico Department of Game and Fish
640 acres.

From Artesia on US 285, N 2 mi. on 285, then E 2.4 mi. on local road.

Several waterfowl areas are along the Pecos River. This small one, on river bends, offers good birding in the fall and winter. No hunting. 156 acres are cultivated for feed crops. Sandhill cranes and snow geese are among the visitors.

BITTER LAKE NATIONAL WILDLIFE REFUGE
U.S. Fish and Wildlife Service
23,350 acres.

From Roswell, N about 2 mi. on US 285, then right on Old Roswell-Clovis Highway and follow signs 9 mi. to Refuge HQ.

Open: One hour before sunrise to one hour after sunset.

The main portion of the Refuge has a self-guiding auto tour route around 5 small impoundments. Visitors can walk wherever they wish, except in posted areas. Bitter Lake itself is a small alkaline playa fed by intermittent springs. It is surrounded by a small Research Natural Area, closed to visitors. The impoundments, lying within the old bottomlands of the Pecos River, are fed by seeps and springs, and contain brackish water. When the ponds and playa are full, total water surface is 750 acres.

The Refuge lies astride the Pecos River. The river water is often very muddy during summer periods of high flow; during the winter there is little flow. Ground water can no longer be pumped for irrigation on the Refuge because of its high sodium content.

In this arid region, even pools of casual water attract migrating waterfowl and shorebirds. The ponds of Bitter Lake may be thronged with over 100,000 ducks and 65,000 geese during the fall migration. Up to 5,000 Canada geese have wintered here since the ponds appeared. Since the early 1960s, the number of migrating snow geese in the Pecos Valley has risen to as many as 65,000. Up to 70,000 sandhill cranes visit the refuge, numbers peaking in mid-Nov.

Elevation at the Refuge is about 3,500 ft. Average annual precipitation is about 12 in. Summer average daily maximum temperatures are in the 90's, winter lows in the high 20's.

Birds: Waterfowl are most numerous in late fall. Some winter here. These migrants are on their way N in Feb., but many other species are all-year residents. The Refuge checklist notes relative abundance for each season. Seasonally common or abundant species include eared and pied-billed grebes, white pelican, double-crested cormorant, great blue heron, snowy egret, black-crowned night-heron, Canada and snow geese. Ducks: mallard, gadwall, pintail; green-winged, blue-winged, and cinnamon teals; American wigeon, northern shoveler, redhead, ring-necked duck, canvasback, common goldeneye, bufflehead, ruddy duck. Turkey vulture, northern harrier, American kestrel, scaled quail, ring-necked and white-winged pheasants, sandhill crane, Virginia rail, sora, American coot, snowy plover, killdeer, willet, greater yellowlegs, least and western sandpipers, long-billed dowitcher, American avocet, black-necked stilt, Wilson's phalarope, ring-billed gull, least and black terns. Also mourning dove, roadrunner, barn and great horned owls, common nighthawk, western kingbird, Say's phoebe, horned lark; rough-winged, barn, and cliff swallows; Bewick's, marsh, and rock wrens; mockingbird, sage thrasher, water pipit, loggerhead shrike. Warblers: yellow-rumped, common yellowthroat, Wilson's. Eastern and western meadowlarks, red-winged and Brewer's blackbirds, brown-headed cowbird, house finch, green-tailed towhee, lark bunting. Sparrows: savannah, lark, Cassin's, sage, clay-colored, Brewer's, white-crowned, swamp, song.

Mammals: No checklist. Noted: abundant desert cottontail and occasional blacktail jackrabbit; mule deer, coyote, bobcat, and badger present, seldom seen. A blacktail prairie dog village is just outside the Refuge, near entrance, on private and public land.

FEATURES

Auto tour route, 8 1/2 mi., passes all 5 impoundments at close range. Turnoffs, overlooks.

Desert garden at HQ.

Salt Creek Wilderness, 9,620 acres, is 4 mi. N, on the N side of US 70. Salt Creek, an intermittent, normally dry tributary of the Pecos River, crosses the site. A red bluff, brushy sand dunes, grasslands, alkali flats. Foot and horse access only.

Hunting: Waterfowl.

NEARBY: Bottomless Lakes State Park (see entry).

PUBLICATIONS

Leaflet with map.
Self-guiding auto tour leaflet.
Bird checklist.
Checklist of most common species.
Public recreational uses and regulations.

HEADQUARTERS: P.O. Box 7, Roswell, NM 88201; (505) 622-6755.

BOTTOMLESS LAKES STATE PARK
New Mexico State Park and Recreation Division
1,611 acres.

16 mi. SE of Roswell via US 380 and SR 409.

These seven small lakes are natural, formed by the collapse of underground caverns. Picnicking and other day use is heavy from Roswell and smaller towns nearby. We stopped overnight on a Sept. weekday and were alone in the campground.

Lea Lake is the center of activity, with campground, concession building, boat rentals. Park HQ at Cottonwood Lake has exhibits; several trails are nearby. The setting is low desert hills, sparsely vegetated.

When uncrowded, it's a pleasant area for an overnight stop or a lakeside stroll. We saw some waterfowl, but birding is better at nearby Bitter Lake National Wildlife Refuge.

HEADQUARTERS: Auto Route E, Box 1200, Roswell, NM 88201; (505) 622-3636.

CARLSBAD CAVERNS NATIONAL PARK
National Park Service
46,755 acres.

On US 62/180, 20 mi. SW of Carlsbad.

Most visitors come to the visitor center, take the elevator down 750 feet to the cavern, and follow a guide for the 1 1/2 mi. walk through chambers and passages and around the Big Room. It's impressive, even for those who have been in other large caves, but this tour is only a part of what Carlsbad has to offer. One can visit another large cavern, New Cave, by lantern light, watch great clouds of bats pouring from the mouth of the main cavern at dusk, drive through Walnut Canyon and up to the top of the Capitan Reef escarpment, or go hiking or backpacking in the Park's rugged backcountry. Qualified spelunkers can get permits to enter several of the 72 other protected wild caves within the Park boundaries. Birders flock to Rattlesnake Springs and Oak Springs, in a tributary of Walnut Canyon, W of the Visitor Center.

The Carlsbad Caverns National Park, Guadalupe Mountains National Park, and the Guadalupe District of the Lincoln National Forest share much of one of the world's largest known limestone reefs, formed near the margin of the sea about 250 million years ago. Limestone dissolves slowly, but over millions of years water seeping underground has formed caverns with fascinating formations.

The Park's terrain is mostly steep rocky ridges and rugged canyons. Elevations in the Park are 3,600 ft. at the base of the escarpment on the E boundary, 4,406 ft. at the Visitor Center, 6,350 ft. on Guadalupe Ridge.

Summer days are warm, winter days usually mild, but extreme changes can occur suddenly. In winter a brief snowstorm or cold front may be driven by gale-force winds. Average annual precipitation is 14 in., most coming in summer. Summer afternoon thundershowers occur, sometimes causing flash floods. Temperature in the caverns remains the same all year: 56°F.

Plants: Vegetation at lower elevations is typical of arid country, creosote the most common plant. Canyon bottoms have black walnut, hackberry, oak, desert willow. Canyon walls and ridge tops are vegetated with agave, yucca, sotol, ocotillo, and desert grasses. At the high elevations are juniper, pinyon pine, Texas madrone, occasional ponderosa pine and Douglas-fir.

Birds: Checklist available with 1981 supplement, totaling 304 species. *Rattlesnake Springs,* a desert oasis, is one of the best birding spots in NM. The entry for Lincoln NF includes an extensive list of birds common to this area, which need not be repeated here. Other common species found here, most of them attracted by the oasis: mallard, gadwall, green-winged and blue-winged teal, Swainson's hawk, American coot, killdeer, yellow-billed cuckoo, roadrunner.

Mammals: no printed checklist available, but a 1965 mimeographed version can be copied on request. Often seen, jackrabbit, ringtail, raccoon, skunk, fox, gopher, woodrat, mice, squirrel, porcupine, mule deer. Present but seldom seen: coyote, badger, bobcat, mountain lion.

FEATURES

The Main Cave: Carlsbad's T-shaped big room is huge, a floor area of 14 acres, with much of its ceiling 200 ft. above the walkway. Formations in caves are always named, and Carlsbad's have some of the same names as cave formations in Majorca, Virginia, and New Zealand. They are impressive anyway—the Whale's Mouth, Bashful Elephant, Temple of the Sun, Frozen Waterfall, and Totem Pole.

During most of the year, visitors are not required to wait for a tour guide; Rangers are met at intervals along the route, and are pleased to help and inform. Radio receivers are provided to each visitor for picking up recorded messages through antenna wires buried in the trail surface. One can also come in by the natural entrance rather than taking the elevator, adding 1 3/4 mi. to the walk. The full trip is 3 mi. and takes about 3 hours. Guided tours are offered in lieu of the self-guided trips through this 1 3/4 mi. walk-in portion for about 8 weeks each winter, when visitation is lowest.

New Cave, in a pristine area of the Park, was discovered in 1937 and left undeveloped: no elevators, electric lights, or subterranean refreshment stands. Guided trips by lantern light are available daily during the summer, and on weekends only during the rest of the year. The cave is a corridor 1,140 ft. long with numerous side passages. Outstanding formations are the Christmas Tree, Monarch, Klansman, Tear Drop, and Chinese Wall. All are impressive when seen by lantern light. Lowest point is 250 ft. below the surface.

Bat flights occur from late May through Oct.; these bats winter in Mexico.

They fly out each night to hunt insects, great clouds of them. Rangers conduct programs, which take place about sunset. Program schedules can be obtained at the Visitor Center. (Flights normally occur within 15 minutes of the previous night's flight.)

Wilderness: 33,125 acres, almost 3/4 of the entire Park, is roadless, primitive, closed to all but foot or horse travel.

Loop Road Scenic Drive. A 9 1/2 mi. drive along the eastern escarpment of the Guadalupe Mountains, then through Rattlesnake Canyon. Auto Guide available.

INTERPRETATION

Visitor center has exhibits, information, talks, literature, concessions. Center and caverns are open every day of the year except Dec. 25. Hours vary with seasons and available staffing. In winter, hours generally are from 8 A.M. to 5:30 P.M. for the visitor center and from 8 A.M. to 2 P.M. for complete cave trips. Summer hours are from 7 A.M. to 8 P.M. for the Visitor Center, and 7:30 A.M. to 6 P.M. for complete cave trips. Big Room trips are available about 1 1/2 hr. later on both summer and winter schedules. Complete trips exit the Cave about 3 hrs. after the last visitors enter.

ACTIVITIES

Camping: No car camping.

Hiking and backpacking: Limited only by the hiker's water supply. Permits are required for overnight trips. A wilderness trail links with trails in the Guadalupe Ranger District of Lincoln National Forest (see entry). Popular destinations include Painted Grotto, Upper Painted Grotto, Double Canyon Overlook, Putman Cabin. Some trails are well maintained and heavily used. Others have only an occasional rock cairn or marker. The best hiking seasons are Apr.–May and Sept.–Oct.

Use of the backcountry is increasing.

PUBLICATIONS

Leaflet.

Loop Road Scenic Drive Auto Guide.

Wild Caving at Carlsbad Caverns National Park.

Checklist of Birds.

Mammals of Carlsbad Caverns National Park.

Amphibians and Reptiles of Carlsbad Caverns National Park.

Trail map and information.

Information pages:

  Information background.

  Cavern information; area map.

Wild caving policy and permit information.

The bat flight program.

REFERENCES

Evans, Harry. *50 Hikes in New Mexico.* Pico Rivera, CA: Gem Guides Book Co., 1984, pp. 154–162.

Barnett, John. *Carlsbad Caverns National Park.* Carlsbad, NM: Carlsbad Caverns Natural History Association, 1979.

Barnett, John. *Carlsbad Caverns: Silent Chambers, Timeless Beauty.* Carlsbad, NM: Carlsbad Caverns Natural History Association, 1981.

ADJACENT OR NEARBY

Lincoln National Forest, Guadalupe Ranger District.

Guadalupe Mountains National Park.

Living Desert State Park.

See entries.

HEADQUARTERS: 3225 National Parks Highway, Carlsbad, NM 88220; (505) 785-2232 or 885-8884.

FORT STANTON CAVE
U.S. Bureau of Land Management
Acreage not given.

Between Lincoln and Capitan on US 380.

We were asked not to describe the location of the cave. It is gated, locked, and access is by permit only. Permits must be requested, in person or by mail, at least 10 days in advance. Permits are issued only to visitors having proper equipment and experience.

Fort Stanton Cave is second in size only to Carlsbad Caverns, in New Mexico. This is one of several caves on land administered by BLM that can be entered only by permit.

The cave is at 6,160 ft. elevation in a hilly to rough and mountainous setting, with grassland and medium to dense growths of pinyon and juniper with scattered ponderosa pine.

Although the cave was known to the Indians long ago and visited by white men at least as early as 1855, some passages were not discovered until 1956. Total length of the known passages is 8 mi. Many of these passages are twisting and narrow. Cavers are advised that penetrating to the farthest points is difficult, strenuous, and potentially hazardous.

The cave is noted for its displays of rare velvet formations, as well as helictites, selenite needles, and various forms of gypsum.

The cave is a winter roost for about 700 Townsend big-eared bats. Disturbing hibernating bats can cause their deaths.

Safety requirements call for minimum parties of 3 with adequate lights and hard hats; other equipment, clothing, and emergency supplies are recommended.

Camping: Not permitted in the cave, but informal sites are available on the surface nearby.

PUBLICATION: Leaflet with cave map.

HEADQUARTERS: BLM, Roswell District Office, 1717 West Second, Roswell, NM 88201; (505) 622-7670.

GUADALUPE MOUNTAINS NATIONAL PARK
National Park Service
76,297 acres.

From Carlsbad, NM, 55 mi. SW on US 62/180.

The Park is in Texas, but it is closely linked to New Mexico, an extension of the Guadalupe Mountains and the Capitan Reef. It adjoins Carlsbad Caverns National Park and the Guadalupe Ranger District of Lincoln National Forest, with connecting trails. Visitors may wish to see all three.

The scenic way to approach the Park is from the S on US 62/180. Directly ahead is the S end of this geological intrusion, El Capitan, a whitish, 1,200-ft. sheer cliff. (From the highway in the pass to the summit of El Capitan is 2,790 ft.) Just to the N of it is the highest point in Texas, Guadalupe Peak, 8,749 ft. Along the highway are viewpoints and a picnic area where visitors can stop to enjoy the view.

The establishment of the Park is attributed to an oil company geologist, Wallace Pratt, who had an important role in defining the Capitan Reef, the largest known limestone fossil reef, formed millions of years ago. At Carlsbad Caverns, the reef is underground. Here it rises above, exposed in the walls of McKittrick Canyon. The geologist bought land in McKittrick Canyon and, some years after his retirement, donated it to the government. The owner of a much larger adjoining landholding then offered to sell at a giveaway price, and the Park was formally established in 1972.

It's a hiker's park. The US highway cuts across its SE corner, but the only vehicle road penetrating the interior of the Park is a 4-wheel-drive track to Williams Ranch. The Park Service intends to keep it that way.

The lowest elevation is at the base of the E escarpment, 3,650 ft. The Guadalupe Mountains here are V-shaped, the apex at El Capitan, arms spreading at a 60° angle into NM.

The annual averages suggest a mild climate: highs of 87–88°F in June–July, lows of 28–27° in Dec.–Feb. But swings occur suddenly in this country, and it's colder at the high elevations, especially with gale-force winter winds.

Snows aren't heavy, but accumulations of 2 to 4 ft. may remain for weeks up high. Precipitation is higher than in the nearby desert, averaging 21 in. per year, most of it June–Sept.

Wildlife: Checklists available: birds, mammals, reptiles, and amphibians. Common species are essentially the same as those occurring in the Lincoln NF and Carlsbad Caverns NP (see those entries).

FEATURES

McKittrick Canyon is the most popular day hike, for the best of reasons. Spectacular canyon walls; a variety of trees, shrubs, and wildflowers; a stream in a rocky bed; an easy trail. Because of its popularity and fragile ecology, the canyon is for day use only. Self-guiding pamphlet.

Guadalupe Peak can be reached by a 9-mi. round-trip hike, gaining 3,000 ft. of elevation. Spectacular views.

Devils Hall, a 5-mi. round trip, relatively level hike in Pine Springs Canyon.

Bush Mountain and *Dog Canyon* are among the destinations for backpackers. Dog Canyon, at the N boundary of the Park, is a secluded and forested canyon, elevation 6,300 ft. A mixture of junipers, maples, and oaks offers shade, greenery, and fall colors. It can also be reached by road. From the junction of US 285 and SR 137, 12 mi. N of Carlsbad, S 47 mi. on SR 137, then County Road 414 to the Park boundary. A ranger station and campground are 1 mi. inside the park.

INTERPRETATION

Visitor center at Frijole, in a temporary building. Information, exhibits, publications.

Nature trail and visitor contact station with exhibits at McKittrick Canyon.

ACTIVITIES

Camping: 2 campgrounds, 42 sites. All year.

Hiking, backpacking: 80 mi. of trails. Some, maintained for day use, are easy. Others are steep, rocky, narrow. Permits are required for overnights. Camping is restricted to 10 designated locations with a total of 100 sites. Each site limited to 20 people.

Horse riding: Day use only. Requires a good "rock horse." Riders can cross the Park into the National Forest in 5 to 8 hours. Horse use prohibited in McKittrick Canyon, the Bowl, and a few other trails. Allowed on the remaining 60–70 mi. of trail. No drinking water on the trails.

Pets are not allowed on park trails.

PUBLICATIONS

Park leaflet.

Weatherproof map of Park. $5.

Information pages:

Information background.
Hiking and backpacking information.
About Your Trip to the Williams Ranch.
Winter use facts.
Monthly weather conditions.

REFERENCES

Murphy, Dan. *Guadalupe Mountains National Park.* Carlsbad, NM: Carlsbad Caverns Natural History Association, 1984.

Tennant, Alan, and Michael Allender. *Guadalupe Mountains of Texas.* Carlsbad, NM: Carlsbad Caverns Natural History Association, 1980.

Kurtz, Don, and William Goran. *Trails of the Guadalupes.* Carlsbad, NM: Carlsbad Caverns Natural History Association, 1982.

Warnock, Barton H. *Wildflowers of the Guadalupe Mountains and Sand Dune Country, Texas.* Carlsbad, NM: Carlsbad Caverns Natural History Association, 1974.

Davy, Dava McGahee. *McKittrick Canyon Guide.* Carlsbad, NM: Carlsbad Caverns Natural History Association, 1977.

——————. *Butterfield Overland Mail.* Carlsbad, NM: Carlsbad Caverns Natural History Association, 1977.

Newman, George H. *Checklist of Birds, Guadalupe Mountains National Park.* Carlsbad, NM: Carlsbad Natural History Association, 1974.

HEADQUARTERS: 3225 National Parks Highway, Carlsbad, NM 88220; (505) 885-8884.

LINCOLN NATIONAL FOREST
U.S. Forest Service
1,103,495 acres; 1,271,066 acres within boundaries.

Three areas. The N area, surrounding Capitan, is crossed by US 380 and US 70. The middle area, E of Alamogordo, is crossed by US 82. The S area, W of Carlsbad, is crossed by SR 137.

One can drive through the Lincoln National Forest almost without noticing it. The principal highways are in corridors of privately owned land. Along US 82 between Alamogordo and Artesia, for example, only about 10 mi. of the road are on the Forest. Portions of this highway that were once scenic are now a regrettable clutter of unplanned development. Turn off any of the main roads, however, and you are almost at once in an admirable forest.

The Capitan, Guadalupe, and Sacramento Mountains dominate SW New

Mexico, rising above the extensive surrounding plains. The resident population of the region is small, but the Forest attracts visitors from an area including Texas and northern Mexico. They come to the mountains in summer to escape the heat of the desert, in winter for snow play.

The range of elevations produces variety in climate and vegetation, from Chihuahuan Desert to subalpine zone. Average annual precipitation is 10 in. at low elevations, up to 35 in. on the ridges. Average snowfall is zero down below, 150 in. on the high slopes. Plant zones range from desert association up through pinyon-juniper to ponderosa pine and mixed conifers.

Five rivers flow from near the W boundary of the Forest to the E side: the Bonito, Ruidoso, Hondo, Felix, and Penasco, all small, all tributaries of the Pecos. Three small lakes offer fishing: Bonito, on municipal land within the Forest boundary; Nogal, on Smokey Bear R.D.; and Bear Canyon Lake, on Mayhill R.D. The Forest has no boating or swimming waters.

About 3/4 of the Forest drains eastward to the Pecos Valley, 1/4 to the Tularosa Basin.

One can find good camping, hiking, or backpacking here at any season, but the visitor needs some guidance. The Lincoln has special characteristics. Almost all its campgrounds close in early Sept., but visitors can choose among many informal campsites. They can do so in other National Forests, but few provide as much help as the Lincoln, with handouts including items such as the following, from the Mayhill R.D.:

> Go south from Mayhill on NM Hwy 130. Turn left onto State Hwy 24 and go over Denny Hill. When you reach the sign that says "Weed-Sacramento," turn right onto NM Hwy 521. At the Sacramento turnoff, keep straight ahead on Forest Road 64 for approximately 5 miles. Turn left at Hoosier Canyon. There are some flat areas suitable for camping. In the fall, the trees sport fall colors in that canyon.

When we asked about hiking, one of our Forest advisors cautioned us that almost all trails outside the two Wildernesses are open to motorcycles and other ORV's. Three short trails are not. Hikers are sometimes disturbed by the noise and by being forced aside. "It's the nature of our clientele," he said. "Most of our visitors want motorized travel, not hiking."

The Forest map is not a useful trail guide. (When we made our most recent visit, in 1984, the 1974 edition was in use. A revised edition was in preparation, but no one knew when it would appear.) Several good trails don't appear on it. Also some routes shown on the map as primitive roads, while originally made by motor vehicles, are now used as trails.

However, the Forest has good written guides to trails both inside the Wildernesses and elsewhere. The Guadalupe R.D. guide, for example, offers precise directions to 6 trailheads, with trail descriptions.

The Forest has 237 mi. of managed system trails, about 89 mi. of which are in the two Wildernesses. The Cloudcroft R.D. has two National Recreation Trails, a 13-mi. Rim Trail and a 6-mi. trail dropping down through Dog

Canyon to Oliver Lee Memorial State Park (see entry). About half of the trail mileage, including most wilderness trails, gets at least minimum maintenance. 129 mi. receive little or none; signing is inadequate; and little-used trails are revegetating.

One weekend we explored an area near Cloudcroft and found a delightful trail not shown on the map or mentioned in any guide. It had once been two-track, but trees several years old grew between the tracks. We saw no motorcycle spoor. Most of the trail was through a conifer forest. We crossed several grassy swales and wet our feet in a marshy area. Birding was good.

RANGER DISTRICTS

Smokey Bear R.D.: The District is composed of several connected blocks. Three on the W straddle the Jicarilla, Patos, Carrizo, and Vera Cruz Mountains and the N end of the Sacramento Mountains.

The southern block includes the White Mountain Wilderness. Between it and the SE block is the fast-growing resort town of Ruidoso, at the intersection of US 70 and SR 37. Ruidoso is the recreational center of the District. All of the District's 6 campgrounds are in the Sierra Blanca block. The Ski Apache ski area is said to be one of the best in the SW. The area offers excellent golf and fishing. Ruidoso claims to have the world's richest horserace. (It is quarterhorse racing.)

The largest block, on the E side of the District, includes the Capitan Mountains wilderness. The Capitan Range is one of the few running W–E. Elevations are 5,000 to 10,000 ft. Most of the area is steep and rocky except for open meadows along the main ridgetop. The E end of the range has many rock outcroppings and very rough terrain.

Cloudcroft and Mayhill R.D.'s: The two R.D.'s are a single block on the Sacramento Mountains E of Alamogordo. The W edge of the Forest consists almost entirely of an escarpment that at one point drops 7,000 ft. to the Tularosa Valley. US 82 eastbound climbs 4,315 ft. in 16 mi. to Cloudcroft, a mountain resort. Smaller than Ruidoso, Cloudcroft also has a ski area and boasts the highest golf course in the United States. All but one of the Districts' campgrounds are clustered near Cloudcroft. That one (on Mayhill R.D.) is farther E on US 82, in James Canyon. The National Solar Observatory, Sacramento Peak, used for solar research, is open to visitors daily.

Guadalupe R.D.: The Guadalupe Mountains have some of the wildest and most picturesque country remaining in NM. More isolated than the other R.D.'s, it is crossed by a single paved road. Most of the area, 209,000 acres, is within the R.D., which extends SE to the Texas border, adjoining Guadalupe Mountains National Park and Carlsbad Caverns National Park (see entries). The S end includes about 35 sq. mi. of rugged mountains with sheer cliffs and deep canyons, from the mouth of Gunsight Canyon at 4,800 ft. elevation to Dark Canyon Lookout Tower at 6,950 ft. Highest point is 7,500 ft. This end is part of the same geological formation as Carlsbad Caverns and has many caves. The N portion of the District is a mesa, rolling terrain with many canyons, chiefly on the E side.

The District has no developed campgrounds but many good informal campsites. Good hiking trails, including trails into the Wilderness Area of Guadalupe NP and trails into the backcountry of Carlsbad Caverns National Park. Most of these trails are not on the Forest map, but HQ or an R.D. office can help.

Plants: Life zones are similar to those of other NM mountains. The S end of the Guadalupes is the southern limit of distribution for many species of the Great Plains, Rocky Mountain, and Chihuahuan Desert plant communities.

Tree species include fragrant ash, quaking aspen, Rio Grande cottonwood, corkbark fir, Douglas-fir, white fir; alligator, one-seeded, Rocky Mountain, and red-berry junipers; New Mexico locust, Texas madrone, Rocky Mountain maple, Knowlton's hophornbeam, chinquapin; wavyleaf, Gambel, Arizona white, and gray oaks; pinyon pine, ponderosa pine, Arizona black walnut, pygmy black walnut, southwestern white pine, blue and Engelmann spruces.

No list of flowering plants is available.

Birds: Checklist available: *Birds of the Sacramento Mountains.* Seasonally common species include turkey vulture, red-tailed hawk, American kestrel, scaled and Gambel's quail, wild turkey, band-tailed pigeon, mourning dove. Owls: screech, flammulated, great horned, pygmy. Poor-will, common nighthawk, white-throated swift, black-chinned and broad-tailed hummingbirds. Woodpeckers: acorn, hairy, downy; northern flicker. Western kingbird; Cassin's, western, and ash-throated flycatchers; violet-green, cliff, and barn swallows; Steller's, scrub, and pinyon jays; common raven, mountain chickadee, plain titmouse, common bushtit, white-breasted and pygmy nuthatches, brown creeper. Wrens: house, cactus, canyon, rock, Bewick's. Mockingbird, curve-billed thrasher, American robin, hermit thrush, mountain and western bluebirds, Townsend's solitaire, ruby-crowned and golden-crowned kinglets, loggerhead shrike, solitary and warbling vireos. Warblers: Virginia's, orange-crowned, yellow-rumped, Grace's, MacGillivray's, Wilson's, yellow, black-throated gray. Red-winged blackbird, western tanager, black-headed grosbeak, Cassin's finch, pine siskin, lesser goldfinch, red crossbill, rufous-sided and gray-headed juncos, chipping and white-crowned sparrows.

We obtained a 1977 Christmas bird count that included additional species. Those of which 5 or more were observed included mallard, Say's phoebe, horned lark, white-necked raven, crissal thrasher, European starling, Brewer's blackbird, pyrrhuloxia.

Mammals: No published checklist, but list available at HQ. Includes myotis: California, cave, fringed, little brown, long-legged, small-footed, Yuma. Bats: big brown; big, Mexican, and pocketed freetail; hoary, pallid, red, silver-haired, spotted, western big-eared, western pipistrel. Mexican and long-tail voles. Shrews: desert, dwarf, vagrant. Mice: brush, cactus, deer, house, northern and southern grasshopper, pinyon, rock, western harvest, western jumping. Pocket mice: Apache, hispid, plains, rock, silky. Bannertail and Ord kangaroo rats, hispid cotton rat; Mexican, southern plains, and whitethroat woodrats. Red and rock squirrels, spotted and thirteen-lined ground squirrels, Texas antelope squirrel, gray-footed and least chipmunks, blacktail jackrabbit, desert and eastern cottontails, Mexican and valley pocket gophers. Black bear, coyote, beaver, nutria, raccoon, ringtail, badger, mountain lion, bobcat, gray fox, kit fox, bridled and longtail weasels, porcupine; hognose, striped, and western spotted skunks; javelina, pronghorn, mule and whitetail deer, elk, Barbary and mountain sheep.

Reptiles and amphibians: List can be seen at HQ. Includes Texas banded gecko. Lizards: collared, eastern fence, greater earless, round-tailed horned, short-horned, Texas horned, tree, crevice spiny. Whiptails: Colorado checkered, Chihuahua spotted, little striped, Texas spotted. Great Plains and many-lined skinks, Sacramento Mountain and tiger salamanders, plains and northern leopard frogs, Texas frog, bullfrog, Couch's and Hammond's spadefoots, red-spotted and Woodhouse's toads. Western box turtle. Snakes: blacknecked, western terrestrial, and checkered garter; common and gray-banded kingsnakes, corn, glossy, coachwhip, lined, long-nosed, milk, mountain patch-nosed, night, gopher, plains black-headed, ring-necked, smooth green, striped whipsnake, Texas blind, trans-Pecos rat, western ground, western hog-nosed, western hook-nosed, Mexican black-headed. Rattlesnakes: blacktailed, rock, western diamondback, western.

FEATURES

White Mountain Wilderness, 48,366 acres, is N of Sierra Blanca Peak, NW of Ruidoso. Elevations from 6,500 ft. at the Three Rivers Campground trailhead to 11,260 ft. near Lookout Mountain on the S. The S boundary borders the Mescalero Apache Indian Reservation; Sierra Blanca Peak, 12,003 ft., is just inside the Reservation. The Wilderness is on a single long ridge with branches. The W side is steep and rugged, the E side sloping more gently, with broad forested canyons holding a few tiny streams. Lower slopes have pinyon-juniper woodland, mid-slopes ponderosa pine and pinyon; the main ridgetop has mixed conifers, including Douglas-fir and ponderosa pine. Also spruce and corkbark fir.

The Wilderness has 50 mi. of developed trails, plus trails that are not maintained but often used. One trailhead is at Three Rivers Campground, at the SW corner of the District; from here it's a strenuous hike to the crest. Others are on the E and W sides. Most link with the 21-mi.-long Crest Trail, which crosses subalpine meadows, grass-oak savannahs, and mixed conifer and aspen stands.

In winter the crest may have 6 ft. of snow while it's comfortably warm at the 6,500-ft. elevation. The high trails are usually open by Apr. July and Aug. are the wettest months, with frequent afternoon showers.

Capitan Mountains Wilderness, 34,513 acres, is about 12 mi. E–W, 2 to 6 mi. wide, NE of the town of Capitan. Trailheads are on Forest Roads reached from US 380 on the S, SR 48 on the N. The N side has steep, rocky slopes with numerous canyons. The S face is less rocky, although there are large outcrops. Elevations range from 5,500 ft. on the E side to 10,083 ft. at Capitan Peak. Lower slopes have pinyon-juniper woodlands, mid-slopes ponderosa pine and pinyon. The main ridge has mixed conifers, including Douglas-fir and ponderosa pine.

A 10-mi. trail follows the ridge. Routes from trailheads generally link with this crest trail. Capitan Peak is a popular destination. The only streams are small.

Caves. The geological formation that includes Carlsbad Caverns extends into the S tip of the Guadalupe R.D., which has an extensive array of caverns. The area is famous among spelunkers, who come here from many countries. Not all the caves have been discovered. Some were found by taking infrared aerial photographs in winter, detecting warm air emanating from cave openings. Many openings are in rugged country, difficult to reach. Some can be reached only by roping down vertical cliffs. Some require rope descents inside, some coping with underground streams or lakes.

Many caves house colonies of bats that hibernate in winter. Bats disturbed during hibernation are likely to die. Some caves have been severely vandalized. To protect bats, the caves, and human life, the Forest Service controls access, gating the openings of the more accessible caves and restricting information about others. The Service is not inhospitable to those who understand caving and responsible conduct. A permit is required for entry to any cave. Permits must be requested at least two weeks in advance.

Scenic drives: Best known is the ascent on US 82 from the Tularosa Valley to Cloudcroft. Overlooks. Less traveled scenic drives are described in Forest handouts. An example, from the Mayhill R.D.:

> *Carr Gap Road:* Take US 82 west from Mayhill for about 10 miles. Turn right on Forest Road 175, Sixteen Springs Road. Stay on FR 175 until you come to the sign: "FR 607, Carr Gap Road." Turn right on FR 607 and follow it back to US 82 about 2-1/2 miles northeast of Mayhill.

INTERPRETATION

R.D. and Supervisor's offices serve as visitor centers with information, literature, some exhibits.

Nature trails near Sleepygrass Campground and near the Silver, Saddle, and Apache Campgrounds, all near Cloudcroft.

Campfire programs are sometimes offered, July–Aug.

Cave tours are sometimes available by request, Guadalupe R.D.

ACTIVITIES

Camping: 14 campgrounds, 369 sites. A few all-year, most May 15–Sept. 15. (We found most closed Sept. 1 in 1984.)

Hiking, backpacking: 254 mi. of trails. Carry water.

Horse riding: On all suitable trails. No special facilities.

Hunting: Chiefly mule deer, elk, bear, wild turkey. Some pronghorn and Barbary sheep.

Fishing: Small trout in a few small streams.

Downhill skiing: Ski Apache and Ski Cloudcroft. Usual season: Dec. 1– Apr. 1.

Ski touring: 2 1/2 mi. of trail in the Cloudcroft area. Also on unplowed roads. A number of old railroad grades offer excellent, ungroomed trails, from beginner quality to advanced.

PUBLICATIONS
Smokey Bear R.D. and Sacramento Mountains map. $1.

Guadalupe District map. $1.

Lincoln National Forest and *Guadalupe Journal.* Tabloid newspaper format. Articles, photos, advertisements.

Information pages:
General description.
Camping, trails, scenic drives, etc.:
Smokey Bear R.D.
Cloudcroft R.D.
Mayhill R.D.
Guadalupe R.D.
White Mountain Wilderness, description and trails.
Capitan Mountains Wilderness, description and trails.
Cloudcroft snow play area map.
Trees on the Lincoln N.F.
Dog Canyon Trail. Leaflet with map.
Bird checklist.
Ski Sierra Blanca (now called Ski Apache).
(Wilderness trail maps were not available in 1984.)

REFERENCES
Ganci, Dave. *Hiking the Southwest.* San Francisco: Sierra Club Books, 1983, pp. 265–283.

Evans, Harry. *50 Hikes in New Mexico.* Pico Rivera, CA: Gem Guides Book Co., 1984, pp. 142–153, 163–171.

NEARBY
See entries:
Valley of Fires State Park.
Oliver Lee Memorial State Park, adjacent to Cloudcroft R.D.
Living Desert State Park.
White Sands National Monument.
Guadalupe Mountains National Park, adjacent to Guadalupe R.D.
Carlsbad Caverns National Park, adjacent to Guadalupe R.D.

HEADQUARTERS: Federal Building, 11th and New York, Alamogordo, NM 88310; (505) 437-6030.

RANGER DISTRICTS: Smokey Bear R.D., Drawer F, Ruidoso, NM 88345; (505) 257-4095. Cloudcroft R.D., P.O. Box 288, Cloudcroft, NM 88317; (505) 682-2551. Guadalupe R.D., Federal Building, Carlsbad, NM 88220; (505) 885-4181. Mayhill R.D., P.O. Box 5, Mayhill, NM 88339; (505) 687-3411.

LIVING DESERT ZOOLOGICAL AND BOTANICAL STATE PARK
New Mexico State Park and Recreation Division
1,120 acres.

4 mi. NW of Carlsbad on US 285.

When we visited in 1984, a $750,000 renovation was about to begin. The plans looked great. Even before renovation, it was a good place to visit for an introduction to desert ecology.

It is to the Chihuahuan Desert what the Arizona-Sonora Desert Museum is to the Sonoran, featuring living plants and animals. Exhibits include an aviary, nocturnal house, botanic garden, and enclosures for reptiles, hoofed animals, and other creatures. More to come.

PUBLICATION: Leaflet.

HEADQUARTERS: P.O. Box 100, Carlsbad, NM 88220; (505) 887-5516.

MESCALERO SANDS
U.S. Bureau of Land Management
6,300 acres.

Access corridor extends S from US 380 about 35 mi. E of Roswell, near mile marker 193.

We usually omit sites that are hemmed in by privately owned land. This one is worth noting because BLM hopes to acquire a right-of-way and because one can get there now by a difficult 5 1/2- to 10-mi. hike. (Visitors can sometimes get permission from landowners, but don't count on it.)

The site is near the W edge of the Caprock (Mescalero Ridge) Escarpment. Designated an Outstanding Natural Area in 1980, it contains the largest drifting sand dunes in SE New Mexico. The major dunes in the ONA are protected from incompatible surface uses such as livestock grazing, mineral development, and vehicle use.

The dunes of White Sands National Monument (see entry) are composed of gypsum. The light-colored dunes of Mescalero Sands are composed of white quartz sand. Some of the sandy soils surrounding the dunes are reddish. Among the most unusual aspects of the dunes is the number of cottonwoods, a tree that needs a moist environment. The dunes look desert-dry, but the water table is near the surface, supporting unusual vegetation. Stabilized dunes in the site and nearby are covered with a dense growth of shinnery oak, a small bush that bears full-size acorns. Another curiosity is the occurrence of fulgurite, a glassy, tube-shaped substance formed by lightning strikes in the sand.

Wildlife of the area includes the lesser prairie chicken, the sand dune sagebrush lizard, and a diminishing herd of whitetail deer.

PUBLICATION: Folder with map.

HEADQUARTERS: BLM, Roswell District Office, 1717 West Second St., Roswell, NM 88201; (505) 622-7670.

OLIVER LEE MEMORIAL STATE PARK
New Mexico State Park and Recreation Division
180 acres.

From Alamogordo, 10 mi. S on US 54, then E 5 mi.

This attractive small Park is at the mouth of Dog Canyon, an historical route into the Sacramento Mountains, now a trailhead for hiking into the Lincoln National Forest. (This isn't the Dog Canyon mentioned in the Guadalupe National Park entry.) Elevated a hundred feet or so above the desert floor, the Park overlooks the Tularosa Basin.

The handsome visitor center has exhibits and a film. It is surrounded by a well-labeled desert garden. From here a fine nature trail leads up the canyon, becoming an elevated boardwalk to preserve the lush riparian vegetation. The canyon has a perennial stream rushing over small cascades, and in places the canyon walls are wet, water dripping down over hanging gardens. Many wildflowers, birds.

ACTIVITIES
Camping: 44 sites. All year.
Hiking, backpacking: Backpackers leaving their cars here are asked to register. The Dog Canyon Trail is a strenuous 4.2-mi. hike to Joplin Ridge,

terminating at Forest Road 90B, an elevation gain of 3,130 ft. In places the canyon walls rise 1,500 ft. above the trail. This trail does not appear on the 1974 Forest map. A new map was expected at the time of our last visit.

PUBLICATION: *Dog Canyon Trail.* Leaflet with map, published by Lincoln National Forest.

HEADQUARTERS: P.O. Box 1845, Alamogordo, NM 88310; (505) 437-8284.

PRAIRIE CHICKEN WILDLIFE AREAS
New Mexico Department of Game and Fish

20,000 acres in 9 areas near Milnesand, Crossroads, and Floyd. Most of the tracts are on dirt roads.

With the short-grass prairies dwindling, the once-abundant prairie chicken has become scarce. The Department began acquiring tracts of prairie in 1940, and a limited population now seems secure.

Birders come from afar in springtime to hear the booming and see the dancing display of the male prairie chicken's courtship. During this period, the birds are easy to approach. The activity usually peaks about Apr. 15. There is also a false booming period in late Sept. and Oct. when the male birds do their booming and dance, but the hens never come into the booming grounds. The cocks may be photographed at this time as well as in the spring. The false boom period is never so big or widespread as in the spring, but it occurs on a number of the booming grounds. Inquire locally for the best areas.

Elevations are 4,000 to 4,200 ft. The habitat includes sandhills and sand plains with sparse vegetation.

There is a short fall hunting season.

HEADQUARTERS: Box 361, Dora, NM 88115.

VALLEY OF FIRES STATE PARK
New Mexico State Park and Recreation Division
463 acres.

On US 380, 1 mi. W of Carrizozo.

The fires are long since out. The Park overlooks the Carrizozo Lava Flow, a 44-mi. river of basalt that flowed S from Black Peak, covering more than 80,000 acres. It is one of the youngest lava flows of the continent, occurring 1,500 to 2,000 years ago. The flow is shown on highway maps as "The Malpais."

The lava flow has a variety of interesting formations, though no features as dramatic as the lava tubes and ice caves of El Malpais in Zone 1 (see entry). Windblown soil has settled in crevices, and a variety of colonizing plants have taken root. These in turn support modest wildlife populations, chiefly small mammals and their predators.

A nature trail leads from the group campground for 3/4 mi. through the nearby lava field. An exhibit stands at the beginning of the trail. The receptacle that once held brochures was missing when we visited.

Almost every point in the Park offers splendid views. It's an exposed site, and camping might be uncomfortable in the strong winds that occur often in spring.

Camping: 50 sites. All year.

ADJACENT

Most of the lava field is public land managed by BLM. An area of 15,570 acres N of US 380 has been considered for Wilderness status. Little Black Peak, 5,679 ft., in the N of the unit, is the most prominent lava cone. Jeep trails on the boundaries of the unit offer possible hiking routes. A larger area S of US 380 extends to the White Sands, where the dominant color shifts suddenly from black to white. An 11,000-acre area adjoining the Park has been proposed for wilderness status. Jeep trails and primitive roads are possible hiking routes.

Don't try hiking on lava in ordinary footgear or in your best boots. Sharp edges cut; rough surfaces abrade.

HEADQUARTERS: P.O. Box 871, Carrizozo, NM 88301; no telephone.

WHITE SANDS NATIONAL MONUMENT
National Park Service
144,420 acres.

15 mi. SW of Alamogordo on US 70/82.

The Monument includes 228 sq. mi. of sparkling white gypsum sand dunes, the gypsum crystals blown from the lakebed of Lake Lucero. This shallow lake is the lowest point in the Tularosa Basin, which lies between the San Andres and Sacramento Mountains. The lake holds up to 10 sq. mi. of very alkaline water. Gypsum crystals form along the shore and on the bed as the lake dries.

Dunes are 10 to 60 ft. high. Sand blown from the windward side is dropped on the other, causing dunes to move as much as 35 ft. per year. As they move, new dunes are forming near the lake.

Just off the highway is the visitor center and concession building. Outside is a well-labeled desert garden with plants common to the area, including sand verbena, rosemary mint, cholla, soaptree yucca, evening primrose, broom snakeweed, mesquite, creosote bush.

A 16-mi. round-trip scenic drive into the heart of the dunes begins here. Numbered posts keyed to the Monument leaflet call attention to dunes stabilized by vegetation, moving dunes, and other features, including dune pedestals—columns of sand held by plant roots after dunes moved on. Hiking is permitted, and most visitors climb at least one of the high dunes.

Lake Lucero cannot be seen without crossing the White Sands Missile Range. This can be done only on one of the bi-monthly guided auto caravans.

Wildlife: Exhibits in the visitor center portray the Monument's animals, few of which visitors are likely to see in the heat of the desert day. About 190 bird species have been recorded, including larks, doves, waterfowl, flycatchers, nighthawks, owls, plovers, wrens, thrashers, shrikes, blackbirds, orioles, finches, warblers, vireos. The mammal list includes 27 species, among them pallid and Brazilian freetail bats, kit fox, coyote, badger, ringtail, porcupine, plains pocket mouse, northern and southern grasshopper mice, bannertail kangaroo rat, deer mouse, white-footed and western harvest mice. Reptiles and amphibians include lesser earless and desert side-blotched lizards, New Mexico whiptail lizard, gopher snake, ground snake, prairie and diamondback rattlesnakes, desert massasauga.

INTERPRETATION

Visitor center has outstanding exhibits, naturalist talks, literature. Open daily except Christmas, 8:30 A.M.–5 P.M., to 7 P.M. in summer.

Evening programs in the dune area, Memorial Day–Labor Day. Special full-moon programs in summer.

Guided walks in the dune area, evenings, Memorial Day–Labor Day.

Auto caravans, guided, to Lake Lucero, bi-monthly; see schedule. By reservation.

Conducted bus tours. No fixed schedule. Inquire.

Nature trail: From Dunes Drive, 3 mi. from visitor center. 1 mi. long.

Hiking, backpacking: 1-mi. hike to primitive camp; registration required. Short trails. Hiking over and among dunes.

PUBLICATIONS

Leaflet with map and tour guide.

Information pages:

Visitor center.

Backcountry campsite.

Programs and hours.

REFERENCES

Atkinson, R. *White Sands, Wind, Sand, and Time.* Globe, AZ: Southwest Parks and Monuments Association, 1977.

Borell, A. E. *Birds of White Sands National Monument.* Unpublished, but available in White Sands NM library.

Dodge, Natt Noyes. *The Natural History of White Sands National Monument.* Globe, AZ: Southwest Parks and Monuments Association, 1971.

Hendrickson, P. *Lake Lucero.* Globe, AZ: Southwest Parks and Monuments Association, 1976.

Big Dune Trail Guide. Globe, AZ: Southwest Parks and Monuments Association.

HEADQUARTERS: P.O. Box 458, Alamogordo, NM 88310; (505) 437-1058.

ARIZONA

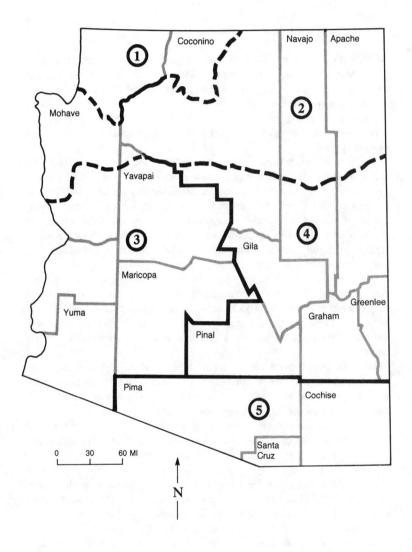

Coconino

Navajo Apache

①

Mohave

②

Yavapai

③

Gila

④

Maricopa

Yuma

Greenlee

Graham

Pinal

Pima

Cochise

⑤

Santa
Cruz

0   30   60 MI

N

ARIZONA

No state is more photographed. No state attracts more outstanding photographers. Many come here on assignment, look through their viewfinders, and decide to stay. Their work appears monthly in *Arizona Highways* magazine, the state's best advertisement.

Any time of year is delightful somewhere. When the desert is too hot, it's cool in the high country. When snow falls on the mountains, the deserts are pleasantly mild.

The Sun Belt boom began in the 1950s, and Arizona got most of it. By 1980, the state had 5 1/2 times as many residents as in 1950, and still they come. Many newcomers have congregated in cities, notably Phoenix and Tucson, but new communities have mushroomed. In the mid-1970s we saw a lonely cluster of half a dozen houses in an otherwise empty desert. Now there are thousands, plus a bustling downtown area, three or four shopping malls, schools, two golf courses, a hospital, an airfield, and other establishments, with more under construction.

We found no reliable count of winter visitors. Many, the "snowbirds," come here when the first frost threatens back home. Others vacation here until they can retire. Some RV parks have little space for transients in winter. The same snowbirds return year after year, often leaving their RVs between seasons. Budget-minded snowbirds assemble in huge masses on the western desert.

What do Arizonans do on vacation? Nearly half take their vacations in summer, and most travel outside the state! Even so, residents are the primary users of the state's outdoor recreation areas. Almost every household owns gear for fishing, hunting, camping, boating, or backpacking.

Some outdoor recreation areas are seasonally crowded, chiefly the most accessible lakes and campgrounds. A few wilderness areas are overused. But one can find as much isolation as one wishes, in magnificent settings. Some mountain ranges have less than a dozen visitors in a year. Even the rim of the Grand Canyon has miles where one is unlikely to meet another hiker. Many delightful places are quite accessible. One August afternoon we drove our motor home to the top of a pine-clad mountain, parked where we could see forever, and had the mountain to ourselves that night.

To most people, Arizona's image is desert. Travelers on the principal highways see little but desert, because road planners avoid mountains. Three deserts, the Great Basin, Mohave, and Sonoran, occupy almost half of the state, chiefly the southern sector and a wide strip along the western border. But the desert region is not all desert; within it are many mountain ranges, some high enough to trap enough moisture for trees to grow.

Except for the mountains, most of the southern and western desert regions are below 2,000 ft. elevation. In the N, the Colorado Plateau, more than a mile high, occupies two-fifths of the state. The plateau region is marked by high mountains, notably the San Francisco Peaks, and by dramatic canyons, chiefly the Grand Canyon of the Colorado. On this high tableland is the world's largest ponderosa pine forest. More than one-fourth of the state's land is forested, a larger area, they say, than the forests of Wisconsin or Maine.

On occasion, Arizona records the nation's highest and lowest temperatures on the same day. Many desert dwellers take to the highlands in summer. It can be a short trip, especially along the 200-mi. Mogollon Rim, where the plateau drops sharply 2,000 ft. to the desert floor.

The entire state is within the drainage basin of the Colorado River. The river, impounded at Glen Canyon Dam, flows S and W through the Grand Canyon to Lake Mead, then S along the California boundary through Lake Mohave, Lake Havasu, and Martinez Lake. All other rivers, though some flow bravely in their upper reaches, dry up or vanish underground during most of the year. Several offer whitewater rafting during spring runoff.

Most lakes are man-made. The largest are shared with bordering states. Roosevelt is the largest lake wholly within the state. Most lakes are in the central and E central regions. Motors can be used on 29 of them.

The great range of elevation, climate, and soils has produced as great a range of plant communities as can be found in any state. These, in turn, support an exceptionally great variety of wildlife species, including about 500 bird species, almost 150 species of mammals, over 100 species of reptiles and amphibians. Arizona attracts both the big-game hunter and the birder seeking additions to his life list.

MAPS

Arizona's official highway map is an adequate if sometimes exasperating guide to Interstate and U.S. highways and most state highways. Its representations of county roads are inadequate and sometimes misleading. Like most official state highway maps, it doesn't show the network of back roads. It has some minor but annoying errors; Mt. Trumbull's elevation is shown as 7,700 ft.; the U.S. Geological Survey (USGS) makes it 8,029.

Some years ago the members of the Four Corners Regional Commission —the tourist bureaus of Utah, Colorado, Arizona, and New Mexico—proposed production of some remarkable *Multipurpose and Outdoor Recreation Facilities Maps.* Colorado and New Mexico dropped out before the maps were made. Utah completed its set of 8 maps, and its tourist bureau still supplies them. They're great; we've found nothing to equal them in any state. Arizona's maps were completed but printed and sold commercially. They, too, were excellent, with details for 7 regions in full color. Now they are out of print. By persistent searching, we found a set, in an improbable place that no longer has any. Some libraries have them. We heard rumors that they may be revised and reprinted.

National Forest maps are indispensable, even though some are more than 10 years old. They show many back roads in adjoining areas.

To find your way in the backcountry, inquire locally, at the BLM office if there's one handy. Always inquire locally before venturing far on unpaved roads, where road conditions can change overnight.

FEDERAL LANDS

Less than one-tenth of Arizona's land is privately owned. About 45% is federal. The largest holding is what remains of the public domain, managed by the Bureau of Land Management, more than 12 1/2 million acres, most of it in the strip that is our Zone 1, the western desert, and the southeast. Many tracts meet the minimum requirements for consideration as wilderness areas: 5,000 or more roadless acres in essentially natural condition. BLM's studies of these areas were a great help to us, as were our talks with the people who made the studies. When the Arizona Wilderness Act of 1984 was signed, however, only 9 BLM tracts were included, 8 of them in the Arizona Strip (Zone 1). The others, though lacking this legal protection, are still there to enjoy.

The 6 National Forests include almost as much land, 11,221,000 acres, as the public domain. The main portion of Grand Canyon National Park was carved from the Kaibab National Forest, which now has Districts N and S of the Park. The Coronado National Forest is distributed over numerous mountain ranges in the SE. The others, including a third piece of the Kaibab, form a huge mass, most of it mountainous, in the central and E central regions.

Some parts of the Forests, especially those on the outskirts of Phoenix and Tucson, are heavily used, but there are countless ridges, canyons, and trails where solitude can be found. The 1984 Arizona Wilderness Act added 25 Wildernesses with more than 500,000 acres to the established 553,000 acres of National Forest Wildernesses.

Almost 3 million acres are in the two National Parks, 15 National Monuments, and 2 National Recreation Areas of the National Park Service. By far the largest site is Grand Canyon National Park. We have entries for 12 of these sites; 7 of the National Monuments are historical sites with no significant natural areas.

The two National Recreation Areas and the Grand Canyon National Park form an immense continuous strip of parkland along the Colorado River from the Utah border to Davis Dam, W of Kingman. Five National Wildlife Refuges include more than 1,500,000 acres. All but 66,000 acres is in two huge desert areas, Cabeza Prieta and Kofa. A small new Refuge near Douglas, San Bernardino, is scheduled to open to visitors in 1990. More than 3,600,000 acres are in military bases. One, Fort Huachuca, welcomes visitors and is of considerable interest to birders.

STATE LANDS

Almost 9 million acres of state lands are administered for revenue production and are not open for public recreation. Arizona has no state forests, as such.

The State Parks system was initiated in 1957. The legislature has not been generous. Only 34,000 acres have been acquired, in 19 parks, 7 of which have less than 12 acres. We visited the larger parks, enjoyed them, and have entries for those which have or adjoin interesting natural areas.

State wildlife areas total 24,584 acres, according to one official document, 282,706 acres according to another. The difference, in large measure, is because the Game and Fish Department has wildlife management responsibility for lands it doesn't own.

Our first exchanges with Game and Fish were discouraging. They supplied little information, said they had no more, and plainly wished we'd stop bothering them. We soon realized the professional staff was doing what it could with few resources. Most Game and Fish sites are small, less than 1,000 acres, widely scattered, and accumulated by chance. "Here's a corner of a ranch," one staff member told us. "It wasn't good for much so they gave it to us." He characterized most sites as "maintenance operations."

We asked how anyone, including a hunter or fisherman, could find a Game and Fish area. "Pure persistence," was the reply. The Department has nothing to hand out, no site descriptions, no maps, no advice. The Department has not been included in Arizona's efforts to attract visitors.

When we made our final field trip, things were changing. The Department was broadening its constituency to include hikers, birders, and other nonconsumptive users. A nongame program had been launched, as well as a broader publications program. We were encouraged and helped.

We have entries for a selection of G&F sites, most of which we visited. Most Game and Fish sites are open to visitors, not necessarily to vehicles. Some areas are closed when elk are calving.

INDIAN RESERVATIONS

More than a quarter of the entire state is included in Indian Reservations. We sent inquiries to each tribal office and received few replies. Each tribe decides whether it wishes to make money by promoting some aspect of tourism. Some sell hunting and fishing licenses. Some have trading posts. We have entries for several where visitors have access to attractive natural features.

This is not an adequate guide to the Reservations. Hunters and fishermen, especially, should make further inquiries.

Indian Reservations are not public lands. The visitor is subject to tribal laws and regulations.

GOVERNMENT OFFICES

U.S. Bureau of Land Management
State Headquarters
3707 N. 7th
Phoenix, AZ 85014
(602) 241-5504

U.S. Forest Service
Southwestern Region
Federal Building
517 Gold Ave. SW
Albuquerque, NM 87102
(505) 766-2401

PUBLICATIONS
Recreation Sites in Southwestern National Forests.
On Your Own in Southwestern Mountains.

National Park Service
Western Regional Office
Box 36063
450 Golden Gate Ave.
San Francisco, CA 94102
(415) 556-4196

U.S. Fish and Wildlife Service
Regional Office
Box 1306
Albuquerque, NM 87103
(505) 766-2321

Arizona State Parks
1688 West Adams

Phoenix, AZ 85007
(602) 255-4174

PUBLICATION: List of parks; brief descriptions.

Arizona Game and Fish Department
2222 W. Greenway Rd.
Phoenix, AZ 85023
(602) 942-3000

PUBLICATION: *Arizona Wildlife: Mammals.*

REFERENCES

GENERAL

Boyd, Thomas D. *Sunset Travel Guide to Arizona.* Menlo Park, CA: Lane, 1978.
Dedera, Don. *Discover Arizona Uplands.* Phoenix: Arizona Highways, 1979.
Hait, Pam, William Breed, and E. Linwood Smith. *Discover Arizona Canyons.* Phoenix: Arizona Highways, 1979.
Lowe, Sam. *Discover Arizona Deserts.* Phoenix: Arizona Highways, 1979.
Reed, Allen C. *Grand Circle Adventure.* Las Vegas, NV: KC Publications, 1983.

BIRDS

Davis, William A. *Birds in Southeastern Arizona.* Tucson, AZ: Tucson Audubon Society, 1979.
Lane, James A. *A Birder's Guide to Southeastern Arizona.* Denver: L & P Photography, 1974.
Monson, Gale, and Allan R. Phillips. *Annotated Checklist of the Birds of Arizona.* Tucson: University of Arizona Press, 1981.
Phillips, Allan, Joe Marshall, and Gale Monson. *The Birds of Arizona.* Tucson: University of Arizona Press, 1964.

MAMMALS

Cockrum, E. Lendell. *Mammals of the Southwest.* Tucson: University of Arizona Press, 1982.

HIKING

Bunker, Gerald. *Arizona's Northland Trails.* Glendale, CA: La Siesta Press, 1972.
Ganci, Dave. *Hiking the Southwest.* San Francisco: Sierra Club Books, 1983.
Mazel, David. *Arizona Trails.* Berkeley, CA: Wilderness Press, 1983.
Nelson, Dick. *50 Hikes in Arizona.* Pico Rivera, CA: Gem Guide Book Co., 1976.

ZONE 1

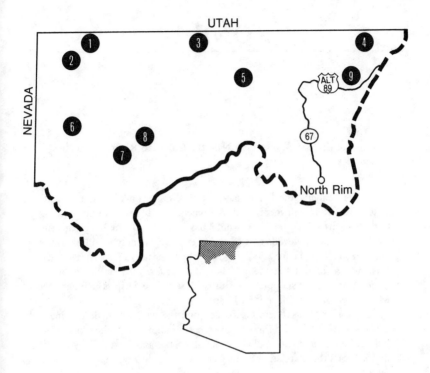

ZONE 1

NW corner of the state; everything N of the Colorado River. N portions of these counties:

Mohave   Coconino

It has been called "the lonely land," "back of beyond," "the lonesome triangle." Mostly it isn't mentioned. An official of Mohave County wishing to visit this part of his territory would have to drive from Kingman, the county seat, through Nevada and Utah to get there. Its only land link to the rest of Arizona is by the Navajo Bridge over Marble Canyon. Its largest town has just over a thousand residents. They and the few other residents of the Strip do their serious shopping in Utah. Most of the Strip is managed by BLM, and its District Office is in Utah.

The Strip is in Mohave and Coconino counties; we have made it Zone 1. Clearly it stands alone, with three large exceptions: portions of the Lake Mead National Recreation Area, Kaibab National Forest, and Grand Canyon National Park. All three are adjuncts of principal areas in Zone 2, and we have not split those entries.

Most of the Strip, 2,737,000 acres, is public domain managed by the Bureau of Land Management. In 1984, eight areas totaling 288,450 acres (including some adjacent lands in Utah), were included in the Arizona Wilderness Bill. We have chosen these new Wildernesses for our entries because they include interesting natural features, but most of the other 2 1/2 million acres is also available for outdoor recreation.

The Strip is a series of high plateaus: the Shivwits, Uinkaret, Kanab, Kaibab, and Paria. The Virgin River cuts across the NW corner, paralleled by I-15 and the Virgin Mountains, which rise to 8,350 ft. from a base elevation of about 2,500 ft. on the river side. To the S are the Grand Wash Cliffs and Upper Grand Wash Cliffs, two steps up to the 5,000-ft.-plus elevation of the Shivwits Plateau.

In the central portion of the Strip are the 1,000-ft. N–S Hurricane Cliffs and scattered mountains, notably 8,029-ft. Mount Trumbull and 7,866-ft. Mount Logan. The plateaus are cut by canyons draining to the Colorado River through Grand Canyon National Park. In the far E of the Strip, the Paria Plateau steps down over the Vermilion Cliffs to House Rock Valley at the edge of Marble Canyon.

Average annual precipitation is about 8 in. at the Virgin River, increasing gradually toward the E, to 14–16 in. on the Kaibab Plateau, up to 20–22 in. on the highest mountains.

By far the most traveled route in the Strip is that leading to the North Rim and Grand Canyon National Park. Most visitors cross the Navajo Bridge over Marble Canyon, passing S of the impressive Vermilion Cliffs, entering the Kaibab National Forest, turning S at Jacob Lake on SR 67 to the Park.

The only other paved roads in the Strip are I-15, crossing the NW corner, and SR 89, looping S from Utah through Fredonia and back to Utah again. All other roads shown on the highway map are keyed "graded, inquire locally." On BLM's *Visitor's Map,* these are called "seasonal roads." Ordinary cars can travel on most of these roads in dry weather; how comfortably depends on when they were last bladed. BLM's map also shows some jeep trails, and there are undoubtedly other tracks. ORV's are restricted to existing roads and trails.

At least two of these seasonal roads enter the undeveloped western area of Grand Canyon National Park, one of them to the Tuweep Area, labeled "Grand Canyon National Monument" on pre-1975 maps. The information page listed in the Grand Canyon NP entry (Zone 2) has a rough map showing roads across the Strip from St. George, UT, Colorado City, and Fredonia to the Park entrance. The roads are labeled, respectively, Routes 3, 2, and 1, the only time we have seen them thus dignified. (BLM's *Visitor's Map* labels them 59, 63, and—yes—59, but they don't look quite the same.) Inside the entrance is the Tuweep Ranger Station, beyond, near the canyon rim, a small campground. At Toroweep Point, the Grand Canyon is less than a mile wide, nearly 3,000 ft. deep. No crowds here!

Driving the Strip requires a full gas tank and a car in good condition. You'll find no service stations and almost no telephones. If it rains, you may have to wait until the roads are dry again.

Plants: BLM's 52-page *Plants of the Virgin Mountains* has wider application, since the range is from the low desert life zone to pine and fir forests at high elevations. From the river up to 4,500 ft., the principal plant association is Joshua tree, barrel cactus, creosote. This merges into the pinyon-juniper-live oak association up to about 5,800 ft. Ponderosa pine then predominates to about 7,500 ft. On Mount Bangs, white fir and Douglas-fir are at the highest elevations. The guide has illustrations and descriptions of plants typical of each association. For plants of the higher plateaus, see entries for Kaibab National Forest and Grand Canyon National Park in Zone 2.

Birds: Checklist available, noting abundance, seasonality, and preferred habitat. Species are much the same as those noted in entries for Kaibab National Forest and Grand Canyon National Park.

Mammals: Checklist available, noting abundance and preferred habitats. Abundant or common species include California myotis, western pipistrel; big brown, pallid, Brazilian and American freetail bats. Desert cottontail, blacktail jackrabbit, cliff chipmunk, rock squirrel, pocket gopher; Great Basin, little, longtail, and desert pocket mice; Ord, desert, and Merriam kangaroo rats. Mice: canyon, cactus, deer, brush, pinyon. Desert woodrat, coyote, gray fox, badger, mule deer. Several transplants of pronghorn have been made, and bighorn sheep have been reintroduced.

Reptiles and amphibians: Checklist available, noting abundance and preferred habitats. Abundant and common species, including those locally common, include Great Basin spadefoot, Woodhouse's, and red-spotted toads; leopard frog; spiny softshell turtle, desert tortoise. Lizards: banded gecko, desert night, chuckwalla, desert iguana, zebra-tailed, leopard, collared, desert spiny, eastern fence, sagebrush, side-blotched, mountain short-horned, desert horned, western tiger and plateau whiptails. Snakes: coachwhip, striped whipsnake, western patch-nosed, glossy, common kingsnake, long-nosed, desert night. Great Basin and Mojave rattlesnakes, Mojave Desert sidewinder.

PUBLICATIONS
Visitor's Map; The Arizona Strip.
Checklists: birds, mammals, reptiles and amphibians.
This Land is Your Land. Leaflet.

HEADQUARTERS: 196 E. Tabernacle, St. George, UT 84770; (801) 673-3545.

COTTONWOOD POINT WILDERNESS
U.S. Bureau of Land Management
6,500 acres.

Just E of Colorado City, on the Utah border. The map shows no trails or trailheads, but contours indicate possible access from Colorado City. Inquire at BLM office or locally.

The AZ portion of a far larger roadless area in Utah, between the town of Colorado City and the Kaibab Indian Reservation. The map shape is that of two peninsulas projecting into AZ, divided by Cottonwood Canyon. The larger of the two rises from about 5,200 ft. on the canyon floor to 6,322 ft. on Cottonwood Point.

The roadless area as a whole is an irregular plateau capped by massive exposures of Navajo sandstone. The plateau is surrounded by high, dissected cliffs and cut by deep, narrow canyons with dense riparian vegetation. BLM's evaluation said, "the landscape is somewhat reminiscent of the landscapes in Zion National Park. The quality of scenery is equivalent to that found in Zion National Park." Excellent opportunities for hiking, backpacking, horsepacking.

GRAND WASH CLIFFS WILDERNESS
U.S. Bureau of Land Management
36,300 acres.

20 mi. N of the Colorado River, 12 to 18 mi. E of the NV border.

The southern Grand Wash Cliffs are an entry in Zone 2. It's easy to be impressed by them there, because a serviceable road runs near their base. There are seasonal access roads to this area, but we could find no reliable map to guide us. Asking directions at the BLM office is the best way.

The Grand Wash Cliffs are cut by the Grand Canyon; it is only the boundary of the Wilderness that lies 20 mi. N of the river. The cliffs are the E boundary of the basin and range province. The top of the cliffs is the edge of the Colorado Plateau province.

The cliffs make two giant steps up from the Grand Wash. The first is about 2,000 ft. high. Then comes a shelf 1 to 3 mi. wide before a 1,000-ft. step up to the Shivwits Plateau. The cliffs are cut by several canyons, hiking or scrambling routes to the top.

KANAB CREEK WILDERNESS
U.S. Bureau of Land Management; Kaibab National Forest
77,100 acres.

S of Fredonia.

The Creek runs S from Fredonia, forming the boundary of Mohave and Coconino counties. It crosses the Kaibab Indian Reservation, and runs S across BLM lands, cutting deeper and deeper into the plateau. Then for about 10 mi. the canyon is just inside the Kaibab National Forest, finally entering Grand Canyon National Park. The Wilderness, established in 1984, begins at the S boundary of the Indian Reservation and continues through the Forest to the Park.

A few people have made the difficult backpacking journey down Kanab Creek to the Colorado River, up the Colorado to Deer Creek, and up out of the canyon by the Thunder River Trail.

There are several ways to enter the Kanab Creek Canyon and several possible routes within the Grand Canyon. None are casual strolls, and none should be attempted in summer. The journey demands careful preparation including, if possible, talk with someone who has been there.

REFERENCE: Butchart, J. Harvey. *Grand Canyon Treks.* Vols. I, II, and III. Glendale, CA: La Siesta Press, 1983.

MT. LOGAN WILDERNESS
U.S. Bureau of Land Management
14,600 acres.

6 mi. SW of Mt. Trumbull.

When the Arizona Wilderness Act was signed in 1984, some people asked, "Where's Mt. Logan?" It isn't shown on the official highway map or BLM's *Visitor's Map.* A third map we consulted shows its contours but not its name. It is on the Geological Survey's 500,000 series map.

Finding it can be even more interesting. Mapmakers have used more imagination than information in plotting the seasonal roads of the area. However, several of them agree that there is a spur road of sorts from the S side of Mt. Trumbull to somewhere near Mt. Logan.

At 7,966 ft., Logan isn't quite as high as Trumbull. Its base is much larger, slopes gentler. Like Trumbull, it has ponderosa pine on top, pinyon-juniper on the lower slopes. Perhaps it was logged in the past, but its new Wilderness status indicates it is in substantially natural condition. An unusual scenic feature, on the W slope, is Hells Hole, a large, colorful amphitheater.

MT. TRUMBULL WILDERNESS
U.S. Bureau of Land Management
7,900 acres.

Seasonal roads S from St. George, UT.

According to the official highway map, Mt. Trumbull's elevation is 7,700 ft., a figure also used in two articles we read about the mountain. Thus we were fascinated to find in another document that there's a splendid ponderosa pine forest above the 7,800-ft. contour! The U.S. Geological Survey brought us back to earth: the true elevation is 8,029 ft.

It's the highest point for miles around. Although there was once a sawmill not far away, the upper slopes have never been logged, and some of the ponderosa pines there are exceptionally large. Because of its undisturbed condition, it was proposed as a Natural Area, "an ideal benchmark for studying the effects of human activities in other pine forest areas." Wilderness designation may attract a few more hikers.

The steep, rocky S- and W-facing slopes support pinyon-juniper woodland with manzanita, silktassel, cliff rose, and shrub live oak. Other species on exposed slopes include Gambel oak, locust, barberry, big sage, agave, and cacti. Ponderosa on N-facing slopes and high elevations in an almost pure stand.

Birds: Characteristic birds seen on the mountain include red-tailed hawk, great horned owl, wild turkey, northern flicker, ash-throated flycatcher, violet-green swallow, Steller's jay, plain titmouse, white-breasted nuthatch, American robin, western bluebird, solitary vireo, western tanager, chipping sparrow.

Mammals: Include California myotis, big brown bat, blacktail jackrabbit, rock squirrel, cliff chipmunk, valley pocket gopher, rock pocket mouse, northern grasshopper mouse, western harvest mouse; deer, brush, and pinyon mice; porcupine, coyote, spotted skunk, mountain lion, bobcat, mule deer.

Reptiles and amphibians: Include Great Basin spadefoot; eastern fence, sagebrush, and short-horned lizards; many-lined skink, gopher snake, Sonora mountain kingsnake, western rattlesnake.

ACTIVITIES

Camping: BLM maintains a small campground near the bottom of the mountain. It has water.

Hiking, backpacking: A trail to the summit was built in 1976, and Nixon Spring was developed for visitor use.

PAIUTE WILDERNESS
U.S. Bureau of Land Management
84,700 acres.

NW corner, extending S along the Virgin Mountains for about 10 mi. Seven trailheads, on the N, S, and W. Principal trailhead is reached from Bloomington exit on I-15. S on Quail Hill Rd. to Wolf Hole, then W, following trail map.

The Virgin Mountains are indeed virginal, almost undisturbed by past or present mining and grazing. Rugged, geologically complex, topped by sharp backbone ridge of granite, gneiss, and limestone. The highest point, Mt. Bangs, 8,012 ft., stands 6,300 ft. above the Virgin River. Life zones range from Mohave Desert at the river to spruce-fir on Mt. Bangs.

N access is through Sullivan Canyon, about 2 mi. S of I-15, from the Virgin River Canyon Recreation Area on I-15 if the river can be crossed. Some of the most spectacular scenery is along this canyon, which is strewn with boulders and oven-hot in summer. The usual ascent of Mt. Bangs is from the S, up to and along the ridge. A trail from Mt. Bangs drops 6,000 ft. to the river.

Designated a Wilderness in 1984, this had previously been the Paiute Primitive Area, well and favorably known to a small but growing number of backcountry travelers.

Spring and fall are the best hiking seasons; summer days can be blazing hot, winter nights bitter cold on the mountains. Annual precipitation is 8 to 14 in., in summer thunderstorms and winter snow. May–June are the driest months.

Water is available at springs, several of them marked on the trail map; water must be treated.

Camping is permitted anywhere. The problem is to find a flat, level spot. The best sites are along the backbone ridge.

PUBLICATIONS
The Paiute Primitive Area. Folder with trail map.
Plants of the Virgin Mountains. Pamphlet.

REFERENCE: Ganci, Dave. *Hiking the Southwest.* San Francisco: Sierra Club Books, 1983, pp. 167–170.

PARIA CANYON
U.S. Bureau of Land Management
Included in Paria Canyon-Vermilion Cliffs Wilderness (see entry).

From Kanab, UT, 43 mi. E on US 89. Beyond the Paria River crossing, look for sign; S 3 mi. on an unpaved road to the White House entrance. An alternative hiking route begins in Buckskin Gulch. From US 89 about 38 mi. E of Kanab, S on House Rock Valley Road; access points at 4 and 8 mi. S of US 89.

This entry is adapted from our Sierra Club Guide to the Natural Areas of Colorado and Utah. The hike is always made from Utah into Arizona. For safety reasons, hiking upstream is prohibited.

One of the classical backpacking treks, a 4- to 6-day 35-mi. journey through a rugged, spectacular canyon, ending at Lee's Ferry, AZ, below Glen Canyon Dam. It was designated a Primitive Area in 1969 to preserve its wilderness qualities.

The hike is considered moderately strenuous. There are no major obstacles for the first 23 mi. At a boulder slide, most hikers detour. About 2,000 hikers per year make the trip. Mar.–June and Sept.–Oct. are the popular seasons. Summers are hot, and the water is cold in winter. Spring hiking is in ankle-deep water with possible waist-deep crossings. The upper river is dry in summer, with shallow water below. However, flash floods are frequent from July through Sept., and hiking requires caution then.

The Narrows begins 4.2 mi. from the White House ruins. For the next 5 mi., there is no possible escape if a flash flood occurs. The hiker must get a weather forecast before setting out, and at 3.9 mi. must decide whether to camp or continue to the next possible campsite at 9.0 mi. Hiking upstream from Lee's Ferry is prohibited because the hiker's weather information would be outdated when he approached The Narrows.

The Buckskin Gulch route is about 10 mi. longer and much more difficult. Under the best conditions, the gorge can be traversed in 12 hours of hard going. The 12-mi.-long canyon is highly dangerous in flash floods. Swift, turbulent water can reach depths of 20 ft., and there are few places where one can climb. At The Dive, the canyon narrows to as little as 3 ft., and average width beyond is less than 15 ft. Near the confluence with the Paria, a rock jam with a 30-ft. drop.

Drinking water is available at the entrance station. The first reliable water source in Paria Canyon is 11 mi. downstream; no water is available in the last 11 mi. All water should be treated.

Plants: Vegetation is typical of the semidesert region. Pinyon-juniper with occasional ponderosa pine dominates the canyon rims. Areas of relatively heavy clay soils support sparse stands of sand dropseed, shadscale brush, pricklypear. Looser sandy soils support fair stands of Indian ricegrass with buckwheat, rabbitbrush, four-wing saltbush. Riparian species include cottonwood, willow, boxelder.

Wildlife: No inventory has been made. Observed bird species include eagles, raven, hawks, dove, killdeer, white-throated swift, cliff swallow. Mammals mentioned include raccoon, fox, beaver, bobcat, mule deer. Desert bighorn were reintroduced in 1984.

FEATURE: *Wrather Arch,* a 200-ft. natural formation, is 2 mi. up a side canyon.

Backpacking: Permit required. Can be obtained at the Kanab office during regular office hours or by telephone, no more than 24 hrs. before departure. During the high season (late Mar. through Oct.) permits may be obtained from a Ranger at the Canyon entrance Thurs. through Mon., 8 A.M.–11 P.M.; however, funding for this service is not assured.

PUBLICATION: *Hikers Guide to Paria.* Folder with map.

REFERENCES

Ganci, Dave. *Hiking the Southwest.* San Francisco: Sierra Club Books, 1983, pp. 162–167.

Hall, Dave. *The Hiker's Guide to Utah.* Billings, MT: Falcon Press, 1982, pp. 150–154.

HEADQUARTERS: BLM, Cedar City District, 1579 North Main, Cedar City, UT 84720; (801) 586-2401. Kanab Area Office, 320 North First East, Kanab, UT 84741; (801) 644-2672.

PARIA CANYON-VERMILION CLIFFS WILDERNESS
U.S. Bureau of Land Management
110,000 acres.

N of Alt. US 89, between the Kaibab National Forest and Marble Canyon.

The Vermilion Cliffs were designated a Natural Area in 1969. They are the principal scenic feature between Marble Canyon and the North Rim of the Grand Canyon, massive, multicolored, rising 1,000 to 3,000 ft. above the highway. Desert vegetation at the base.

The Arizona Wilderness Act of 1984 combined this area with the Paria Canyon (see entry), adding acreage between them on the Paria Plateau.

The Paria Plateau above the Cliffs and Canyon is also public land. The *Visitor's Map* shows 4-wheel-drive tracks on the plateau, accessible from the road shown on the highway map skirting the National Forest.

VIRGIN RIVER GORGE
U.S. Bureau of Land Management
23,070 acres.

Along I-15, NE of the US 91 intersection.

The Virgin River Gorge, described as one of the most spectacular river canyons in the SW, is between the Virgin Mountains and Beaver Dam Mountains. BLM designated a Virgin River Canyon Recreation Area here in 1973, providing opportunities to pause, picnic, camp, hike, or backpack S into the

Paiute Wilderness (see entry). In 1984 most of this area was incorporated in the Paiute Wilderness and Beaver Dam Mountains Wilderness. The two are separated by I-15.

The Beaver Dam Mountains Wilderness includes 19,600 acres in Arizona and Utah. The area is immediately N of I-15, E of US 91.

ZONE 2

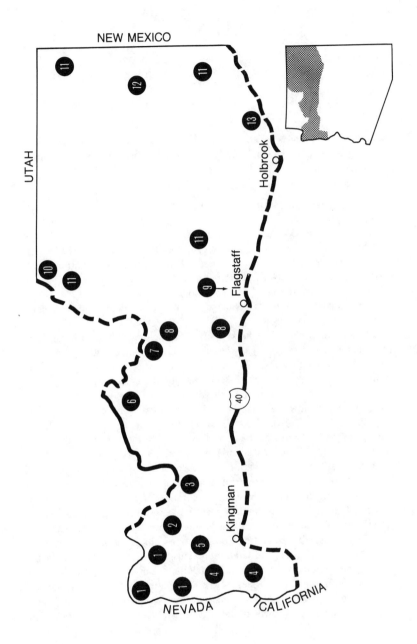

NEW MEXICO

UTAH

Holbrook

Flagstaff

40

Kingman

NEVADA   CALIFORNIA

ZONE 2

Includes everything N of I-40 except the Arizona Strip, the NW corner of Arizona isolated by the Colorado River. Includes portions of these counties:

Mohave	Coconino
Navajo	Apache

The zone boundary extends from Lake Powell and Glen Canyon Dam along the Colorado River through the Grand Canyon, into Lake Mead, then S along the Colorado River and Lake Mohave. Almost the entire E portion is within the Navajo and Hopi Indian Reservations. In the W portion, the largest blocks are parts of the Coconino and Kaibab National Forests, Grand Canyon National Park, the Hualapai and Havasupai Indian Reservations, and the Lake Mead National Recreation Area. Grand Canyon National Park extends about 50 mi. W from Grand Canyon Village, where travelers congregate.

In the W, rising from the flood plain of the Colorado River, are the Black Mountains. This western area is largely public domain, but with many scattered private landholdings. The BLM-managed public domain includes a number of roadless tracts; we have entries for three of them.

Much of the central portion of the zone is on the Coconino Plateau. Just N of Flagstaff, however, are the highest mountains in the state, the San Francisco Peaks. This part of the Coconino National Forest is a volcanic landscape studded with about 400 cinder cones. The most recent is the central feature of Sunset Crater National Monument.

The Navajo Indian Reservation occupies about one-fifth of the entire state. Visitors to the North Rim see a fragment of it as they travel N on US 89, then NW along the canyon of the Little Colorado River. This route skirts the colorful Painted Desert. Secondary roads in the reservation offer better views, but the easiest place to see it is in the N end of Petrified Forest National Park.

US 160 crosses the reservation from US 89 to Four Corners, where Arizona, New Mexico, Colorado, and Utah meet. Turning N through Kayenta brings one to much-photographed Monument Valley. Canyon de Chelly National Monument, in the E central part of the Reservation, is both spectacular and unique, the only National Monument we know of which is on nonfederal land; the Navajo Tribe owns it and Navajos still live within the Monument.

BLACK MOUNTAINS
U.S. Bureau of Land Management
About 200,000 acres.

W of Kingman. Within the triangle formed by the Colorado River, I-40, and US 93. N boundary is the Cottonwood road, W from US 93, 28 mi. NW of Kingman. Crossed by SR 68 and old Route 66, the Golden Shores-Oatman-Kingman road.

At BLM's Kingman office, we were told hiking and backpacking aren't popular locally. Some of the staff members are hikers, however, and they were enthusiastic about the Black Mountains. This entry describes three large roadless tracts: *North,* between the Cottonwood road and SR 68; *Middle,* from SR 68 to old 66 near Oatman; and *South,* from there S to I-40.

North: The NE corner of this tract is a plateau rising gradually from the Detrital Valley to the crest of the Black Mountains at about 4,000 ft. elevation. Highest point is 4,801 ft. On the W is a dramatic drop of 2,000 ft. to a volcanic plain. The mountains have rugged, craggy peaks with volcanic plugs and dikes, steep V-shaped canyons, varied colors and textures. Many narrow canyons widen into sandy washes trending W on the outwash plain.

Some of the higher canyons have perennial springs. Usually the water soon vanishes underground, but pools and waterfalls appear after a storm.

Vegetation includes juniper, Mojave yucca, catclaw, white bursage, creosote, grasses. Where springs occur, riparian vegetation includes willow, nettle, watercress. Wildlife includes resident bighorn sheep.

The tract adjoins an area of the Lake Mead National Recreation Area proposed for wilderness status.

Good opportunities for day hikes and overnights.

Middle: The smallest of the tracts is directly W of Kingman, and development is expanding through the Sacramento Valley at the mountain's base. Even so, our BLM advisor said this is his favorite place for hiking. "Beautiful! . . . Spectacular canyons, scores of springs. . . . In wet years, some of the streams flow for four months or more, January through April."

Between North and Middle, where SR 68 crosses, the ridge drops below 4,000 ft. Between Middle and South, old Route 66 crosses the mountains through Sitgreaves Pass, elevation 3,550 ft. The mountains between these crossings are rugged, rising to 5,216 ft., composed chiefly of complex volcanic flows. NE of Sitgreaves Pass, the descent from summit to bordering canyons and the valley is a series of terraced slopes, with some escarpments 200 to 300 ft. high.

ARIZONA 156

South: From the tract's SW corner near the Colorado River, the land slopes upward gradually from about 500 ft. elevation to the foot of the Black Mountains at about 1,500 ft. From here the land rises steeply, with large cliffs and sharp peaks, none especially high. The mountains are penetrated by small valleys separated by steep ridges, which narrow into winding canyons. Warm Springs Wash runs from the central portion of the unit to its SW corner. Much of the high ground, at about 3,500 ft. elevation, is occupied by Black Mesa, an extensive grassy area with many wildflowers and occasional stands of yucca and cholla. On the E side of Black Mesa are 1,800-ft. bluffs dropping down into the Sacramento Valley. The bluffs are dissected by numerous canyons that twist and turn. On the W side, mesas drop suddenly into wide canyons over 800 ft. deep, with numerous side canyons.

Plants: Typical of the Mohave Desert. At the higher elevations, blackbrush, Mexican bladder sage, grasses, Indian paintbrush, and other forbs. In the lower SW portion, mesquite, palo verde, ocotillo, brittlebush, beavertail, pricklypear, and hedgehog cactus. Smoketree and catclaw in the washes.

Birds likely to be in the area include turkey vulture, red-tailed hawk, prairie falcon, Gambel's quail, mourning dove, roadrunner, great horned owl, lesser nighthawk, common raven, verdin, canyon and rock wrens, mockingbird, hooded oriole.

Mammals likely to be in the area include bats: California and Yuma myotis, western pipistrel, pallid, California leafnose, Mexican freetail. Blacktail jackrabbit, cottontail, rock squirrel, Harris antelope ground squirrel, valley pocket gopher, rock pocket mouse, Merriam kangaroo rat, deer and cactus mice, whitethroat woodrat, coyote, gray fox, badger, spotted skunk, bobcat, mule deer.

Reptiles likely to be in the area include lizards: zebra-tailed, collared, chuckwalla, desert spiny. Diamondback and speckled rattlesnakes, desert patch-nosed snake, desert kingsnake, bull snake.

ACTIVITIES

Camping: No campground. Numerous short unmapped ways and unmaintained roads enter from the perimeter, providing suitable informal campsites.

Hiking, backpacking: No maintained trails, but they aren't needed. Staff members at the BLM office can suggest routes, including an historical trail. Numerous canyons provide access to the high country.

HEADQUARTERS: BLM, Kingman Resource Area, 2475 Beverly Ave., Kingman, AZ 86401; (602) 757-4011.

CANYON DE CHELLY NATIONAL MONUMENT
National Park Service
83,840 acres.

From Chambers on I-40, N 75 mi. on US 191 (SR 63 on some maps, Navajo Route 8 on the Monument leaflet map).

We know of no other National Monument on nonfederal land. The canyon is part of the vast Navajo Indian Reservation. By agreement, the National Park Service manages the prehistoric sites and ruins; Navajo still live and farm here. Visitor movements are restricted, partly for safety reasons, partly because the Navajo want it that way.

Among Arizona's tens of thousands of canyons, about a dozen have top rank: most scenic, most photographed, best known. De Chelly is clearly among these. From Chinle, at the entrance, the Monument branches in crooked fingers along Monument Canyon, Canyon del Muerto, and Canyon de Chelly, which meet here. The main canyon has vertical sandstone walls up to 1,000 ft. high, colorful layers in shades of red and brown with vertical stripes of mineral stain. Present-day Navajo homes and farms are on the canyon floor. In the canyons and on high ledges are the ruins of past Indian dwellings.

The canyon streams flow in periods of rain and in spring runoff. Especially in summer, flash floods are a hazard.

Two rim drives have spurs to overlooks. A trail leads down to the White House Ruin, a 2 1/2-mi. round trip. While the overlooks have splendid vistas, the best way to see the canyon is from below, and this requires a guide; visitors are not permitted inside the canyon on their own, except at the White House Ruin. Park Rangers lead tours. Arrangements can be made at the visitor center for a Navajo guide. A concessioner offers periodic bus tours on the canyon floor.

As photographs of the canyon demonstrate, a long look isn't enough. To appreciate the full range of shapes and colors, one must see it at dawn and dusk, in sunshine and by moonlight, after a summer storm and when it is blanketed by winter snow.

Open all year. Average annual precipitation is about 6 1/2 in. July–Oct. are the wettest months. July–Aug. are the warmest months: average daily highs in the low and mid 90s. May and Sept. are most favored by visitors. Winter visitation is light.

INTERPRETATION

Visitor center is open daily except Thanksgiving, Christmas, and New Year's Day. 8 A.M.–5 P.M., except to 6 P.M. in summer.

Campfire programs and *guided hikes* are offered seasonally.

Camping: 90 sites. All year. (Lodge and motel at Chinle.)

A Navajo guide is required for hiking or off-road driving in the Reservation. Can be arranged at the visitor center.
Pets are not allowed within the canyon. Elsewhere on leash.

PUBLICATION: Leaflet with map.

HEADQUARTERS: P.O. Box 583, Chinle, AZ 86503; (602) 674-5436.

GLEN CANYON NATIONAL RECREATION AREA
National Park Service
1,157,463 acres, of which 1,061,738 acres are in Utah.

Glen Canyon Dam is near Page on US 89. *In Utah:* SR 95 crosses the upper end of the impoundment, Lake Powell. From SR 95, SR 276 goes S to Bullfrog Basin Marina, SR 263 to Halls Crossing Marina on the opposite shore. Jeep trails to a few other points on the shore or to foot trailheads.

The largest recreation center is near the dam, in Arizona. Boaters leaving from here are almost immediately in Utah. The following entry is from our Sierra Club Guide to the Natural Areas of Colorado and Utah.

Glen Canyon Dam, built between 1956 and 1964 across the Colorado River, has backed up a pool, Lake Powell, 186 mi. long, in a narrow, twisting canyon. With many even narrower side canyons, it has a shoreline of about 2,000 mi., depending on the height of the pool. Conservationists, valuing Glen Canyon, fought unsuccessfully to block the project. They were dismayed when the pool first reached maximum height 17 years later, flooding the lower portions of Coyote Gulch and Escalante Canyon; they thought they had been assured this wouldn't happen. They argued that federal law prohibited flooding any part of a National Monument, but the lake waters extend under Rainbow Bridge.

The lake quickly became a popular boating and fishing area. On weekends, processions of cars with boat trailers can be seen on nearby desert highways. But as yet there are only 4 marinas on the lake and less than a dozen places where a car can be driven to the lakeshore. Speedboats and water skiers don't venture far from their marinas. Most of the lake is quiet, much of the shore wilderness. Almost all the surrounding land is public, including wilderness areas of Capitol Reef National Park, Canyonlands National Park, Dark Canyon Primitive Area, Grand Gulch Primitive Area, and various roadless areas administered by the Bureau of Land Management. Camping from boats is permitted, and one can hike or backpack into many roadless areas from the shore.

In addition to flooding Glen Canyon, the dam also backed up a pool on the San Juan River. The National Recreation Area includes the N shore of the San Juan all the way to the Goosenecks State Reserve; the S shore is the Navajo Indian Reservation.

Glen Canyon was carved by the Colorado River in sedimentary rock, much of it brick-red Navajo sandstone. It is a region of canyons, large and small, many of them deep and steep-walled, separated by narrow ridges or broader mesas. Most of the land area is between 4,500 and 5,500 ft. elevation, with occasional mesas over 6,000 ft. Highest point is 7,451 ft.

Average maximum temperatures are in the 90s in summer, 45–55°F in winter. Average winter lows are 25–35°F. Annual precipitation is about 10 in. Most winters see some snow but no significant accumulation.

Plants: There are five principal associations. (1) *Streamside:* Prominent species are sandbar willow, tamarisk, arrowweed, common reed, saltgrass; may include Gambel oak, hackberry, Fremont cottonwood, cheatgrass, cattail. (2) *Terrace,* old flood plains now above flood level. Prominent species are greasewood, rabbitbrush, sand sagebrush, dropseed grass, Indian ricegrass; may include arrowweed, shadscale, hackberry, blackbrush, snakeweed. (3) *Hillside association,* chiefly widely spaced low shrubs. Prominent species: snakeweed, shadscale, hackberry, blackbrush; may include Indian ricegrass, pricklypear, hedgehog cactus, serviceberry, silver buffaloberry, cliff rose. Also sego and mariposa lilies, eriogonum, prickly poppy, prince's plume, gaillardia, lupine, locoweed, euphorbia, globemallow, blazing star, evening primrose, gilia, penstemon, Indian paintbrush, golden aster. (4) *Hanging gardens,* where moisture seeps from canyon walls. Species include maidenhair fern, columbines, red monkeyflower, cardinal flower, false solomonseal, evening primrose. (5) *Plateau:* Pinyon-juniper association includes bitterbrush, cliff rose, galleta, blue grama, Indian ricegrass.

Birds: Checklist of 65 water or shore birds, 127 land species, plus 58 species known to occur in immediately adjacent areas. Seasonally common species include western, eared, and pied-billed grebes; American white pelican, great blue heron, snowy egret, Canada goose, mallard, green-winged and cinnamon teals, shoveler, ring-necked duck, common goldeneye, turkey vulture, red-tailed and Swainson's hawks, northern harrier, prairie falcon, American kestrel, American coot, American avocet, black-necked stilt, killdeer, long-billed curlew; spotted, least, and Wilson's sandpipers; California, ring-billed, Franklin's, and Bonaparte's gulls; mourning and rock doves, black-throated gray and MacGillivray's warblers, house sparrow, red-winged blackbird, Cassin's finch; vesper, sage, and chipping sparrows; gray-headed junco, great horned and long-eared owls; black-chinned, broad-tailed, and rufous hummingbirds; downy woodpecker, western and Cassin's kingbirds, Say's phoebe, dusky flycatcher, western wood-pewee, horned lark, violet-green and cliff swallows, American crow, mountain chickadee, pygmy nuthatch, mockingbird.

Fall migration of many species begins in late June or July. Canyons and shoreline of Lake Powell are fall and winter habitat. Sandbars and beaches are resting places for migrants.

Mammals: Checklist available; does not indicate whether common or rare, but does state habitats. Includes 5 species of shrews, 13 of bats. Pika, whitetail and blacktail jackrabbits, mountain and desert cottontails. Squirrels: Abert, red, rock. Spotted and antelope ground squirrels, golden-mantled squirrel, whitetail prairie dog; least, Uinta, Colorado, and cliff chipmunks; northern and Botta pocket gophers. 5 species of pocket mice, Ord kangaroo rat, beaver, 10 species of mice, 5 species of wood rats, muskrat, heather and Mexican voles, porcupine. Also coyote, red and gray foxes, black bear, ringtail, longtail and shorttail weasels, badger, striped and spotted skunks, river otter, bobcat, mountain lion, mule deer, pronghorn, elk.

Lizards: Checklist includes chuckwalla, collared, leopard, lesser earless, side-blotched, eastern fence, desert spiny, western whiptail, plateau striped whiptail, desert horned.

Snakes: Checklist includes striped whipsnake, western patch-nosed, gopher, common kingsnake, western diamondback rattlesnake, western rattlesnake.

FEATURES

Wahweap is the principal recreation area, with marina, campground, lodge, other facilities. Reached by a short scenic drive from the dam.

Warm Creek–Smokey Mountain road is a scenic route from Big Water (formerly Glen Canyon City). "Moonscape" scenery.

Rainbow Bridge National Monument is 45 mi. uplake from the dam. The huge red and yellow natural sandstone arch is the largest yet discovered. Getting there by land is difficult. The bridge now spans a flooded canyon, and boat access is easy. Floating marina at Dangling Rope Canyon has Ranger Station, restrooms, boat fuel, camp supplies, emergency communications. Courtesy dock a short hike from the Bridge.

Hole-in-the-Rock, 60 mi. uplake from the dam, is a slot in the canyon wall through which Mormon pioneers lowered wagons to the river for ferrying. The Hole-in-the-Rock Trail, a county-maintained graveled road, extends 61 mi. to Escalante, between the Straight Cliffs of the Kaiparowits Plateau and Escalante Canyon, one of UT's best-known and most-visited backcountry areas.

Hurricane Wash is a route from Hole-in-the-Rock Trail into Coyote Gulch, an area with several natural arches. Trailhead is 20 mi. from the lake shore. The trail down Coyote Gulch connects with the Escalante Canyon Trail.

Escalante River enters Lake Powell about 63 mi. from the dam. About 3 mi. up this river, on the left, is the mouth of Davis Gulch, with several natural arches nearby. About 9 mi. upstream, how far depending on the lake level, is the beginning of the trail up Escalante Canyon.

Bullfrog is 96 mi. up-lake, on the N side, at the end of SR 276. Campground, marina, store, service station, lodge, ranger station.

Halls Crossing, across the lake at the end of SR 263, also has campground, marina, store, lodge.

Hite is at the head of the lake, 156 mi. from the dam, at the end of Cataract Canyon. SR 95 crosses here. Primitive campground, store, boat-fuel service. Boats can travel 30 mi. up Cataract Canyon. Hite is the take-out point for float trips down the canyon.

Dark Canyon ends in Cataract Canyon. (See entry, Dark Canyon Primitive Area.) The only boat-hiker contact in Cataract Canyon is here, about 1 1/2 mi. from the river channel.

San Juan River (see entry) is backed up 71 mi. from its confluence with the Colorado. No facilities available. Raft trips from upstream on the San Juan often take out at Clay Hills Crossing.

Orange Cliffs district extends about 30 mi. N from Cataract Canyon along the entire W boundary of Canyonlands National Park. Many 4-wheel-drive routes and hiking possibilities.

ACTIVITIES

Camping: 4 campgrounds with 156 spaces; 1 primitive campground with no marked sites. No reservations. Informal camping is permitted except in or adjacent to developed areas. Camping from boats is permitted, but campers are warned that some sites are hazardous.

Hiking, backpacking: The site map shows several hiking trails, but handout information is available only for the most popular: those in the Escalante Canyon area. Many opportunities for day hikes, up canyons from the lake shore or from unpaved roads. For longer hikes, consult ranger.

Fishing: Rainbow and brown trout, largemouth bass, black crappie, channel catfish, walleye, bluegill, striped bass.

Boating: Houseboating is one of the best ways to enjoy the remote areas of the lake. Rentals at major marinas. Other craft can also be rented. While narrow, the lake is often windy and rough. Sailing is best in the three large bays, canoeing in side canyons.

Swimming: Favorable water temperatures June–Sept. Beach at Wahweap, unsupervised.

PUBLICATIONS

Folder with map.
Checklists: Plants, birds, mammals, lizards, snakes, fishes.
Information pages:
  Geology.
  Climate.
  Hiking the Escalante River Canyon Country.

REFERENCE: *Glen Canyon–Lake Powell: The Story Behind the Scenery.* Las Vegas, NV: KC Publications, 1980.

HEADQUARTERS: P.O. Box 1507, Page, AZ 86040; (602) 645-2471.

GRAND CANYON NATIONAL PARK
National Park Service
1,189,636 acres.

South Rim: NW on US 180 from Flagstaff. North Rim: N on US 89 from Flagstaff to Alt. US 89; W to Jacob Lake; S on SR 67.

Arizona's premier attraction. In the view of many, America's. One of the Seven Wonders of the World. A highlight of the Grand Tour. Possibly the most-photographed setting in the universe. Subject of countless books and articles, exhausting all superlatives; we have none to add.

Other entries mention impressive canyons a thousand feet deep. Here the river is more than a mile below, at one point 6,200 ft. The canyon is 280 miles long, as much as 18 mi. wide.

Almost all first-time visitors go to the South Rim, Grand Canyon Village. They should, although it's a bustling little town, crowded in season. The visitor center, museums, amphitheater, and surrounding area provide the best introduction to the Canyon's history and natural history. The views from the Rim Trail are unequaled, and we've never found the trail unpleasantly crowded. Even here one can escape the crowds. One day we walked along the rim and found an unmaintained trail down into the canyon. We didn't walk far down, partly because we were fascinated by the many fossils in the rock, but in four hours we met no other hikers. One can also turn one's back on the canyon and hike into the forest; no one is there.

If you weigh less than 200 pounds, you can ride a mule down to Phantom Ranch and spend the night there. You can also hike down Bright Angel Trail or Kaibab Trail and, if you're in excellent physical condition, hike back. Don't hurry. One can hike for days down there or make the crossing to the North Rim.

We urge the first-time visitor to spend a minimum of two full days at the South Rim, preferably more. Take all the scenic drives; stop at every overlook; walk every foot of the Rim Trail; listen to every talk; study every exhibit; look out from the rim at dawn and dusk and by moonlight.

Next time, the North Rim. This is the Kaibab Plateau, at the lodge 1,300 ft. above the South Rim. Back of the South Rim is pinyon-juniper or ponderosa forest; here it's spruce-fir or ponderosa. Read the entry for the Kaibab National Forest, which describes the area visitors pass through on their way to the North Rim.

North Rim development is much simpler than Grand Canyon Village. It includes the venerable Grand Canyon Lodge, a campground, ranger station, and public garage. Only a tenth as many people come here. It's about 7 degrees F cooler in summer. There are many pleasant trails into the canyon and along the rim. Here, too, you can ride a mule down to the bottom. Once we rented horses and rode in the forest for a day. The road to the North Rim is closed when the first snow flies.

Plants: A satellite photo shows a thin strip of green along the river with short spurs extending up side canyons; this marks the riparian vegetation of cottonwood, acacia, mesquite, willow, and salt cedar. Large blocks of green mark the Kaibab Plateau forest back of the North Rim, the Coconino Plateau forest behind the South Rim. Between are the colors of the rocks, and bare rock is what one seems to see looking into the canyon. Look more closely. More than a thousand plant species have been found within the Park, including many seasonal wildflowers.

The Inner Canyon has plants typical of the Sonoran Desert, such as cacti, creosote, bursage, ocotillo, agave, and yucca. Higher on the slopes are blackbrush, pinyon pine, and juniper, often growing from cracks and on tiny ledges. Cliff rose is common on both rims and for a short distance below.

Birds: Checklist available notes abundance, seasonality, and preferred habitats. Common on the river and other wetlands: great blue heron, mallard, common goldeneye, common merganser, spotted sandpiper, dipper, common yellowthroat, yellow-breasted chat, blue grosbeak, lazuli bunting, lesser goldfinch. Common in other habitats: red-tailed hawk, American kestrel, Gambel's quail, wild turkey, mourning dove, great horned owl, poor-will, common nighthawk, white-throated swift; black-chinned, broad-tailed, and rufous hummingbirds; northern flicker, yellow-bellied sapsucker, hairy woodpecker, ash-throated flycatcher, Say's phoebe, western wood-pewee, horned lark, violet-green swallow; Steller's, scrub, and pinyon jays; common raven, Clark's nutcracker, mountain chickadee, bushtit, white-breasted and pygmy nuthatches, canyon and rock wrens, American robin, western and mountain bluebirds, blue-gray gnatcatcher, ruby-crowned kinglet, solitary vireo. Warblers: Virginia's, Lucy's, yellow, yellow-rumped, black-throated gray, Grace's. Western meadowlark, Brewer's blackbird, brown-headed cowbird, western tanager, black-headed grosbeak, Cassin's and house finches, pine siskin, rufous-sided towhee, dark-eyed and gray-headed juncos; black-throated, chipping, white-crowned, and Lincoln's sparrows.

Mammals: Checklist available notes abundance and preferred habitats. Common species include Yuma, long-legged, and California myotis; western pipistrel, big brown and pallid bats, desert cottontail, rock and golden-mantled squirrels, antelope squirrel; least, Uinta, and cliff chipmunks, Abert and red squirrels, pocket and northern pocket gophers, rock pocket mouse. Mice: western harvest, canyon, cactus, deer, brush, pinyon. Woodrats: whitethroat, desert, Stephens, Mexican, bushytail. Longtail and Mexican voles, porcupine, coyote, ringtail, striped and western spotted skunks, gray fox, bobcat, mule deer.

Reptiles and amphibians: Checklist available notes abundance and preferred habitats. Common species include Rocky Mountain and red-spotted toads, canyon tree frog. Lizards: collared, black-collared, yellow-backed spiny, northern and southern plateau, northern sagebrush, tree, desert and northern side-blotched, mountain short-horned. Northern whiptail. Snakes: desert striped whipsnake, Sonoran and Great Basin gopher, California kingsnake.

FEATURES

Visits to the main activity centers on South and North Rims are mandatory introductions to the canyon. Most people stop there. But the canyon and the Park extend far beyond what one can see from these vantage points, substantially beyond the huge area shown on the maps included in Park leaflets. To see more:

From the air: Scenic flights are available daily from Grand Canyon Airport and Tusayan. You can also fly to the North Rim.

By raft: Glen Canyon Dam now regulates the Colorado River flow in the canyon and, some fear, is inflicting serious damage on its ecology. Damage has also been done by the large number of raft parties journeying through the canyon. There are no trash barrels or flush toilets along the river. A permit system now limits use: commercial to 106,156 user-days during the busy season, noncommercial to 43,920 days. The Park Service tried to phase out motorized craft, but Congress blocked the move.

Much of the canyon can be seen only by boat. River trips last from 2 to 18 days. Ask for a list of the licensed concessioners, and make reservations as early as you can.

On foot: The hiking and backpacking possibilities are almost unlimited. From the South Rim, two popular trails, Bright Angel and South Kaibab, descend to the river. They are linked partway down by the Tonto Trail, making possible a 13-mi. loop hike—possible for people in excellent condition who have sense enough not to try it in summer.

Permits aren't required for day hikes in the canyon on the principal trails. They are required for overnight trips or day hikes on other canyon trails. Three campgrounds are in the canyon; reservations are required and should be made 6 months or more in advance.

J. Harvey Butchart, author of the most comprehensive Grand Canyon trail guide, has defined 96 rim-to-river routes. These and the many trails and tracks within the canyon are for the fit, experienced, and careful. Hikers have died in the canyon because they carried too little water, became disoriented, or fell.

On muleback: Day, overnight, and longer trips are available.

On horseback: You can arrange to ride your own horse down Bright Angel Trail or North and South Kaibab Trails, if your horse is properly conditioned to Canyon trails and climate.

By car: Several scenic drives are on South and North Rims. You can also drive on fair-weather roads to remote points on the rim, such as the Tuweep Area in the western sector of the North Rim. See the Arizona Strip (Zone 1) preface and the Tuweep information page listed below.

Believe it or not, it is possible to drive into the Grand Canyon, depending on road conditions. *See entry: Hualapai Indian Reservation.*

INTERPRETATION

On the South Rim:

Visitor center has information, publications, talks, museum. Open 7 A.M.–7 P.M.

Yavapai Museum. Natural history. Open 9 A.M.–4:30 P.M.

Tusayan Museum. Archaeological exhibits, talks, tours.

Ranger talks, guided walks, other naturalist programs are frequent; schedules change from week to week.

On the North Rim:

Ranger talks, guided walks, other naturalist programs are frequent in summer; schedules change from week to week.

ACTIVITIES

Camping: South Rim: 2 campgrounds, 208 sites; one open all year. 7-day limit. Reservations advisable Memorial Day–Labor Day: Grand Canyon National Park, Box 129, Grand Canyon, AZ 86023. North Rim: one campground, 82 sites; May 15–Oct. 15; no reservations, usually filled by 9 A.M. Camping is available in the adjacent Kaibab National Forest (see entry).

For information about commercial campgrounds in Grand Canyon Village: Chamber of Commerce, Box 507, Grand Canyon, AZ 86023.

Hiking, backpacking: For reservations in the 3 campgrounds below the rim: Backcountry Reservation Office, Box 129, Grand Canyon, AZ 86023.

For information on trail conditions: (602) 638-2473 or 638-2622 (summer only).

PUBLICATIONS

General information pamphlet.

Free leaflets and sheets on: South Rim and North Rim camping, hiking, backcountry permits, river running, climate. (Allow two weeks for response.)

Tuweep information (North Rim, remote area).

Bird, mammal, reptile and amphibian checklists.

REFERENCES

Many books are in print about the Grand Canyon's history, geology, fauna and flora, etc. The Grand Canyon Natural History Association has a bibliography and list of publications available by mail order. Those below marked * are on the Association list.

*Beal, Merrill D. *Grand Canyon: The Story Behind the Scenery.* Las Vegas, NV: KC Publications, 1978.

Hamblin, W. Kenneth, and J. Keith Rigby. *Guidebooks to the Colorado River,* Parts I and II. Provo, UT: Brigham Young University Press, 1970.

Grater, Russell K., James A. Holland, David H. Huntzinger. *Flowering Plants of the Lake Mead Region.* Globe, AZ: Southwest Parks & Monuments Association, 1978.

Phillips, Arthur M., III. *Grand Canyon Wildflowers.* Grand Canyon Natural History Association, 1979.

*Brown, Bryan T., Peter S. Bennett, Steven W. Carothers, Lois T. Haight, R. Roy Johnson, and Meribeth M. Riffey. *Birds of the Grand Canyon Region.* Grand Canyon Natural History Association, rev. 1984.

*Miller, Donald M. *Amphibians and Reptiles of the Grand Canyon National Park.* Grand Canyon Natural History Association.

Butchart, J. Harvey. *Grand Canyon Treks.* Vols. I, II, and III. Glendale, CA: La Siesta Press, 1983.

Mazel, David. *Arizona Trails.* Berkeley, CA: Wilderness Press, 1981, pp. 225–266.

Stohlquist, Jim. *Colorado Whitewater.* Denver: American Canoe Association, 1977.

HEADQUARTERS: Grand Canyon, AZ 86023; (602) 638-2411.

GRAND WASH CLIFFS
U.S. Bureau of Land Management
128,000 acres.

From Kingman, 27 mi. NW on US 93, then 20 mi. NE toward Pearce Ferry. At 20 mi. is a road SE through the Hualapai Valley to US 66. The Pearce Ferry road parallels the N portion of the Cliffs.

The cliffs are a magnificent escarpment, 3,000 to 4,000 ft. high, the boundary between the basin and range province and the Colorado Plateau. A dramatic transition from hilly forest land above to the desert plain below. A great fault line, the cliffs extend for 50 mi. from the mouth of the Grand Canyon S and E to the Music Mountains, and N through the Arizona Strip (Zone 1) to southern UT.

From the top, the cliff descends almost vertically for about 1,500 ft., composed here of horizontal layers of limestone, sandstone, and shale. Just below is a layer of about 1,000 ft. of gneiss and schist. The lowest portion of the cliffs is less steep, irregular, hills and ridges with alluvial fans. Cut back into the cliffs are several short, deep canyons. Foot access to the top of the cliffs is easy from the N.

Plants: The lower portion is dominated by Joshua tree, blackbrush understory, with banana yucca, beavertail cactus, cholla, turpentine-broom. Juniper and Joshua tree intermix in canyons and on rocky slopes. Vegetation on the washes includes desert willow, penstemon, acacia, shrub oak, mesquite. *Wildlife:* No species lists available. The cliffs appear to be fine raptor habitat. The contrast between the woodland above and desert below is undoubtedly reflected in the fauna of these different habitats. Bighorn sheep were transplanted here in 1983.

NEARBY: *Red Lake,* shown on the highway map, is a playa, a dry lake bed, about 10 mi. by 16 mi., with vegetation of interest to botanists.

HEADQUARTERS: BLM, Kingman Resource Area, 2475 Beverly Ave., Kingman, AZ 86401; (602) 757-4011.

HAVASUPAI INDIAN RESERVATION
Havasupai Tribe
188,077 acres.

S of the Colorado River, between the Hualapai Indian Reservation and Grand Canyon National Park. From Peach Springs on US 66, NE through Fraziers Well to Hualapai Hilltop, the trailhead. Ask about road conditions.

A friend once spent several weeks living in the tiny village of Supai. He remembers it fondly. Some 400 members of the tribe live on the floor of Havasu Canyon tending gardens and orchards beside blue-green Havasu Creek. The only ways to the village are on foot or horseback, or—in a pinch —by helicopter.

In the canyon below the village, the creek plunges over three waterfalls. Havasu, the most photographed, is about 2 mi. downstream; 1 mi. beyond is 196-ft. Mooney Falls. Natural travertine dams below the falls have formed large pools deep enough for swimming. Gardens, orchard trees, and lush riparian vegetation make a green landscape under the red canyon walls. In the canyon are hiking and horseback trails.

Accommodations include a lodge and two campgrounds, including one at Navajo Falls.

Reservations are necessary. You must hike down or make arrangements to meet the pack train for the 6-mi. descent, 2,000 ft. down to the creek, then 2 mi. more to the village.

PUBLICATION: Brochure.

HEADQUARTERS: Havasupai Tourist Enterprise, Supai, AZ 86435; (602) 448-2121.

HUALAPAI INDIAN RESERVATION
Hualapai Tribe
993,173 acres.

US 66 crosses the Reservation.

The Reservation is on the S side of the Colorado River, with about 110 mi. of riverfront between Lake Mead National Recreation Area and Grand Canyon National Park. The visitor's first stop is at the tribal office in Peach Springs. Fees are charged for visiting the Reservation, camping, hunting, and fishing. With a permit, one can hike or camp almost anywhere within the Reservation. Permits are obtainable at Hualapai Wildlife Office, P.O. Box 168, Peach Springs, AZ 86434; (602) 769-2347.

Here is the only motor vehicle road to the bottom of the Grand Canyon, a 22-mi. gravel route suitable for light cars and pickups except after rain. (A more cautious judgment: pickups or 4-wheel drive.) It ends at the river where Diamond Creek enters. Once a hotel was here. There's not much now except the magnificent canyon, the river, and a quiet place to camp. Occasionally a raft party passes or stops to rendezvous with a supply vehicle.

The uplands are rolling grasslands and forest. SR 18 runs NE from Peach Springs to Fraziers Well, where water can be obtained. An unpaved road runs NW from Peach Springs, above the Grand Wash Cliffs, to Quartermaster Point, a canyon overlook. Other roads, unmapped and unimproved, cross the Reservation, some meeting small canyons tributary to the Colorado.

Hualapai River Running Enterprise, a tribal business, offers raft trips through the lower gorge of the Colorado.

HEADQUARTERS: Hualapai Tribe, Hualapai River Running Department, P.O. Box 168, Peach Springs, AZ 86434; (602) 769-2347.

KAIBAB NATIONAL FOREST
U.S. Forest Service
1,556,465 acres; 1,600,075 acres within boundaries.

Three large blocks: (1) North Kaibab Ranger District, on the N boundary of Grand Canyon National Park. Crossed by SR 67, access route to the

Park's North Rim. (2) Tusayan Ranger District, on the S boundary of the Park. Crossed by US 180 and SR 64, access routes to the South Rim. (3) Chalender-Williams Ranger Districts, surrounding Williams, AZ. Crossed by I-40.

Grand Canyon National Park was carved from the Kaibab National Forest. Visitors to the Canyon's South Rim pass through the Tusayan Ranger District on the way. Those visiting the North Rim pass through the North Kaibab Ranger District. The SE corner of the North Kaibab has some frontage on the Rim, but few visitors find their way there.

By official count, the Kaibab has a large number of visitors, but the Forest Service counting method includes anyone driving through. Here it counts visitors on their way to Grand Canyon National Park and motorists on I-40. The Forest campgrounds along the routes to the Grand Canyon are popular. Away from the main roads, the North Kaibab and Tusayan Ranger Districts are uncrowded. Hiking is estimated at less than 8,000 visitor-days per year. The outfitter renting horses on the North Kaibab had 300 riders in 1984. A forested plateau without conspicuous features can't compete with the Grand Canyon, but the North Kaibab, especially, offers opportunities and challenges for those who seek solitude.

The third block, the Chalender-Williams Ranger District, has notable features, and it attracts many day hikers.

FEATURES:

North Kaibab Ranger District. The Kaibab Plateau has been called an "island in the sky." High, forested, rolling, it is surrounded by canyons and deserts. The Kaibab squirrel is an example of the divergent evolution that occurs in such isolation. The natural barriers also prevented colonization by some species for which the habitats are suitable.

Elevations range from about 4,000 ft. at Kanab Creek on the W boundary to 8,982 ft. at VT Ridge near SR 67.

Summer temperatures can reach 110–120°F in the inner canyons while the plateau above is a cool 70–80°. Annual precipitation is 14 to 27 in. Snowfall is heavy, more than 100 in., at high elevations. Despite this precipitation, the plateau is almost entirely lacking in streams. Springs are few, and their water is usually highly alkaline. Moisture seeps rapidly through the plateau's limestone surface.

Life zones range from the Sonoran Desert at Kanab Creek to the subalpine in the S central portion. Ponderosa pine is the principal species in the extensive conifer forest, with pinyon-juniper on lower slopes, spruce-fir in the high country.

Some tourists are too intent on getting to the canyon to appreciate the passing scene, which one writer called "the most pleasant 44 miles in America." Passing first through a forest of ponderosa and aspen, it ascends from 7,921 ft. at Jacob Lake to 9,000 ft. at the Park boundary, emerging from forest into meadows often colorful with wildflowers.

Birds: Checklist available; notes abundance and seasonality. Species common or fairly common in the North Kaibab include turkey vulture, red-tailed hawk, American kestrel, blue grouse, Gambel's quail, chukar, wild turkey, killdeer, mourning dove; flammulated, great horned, and saw-whet owls; poor-will, common nighthawk, white-throated swift; black-chinned, broad-tailed, and rufous hummingbirds; northern flicker, Lewis' and hairy woodpeckers, Williamson's and yellow-bellied sapsuckers, western kingbird, black and Say's phoebes, Hammond's and western flycatchers, western wood-pewee, horned lark, violet-green and tree swallows; Steller's, scrub, and pinyon jays; common raven, common crow, Clark's nutcracker, mountain chickadee, plain titmouse, bushtit, white-breasted and pygmy nuthatches, brown creeper, house and rock wrens, American robin, hermit thrush, western and mountain bluebirds, Townsend's solitaire, blue-gray gnatcatcher, ruby-crowned kinglet, European starling, solitary and warbling vireos. Warblers: yellow, yellow-rumped, black-throated gray, Townsend's, hermit, Grace's, Wilson's. Also western meadowlark; yellow-headed, red-winged, and Brewer's blackbirds; brown-headed cowbird, western tanager, black-headed grosbeak, Cassin's finch, pine siskin, lesser goldfinch, green-tailed and rufous-sided towhees, dark-eyed and gray-headed juncos; lark, chipping, white-crowned, and song sparrows.

Mammals: No checklist available. The case of the Kaibab deer is discussed in many ecology texts. After the area became a National Game Preserve in 1906, deer hunting was prohibited and large predators were suppressed. The deer herd multiplied. Overbrowsing curtailed annual plant growth, and starvation caused a deer population crash in 1924. Hunting is now managed; the habitat has gradually recovered; and the North Kaibab is producing world-record trophy mule deer.

The tassel-eared Kaibab squirrel is found only here.

The Rim: On the SE, the District has several mi. of frontage on the Rim overlooking the Grand Canyon. Forest Road 445 leads to this part of the Rim. It's more than 20 mi. from US Alt. 89, and it would be advisable to ask about road conditions. Views from the Rim are spectacular, and there are no crowds.

Saddle Mountain Wilderness, 40,600 acres, is at the Rim. Access by Forest Road 445.

Kanab Canyon, W boundary of the district, is a principal tributary of the Grand Canyon. Kanab Creek has cut a huge basin between the Kanab and Kaibab plateaus. The lower portion of the canyon is within the National Park. Several trails lead from the Kaibab Plateau down into the canyon. They are mapped but not well marked or maintained. Some adventurous souls make the hike down to the river, upstream, and out by the Thunder River Trail.

It's not easy hiking, but the canyon is dramatic, at times as narrow as 40 ft., walls as high as 1,000. Water is scarce; hikers are warned not to rely on finding any. Travel through the canyon is strongly discouraged in summer because of the fierce heat and lack of water. Permits are required for entry to the National Park portion of the canyon. "Every visitor is in a sense a pioneer," warns a Forest brochure. "He must possess the resourcefulness, initiative and endurance that the word implies."

North Canyon Trails, E of DeMotte, are unique in having a small spring-fed stream. It flows for about a mile through a forested canyon before vanishing. The trail loop can be hiked in a day.

House Rock Buffalo Ranch, 40,420 acres, 80 mi. SW of Page, on the road to the Forest's portion of the North Rim. (Shown on NF and highway maps.) Operated by Arizona Game and Fish Department on a grazing permit. Terrain is rolling to sharply breaking, steep mountains on the SW and S, vertical cliffs dropping from the Rim to the Colorado River on the E. Semidesert shrub-grassland with pinyon-juniper at upper elevations. Bison were introduced here some years ago, now number 75 to 100. The herd is cropped periodically by hunting. Visitors other than hunters number about 500 per year.

Jacob Lake is a commercial development on the way to the North Rim: inn, RV park, etc. The Forest has an information center here, two campgrounds.

Demotte Park, about 4 mi. from the Park boundary on SR 67 has a lodge, store, campground.

Hiking: The Forest's only printed trail guide describes about 40 mi. of trails on the Kaibab, mostly in low desert canyons, too hot for pleasant hiking in summer. Sierra Club volunteers are building a new Rim Trail.

SR 67 is closed beyond Jacob Lake when the first snow falls, usually mid-Nov. to mid-May. US Alt. 89 is kept open.

Tusayan Ranger District adjoins the National Park on the S. SR 64, joining US 180, crosses the W side of the District en route to Grand Canyon Village on the South Rim. SR 64 then turns E and cuts across the NE corner of the District.

The District is on the Coconino Plateau, a relatively flat expanse of ponderosa forest with no peaks. The Forest map shows a network of unpaved roads but no trails or features of special interest. Elevation is about 7,000 ft. A Forest campground is on SR 64 about 4 mi. S of the Park boundary. Just before the boundary is the community of Tusayan, with airport, shops, motel, etc.

The *Chalender* and *Williams Ranger Districts* surround the city of Williams. They are crossed by I-40 and other paved roads and have many scattered inholdings, chiefly along these roads.

Here there are mountains. The Districts, generally above 7,000 ft. elevation, have a number of scattered volcanic peaks. Highest are Kendrick Peak,

10,418 ft., Sitgreaves Mountain, 9,388 ft., and Bill Williams Mountain, 9,256 ft. The Forest map shows short trails ascending the principal peaks, but no long trails. The District adjoins the Coconino and Prescott National Forests.

Sycamore Canyon Wilderness, 7,125 acres, plus 48,818 acres in the Prescott and Coconino National Forests, is among the most famous of the state's dramatic gorges. The 21-mi.-long canyon is carved deep into the Colorado Plateau. The widest point is 7 mi. from rim to rim. High cliffs, spectacular formations of red and white sedimentary rock. The canyon floor is green with riparian vegetation. Douglas-fir and ponderosa pine at 7,000 ft. on the N rim.

Various access points, including roads SE from Williams and SW from Flagstaff, offer opportunities for day hikes or a complete transit of the canyon, which can take 5 days or more.

Hiking in summer is not recommended; daytime temperatures often exceed 100°F. Apr. through June and Sept. to mid-Nov. are best. Visitors must carry their own water; the canyon has few springs. Horses require supplemental feed.

A small area at the S end of the canyon is closed to overnight camping.

White Horse Lake, a small lake with a Forest campground, is on Forest Road 109 near the head of Sycamore Canyon.

Kendrick Mountain Wilderness, 6,510 acres, with part in the Coconino National Forest. The highest point in the Kaibab, rising 3,000 ft. from its base. A 4-mi. trail to the top, through ponderosa pine and mixed conifer forest with some open meadows. Two other trails, totaling 8 mi.

Bill Williams Mountain catches enough snow to make it a ski area. Usual season Nov. 1–Mar. 1. Road to the top. About 8 mi. of trails on the N and E sides.

I-40 Parks Rest Area Trail. A short nature trail, paved for the handicapped, designed to attract motorists who pause here.

Camping: North Kaibab: 3 campgrounds; 71 sites. Tusayan R.D.: 1 campground; 70 sites. Chalender-Williams R.D.: 4 campgrounds, 162 sites; plus 1 campground without designated sites. Season is generally May–Oct.

PUBLICATIONS
Forest maps, North and South sections. $1 each.
Bird checklist.

REFERENCE: Ganci, Dave. *Hiking the Southwest.* San Francisco: Sierra Club Books, 1983, pp. 64–68.

HEADQUARTERS: 800 S. 6th St., Williams, AZ 86046; (602) 635-2681.

RANGER DISTRICTS: North Kaibab R.D., P.O. Box 248, Fredonia, AZ 86022; (602) 643-5895. Tusayan R.D., P.O. Box 3088, Tusayan, AZ 86023; (602) 638-2443. Chalender R.D., 501 W. Bill Williams Ave., Williams, AZ 86046; (602) 635-2676. Williams R.D., P.O. Box 434, Williams, AZ 86046; (602) 635-2633.

LAKE MEAD NATIONAL RECREATION AREA
National Park Service
896,230 acres in AZ, 586,006 acres in NV.

From Kingman, NW on US 93.

See entry in NV Zone 6. Most visitors come through NV. Most of the marinas and other recreation sites are in NV. NV has the larger portion of the lake.

However, AZ has a majority of the uplands, and fair-weather roads on the AZ side lead to uncrowded places on the shore.

MOUNT TIPTON
U.S. Bureau of Land Management
19,550 acres.

N of Kingman. Mt. Tipton appears on the highway map, which also shows a road from US 93 E to Chloride. About 2 mi. N of this intersection is Big Wash road, an unpaved road NE to Packsaddle Mountain, the unit's S boundary.

The chief attractions here are 7,148-ft. Mt. Tipton and other peaks of the Cerbat Mountains. (The official highway map says Tipton is 6,900 ft. We rely on the U.S. Geological Survey.) Splendid views from the peaks and ridges.

The general appearance of the Cerbats differs from that of the nearby Black Mountains (see entry). Here the upper slopes are highly vegetated with pinyon pine, shrub live oak, manzanita, beargrass, and desert ceanothus. Large granite outcrops on the ridgeline. Gray and red rock contrast with the green of plants.

Deep washes are divided by descending ridges. Small valleys and bowls throughout the unit. Good habitat for mule deer, kit fox, bobcat, many raptors, Gambel's quail, cactus wren.

Camping: The Big Wash road leads to two BLM-maintained dry campgrounds. Spectacular ridgetop views.

HEADQUARTERS: BLM, Kingman Resource Area, 2475 Beverly Ave., Kingman, AZ 86401; (602) 757-4011.

NAVAJO INDIAN RESERVATION
Navajo Tribal Council
Over 16,000,000 acres, including acreage in Utah and New Mexico.

NE Arizona. Crossed by US 89, US 160, US 191, and several state routes.

Covering about one-fifth of the state, the Reservation is the largest in the Lower 48. Within this huge area are only a few small centers, such as Tuba City and Kayenta. Most of the Navajo population is dispersed. Average population density is about 6 per sq. mi.

The area is scenic but dry. No part of the Reservation receives more than 12 in. of precipitation per year, and some as little as 6. Dust plumes mark the passage of cars on other than the paved roads.

Much of the reservation is high plateau, elevations about 5,000 ft., with many hills and mesas in the 5,500–6,500 ft. range. The land slopes upward toward the N and E. Here there are high mesas and mountains, a number of peaks exceeding 9,000 ft. In the NW corner the Reservation adjoins the Glen Canyon National Recreation Area. Travelers on SR 64 between Grand Canyon Village and US 89 cross the Reservation beside the Little Colorado River Gorge and may pause at the overlook. Most other streams are intermittent, but the Reservation has a number of small lakes used for fishing. Much of the landscape is red sandstone, often in dramatically sculptured formations, the most massive of which are in Monument Valley.

When to go? Winter is cold, often wet or snowy. Thaw and rain make most unpaved roads impassable in spring, though travel on pavement is no problem. High winds in Mar.–Apr. can produce dust storms. Mid-Apr. through May is a season favored by Arizonans, before the summer heat. Fall is also delightful.

Tourism is an important source of tribal revenue. Visitors are welcome at the several centers, such as Window Rock and Hubbell Trading Post. Rodeos, fairs, and other special events attract many visitors. Tours are available, from a few hours to several days. Wandering on your own off the main routes is inadvisable. Unescorted visitors should confine their travels to roads shown on the highway map.

Tribal permits are required for hunting and fishing.

FEATURES

Canyon de Chelly. See entry.

Monument Valley. On US 163 at the Utah border. Everyone has seen these huge red sandstone pillars in television commercials. They're even more impressive without the automobiles on top. Many of them can be seen from the highway. For a fee you can drive the tour route among the monuments, or you can book a more extensive guided tour. The campground, where we spent the night, is on a promontory, a fine vantage point for seeing the changing colors and patterns at dusk, by moonlight, and at dawn.

Navajo National Monument, 360 acres. Well-preserved cliff dwellings, some of which can be seen only by hiking or horse riding. Visitor center.

Painted Desert. Colorful desert formations of sandstone and clay, how colorful depending on the play of light. The colors are most subdued at midday, bright near dawn and dusk, brightest after rain. The Painted Desert is in the SW corner of the Reservation and extends into the N half of Petrified Forest National Park (see entry).

HEADQUARTERS: The Navajo Tribe, Visitor Services, P.O. Box 308, Window Rock, AZ 86515; (602) 871-6436.

PETRIFIED FOREST NATIONAL PARK
National Park Service
93,493 acres.

See entry in Zone 4.

SUNSET CRATER AND WUPATKI NATIONAL MONUMENTS
National Park Service
3,040 acres and 35,253 acres.

From Flagstaff, 15 mi. N on US 89.

Linked by a 36-mi. loop road, the Monuments are under common management. Sunset Crater features a large volcanic cinder cone, Wupatki the ruins of red sandstone pueblos. Sunset Crater is within the Coconino National Forest; Wupatki is at the NE corner.

Some 400 dead volcanoes, including 200 cinder cones, surround the towering San Francisco Peaks (see entry, Coconino National Forest, Zone 4). Sunset Crater, about 1,000 ft. high, is the most recent and dramatic, its name derived from the red iron oxide stains around its top. Elevation at the crest is 8,029 ft. Other volcanic features of the Monument include lava flows, a lava tube, and spatter cones.

The eruption forced the Indians living nearby to flee, but the widespread ashbed formed an excellent mulch, and other Indians moved into the area to farm. The settlement at Wupatki became the largest, with a 3-story structure containing more than 100 rooms, open-air amphitheater, and ball court. The Monument includes about 800 Indian ruins. Some ruins are not yet excavated.

Annual precipitation in the Sunset Crater area is about 16 in. per year, enough to support a rich vegetation; at Wupatki it's half that. Summers are warm rather than hot, average daily high temperatures in the low 80s. Brief, scattered afternoon thundershowers occur almost daily. Winters are cold, with daytime temperatures usually below freezing for several hours. Subzero readings are not uncommon. Snowfall averages 60 to 70 in.

Sunset Crater Area

Plants: Lichens are first to colonize after such an eruption, followed by such small pioneering plants as mosses, galleta grass, buckwheat, globemallow, and Indian paintbrush. Next in succession are such shrubs as Apache plume, rabbitbrush, four-wing saltbush, and wax currant. Finally are trees: one-seed juniper, pinyon pine, and ponderosa pine. About one-third of the area is forested. Flowering plants include, in June, pink beardtongue, scarlet beardtongue, Apache plume. In July: scarlet beardtongue, cranesbill, skyrocket gilia, loco. In Aug., the peak blooming season: various sunflowers, Rocky Mountain beeplant, skyrocket gilia, loco, many others.

Birds: Checklist available, covering a 20-sq.-mi. area. On our most recent visit, we were lucky enough to spot a pair of golden eagles on the rim of a small cinder cone; we were told it was the first sighting of the year. Seasonally common species include American kestrel, mourning dove, common nighthawk, broad-tailed hummingbird, northern flicker, violet-green swallow, Steller's and pinyon jays, mountain chickadee, white-breasted and pygmy nuthatches, American robin, western bluebird, yellow-rumped warbler, western meadowlark, Oregon junco.

Mammals: Checklist available. Often or occasionally seen: blacktail jackrabbit, cliff chipmunk, Abert squirrel, coyote, mule deer, pronghorn.

Reptiles and amphibians: Checklist includes short-horned, eastern fence, and tree lizards; many-lined skink. Arizona mountain kingsnake, gopher snake, black-necked and wandering garter snakes, Arizona black rattlesnake.

Wupatki Area

Plants: Typical of the Upper Sonoran Desert region: juniper, yucca, Mormon tea, Apache plume, saltbush, rabbitbrush, snakeweed. Flowering plants include mallow, four o'clock, beeweed, prince's plume, sacred datura.

Birds: Checklist available. Seasonally common: red-tailed hawk, American kestrel, mourning dove, poor-will, common nighthawk, broad-tailed hummingbird, northern flicker, Say's phoebe, horned lark, common raven, rock and canyon wrens, American robin, Townsend's solitaire, mountain bluebird, ruby-crowned kinglet, house finch, dark-eyed junco.

Mammals: Checklist available. Desert species, seldom seen by day. Included are various species of shrews, bats, mice, woodrats. Pocket gopher, whitetail prairie dog, rock squirrel, spotted and whitetail antelope ground squirrels, porcupine, blacktail jackrabbit, desert cottontail, bobcat, mountain lion, gray fox, coyote, badger, striped and spotted skunks, longtail weasel, pronghorn, mule deer.

Reptiles and amphibians: Checklist available. Most common are side-blotched, collared, and leopard lizards; western whiptail, desert spiny lizard. Gopher snake, common kingsnake, Hopi rattlesnake.

INTERPRETATION
Visitor centers at both Monuments. Exhibits, talks, literature. Open 8 A.M.–
5 P.M. daily except Christmas and New Year's days, 7 A.M.–7 P.M. in summer.
Campfire programs and *guided hikes,* mid-June–Labor Day.
Bus trips: mid-June–Labor Day.
Lava Cave tours: mid-June–Labor Day.
Nature trail 1 1/2 mi. E of Sunset Crater visitor center.

Camping: Campground at Sunset Crater. 44 sites. Apr. 15–Nov. 15.

*Hiking and climbing on Sunset Crater, once permitted, now prohibited
because of its fragile nature. Hiking is not restricted in the National Forest
between the Monuments.*
Snow occasionally closes the site in winter.

PUBLICATIONS
Leaflet with map.
Information pages, Sunset Crater:
  General information.
  Geology.
  Dating Sunset Crater.
  Natural history.
  Checklists of birds, mammals, reptiles and amphibians.
  Weather.
  Camping information.
  Checklist of vascular plants.
Information pages, Wupatki:
  General information.
  Blowholes of the Wupatki Area.
  Perennial Plants of Wupatki National Monument.
  Roadside Plants of Wupatki National Monument.
  Bird, mammal, reptile checklists.

REFERENCES
Plateau Magazine. *Wupatki-Sunset Crater.* Flagstaff: Museum of Northern
  Arizona, 1979.
Schroeder, Albert. *Of Men and Volcanoes.* Globe, AZ: Southwest Parks
  and Monuments Association, 1977.
Krutch, Joseph Wood. *The Paradox of a Lava Flow.* Globe, AZ: Southwest
  Parks and Monuments Association, 1958.

HEADQUARTERS: Route 3, Box 149, Flagstaff, AZ 86001; (602) 526-0586.

WUPATKI NATIONAL MONUMENT
National Park Service
See entry, Sunset Crater National Monument.

ZONE 3

1. Hualapai Mountain Park
2. Wabayuma Peak
3. Havasu National Wildlife Refuge
4. Crossman Peak
5. Burro Creek
6. Peoples Canyon
7. Joshua Forest Parkway
8. Prescott National Forest
9. Dead Horse Ranch State Park
10. Tuzigoot National Monument
11. Lake Havasu State Park
12. Buckskin Mountain State Park
13. Bill Williams River
14. Alamo Lake State Park
15. Gibraltar Mountain
16. Cactus Plain
17. Lake Pleasant Regional Park
18. Tonto National Forest
19. Lower Colorado River
20. La Posa Plain
21. New Water Mountains
22. Harquahala Mountains
23. Kofa National Wildlife Refuge
24. Eagletail Mountains
25. White Tank Mountains Regional Park
26. Robbins Butte
27. Estrella Mountain Regional Park
28. McDowell Mountain Regional Park
29. Desert Botanical Garden
30. Phoenix South Mountain Park
31. Cibola National Wildlife Refuge; Imperial National Wildlife Refuge
32. Mittry Lake Wildlife Area
33. Green Belt Resource Conservation Area
34. Painted Rocks State Park
35. Luke Air Force Range
36. Cabeza Prieta National Wildlife Refuge

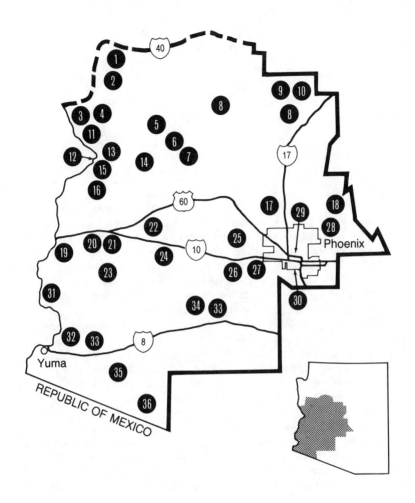

ZONE 3

Includes these counties:

Mohave (S portion)	La Paz	Maricopa
Yuma	Yavapai	

This is our largest and most complex zone in Arizona, with a great variety of settings and remarkable contrasts. It includes high, pine-clad forests with clear streams and waterfalls, and the state's hottest, driest desert. Its eastern boundary is high and mountainous, its western the Colorado River and Lake Havasu. It is crossed by several Interstate and U.S. highways but contains some of the state's wildest and least accessible wildernesses.

We found one contrast in Maricopa County. Phoenix is horrifying. The city and its satellites have grown explosively, with no coherent plan or regard for such necessities as water. It is often likened to Los Angeles, and one hears jocular speculation about when these two sprawling monsters will merge.

Yet around Phoenix is one of America's finest county park systems. Until now we haven't included county parks in our guides, but how can you ignore a county system whose 5 largest units have almost 2 1/2 times the acreage of all Arizona's State Parks combined? These county parks are huge, with large areas of virtual wilderness.

The eastern portion of the zone is mostly in the Prescott and Tonto National Forests. Both include popular, sometimes crowded, recreation areas, but we also found little-used trails. Both have splendid Wildernesses.

I-8 crosses the S part of the zone, paralleling the Lower Gila River, which is usually dry or nearly so, but has some interesting natural areas adjacent and more white-winged doves than you'll find anywhere else. S of the highway is the Luke Air Force Base and part of the huge Cabeza Prieta National Wildlife Refuge. At the Colorado River is Yuma, almost the lowest point in the state, hot and dry.

The Colorado River isn't its old self. Sections of it attract great concentrations of people. One is just below Parker Dam, where development crowds every inch of river bank and boat motors create a day-long din. Even the several wildlife refuges along the river have no defense against this boat traffic. There are quiet times and places.

The western third of the zone is strewn with mountains, ranges with no prevailing orientation, some rising to only 1,500 ft. elevation, many between 3,000 and 4,000 ft., a few higher than 7,000 ft. Most of this land is public domain, and here BLM found many tracts meeting the preliminary requirements for Wilderness study: 5,000 or more roadless acres in essentially natural condition. Seen from a distance, these mountains look much alike, and many of BLM's field descriptions have a family resemblance. Almost any one of these desert mountains would be a good entry for us if it stood alone, but would readers want two or three dozen quite similar entries? We chose those which had features of special interest. If two sites had similar qualities except that one could be reached only by hours of hot and difficult scrambling, we chose the more accessible. In this country, such accessibility does not mean crowds. Many of these sites are rarely visited except in hunting season.

Not all these mountains are hot and dry. A few offer relief from desert heat in their cool pine forests with trickling streams. We have entries for those.

ALAMO LAKE STATE PARK
Arizona State Parks
5,642 acres.

From Wendon on US 60, 38 mi. N.

The road N from Wendon to the lake is a scenic drive, through the Harcuvar Mountains and skirting the E end of the Buckskin Range. The desert landscape is well vegetated with saguaro of all ages, many chollas, and ocotillo.

The park isn't a natural area, but it adjoins large areas of attractive public lands. The lake, an Army Corps of Engineers flood control project, varies in size. The minimum pool, not seen since 1970, is only 500 acres. Floods in 1980 increased it to over 10,000 acres. "Normal" is about 4,300 acres (3,530 acres according to the Arizona Outdoor Recreation Coordinating Commission). The park was designed for intensive water-based recreation. It has more campsites than any other AZ state park except Lake Havasu, plus ramp, boat rentals, store, and other facilities.

Summer isn't the busy season; that begins in mid-Oct. Visitation drops off before Christmas, then increases in late Jan. for a spring season. We arrived on a Sunday afternoon in early Oct., and most weekend campers had left. Only 6 boats were on the lake.

The lake was formed by damming the Bill Williams River. The park is surrounded by low, rolling hills cut by small dry washes, beyond which are virtually undisturbed mountains. A scenic overlook has good views of the lake and environs.

ADJACENT

Arrastra Mountain, U.S. Bureau of Land Management, 108,285 acres. This huge area of public land is upstream from the lake. The Big Sandy and Santa Maria rivers, both perennial, join to form the Bill Williams; their confluence is now submerged. Above the lake, they approximate the S and SW boundaries of the site, which extends N to US 93. Burro Creek (see entry) is just N of the unit.

Elevations from about 1,235 ft. at stream level to 4,807 on Poachie Peak. The terrain is rough and irregular, with granitic outcrops, several peaks over 4,000 ft., volcanic hills and mesas, numerous washes, winding canyons.

Vegetation includes species typical of both Upper and Lower Sonoran life zones: chiefly Sonoran Desert scrub with Mohave Desert scrub influence and chaparral. The SW sector supports a palo verde-saguaro association. Joshua tree, Bigelow nolina, and bladder-sage intermix with this association in the N and W. Cottonwood-willow and mesquite bosque occur along the two rivers. Feral burros damaged much of the native vegetation, but most of them have been removed.

The area is rated "outstanding" for birding. Water and vegetation attract a variety of wildlife species.

The washes are natural hiking routes. Jeep tracks to abandoned mines are revegetating but can often be hiked.

Bill Williams Gorge, U.S. Bureau of Land Management, 71,900 acres. Downstream from Alamo Lake. The river meanders for 8 mi. through a 600-ft.-deep canyon. A roadless area of public land extends for 8 mi. NW of the canyon along the Rawhide Mountains, 9 mi. to the SE on the E end of the Buckskin Mountains. The Rawhide Mountains are low hills with numerous rugged outcrops, the highest point 2,430 ft. Several small washes and canyons, notably Mississippi Wash, which winds down a narrow canyon with several small waterfalls. The Buckskins are a larger and higher range, mostly lying W of this unit.

The perennial stream, colorful bluffs, and riparian vegetation make the Bill Williams Gorge and its side canyons the principal attraction. We were told that in dry weather ORV's have occasionally made their way up from the mouth, 35 mi. away, to within a few mi. of the dam. The state park boundary extends 1 mi. below the dam, and park visitors sometimes fish the river.

Getting down to the river takes a little scrambling. The road to the dam is gated and locked. Park employees may not be familiar with the BLM areas.

Camping: 292 sites. All year.

HEADQUARTERS: Park: Box 38, Wendon, AZ 85357; (602) 669-2088. BLM: Phoenix District Office, 2015 W. Deer Valley Rd., Phoenix, AZ 85027; (602) 241-2501.

BILL WILLIAMS RIVER

U.S. Bureau of Land Management and others.
Indeterminate acreage.

> From SR 95 near Parker Dam. Planet Ranch Road, access to the Bill
> Williams Unit of the Havasu National Wildlife Refuge (see entry), enters
> private land. Inquire at BLM office or locally for routing beyond this point.

Lake Havasu, formed by Parker Dam, inundated the original mouth of Bill
Williams River, which flows from Alamo Lake State Park (see entry) between
the Rawhide and Buckskin Mountains. The present mouth and 6,105 acres
of riparian land are part of the Havasu National Wildlife Refuge. Most of the
area upstream is public land, although there are private holdings. Sections of
the river are confined in colorful, narrow, steep-walled canyons. Others cross
a fairly broad flood plain.

Banded Canyon, 15 mi. long, is a principal feature of the area, a constriction
in the drainage for all of west central AZ. It is named for the layers of schists
and gneisses in the canyon walls. Canyon plants are transitional between the
Sonoran and Mohave deserts. The canyon has been proposed as a National
Natural Landmark.

The river's course can be hiked, and we were told ORV's occasionally
manage to reach Alamo Dam or almost that far. Side canyons offer routes
into the mountains. On the N side, two large washes, Castaneda and Centen-
nial, are natural trails. Water and riparian vegetation attract wildlife.

We had no opportunity to hike the river, and information about it was
scanty. Almost everyone comes here because of the lake and the Colorado
River; the mountains are just background. But we found one enthusiast:
"Hey! That's a neat place!"

For Bill Williams Gorge, see entry, Alamo Lake SP.

NEARBY
See entries:
Lake Havasu National Wildlife Refuge.
Havasu Lake State Park.
Buckskin Mountain State Park.

HEADQUARTERS: BLM, Havasu Resource Area, 3189 Sweetwater Ave., Lake
Havasu City, AZ 86403; (602) 855-8017.

BUCKSKIN MOUNTAIN STATE PARK
Arizona State Parks
1,677 acres.

11 mi. N of Parker on SR 95.

The park fronts on the Colorado River below Parker Dam. An intensive-use area on a busy river. The park leaflet doesn't mention it, nor does the leaflet map show it, but there's a substantial block of undeveloped acreage E of the highway, with trails leading into an attractive area of desert hills.

ACTIVITIES
Camping: Two areas, 80 sites.
Hiking: A 1-mi. trail at the park entrance provides access to the Buckskin Mountains.

NEARBY
See entries:
Bill Williams River.
Havasu National Wildlife Refuge.

HEADQUARTERS: Box 664, Parker, AZ 85344; (602) 667-3231.

BURRO CREEK
U.S. Bureau of Land Management
49,690 acres.

On and NE of US 93, about 62 mi. NW of Wickenburg.

The Burro Creek watershed is one of the most fascinating areas in this part of AZ, with dramatic scenery, perennial water, springs, a great diversity of plant and animal life, and exceptional opportunities for backcountry recreation.

This site is just NW of the Joshua Forest Parkway (see entry). BLM has a popular campground on the W side of the road. The roadless portions of the Burro Creek watershed described here are E of the highway. Upper Burro Creek is 18 mi. E of Wikieup, 4 mi. NW of Bagdad. Primary access is by Pipeline road, which intersects US 93 about 300 ft. N of Signal Rd. Lower Burro Creek is 10 mi. SE of Wikieup; a portion of the site boundary is on US 93. Good access from the same road.

The upper part of the site includes a bit of Goodwin Mesa, a large, rolling, grassy area. Burro Creek Canyon drops down from the mesa over several vertical rock faces, descending 1,500 ft. in a half mile. Francis Creek is a rugged tributary canyon. The site includes several smaller canyons, a complex system of small hills, and a large butte rising 800 ft. above the hills.

The principal feature of Lower Burro Creek is a large volcanic butte. Seven small canyons descending from the tableland at the N end of the unit have carved an intricate maze of overhangs, spires, and ridges (called Hell's Half Acre), all dropping almost vertically into a basin just above the creek. This segment of Burro Creek meanders into an open but often steep-walled canyon for about 8 mi. through the unit. S of the creek is a relatively flat plain with huge granitic boulders.

Elevations range from about 2,000 to about 5,000 ft., with much of the site at about 2,500. Annual precipitation is about 10 in. Summers are too hot for serious hiking. Occasional thunderstorms. Winters are relatively mild, with widespread showers. Spring and fall are the favored hiking periods.

Some degradation of the watershed, especially riparian habitats, has occurred because of overgrazing, including the impact of feral burros. ORV activity is as yet a minor problem but on the increase. Two areas have been defined as worthy of protection as unique Natural Areas. Both Upper and Lower Burro creeks have been considered for Wilderness status. BLM has also prepared a Riparian Management Plan.

Plants: Seven major plant communities are represented: palo verde-saguaro, chaparral, arid grassland, pinyon-juniper, and three riparian types: cottonwood-willow, mesquite bosque, and mixed broadleaf. Over 250 plant species recorded. Topography creates many microhabitats in which unusual mixing of communities occurs.

Perennial water and this diversity of plant life attracts and supports 278 species of vertebrates.

Birds: No checklist. 150 species recorded. Noted: cactus wren, white-winged dove, Gambel's quail, scrub jay, dipper, great and snowy egrets, black-crowned night-heron, gray vireo, bushtit, ladder-backed woodpecker, mockingbird, brown towhee, roadrunner, bald eagle, osprey, prairie falcon, American kestrel; black, zone-tailed, Cooper's, sharp-shinned, and red-tailed hawks; turkey vulture.

Mammals: No checklist. Noted: beaver, raccoon, desert cottontail, ringtail, badger; spotted, striped, and hognose skunks; gray fox, javelina, bobcat, mountain lion, mule deer, pronghorn. Also feral burros.

ACTIVITIES

Camping: 32 sites, all year, at Burro Creek Campground, shown on highway map. Popular except in summer. Scenic location. Desert garden. Occasional naturalist programs.

Hiking, backpacking: Most hikers choose the canyons. Water in stream and springs should be treated. Upland areas have a few jeep tracks, but strangers would do well to consult the BLM office before going far.

HEADQUARTERS: BLM, Kingman Resource Area, 2475 Beverly Ave., King-man, AZ 86401; (602) 757-3161.

CABEZA PRIETA NATIONAL WILDLIFE REFUGE
U.S. Fish and Wildlife Service
See entry in Zone 5.

CACTUS PLAIN
U.S. Bureau of Land Management
84,095 acres.

Shown on the highway map, about 10 mi. SE of Parker, just N of SR 72. Bounded by maintained roads.

An immense area of stabilized and partially stabilized sand dunes. Botanists find much of interest here. Hikers will find it most attractive in the early morning and late afternoon, when the angle of sunlight accentuates the pinkish dunes.

The undulating terrain quickly provides a sense of isolation from outside sights and sounds. We were reminded of the time we were "lost" among the dunes of a small barrier island, a heavy cloud cover hiding the sun, surf sounds echoing from all around us, no vantage point. Here one would almost always have the sun, but a compass is reassuring.

Mixed duneshrub plant community. Species of special interest include wooly heads, sand flat milkvetch, Death Valley Mormon tea, linearleaf sand spurge. Wildlife species of special interest include elf owl, Mohave Desert fringe-toed lizard, flat-tailed horned lizard.

HEADQUARTERS: BLM, Havasu Resource Area, 3189 Sweetwater Ave., Lake Havasu City, AZ 86403; (602) 855-8017.

CIBOLA NATIONAL WILDLIFE REFUGE;
IMPERIAL NATIONAL WILDLIFE REFUGE
U.S. Fish and Wildlife Service
Cibola: 7,786 acres, plus 3,647 acres in CA.
Imperial: 17,806 acres, plus 7,958 acres in CA.

Adjoining, on the Colorado River. For Cibola, best road access is from CA side. From I-10 W of Blythe, S on SR 78. 3 mi. beyond Palo Verde, turn left. Left at the river, cross the bridge into AZ, and turn right. For Imperial, N from Yuma about 25 mi. on US 95. Turn left at the Martinez Lake Road and follow Refuge signs.

Cibola NWR was established to mitigate losses of wildlife habitat caused by channelizing 50 mi. of the Colorado River. Its mission is to maintain Canada goose and field-feeding ducks during the winter, and to this end 2,000 acres of feed crops are cultivated. The Refuge includes the dredged and diked channel, the old channel, river bottomland, a small lake, and marshes. Visitors are permitted to drive on the dike but warned that refuge roads have low and sandy places. Refuge HQ on site. The best way to see the refuge is by boat. The old channel is canoeable. The best time for birding is Dec.–June. A self-guided tour loop to view the Canada geese is provided during the wintering period. Most visitors come in summer for boating and fishing.

Imperial NWR includes about 30 mi. of the river below Cibola, together with adjacent backwater lakes. Most of the area is river bottomland and low, rolling desert. Bottomland vegetation is largely giant cane, willow, arrowweed, cattails, salt cedar. Desert species include ironwood, palo verde, mesquite, smoke tree, creosote, brittlebush, lycium, and cacti. Here, too, best birding is winter and spring; summer visitors come to boat and fish. On our most recent visit, in Oct., no visitors were present. The visitor center is open from 7 A.M. to noon and 12:30 to 3:30 P.M., Mon.–Fri. Leaflets and an informational sign are located on the entrance road. Birding is best along the desert washes N of the information sign, Nov.–Feb.

For both refuges, heavy and noisy boat traffic on the river is a growing problem. In the past, canoeing the river has been delightful. Many float trips begin at Blythe. Picacho State Recreation Area in CA is a convenient overnight stop. Take-out at Martinez Lake or Imperial Dam. Canoeing amid power boat traffic is neither pleasant nor safe. Fortunately this traffic abates in winter, the best time for birding.

Birds: Both refuges have bird checklists, which are almost identical, including 232 species. Both provide habitat for the endangered Yuma clapper rail. The sandhill crane has become common on Cibola, nesting here. Seasonally common or abundant species include eared and pied-billed grebes, white pelican, great blue heron, great and snowy egrets, Canada goose, gadwall, pintail, green-winged and cinnamon teals, American wigeon, shoveler, redhead, lesser scaup, bufflehead, ruddy duck, common merganser, turkey vulture, Gambel's quail, common moorhen, American coot, killdeer; spotted, least, and western sandpipers; black-necked stilt, Wilson's phalarope, ring-

ARIZONA ◀§ 188

billed gull, Forster's and black terns. Also mourning and white-winged doves, roadrunner, screech and great horned owls, lesser nighthawk, Costa's hummingbird, belted kingfisher, northern flicker, Gila and ladder-backed woodpeckers, western kingbird; ash-throated, willow, and western flycatchers; black and Say's phoebes, western wood-pewee. Swallows: tree, rough-winged, barn, cliff. Verdin, house wren, marsh wren, mockingbird, crissal thrasher, black-tailed gnatcatcher, ruby-crowned kinglet, water pipit, phainopepla, loggerhead shrike, warbling vireo. Warblers: orange-crowned, yellow, yellow-rumped, MacGillivray's, yellowthroat, yellow-breasted chat, Wilson's. House sparrow, western meadowlark; yellow-headed, red-winged, and Brewer's blackbirds; brown-headed cowbird, western tanager. Also black-headed and blue grosbeaks, house finch, Abert's towhee. Sparrows: savannah, chipping, Brewer's, white-crowned, song.

Mammals: Annotated checklist of 39 species available. Excluding those called rare, the following are noted: leafnosed bat, western pipistrel, pallid bat, Mexican freetail bat, blacktail jackrabbit, desert cottontail, Yuma and whitetail antelope squirrels, roundtail ground squirrel. Pocket mice: little, longtail, desert, rock, spiny. Merriam kangaroo rat, beaver, western harvest mouse; canyon, cactus, and deer mice; hispid cotton rat, white-throat and desert woodrats, muskrat, coyote, kit fox, gray fox, ringtail, raccoon, striped skunk, bobcat, mule deer, bighorn sheep. Also feral horse, hog, and burro.

Amphibians and reptiles: Checklist available. Includes Great Plains, red-spotted, and Woodhouse's toads; bullfrog, leopard frog. Spiny softshell turtle. Lizards: banded gecko, desert iguana, chuckwalla, zebra-tailed, collared, leopard, desert spiny, side-blotched, long-tailed brush, ornate tree, desert horned, western whiptail. Snakes: western blind, coachwhip, western patch-nosed, glossy, gopher, kingsnake, long-nosed, checkered garter, western ground, western shovel-nosed, spotted night, western diamondback, sidewinder, Mojave rattlesnake.

ACTIVITIES

Hunting: Designated areas; special rules. Waterfowl, quail, dove, cottontail, mule deer.

Fishing: River and backwaters. Largemouth bass, flathead, channel cat, bullhead, crappie, bluegill, carp.

Boating: Ramp at Imperial.

Summers are hot, mosquitoes abundant.

PUBLICATIONS

Cibola:
　　Leaflet with map.
　　Bird checklist.
　　Amphibians and reptiles checklist.
　　Public use regulations, including hunting and fishing.

Imperial:
  Bird checklist.
  Mammal checklist.
  Public use regulations, with Refuge map.

REFERENCES
  Colorado River from Blythe to Imperial Dam. Map, float information, facilities, etc. Available locally or from Arizona Game and Fish Department, 3005 Pacific Ave., Yuma, AZ 85364; (602) 344-3436.
  Ganci, Dave. *Hiking the Southwest.* San Francisco: Sierra Club Books, 1983, pp. 157–158.

HEADQUARTERS: *Cibola:* P.O. Box AP, Blythe, CA 92226; (602) 857-3253.
  Imperial: P.O. Box 72217, Martinez Lake, AZ 85364; (602) 783-3371.

CROSSMAN PEAK
U.S. Bureau of Land Management
22,915 acres.

  Shown on highway map, 10 mi. NE of Havasu City. A maintained local road penetrates the area.

An imposing backdrop for the fast-developing Lake Havasu City. The Environmental Impact Statement reviewing this area's suitability for Wilderness status commented, "appears to be more attractive for primitive recreation when examined in detail than it does when observed from a distance. From within, its surprising diversity of terrain, vegetation, and wildlife make it highly desirable for activities involving foot or horseback travel."

Seen from a distance, this section of the Mohave Mountains appears rugged, steep, and barren. Average annual rainfall is only 5 in., supporting a sparse cover of desert shrubs, grasses, cholla, pricklypear, scattered pinyon and Joshua trees. Greater density and diversity occur in the many narrow canyons and drainages. Fourteen natural springs occur on the E side of the site.

Its chief attraction is Sunrise Road from the W side to the top of Crossman Peak. When we visited, this was a trail used by hikers and horsemen; the BLM office, reviewing this entry, noted that it is now a road.

HEADQUARTERS: BLM, Havasu Resource Area, 3189 Sweetwater Ave., Lake Havasu City, AZ 86403; (602) 855-8017.

DEAD HORSE RANCH STATE PARK
Arizona State Parks
320 acres.

In Cottonwood off US 89 Alt., out N 5th St.

Permits are sold for day use and camping; Park is closed when sites are filled.

The Park is on the Verde River, just across from the town. It is close to the Prescott National Forest, though it does not adjoin, and makes a good base for tours into the Forest, as well as to Tuzigoot National Monument and other nearby sites. It borders the Coconino National Forest to the N.

One can stroll for a mile or more along the river. Large cottonwoods on the banks. Good birding here and around Peck's Lake, a small pond in the day-use area. The bird checklist for Tuzigoot National Monument (see entry) is largely applicable here.

ACTIVITIES
Camping: 45 sites. All year.
Hiking, horse riding: Trails into the National Forest.

PUBLICATION: Leaflet with map.

HEADQUARTERS: P.O. Box 144, Cottonwood, AZ 86326; (602) 634-5283.

DESERT BOTANICAL GARDEN
Independent
150 acres.

In Papago Park, Phoenix. On Galvin Parkway, S of McDowell Rd. and 64th St.

Open: 9 A.M.–sunset daily, except 7 A.M.–sunset July–Aug.

A well-known exhibition, education, and research center for desert plants, native and foreign. Splendid gardens, including both natural and landscaped areas. The self-guiding tour has 46 stations. Some species are in bloom in any season, but the peak period is Mar.–July. The Garden has had an important role in propagating native species to revegetate mined areas, providing seeds for commercial production of jojoba, conducting research on desert plants for food, and conserving endangered plant species.

Lectures and other programs are scheduled throughout the year. Visitors are welcome at meetings of the Central Arizona Cactus and Succulent Society and the Arizona Native Plant Society. Guided walks with docents, courses, and field trips are also offered.

ADJACENT: Papago Park also includes the Phoenix Zoo, hiking and bicycle trails, stable, etc.

PUBLICATIONS
Leaflet.
Bird checklist.
Guide to the Garden (walking tour) with map.
Guide to Desert Landscape Plants (walking tour) with map.
Catalog of the Flora of Arizona.

HEADQUARTERS: 1201 N. Galvin Parkway, Phoenix, AZ 85008; (602) 941-1225.

EAGLETAIL MOUNTAINS
U.S. Bureau of Land Management
120,925 acres.

S of I-10, about 65 mi. W of Phoenix, on the Yuma-Maricopa-La Paz county lines. Access from the E by Harquahala Valley Rd. or Courthouse Rock Road.

This huge roadless area, 188 sq. mi., includes the SE portion of the Eagletail Range, Cemetery Ridge to the S, and desert plain between. Both ranges are oriented NW–SE. Elevations from 1,200 ft. on the plain to 3,300 ft. on Eagletail Peak. The S slopes are gradual. The N face rises almost vertically from the desert floor. Courthouse Rock, a massive granitic monolith N of Eagletail Peak, rises 1,274 ft. above the flats. Weathering and erosion have created spectacular landforms, including natural arches, huge spires, monoliths, sawtooth ridges.

The site has been considered for Wilderness status and recommended for protection as a Scientific or Scenic Natural Area. One of our informants was concerned that such designation might attract too many people. At present few come here.

Summer is not the time for a visit. Daytime temperatures usually reach 100°F and at times 115°. Winters, however, are pleasant; night temperatures sometimes drop below freezing, but briefly, and days are often above 70°. Average annual precipitation is 5 to 10 in., most of it during the winter.

Plants: Vegetation is typical of the Sonoran Desert. On the lower slopes, creosote, bursage, ocotillo, teddybear cholla. The more heavily vegetated washes are dominated by palo verde, ironwood, smoketree, and catclaw, with occasional mesquite. On the steep hillsides: palo verde; barrel, staghorn, and hedgehog cacti; Mormon tea, saguaro.

Wildlife: Includes great horned owl, coveys of Gambel's quail, numerous raptors, jackrabbit, coyote, ground squirrel. Desert bighorn sheep are seen occasionally.

HEADQUARTERS: BLM, Phoenix District Office, 2015 W. Deer Valley Rd., Phoenix, AZ 85027; (602) 863-4464.

ESTRELLA MOUNTAIN REGIONAL PARK
Maricopa County Parks & Recreation Department
18,600 acres.

12 mi. W of Phoenix. From SR 85 at Goodyear, 3 mi. S on Bullard Ave.

On the N end of the Sierra Estrella, a NW–SE range. E boundary is the Gila River Indian Reservation. The Gila River, here an intermittent stream, is just outside the N boundary, crossed by the access road. Elevations from 900 ft. to 3,650 ft. on Squaw Tit Peak.

The entrance road divides, the right fork going to the golf course and associated facilities, the left into a loop around which are camping and picnic sites. All this development is on the alluvial plain. Only foot and horse trails go into the hills.

Average annual precipitation is only 6 in. June and July are hot and dry. Most visitors come Oct.–Nov. and Feb.–May. The peaks have an occasional dusting of snow in winter.

Plants: Vegetation is typical of the Sonoran Desert, dominated by palo verde, mesquite, saguaro, and ironwood, with brittlebush, creosote, ocotillo; hedgehog, barrel, fishhook, and pincushion cacti; cholla, pricklypear, desert poppy, lupine, blue-dicks, globemallow, goldfields, paintbrush, fiddleneck, desert buckwheat, gourds, senna.

Birds: No checklist. Noted: white-winged dove, Gambel's quail, Gila woodpecker, cactus wren, northern flicker, roadrunner, phainopepla, owls, redtailed and Cooper's hawks, American kestrel, turkey vulture, great blue heron, pintail.

Mammals: No checklist. Noted: roundtail ground squirrel, desert cottontail, blacktail jackrabbit, kit fox, gray fox, coyote, bobcat, javelina. Mountain lion, mule deer, and bighorn sheep inhabit the range but are seldom seen.

Reptiles and amphibians: No checklist. Noted: desert horned toad, Gila monster, desert tortoise, diamondback, Mojave rattlesnake.

ACTIVITIES
Camping: Small campground, undesignated sites.
Hiking, backpacking: 26 mi. of trails. We were told use of the trail system is light but increasing slowly.
Hunting: Small game, quail, rabbit. Special rules.
Horse riding: 26 mi. of trails.

PUBLICATIONS
Site map with regulations.
Map of developed area.

HEADQUARTERS: 3355 W. Durango, Phoenix, AZ 85009; (602) 262-3711. Park office on Casey Abbott Drive; (602) 932-3811.

GIBRALTAR MOUNTAIN
U.S. Bureau of Land Management
7,870 acres.

   About 10 mi. NE of Parker. Access via Shea Road, which runs E from SR 95 about 1 mi. S of Parker.

Its elevation is only 1,568 ft. The mountain is a rugged mass of volcanic rock dissected by deep, sandy washes. Vegetation is typical of the region: a sparse cover of creosote, staghorn cholla, barrel cactus, palo verde. Just another hill among many. But those who know the place praise it: "Some of the best natural recreation opportunities in the district." ". . . highly attractive for recreation activities involving foot and horse travel. . . . The winding courses taken by most drainages provide ever-changing landscape and vegetation patterns which make the area attractive for photography and sightseeing." "The mountainous areas, although of low elevation, stand out dramatically. When hiking along the high ridges and peaks, one is treated to broad, constantly changing panoramas."
   The area is the western edge of the desert bighorn sheep range in the Buckskin Mountains.
   The acreage given is just for the roadless area considered for Wilderness status. Most of the surrounding land is also public, including the eastward extension of the Buckskin Mountains. Portions of the site have unmaintained trails, but canyon bottoms and washes are natural routes. Parts of the site have been marred by ORV's.

Present visitation by hikers, hunters, horse riders, rockhounds, and ORV operators is estimated at 500 to 1,000 annually.

ADJACENT

Buckskin Mountain State Park (see entry).

La Paz County Park.

HEADQUARTERS: BLM, Havasu Resource Area, 3189 Sweetwater Ave., Lake Havasu City, AZ 86403; (602) 855-8017.

GREEN BELT RESOURCE CONSERVATION AREA
U.S. Bureau of Land Management
62,735 acres.

> About 100 mi. along the Gila River, from about 10 mi. W of Phoenix downstream to near Date Palm.

The Green Belt is a strip of dense vegetation along the Gila River. The river here is often dry, or nearly so, in a wide, sandy flood plain. Numerous potholes still hold water after the river is dry, attracting waterfowl and other wildlife.

The Fred J. Weiler Overlook on SR 85, 29 mi. N of Gila Bend, offers a sweeping view of the area. Visitors can reach the area by local roads and tracks from SR 85, I-8, and other roads. Some access routes require 4-wheel drive. Bring plenty of water.

Birds: The area is known to hunters for its large white-winged dove population, which often has a hundred nests per acre in the thickets of mesquite, salt cedar and other riparian species. Mourning dove also nest. Good population of Gambel's quail. Songbirds are abundant, including pyrrhuloxia, cardinal, finches, orioles, tanagers, woodpeckers, northern flicker, hummingbirds, roadrunner, phainopepla. Waterfowl visiting seasonally include mallard, pintail, teal, redhead, canvasback, Canada goose. Also common: herons, egrets, yellowlegs, Wilson's snipe.

Mammals: Include fox, coyote, raccoon, bobcat, mule deer, javelina.

Camping: Permitted almost anywhere except—as prohibited by state law —within a quarter-mile of any waterhole.

INCLUDES: Robbins Butte, Painted Rocks State Park (see entries).

PUBLICATION: Leaflet with map.

HEADQUARTERS: BLM, Phoenix District Office, 2015 W. Deer Valley Rd., Phoenix, AZ 85027; (602) 863-4464.

HARQUAHALA MOUNTAINS
U.S. Bureau of Land Management
73,875 acres.

10 mi. E of Wendon, S of US 60. Eagle Eye Rd., from US 60, is the E boundary.

One of the largest ranges in SW AZ, with many unusual attributes. Foremost is the availability of water; "running water up high" was the translation of its Indian name. Many of its canyons have perennial springs and seeps, as well as seasonal waterfalls.

Harquahala Peak, 5,681 ft., is the highest point in SW AZ. On top are the ruins of a solar observatory built by the Smithsonian Institution in 1920; the equipment was packed in by mule. We were told that a miner has since built a rough road up the mountain from Blue Tank Wash, on the S side. Traces of old mines are found at many points on the site.

The site includes high peaks, foothills, ridges, canyons, valleys, and surrounding bajadas. The highest peaks and several deep, rocky canyons are on the W side. Sunset Canyon drops over 1,600 ft. from the steep E rim. Brown's Canyon, in the NE sector, is 9 mi. long.

Plants: Several plant communities. The bajadas and valleys have a dense community of Lower Sonoran Desert scrub, with palo verde, saguaro, buckhorn and teddybear cholla, and many species of cacti, together with acacia, buckwheat, brittlebush, wolfberry, ocotillo, creosote, bursage, and a variety of wildflowers. Riparian vegetation includes ironwood, mesquite, acacia, palo verde, baccharis, canyon ragweed, wolfberry. Above 3,000 ft. vegetation is sparser and includes palo verde, agave, ephedra, ocotillo, brittlebush, jojoba, calliandra, and cacti. At this elevation the riparian communities include cottonwood, hackberry, mountain-mahogany, penstemon, occasional willow. High elevations feature canotia, agave, nolina, scrub live oak, ceanothus, perennial grasses.

Wildlife: No checklists are available, but the area is said to have an exceptional variety of vertebrates, more than most desert ranges. The site has the highest mule deer density in the western AZ desert and one of the few increasing bighorn sheep populations. It is considered a major area for raptors. Brown's Canyon is desert tortoise habitat.

The site offers excellent opportunities for hiking and backpacking, with little likelihood of encountering other visitors. From the peak, atmospheric conditions permitting, one can see many distant ranges, from Table Top, more than 100 mi. to the SE, to the Chemehuevis, 90 mi. to the NW. Few desert ranges combine such scenic splendor with available water and green campsites.

Hiking not recommended May–Oct., due to hot weather and scarcity of potable water.

HEADQUARTERS: BLM, Phoenix District Office, 2015 W. Deer Valley Rd., Phoenix, AZ 85027; (602) 863-4464.

HAVASU NATIONAL WILDLIFE REFUGE
U.S. Fish and Wildlife Service
35,323 acres in AZ; 7,747 acres in CA.

Along the Colorado River S of Needles, CA. Three units: Topock Marsh, N of I-40; Topock Gorge, from I-40 to Mesquite Bay on Lake Havasu; Bill Williams Unit, 10 mi. long, from the mouth of Bill Williams River near Parker Dam.

The Refuge was established in 1941 to compensate for the wildlife habitat flooded by Parker Dam. Portions of the Refuge can be visited by land, but much more of the two northern sections can be seen by boat.

At one time the Refuge included Lake Havasu. It now includes only a bit of the upper end, to a point about 3 mi. S of the gorge. On the AZ side of the gorge, the Refuge includes part of the Mohave Mountains.

Topock Marsh lies at the apex of the Mohave Valley. It is bordered on the E by a narrow buffer of desert outwash plain, on the W by the channelized Colorado River. The heart of the unit is an impounded 4,000-acre marsh, a network of open-water bays, ponds, and channels laced by vast stands of cattail and bulrush. Drier sites have thickets of willow, mesquite, salt cedar, and arrowweed. Although this marsh replaces only a fraction of the marshes and oxbow lakes destroyed by flooding and channelization, it is an important wintering area for migrating waterfowl. Great blue heron nest in mesquite snags. Bulrush stands are habitat for Yuma clapper and Virginia rails.

Those canoeing the river can decide at Needles whether to stay in the channel or visit the marsh, a trip requiring two short portages. Access to the marsh is through the 4-mi. Inlet Canal, often shallow in winter. About halfway through the marsh is Five Mile Landing, off SR 95, a concession and the only camping place on the route. Boats can be launched here and at Catfish Paradise, near the S end of the marsh, a day-use area. The marsh has numerous stubs and snags, menacing to propellers. The route through the marsh is about 13 mi., assuming no detours. Portions of the marsh are closed seasonally; the main route is open. Those who choose the river route have only a 10-mi. run to Park Moabi, a county park, 1 mi. N of the Topock bridge, where camping is available.

Topock Gorge is the last remaining free-flowing segment of the Colorado River. It extends S from the Topock bridge to Lake Havasu, a 16-mi. trip. Some enthusiasts call this the most scenic section of the Lower Colorado. Others limit this superlative to the 7 mi. of colorful rock cliffs in Mohave Canyon. The 16 mi. can be made by canoe in a day, if one starts early. There is little choice, because camping is prohibited in the gorge. Take-out is at Castle Rock, on the AZ side, unless one is continuing on through Lake Havasu, inadvisable in windy weather. Beyond the buoys marking the end of the Gorge, camping is allowed on the AZ side, except at Mesquite Bay.

The CA side of the gorge is the E edge of the Chemehuevi Mountains. The strip of desert upland on the W side of the river, generally less than 1 mi. wide, is the only land area of the Refuge in CA.

The dam has created a number of backwater bays that are good wildlife habitats. Motors are allowed on the river, and boat traffic has increased year by year since the dam was built. The strip of land along the gorge is closed to hunting. This part of the Refuge is roadless.

Bill Williams Unit, the third unit, on the delta of the Bill Williams river, is near Parker Dam at the S end of Lake Havasu. Turn SE on Planet Ranch Rd., the E boundary of the unit. The unit, 4,356 acres, includes four major habitat types: high, rocky desert with scant vegetation; mesa desert floor, with creosote bush-ocotillo association; pockets of saguaro cactus and blue palo verde; river bottomland with open water, extensive cattail marsh, and cottonwood groves. This unit has a greater variety of flora and fauna than the other two. It is best explored on foot. (See entry, Bill Williams River.)

Elevation at the river is about 500 ft. Annual precipitation is about 4 in. Rainfall occurs chiefly in early spring and later summer during violent thunderstorms.

Plants: Extensive areas of bulrush and cattail. Bottomland in the Bill Williams unit has one of the last large stands of Fremont cottonwood on the Lower Colorado. Desert plant communities include creosote bush, ocotillo, brittlebush, palo verde, saguaro, white bursage, desert lavender, desert holly. Cacti include saguaro, cholla, jumping cholla, barrel, beavertail, hedgehog. Wildflowers include phacelia, evening primrose, desert trumpet, snapdragon, globemallow, golden aster, California poppy, lupine, milkvetch, desert lily, sand verbena.

Birds: Of the 276 species recorded, 64 are known to nest on the refuge. Most are seasonal visitors. Best period to see waterfowl is Oct. to mid-Mar. Wintering snow and Canada geese usually arrive early Nov. An observation tower near the levee road in the Topock Marsh unit offers a view of geese grazing on the refuge fields. Migrating bald eagles are sometimes seen at the marsh during winter and early spring. Active rookeries of great blue heron and double-crested cormorant can be seen here between Feb. and May. Western grebe colonies are best seen in the backbays of the Gorge in summer. The Refuge is a major nesting area for the endangered Yuma clapper rail, but these solitary, secretive birds are seldom seen. Checklist available. Seasonally common or abundant species include eared, western, and pied-billed grebes; white pelican, green heron, great and snowy egrets, black-crowned night-heron, least bittern, mallard, gadwall, pintail, green-winged and cinnamon teals, American wigeon, shoveler, redhead, ring-necked duck, lesser scaup, bufflehead, ruddy duck, common and red-breasted mergansers. Also sora, common moorhen, American coot, snowy plover, spotted sandpiper, willet, greater yellowlegs, least sandpiper, long-billed dowitcher, western sandpiper, marbled godwit, avocet, black-necked stilt, Wilson's and northern phalaropes. Raptors include Cooper's, sharp-shinned, red-tailed hawks; northern harrier, American kestrel. Upland species include Gambel's quail; white-winged, mourning, and Inca doves; roadrunner, lesser nighthawk, white-throated swift, Costa's hummingbird, northern flicker, Gila and ladder-backed woodpeckers, western kingbird; ash-throated, willow, Hammond's, and western flycatchers; western wood-pewee; violet-green, tree, rough-winged, and cliff swallows. Common raven, verdin, house and rock wrens, marsh wren, black-tailed gnatcatcher, ruby-crowned kinglet, phainopepla, loggerhead shrike, starling, warbling vireo. Warblers: orange-crowned, yellow, yellow-rumped, MacGillivray's, yellowthroat, yellow-breasted chat, Wilson's. Also western meadowlark, yellow-headed and red-winged blackbirds, hooded and northern orioles, western tanager, black-headed and blue grosbeaks, house finch, Abert's towhee; savannah, black-throated, sage, Brewer's, white-crowned, Lincoln's, and song sparrows.

Mammals: Include California myotis, western pipistrel, Mexican freetail bat, blacktail jackrabbit, cottontail, antelope squirrel, roundtail ground squirrel, valley pocket gopher, pocket mice, Merriam and desert kangaroo rats, beaver, western harvest mouse; canyon, cactus, and deer mice; hispid cotton rat, whitethroat woodrat, muskrat, porcupine, coyote, kit fox, gray fox, ringtail, raccoon, badger, striped skunk, bobcat, mule deer, bighorn sheep. Also feral horse, hog, and burro.

Amphibians and reptiles: Include desert banded gecko, desert iguana, western chuckwalla; zebra-tailed, collared, long-nosed, yellow-backed spiny, desert side-blotched, western brush, tree, Mojave fringe-toed, and southern desert horned lizards. Great Basin whiptail, many-lined skink, Gila monster; spadefoot, Great Plains, red-spotted, and southwestern toads; canyon treefrog, bullfrog, leopard frog. Texas and spiny soft-shelled turtles, Sonoran and yellow mud turtles, western worm snake, desert rosy boa, glossy snake, western shovel-nosed snake, spotted night snake, California kingsnake, common whipsnake, spotted leaf-nosed snake, gopher snakes, western ground snake, desert and Mojave patch-nosed snakes, checkered garter snake, Arizona lyre snake, desert sidewinder, Mojave rattlesnake, western diamondback rattlesnake.

ACTIVITIES

Camping: In Topock Marsh, at the concession. In Gorge, on the AZ shoreline below the buoys marking the S end of the Gorge, but not in Mesquite Bay.

Hunting: In designated areas, during current seasons for the Refuge complex.

Fishing: In all waters except as posted. Largemouth and striped bass, bluegill, crappie, catfish, rainbow trout.

Boating: On all waters, except as posted. Water skiing on the river only, and not in the Gorge. Boat traffic has become so heavy at peak periods that regulations have been adopted to minimize accidents. Boaters should be aware of these before launching.

Canoeing: Mar.–Apr. is the best time to canoe the Gorge. Power boat traffic is light. Desert plants bloom. Climate is good. Powerboat traffic is heavy on summer weekends.

PUBLICATIONS (REFUGE)

Public use regulations; information; map.
Leaflet.
Partial plant list (photocopy).
Bird checklist.
Mammal list.
Fish, amphibians, and reptiles list.
Hunting information.
Fishing information.
Canoe and float trip information.

HEADQUARTERS: P.O. Box A, 1406 Bailey Ave., Needles, CA 92363; (619) 326-3853.

HUALAPAI MOUNTAIN PARK

Mohave County Parks Department
2,200 acres.

From I-40 in Kingman, Stockton Hill exit. S-bound, this becomes Hualapai Mtn. Rd. 14 mi.

Enthusiastically endorsed by our black Labrador. It had been a hot day in Kingman. Suddenly we were in a cool forest. This transition, 30 minutes from

Joshua tree desert to Canadian life zone, is not unique, but nowhere is it more dramatic. Summer and fall are the busy seasons, but on a weekday in early Oct. we were the only campers; our motor home was parked on a knoll with a tremendous view.

Elevation at Kingman is 3,340 ft., 4,984 ft. at the Park boundary. The paved road climbs steeply, with some sharp turns, but almost any RV can make it if carefully driven. Highest point within the park is 8,417 ft.

We were impressed by the park planning. Developments include picnic and camping areas, group camps, summer cabins, a recreation area with play-fields. These are fitted unobtrusively into the rugged mountain contours, and most of the park is virtually wilderness, marked only by 10 mi. of hiking trails.

Park personnel have developed plant and animal checklists. No scheduled naturalist programs, but "We are more than willing to conduct tours and hikes for campers and park users when time permits."

Annual precipitation up here is 12 to 16 in., most of it in winter and spring. Annual snowfall is 1 to 2 ft.

Camping: 70 sites, all year, weather permitting.

PUBLICATIONS
   Brochure.
   Trail map.
   Plant checklist.
   Checklist of birds, mammals, reptiles.

NEARBY: BLM's Wild Cow campground. 5 mi. beyond the park on a winding dirt road that isn't for the fainthearted or foolish.

HEADQUARTERS: Pine Lake Star Route, Kingman, AZ 86401; (602) 757-3859. For cabin reservations: Mohave County Parks, (602) 753-9141, ext. 215.

IMPERIAL NATIONAL WILDLIFE REFUGE
U.S. Fish and Wildlife Service
See entry, Cibola National Wildlife Refuge.

JOSHUA FOREST PARKWAY
Arizona State Reserve
16 road miles.

Along US 93 NW of Wickenburg, S from the Santa Maria River.

The state established this roadside reserve to safeguard the unusually dense stand of Joshua trees on both sides of the road.

It is interesting to study the relationship between the Joshua trees and another prominent species: the saguaro cactus. N of the Santa Maria River, saguaros are abundant, Joshua trees few. As the Joshuas become denser, the saguaros decrease sharply. In several places, one sees Joshua trees near the highway, saguaros on slopes a short distance away.

KOFA NATIONAL WILDLIFE REFUGE
U.S. Fish and Wildlife Service
660,000 acres.

Four access roads E from SR 95 between Yuma and Quartzsite.

A 1,000-sq.-mi. mountainous desert wilderness is no place for a casual after-noon visit. Nor is it advisable to explore the Kofa in summer, when the thermometer is likely to register 115°F. Indeed, any visit is a serious undertak-ing. A good map is necessary, but not enough; ask about current road condi-tions. Most roads are one-way trails and many require 4-wheel drive. We tried one of the access roads in our motor home and retreated from a section of soft sand.

Always carry emergency supplies, chiefly plenty of water. Two vehicles are far safer than one, but if that can't be arranged be sure someone knows where you're going and when you plan to return.

Why go? The Kofa is magnificent, unspoiled. Its primary physical features are the rugged Kofa and Castle Dome Mountains, separated by the broad King Valley. Elevations range from 680 ft. to 4,877 ft. on Signal Peak at the NW end of the Kofas. The Kofas are not a well-defined range with a ridgeline, but a huge, irregular mountain mass arising from desert plain, occupying most of the N half of the Refuge.

Average annual precipitation is only 3 to 8 in., chiefly in Dec.–Feb. and Aug.–Sept. The area has no perennial streams. Before the Refuge was estab-lished in 1939, wildlife depended on small, scattered springs and seeps. To increase carrying capacity, these natural sources have been enlarged and new waterholes blasted into the rock.

The Kofa is best known for its bighorn sheep, which inhabit the higher ground. A leaflet published in 1979 estimated their number at 250, a consider-able increase over the 1939 population. By 1982 the estimate had been raised to 700, but part of the increase was attributed to more intensive survey methods.

Plants: Vegetation on the desert flats is sparse, typical of the Sonoran Desert, dominated by creosote, with palo verde and ironwood. On higher ground and in drainages includes saguaro and other cacti, ocotillo, catclaw acacia, mesquite, Mormon tea. Scrub oak occurs in the Kofa Mountains, creating microhabitats typical of the Upper Sonoran zone.

Botanists have a special interest in the vegetation of two canyons. *Palm Canyon* is best known for its groves of native California palms, unique for AZ. This is one of the few places in the Refuge that shows signs of visitor impact. It isn't far from the highway, and it has been publicized. It's a 1/2-mi. hike beyond the parking area.

Fishtail Canyon is an established Natural Area with an exceptionally rich flora. We were asked not to give its location; people who are seriously interested can ask at HQ. It has a small stand of palms. The vegetation of both canyons is dominated by ironwood, palo verde, and catclaw. Other species include bush muhly, big galleta grass, beargrass, chorizanthe, California buckwheat, saltbush, Kofa Mountain barberry, pepper-grass, ratany, crucifixion thorn, jojoba, squawbush, and cacti.

Birds: 161 species recorded. Checklist available. Relatively few are classified as abundant or common. Birders in the Kofa seek the waterholes, which are responsible for rare sightings of great blue heron, snowy egret, white-fronted goose, American avocet, and other species seldom seen far from water.

Seasonally abundant or common: red-tailed hawk, Gambel's quail, white-winged and mourning doves, screech and elf owls, Costa's hummingbird, northern flicker, Gila and ladderbacked woodpeckers; ash-throated, willow, and western flycatchers; western wood-pewee, rock wren, mockingbird, black-tailed gnatcatcher, ruby-crowned kinglet, phainopepla, loggerhead shrike, warbling vireo. Warblers: orange-crowned, Nashville, yellow, yellow-rumped, Townsend's, MacGillivray's, Wilson's. Northern oriole, western tanager, house finch, brown towhee, black-throated and Brewer's sparrows, dark-eyed junco.

Mammals: Checklist available, include 5 bat species, desert cottontail, blacktail jackrabbit, Harris antelope squirrel, roundtail ground squirrel; Arizona, Bailey, and desert pocket mice; Merriam kangaroo rat, cactus mouse, whitethroat and desert woodrats, coyote, kit fox, gray fox, ringtail, badger, spotted skunk, bobcat.

Reptiles and amphibians: Include Couch's spadefoot; Colorado River, Great Plains, and red-spotted toads. Desert tortoise. Lizards: Gila monster, banded gecko, desert iguana, collared, leopard, chuckwalla, zebra-tailed, desert spiny, side-blotched, long-tailed brush, tree, desert horned, western whiptail. Snakes: western blind, California boa, coachwhip, western patch-nosed, gopher, glossy, long-nosed, kingsnake, spotted leaf-nosed, western ground, western shovel-nosed, southwestern lyre, night, western diamondback, Mojave and speckled rattlesnakes, sidewinder.

ACTIVITIES

Camping: One campground, Crystal Hill, near the NW corner of the area; no designated sites. Otherwise, camp anywhere except within 1/4 mi. of a waterhole. Vehicles must remain within 100 ft. of public roads.

Hunting: Limited; special rules.

PUBLICATIONS
Bird checklist.
Mammal checklist.
Public use regulations.
Hunting regulations.

REFERENCE: Ganci, Dave. *Hiking the Southwest.* San Francisco: Sierra Club
Books, 1983, pp. 153–155.

HEADQUARTERS: P.O. Box 6290, Yuma, AZ 85364; (602) 783-7861.

LA POSA PLAIN
U.S. Bureau of Land Management
Extensive area.

N and S of Quartzsite, at the intersections of I-10 and US 95.

The tiny desert crossroads town of Quartzsite has become a gathering-place
for people who sell rocks to each other. Three times a year, we were told, some
250,000 people assemble, parking their RVs in the desert outside town.
Quartzsite's main street is lined with rock shops where one can buy raw
material by the pound or expertly finished stones.

What astonished us even more was the assemblage of winter visitors—
snowbirds. We heard about this at BLM's Yuma office. So many thousands
were coming here for the winter that BLM found it necessary to designate
long-term camping areas rather than allow the entire desert to be degraded.
One of the largest areas is just S of Quartzsite. Park all winter for $25.

Many thousands do, in a section of open desert without water, washrooms,
marked campsites, or other amenities. We were there before the season, so
we couldn't observe how so many people manage to fill and dump their tanks
or even buy supplies. One convenience market owner said she has difficulty
stocking her shelves; groceries are sold almost as fast as they come off the
trucks.

The La Posa Plain has several areas of consolidated sand dunes recommended for protection as natural areas. This is the driest part of Arizona,
annual precipitation less than 5 in. Summers are blazing hot, but winters are
mild, highs normal in the upper 60s and low 70s, night lows in the 30s and
40s.

LAKE HAVASU STATE PARK
Arizona State Parks
13,072 acres.

On 25 mi. of lake shore S from Lake Havasu City.

After the raucous boat traffic on the Colorado River below Parker Dam, Lake Havasu seemed peaceful. One reason is the more limited development on the CA side, where about half of the shoreline is within the Chemehuevi Indian Reservation. The lake is long and narrow, with a surface area of about 25,000 acres. Its widest stretch is at Lake Havasu City. The city, site of transplanted London Bridge, is sprawling but not yet congested.

The Park is AZ's largest and one of its busiest, with a hotel, two restaurants, a golf course, tennis courts, water slide, shops, and huge campground. Most activity is water-based.

Three aspects of the Park make it an entry for us. Large sections of its 25-mi. shoreline are roadless, accessible only on foot or by boat; and along this shore are 250 boat-in campsites. The Park includes the Aubrey Hills Natural Area, rugged hills that form the Park's shoreline below Lake Havasu City. They are attractive for easy day hikes, with lake views and interesting mineral formations. Elevations range from 440 ft. at the lake shore to 1,700 ft. in the hills.

The park is also a convenient base for visiting nearby wildlife refuges and exploring the Bill Williams River (see entries).

Lake Havasu is frequently the summer hotspot of the nation. Temperatures of 115°F are common, 120°F or more recorded. The busy season here is Easter through Labor Day. In summer, however, there's little activity except in or on the water; it's too hot. "The backpacking/hiking potential in the park has hardly been touched," said one advisor. "The largest crowds are here when it's too hot for hiking."

Wildlife: The hills are home for 55–65 head of desert bighorn sheep. During the summer months, when inland water holes dry up, sheep are frequently seen along the shore. In addition to the desert bighorn, wildlife includes mountain lion, bobcat, coyote, mule deer, many smaller mammal species, and wintering waterfowl.

ACTIVITIES

Camping: The largest campground, with 1,250 sites, is a concession. The Park has an outlying campground with 40 sites, plus the boat-in sites. All year.

Boating: 6 ramps, 2 marinas.

Swimming: 6 beaches, 3 concession-operated.

HEADQUARTERS: 1350 W. McCulloch Blvd., Lake Havasu City, AZ 86403; (602) 855-7851.

LAKE PLEASANT REGIONAL PARK
Maricopa County Parks & Recreation Department
14,382 acres.

35 mi. NW of Phoenix. I-17 N to Carefree Highway; W to Lake Pleasant Rd.; then N.

Maricopa County's only regional park for water-based recreation. On the Agua Fria River, Upper Lake has a high-water surface of 3,500 acres. Lower Lake, a holding pool below the dam, is about a mi. long, 300 to 700 ft. wide.

The dam was built for water storage in 1927. Since then the extreme difference between high and low lake levels has been over 120 ft., although average annual drawdown in recent years has been less than 25 ft.

Elevations range from 1,400 ft. below the dam to 2,400 ft. The lake is surrounded by low, irregular desert hills with many large outcrops, including low cliffs on the lake shores. Terrain on the E side of Upper Lake is rough, roadless, described as "pseudo wilderness." Plans are to leave this undisturbed as a primitive area. Vegetation is sparse, typical of the Sonoran Desert, ironwood, palo verde, and mesquite prominent, with saguaro, ocotillo, creosote, brittlebush, Mexican gold poppy, miniature lupine, desert globemallow, barrel cactus, pricklypear.

Average annual precipitation is about 10 1/2 in. Wettest months are Dec.–Mar., but summer thunderstorms sometimes cause flash flooding. Summers are hot; the busiest months are Apr.–June. Lowest visitation time is Dec.–Jan.

INTERPRETATION
Information center on Lower Lake.
Outdoor Education Center is for groups only, by request. Comprehensive environmental program, chiefly for school classes.

ACTIVITIES
Camping: 48 sites. All year. Boat camping on shores.
Hiking, backpacking: No trails, but upland areas are open enough for off-trail hiking.
Hunting: Small game, quail, waterfowl. Special rules.
Fishing: Carp, white bass, largemouth and smallmouth bass, channel catfish, crappie, bluegill.
Boating: Ramps, marina, no hp limit on Upper Lake. Canoeing, sailing, etc., on Lower Lake; electric motors only.
Swimming: Unsupervised.

Lower Lake may be closed for a period due to dam construction.

PUBLICATIONS
Folder with map, description, regulations.
Plant list.
Mammal list.

(A bird list may be available.)
Several items pertaining to the Outdoor Education Center.

HEADQUARTERS: Box 1626, Black Canyon Stage #1, Phoenix, AZ 85029; (602) 583-8405.

LOWER COLORADO RIVER
Mixed ownerships

CA border, S of I-40.

An estimated 17 million people can reach this part of the river within half a day. It seems that most of them do. Wherever commercial development can happen, it has: motels, marinas, RV parks, and other establishments packed tight together at the water's edge. Boat traffic on the river is heavy and noisy from dawn to dusk.

BLM manages some stretches of river front. It has granted 14 commercial concessions and estimates that they attract almost a million visitor-days per year. BLM also manages a number of camp and picnic sites, also kept busy. Winter visitor camping sites are filled to capacity Nov.–Mar. Most of the state, county, and local camps and other facilities on the river are on public land leased from BLM.

Portions of the river are within the Cibola and Imperial National Wildlife Refuges. Here the shoreline remains undeveloped. Boat traffic has not been excluded, but it isn't as heavy as it is in developed areas.

No doubt there are attractive natural sites along the river, probably where the map shows no road access. Boat traffic was so heavy when we were there that we didn't care to launch our inflatable, but there must be quiet times on the river.

PUBLICATION: *The Laguna Martinez National Recreation Lands.* Leaflet. From BLM, Yuma District Office, 3150 Winsor Ave., Yuma, AZ 85364.

LUKE AIR FORCE RANGE
U.S. Air Force

SW Arizona.

This vast area has been closed to the public, except for the portion occupied by the Cabeza Prieta National Wildlife Refuge (see entry in Zone 5). We learned that consideration is being given to limited public use. Naturalists who have visited the site say it has been locked up for so long that the desert is in splendidly pristine condition.

MCDOWELL MOUNTAIN REGIONAL PARK
Maricopa County Parks & Recreation Department
21,099 acres.

E of Phoenix. E on Shea Blvd., continuing on Fountain Hills Blvd. to McDowell Mountain Park Rd.

The McDowells are a moderately low desert range rising abruptly from the desert floor. The Park is a 6-by-6-mi. square on the E side of the range. The Fort McDowell Indian Reservation is on the E, cutting a strip from the square. The Tonto National Forest boundary is 1 mi. E.

Lowest point in the Park is 1,600 ft. on the alluvial plain. Highest is 3,000 ft. along the W boundary, although the McDowells have a maximum height of 4,116 ft. Park terrain is generally sloping. Although there are no outstanding physical features within the site, its setting is pleasantly scenic.

A master plan prepared in 1967 proposed substantial development of recreation facilities. The theme, linked to the area's history, has been maintained: a desert ranch with horses and cattle. Developments include small campgrounds, 35 mi. of trails, picnic grounds, and horse staging area. Most of the site is undeveloped and will probably so remain.

Flora and fauna are typical of the Sonoran Desert. We were told checklists have been prepared, but we could not obtain copies. Species should correspond closely to nearby Estrella and White Tanks Mountain Regional Parks (see entries).

We were also told a visitor center will be built soon.

Climate is similar to that of the other Regional Parks nearby, so summer visitation is light. Most visitors come Oct.–Mar. Although visitation is increasing, visitor impact is still light to moderate.

ACTIVITIES

Camping: 1 campground. 40 sites. Sept. 1–May 30.

Hiking, backpacking: 35 mi. of trails, or off-trail.

Horse riding: On trails only.

Hunting: Small game, quail, rabbit. Special rules.

PUBLICATIONS: We were told site map, flora and fauna checklists, are available on request.

HEADQUARTERS: Maricopa County Parks & Recreation Department, 3355 W. Durango, Phoenix, AZ 85009; (602) 262-3711.

MITTRY LAKE WILDLIFE AREA
Arizona Game and Fish Department
3,575 acres.

From Yuma, E on US 95. N on Ave. 7E, 14 mi. to lake.

A pleasant undeveloped area. The lake is about 3 mi. long, irregular in shape, about 400 acres. An unpaved road follows the S shore. The lake and an associated smaller impoundment were created to help mitigate losses of fish and wildlife habitat caused by channelizing the nearby Colorado River.

The lake is fringed by bulrush, cattail, phragmites, spike rush, pondweed, widgeon grass, with cottonwood, willow, salt cedar, and mesquite on the shores. At the time of our visit, there was an extensive marshy area at the NE end. The only development is a launching ramp with parking area.

Game and Fish once had a campground, but not now. However, numerous pullouts along the shore offer pleasant informal campsites. Most visitors are local fishermen.

According to Game and Fish, migrating waterfowl reach a peak population of about 10,000, shore and marsh birds about 4,000. The endangered Yuma clapper rail breeds here regularly. Estimated populations of land areas include 5,000 dove, 500 quail, 500 rabbit, 10 deer. Many songbirds.

We launched our inflatable and spent several hours before sundown exploring; we saw a number of birds and a muskrat.

HEADQUARTERS: Game and Fish, Region IV, 3005 Pacific Ave., Yuma, AZ 85364; (602) 344-3436.

NEW WATER MOUNTAINS
U.S. Bureau of Land Management
40,375 acres.

See highway map. Between I-10 and Kofa National Wildlife Refuge. Access by Gold Nugget Road and Vicksburg Road S from I-10.

Most of the Kofa NWR has been proposed for Wilderness status. This adjacent tract would be an addition.

The New Water Mountains are a colorful, scenic, W–E string of sharp ridges, craggy spires, large rock outcroppings, steep slick-walled canyons.

Base elevations are 1,000 to 1,500 ft. High point in the mountains is 2,536 ft. Highest point in the area is Black Mesa, on the W side, 3,639 ft.

Day hiking and backpacking opportunities are provided by the many canyons, ravines, valleys, and washes. Movement within the unit is facilitated by about 20 mi. of ways, now little used by vehicles.

Annual precipitation is less than 5 in. Vegetation is sparse, creosote-bursage association. Wildlife includes desert bighorn sheep.

The site is rated outstanding for rockhounding: jasper, quartz, chrysocolla.

HEADQUARTERS: BLM, Phoenix District Office, 2015 West Deer Valley Rd., Phoenix, AZ 85027; (602) 863-4464.

PAINTED ROCKS STATE PARK
Arizona State Parks
2,690 acres.

From I-8 W of Gila Bend, exit 102; N on Painted Rock Road.

In the Green Belt (see entry) along the lower Gila River, on the flood plain. 150-acre lake. Surrounded by undisturbed desert, Lower Sonoran plant association. Includes an historic Indian petroglyph site. Good birding in season.

Camping: 60 sites, all year.

NEARBY: W of Painted Rock Road, between the river and I-8, are the Painted Rock Mountains. They're not impressive, rising to about 1,500 ft. from a base elevation of 740 ft., but they offer some variety of terrain—ridges, canyons, and washes—in a few thousand roadless acres for easy desert hikes.

HEADQUARTERS: P.O. Box 273, Star Rt. 1, Gila Bend, AZ 85337; (602) 683-2151.

PEOPLES CANYON
U.S. Bureau of Land Management
3,400 acres.

Between Kingman and Wickenburg.

We are often asked to omit a site, lest it be damaged by an increase in visitation. (Once a National Monument supervisor asked this, saying 2 million a year was all he could cope with!) Usually we comply, unless the site is already well publicized.

We were asked to omit Peoples Canyon. It is small, attractive, with a unique riparian plant community. "One of my favorite places," several of our advisors said. It has been damaged by heedless hikers. "There are trails now that weren't there three years ago," we were told.

However, it has been given enough publicity so we can't pretend it's not there. We just aren't telling its location. Those with a serious interest can inquire at the BLM office.

Access is difficult, high-clearance 4-wheel-drive only, and the area is subject to dangerous flash floods at any time of year.

HEADQUARTERS: BLM, Phoenix District Office, 2015 West Deer Valley Road, Phoenix, AZ 85027; (602) 863-4464.

PHOENIX SOUTH MOUNTAIN PARK
City of Phoenix
16,000 acres.

On the S edge of the city.

"Steep, remote trails. So wear sturdy shoes, a hat, and take a friend along. Be sure you also take enough water, a gallon a day per person minimum in warm weather." Such advice for a city park? But it is billed as the world's largest municipal park, and most of it is mountainous wilderness with remote canyons. 40 miles of trails. Handsome desert vegetation: saguaro, ocotillo, etc. Unique, admirable, but don't expect to be alone.

PRESCOTT NATIONAL FOREST
U.S. Forest Service
1,250,613 acres; 1,407,528 acres within boundaries.

Two large blocks. (1) The W half is shaped like the figure 8, with the city of Prescott near its center, where it is crossed by US 89. (2) The E half is crossed by I-17. US 89 cuts across its N tip. Alt. US 89 also crosses the E half, from Prescott to Flagstaff.

The two blocks of the Forest are on parallel mountain ranges trending NW–SE, separated by the Chino and Agua Fria valleys. The W half is on the Santa Maria, Juniper, Sierra Prieta, and Bradshaw mountains, the E half on the Black Hills, Mingus Mountain, and Black Mesa. The ranges are not high, their crests below 8,000 ft. Elevations of the surrounding desert are generally 3,000 to 4,500 ft.

The W block has many scattered inholdings and is surrounded by a mix of state and private lands. The E block adjoins the Kaibab and Coconino National Forests on the N and E, the Tonto National Forest on the S. The valleys between the blocks have fast-growing communities and subdivisions.

The climate is generally mild. Depending on elevation, summer days are warm to hot, nights cool to warm. Winters are moderate. Snow seldom lasts more than a few days even on the upper slopes. Annual precipitation is about 6 in. at base elevations, up to 25 in. above.

Climate and accessibility attract visitors all year. Current annual recreational use is about a million visitor-days, about half of this at developed recreation sites. Dispersed recreation is increasing as developed sites become crowded.

Developed recreation areas are clustered near Prescott and to the NE along US 89. Water-based recreation is popular at Lynx Lake, Granite Basin Lake, Horsethief Reservoir, and along the Verde River. Lynx, largest of the lakes, is only 55 acres.

The Forest has a network of roads, some paved or all-weather, others suitable for high-clearance or 4-wheel-drive vehicles. Visitors should not rely on the Forest map as a guide to road conditions. Dense clusters of primitive roads, such as those S of Prescott, are signs of past mining activity. Some of these roads have been abandoned. Throughout the Forest, some roads are deteriorating for lack of maintenance funds.

When we began gathering data, the Forest had only two relatively small Wildernesses. While we were on our last field trip, Congress passed the Arizona Wilderness Act, adding 6 new Wildernesses, bringing the total Wilderness acreage to 104,382.

Although more and more people come to the Forest for recreation, operating funds have been cut. Some of the effects are conspicuous. Trail maintenance has virtually ceased except for the efforts of volunteers. At one time 14 maintenance workers serviced the Forest campgrounds. In 1984 there were two. Wilderness areas are legally closed to motor vehicles, but some ORV operators ignore signs and regulations, and enforcement manpower is lacking.

Plants: About 110,000 acres, less than 10% of the total acreage, is in conifers, such as ponderosa pine, about 640,000 acres in pinyon-juniper, much of which was grassland before cattle came. The Forest has no remaining old-growth stands. Principal plant associations are as follows:

Sonoran Desert scrub, below 3,000 ft. elevation. Cacti, yuccas, agaves, grasses, herbs, drought-resistant trees and shrubs.

Grasslands, from 3,000 to 5,000 ft. Annual precipitation about 11 in. Shortgrasses with scattered yuccas, agaves, cacti.

Chaparral, from 4,000 to 6,000 ft. Annual precipitation about 15 in. Generally dense evergreen shrubs, to 10 ft. tall.

Woodland, from 5,000 to 7,000 ft. Annual precipitation about 17 in. Pinyon pine, juniper, and oak, with understory of grasses.

Evergreen forest, above 6,000 ft. Conifers, ponderosa pine dominant, fir at the highest elevations.

In summer, of course, many visitors seek the coolest areas for hiking and camping: the high country where the conifers grow.

Flowering species include filaree, mustards, owl-clover, lupine, penstemons, fairy duster, Indian paintbrush, skyrocket, evening primrose, poppies, cacti. Peak blooming season is late Mar.–early May. No checklist.

Birds: Checklist of 248 species available. Forest publications include *A Campground Guide to the Most Common Birds of the Area,* describing turkey vulture, red-tailed and sharp-shinned hawks, mourning dove, band-tailed pigeon, common nighthawk, Bullock's oriole, hepatic tanager, black-headed grosbeak, house finch, white-crowned sparrow, brown towhee, violet-green swallow, rufous and black-chinned hummingbirds, northern flicker, acorn woodpecker, mockingbird, American robin, western bluebird, common raven, house sparrow, western kingbird, Say's phoebe, Steller's and Mexican jays, white-breasted nuthatch.

Also common, according to the checklist: eared grebe, great blue heron, American kestrel, Gambel's quail, American coot, great horned owl, broad-tailed hummingbird, vermilion flycatcher, black phoebe, western wood-pewee, horned lark, scrub jay, mountain chickadee, house wren, European starling, solitary and warbling vireos, yellow-rumped and Grace's warblers, Brewer's blackbird, rufous-sided and Abert's towhees, lark bunting, chipping and white-crowned sparrows, dark-eyed and gray-headed juncos.

The Forest issues another mimeographed publication, *Birds of Arizona,* which lists birds typical of various habitats.

Mammals: Checklist of 71 species available. Common species include: bats: Brazilian freetail, hoary, silver-haired, western pipistrel, pallid, Townsend's big-eared, big brown, cave myotis, little brown myotis, Yuma myotis, long-eared myotis, long-legged myotis, California myotis, small-footed myotis, fringed myotis. Desert cottontail, rock squirrel, cliff chipmunk, valley pocket gopher, silky pocket mouse; brush, cactus, deer, pinyon, and house mice; Stephens woodrat, coyote, striped skunk, mule deer.

Reptiles and amphibians: Checklist of 63 species available. Common species include eastern fence, short-horned, and side-blotched lizards. Black-tailed rattlesnake, common and Sonoran mountain kingsnakes, gopher snake. Canyon treefrog, chorus frog, northern leopard frog, tiger salamander, western spadefoot toad, Woodhouse's toad.

FEATURES

The Sycamore Canyon and Pine Mountain Wildernesses were well known to hikers before the 1984 Wilderness Act. The newer ones have had fewer visitors.

Sycamore Canyon Wilderness, 25,870 acres in the Prescott NF, 36,305 adjacent acres in the Coconino and Kaibab NF. The Canyon is at the Prescott NF boundary, SW of Flagstaff. The 21-mi.-long canyon has been carved deep into the Colorado Plateau. The widest point is 7 mi. from rim to rim. Deep gorges, high cliffs, spectacular formations of red and white sedimentary rock. Habitats range from cactus and mesquite at 3,600 ft. elevation in the S portion to Douglas-fir and ponderosa pine at 7,000 ft. on the N rim.

Access is from trailheads on primitive Forest roads. Trailheads for the N and central portions are in the Coconino NF, but the area is shown on the Prescott forest map. Two trailheads are in the Prescott NF: Sycamore Basin, on Forest Road 181, and Packard, where Sycamore Creek joins the Verde River. Ask about road conditions.

Hiking in summer is not recommended; daytime temperatures often exceed 100°F. Apr. through June and Sept. to mid-Nov. are best. Visitors must carry their own water; the canyon has few springs. Horses require supplemental feed.

A small area at the S end of the canyon is closed to overnight camping.

Pine Mountain Wilderness, 8,761 acres in the Prescott NF, 11,301 acres in the Tonto NF. About 65 mi. N of Phoenix. Pine Mountain, 6,814 ft., is the highest point on the Verde Rim, which bisects the area NE–SW. The Wilderness has a small island of tall timber, chiefly ponderosa pine and Douglas-fir. The S portion slopes down sharply toward the Verde River. Moderately steep, rocky slopes. Mesas covered by pinyon-juniper are separated by deep, rugged canyons. Fine views from the Rim, overlooking the Verde River and desert. Wildlife includes mule deer, whitetail deer, black bear, mountain lion, javelina.

Trailheads on the Prescott NF side are at Nelson Place Spring on Forest Road 68 and Hidden Spring on Forest Road 677A. Ask about road conditions.

At this elevation, summer hiking is feasible, though days can be hot. Visitors must carry water; the area has few springs. Horses require supplemental feed.

Castle Creek Wilderness, 25,125 acres. Access is from Mayer, on SR 69, W on Crown King Road. Ask for guidance at HQ or a Ranger District; as of 1985 no Wilderness map was available. The area is at the SE end of the

Bradshaw Mountains. Elevations from 2,800 ft. at the SE corner to 7,000 ft. on Juniper Ridge. Several trails cross the area. Terrain is rugged, steep; elevation changes of 1,000 ft. in 3/4-mi. are not uncommon. There has been little trail maintenance.

Apache Creek Wilderness, 5,498 acres. About 34 mi. NW of Prescott, at the N end of the Santa Maria Mountains, just S and W of inholdings in the Walnut Creek drainage; bounded by Forest roads. Rolling hills, with elevations from 5,200 to 6,900 ft. Mostly pinyon-juniper association. No mapped trails.

Granite Mountain Wilderness, 9,825 acres. About 8 mi. NW of Prescott. Easy access by Granite Basin Road, paved, to Granite Basin Campground. Granite Mountain is an isolated, rugged, boulder-strewn mountain, rising from 5,000 to 7,600 ft. elevation. The SW side is a vertical cliff popular with climbers. Terrain and chaparral vegetation make foot travel difficult. A popular trail goes to the top.

Juniper Mesa Wilderness, 7,554 acres. In the NW sector of the W half of the Forest. The state highway map shows a county road NW of Prescott crossing the Forest from Simmons to the Luis Maria Baca Grant. The Wilderness is N of this road, on the Forest boundary. On the S end of the Juniper Range. An E–W escarpment breaks to steep canyons and rolling hills to the N, drops abruptly to the S. Elevations from 5,650 to 7,050 ft. Recreational use of the area has been small, a few hundred visitors a year, chiefly hunters and—before Wilderness designation—ORV operators.

Cedar Bench Wilderness, 15,999 acres, and *Woodchute Wilderness,* 5,750 acres, were also added. We were unable to obtain descriptions in time to include them here.

Thumb Butte, 1 1/2 mi. W of downtown Prescott, is a volcanic plug rising to 6,522 ft. Near the Thumb Butte picnic site. A 2 1/2 mi. trail to the top. Fine views.

Senator Highway, Forest Road 52 S from Prescott, is a scenic route, unpaved, rough, with many hills and curves, through an area of the Forest that once had many active mines. It leads to *Crown King,* an old mining town kept alive by tourism. This is one of the popular recreation areas of the Forest, with three nearby campgrounds, trails, Horsethief Lake.

Lynx Lake, about 3 mi. SE of Prescott, largest in the Forest, is only 55 acres, but it's popular. The fishing is just as good as the most recent stocking.

Mount Union, 7,979 ft., is the highest point in the Bradshaw Mountains, reachable by car from the Senator Highway. Ask about road conditions. One appreciative writer declared, "There is probably no better place in all Arizona to appreciate its infinite spaces and comprehend its heritage."

Verde River is the Forest's principal perennial stream. It flows from Big Chino Valley N of Prescott, enters the E half of the Forest near Paulden, continues S, becomes the boundary between the Prescott and Coconino National Forests, finally joins the Salt River E of Phoenix. In 1984 much of the river, including 28 mi. within the Prescott NF, was given protection as a Wild and Scenic River. Portions of the river can be rafted at times, beginning at Camp Verde. Usual season is Mar.–Apr.

INTERPRETATION
   The Forest has no naturalist programs except for occasional campfire talks in summer.
   A *nature trail* at Groom Creek, 1,500 ft., has been adapted for handicapped and blind visitors.

ACTIVITIES
   Camping: 15 campgrounds, 380 sites. Official season for most is May–Oct. or Apr.–Nov. Three are open all year. Informal camping almost anywhere.
   Hiking, backpacking: 320 mi. of mapped trails. Trail guides available. A few trails are popular, heavily used at times. Trail maintenance depends almost entirely on volunteers. Some trails are in poor condition. Some unmaintained Forest Roads are suitable hiking routes. Ask HQ or a Ranger District for advice on destinations and trail conditions.
   Horse riding: Most trails are suitable. Local stables are available. Consult District Office for rules governing horse travel.
   Hunting: Deer, antelope, javelina, turkey, quail.
   Fishing: Trout in Lynx Lake and Sycamore Creek. Catfish, carp, and bluegill in Verde River and Granite Basin Lake.
   Boating: Largest lake is 55 acres. Rentals at Lynx Lake; electric motors only.
   Rafting, kayaking: Verde River.

PUBLICATIONS
   Forest map. $1.
   Trail guides:
      Bradshaw R.D.
      Chino Valley R.D.
      Crown King area.
   A Campground Guide to the Most Common Birds of the Area.
   Checklist of vertebrate species.
   Sycamore Canyon Wilderness leaflet with small map.
   Pine Mountain Wilderness leaflet with small map.
   Animal Tales. Leaflet, animals and their habitats.
   River Runners Guide to the Verde River.

REFERENCE: Ganci, Dave. *Hiking the Southwest.* San Francisco: Sierra Club Books, 1983, pp. 83–99.

HEADQUARTERS: 344 S. Cortez, Prescott, AZ 86301; (602) 445-1762.

RANGER DISTRICTS: Bradshaw R.D., RFD 7, Box 3451, Prescott, AZ 86301; (602) 445-7253. Verde R.D., Star Rt. 1, Box 1100, Camp Verde, AZ 86322; (602) 567-4121. Chino Valley R.D., P.O. Box 485, Chino Valley, AZ 86323; (602) 636-2302.

ROBBINS BUTTE
Arizona Game and Fish Department
1,440 acres.

From Buckeye, 31 mi. W of downtown Phoenix, W on SR 85 (US 80 on some maps). Where 85 turns S, continue about 3 mi. Robbins Butte is on the right.

The butte, 1,162 ft. elevation, overlooks the Gila River flood plain. From here to the Colorado River, the Gila is a braided stream, meandering through a wide sandy wash. It is often dry.

Soon after the Department began its nongame program, Robbins Butte was chosen as a demonstration site. The mesquite thickets provide ample cover for wildlife, and cottonwoods have been replanted in a habitat restoration project. "It's our best site along the Gila River for nonconsumptive use," we were told. When we visited, plans were still shaping. It was hoped that nature trails would be in place by 1986.

Winter birding for finches and hawks is excellent.

WITHIN: Green Belt Resource Conservation Area (see entry).

TONTO NATIONAL FOREST
U.S. Forest Service
See entry in Zone 4.

TUZIGOOT NATIONAL MONUMENT
National Park Service
849 acres.

Near Clarkdale on US 89 Alt.

We visited the ruins of this large prehistoric Indian pueblo and were surprised to be shown a bird checklist. The Monument's theme is archeological: the gathering, living, and departure of the Sinagua Indians. They were attracted here by the waters of the Verde River, and it is the river valley that attracts so many birds. The list was compiled at the Monument and at nearby Tavasci Marsh and Peck's Lake. It is also applicable to Montezuma Castle National Monument, Montezuma Well, Dead Horse Ranch State Park, and similar habitats in the valley.

Camping at nearby Dead Horse Ranch SP (see entry).

PUBLICATIONS
Bird checklist. Being reprinted, will sell for $0.15.

HEADQUARTERS: P.O. Box 68, Clarkdale, AZ 86324; (602) 634-5564.

WABAYUMA PEAK
U.S. Bureau of Land Management
37,450 acres.

From milepost 36 on I-40 S of Kingman, E on Walnut Creek Road.

This roadless area is in the Hualapai Mountains, about 5 air mi. SW of Hualapai Mountain Park (see entry). A BLM map shows a tangle of primitive roads in the area between, but for hiking this rugged country compass and topo map are necessities, and we'd suggest a talk with someone at the BLM office who knows the terrain.

Access from the W is straightforward. Wabayuma Peak, 7,601 ft., rises 5,000 ft. in 5 miles. On the steep slopes are five life zones: Sonoran and Mohave desert scrub below 3,500 ft., chaparral and pinyon-juniper from 3,500 to 7,000 ft., ponderosa pine and Gambel oak above 7,000 ft. This is the northernmost site with saguaro cactus. Many wildflowers, blooming seasons extending through summer.

Massive ridges extend W and S from the peak, with outcroppings, spires, and crags, dropping down steeply into canyons. A large basin is at the upper end of Willow Creek.

The site has no perennial streams. Numerous springs, most of them developed in the past for cattle or mining. Numerous vehicle tracks, most now unused and revegetating, but possible hiking routes.

HEADQUARTERS: BLM, Kingman Resource Area, 2475 Beverly Ave., Kingman, AZ 86401; (602) 757-3161.

WHITE TANK MOUNTAINS REGIONAL PARK
Maricopa County Parks & Recreation Department
26,337 acres.

25 mi. W of downtown Phoenix. From Glendale, 15 mi. W on Olive Ave.

Largest Maricopa County park. The mountains are a N–S range about 7 mi. long, separating the Phoenix basin of the Salt River Valley from the Hassayampa Plain. Highest point in the range is 4,083 ft., lowest within the park 1,402 ft. From the E and N boundaries, alluvial slopes rise gently to the foot of the mountains. From this base, the mountain rises sharply; the upper area has irregular rocky ridges and deep canyons. This upper terrain is so difficult that cattlemen had to construct horse trails up the E side. Later two jeep tracks were built on the N side, one to serve a radio beacon. The county has a developed trail system that now includes more than 15 mi.

Annual rainfall is scanty: light winter rains and summer thunderstorms. An occasional torrential summer storm sends flash floods sweeping down canyons, scouring depressions—"tanks"—in white granite rock below. Some of these tanks hold water most of the year. Although the 2,600-ft. rise in elevation means it's significantly cooler on top, summer use of the park is light.

Vegetation on the upper slopes is sparse: grasses, shrubs, cacti, stunted palo verde. Mesquite, willow, and ironwood occur in canyon bottoms. Although this flora seems typical of desert ranges, botanists see much to interest them here. One, in a 2-year study, identified 332 plant species, including one not previously known in AZ, in five distinct life zones. In part because of this work, a site within the Park has been proposed as a Scientific Natural Area.

Preliminary wildlife assessments have identified 40 birds species, 12 mammal species, and 5 reptile species within the Park. These lists will undoubtedly grow.

Development includes a 260-unit picnic area, rest rooms, and campgrounds. Most of the Park is accessible only on foot or horseback.

ACTIVITIES

Camping: 2 campgrounds; 15 tent units, 40 family. Reservations needed in motor home area only.

Hiking, backpacking: Hikers planning to camp backcountry are asked to notify a ranger.

Hunting: Dove, quail, rabbit, mule deer.

Horse riding: 15 mi. of rough trails.

PUBLICATIONS
Site map with regulations.
Road and trail map.

HEADQUARTERS: Maricopa County Parks & Recreation Department, 3355 West Durango, Phoenix, AZ 85009; (602) 262-3711.

ZONE 4

1 Coconino National Forest
2 Oak Creek Canyon
3 Walnut Canyon National Monument
4 Chevelon Creek Wildlife Area
5 Petrified Forest National Park
6 Apache-Sitgreaves National Forest
7 Lyman Lake State Park
8 Tonto Natural Bridge
9 Tonto National Forest
10 Tonto National Monument
11 Fort Apache Indian Reservation
12 Salt River Canyon
13 Lost Dutchman State Park
14 Boyce Thompson Southwestern Arboretum
15 White Canyon
16 Mescal Mountains
17 San Carlos Lake
18 Aravaipa Canyon
19 Gila Mountains
20 Cluff Ranch Wildlife Area
21 Gila Box; Turtle Mountain
22 Javelina Peak; San Simon Valley
23 Table Top Mountain
24 Picacho Peak State Park
25 Peloncillo Mountains

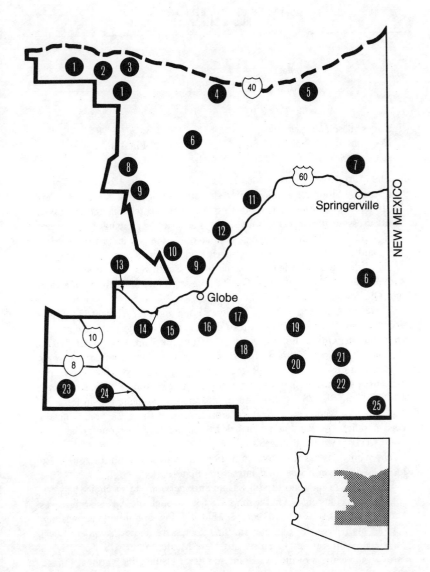

ZONE 4

Includes these counties:
Coconino (S of I-40)   Graham   Pinal
Apache (S of I-40)   Navajo (S of I-40)   Greenlee

The central two-thirds of the zone is occupied by the Coconino, Tonto, and Apache-Sitgreaves National Forests and the Fort Apache and San Carlos Indian Reservations. Most of this is mountainous terrain, and the paved roads crossing it are scenic routes, not speedways. It includes the largest part of the world's largest ponderosa pine forest, the two largest all-Arizona lakes and numerous smaller ones, several rivers and streams, and extensive areas of desert. It also includes some of the Southwest's most spectacular canyons, among them Walnut, Oak Creek, Aravaipa, Salt River, Gila Box, and Chevelon.

The zone is divided by the Mogollon Rim, a giant escarpment more than 200 mi. long, where the high plateau drops abruptly to desert. It's best seen from the air. Only a few roads descend from the Rim. One is Alt. US 89 through Oak Creek Canyon, but here one is more aware of the canyon's unique features. SR 87 and SR 260, converging at Payson, both make the descent, giving the Payson Chamber of Commerce claim to "Rim Country." US 60 S from Show Low drops down into the Fort Apache Indian Reservation and, as a second scenic feature, crosses the Salt River Canyon. No main road parallels the Rim, above or below, and much of the country between main roads is wild and rugged.

Three portions of the Coronado National Forest are within the zone. Also included are several small but interesting State Parks.

In the far E of the zone, driving S from Springerville offers a choice between splendidly scenic routes. On the map, US 666 through the Apache-Sitgreaves National Forest seems the direct way, but it's slow, mountainous, twisting, and its high passes are among the first to receive snow in winter. Local travelers say it's faster to cross into New Mexico along US 180, drive S through the canyon of the San Francisco River in the Gila National Forest, then—if your destination is in Arizona—turn W on SR 78, through Cold Creek Canyon.

APACHE-SITGREAVES NATIONAL FOREST
U.S. Forest Service
2,004,819 acres in AZ; acreage in NM administered by Gila NF.

Two connected parts: (1) W of Springerville, on the Mogollon Plateau; crossed by SR's 260, 277, 77, US 60. (2) S of Springerville, along the NM border; crossed by US 666.

Strangers, thinking of Arizona as desert, are surprised to find here the world's largest ponderosa pine forest. Much of it is within this picturesque National Forest. They may be surprised, too, to learn that one of the principal recreational activities here is fishing, with more than 20 lakes and streams, numerous streams and rivers.

The Forest produces timber. Logging requires road building. When the Wilderness Act mandated a search for roadless areas, the yield in this National Forest was small. One of our advisors said "You can't hike a quarter-mile without hitting a road." Many of these are old roads that are no longer needed. Management would like to obliterate them by revegetating. Budgets are restrictive, however, so the best that can be done is to close them and let nature take over. Far fewer roads are in the S sector.

The area W of Springerville is on the Mogollon Plateau. From about 6,000 ft. elevation at the N boundary, the land slopes gradually up to about 7,000 ft. at the Rim, with a few parks reaching nearly 8,000 ft. The area is best known for its scenic drives and many lakes. Towns such as Lakeside, Pinetop, and Show Low, inholdings within the Forest boundaries, are popular resort areas. Many Arizonans come here in summer to escape the desert heat at lower elevations. This, the smaller portion of the Forest, attracts the majority of visitors.

Summer camping is a major activity, and some areas, notably around Woods Canyon Lake near the Rim, are heavily impacted. "We don't know what to do with them all," we were told, "so they camp anywhere. The campgrounds are usually full in summer." Crowds can be expected at any campsite on the plateau, especially near a lake. The season ends abruptly. When we visited in early Oct., the weather was fine but all campgrounds were closed.

Don't drive on US 666 if you're in a hurry. A fine scenic route, it's narrow and crooked, closed to rigs over 35 ft. The portion of the Forest S of Springerville has much greater topographic variety than the W part. Much of it is rugged and mountainous. Mt. Baldy, 11,590 ft., is the second highest peak in Arizona. Escudilla Mountain is 10,912 ft. Numerous other peaks are above 8,000 ft. The area is carved by numerous streams, seasonal and perennial, many of them tributary to the Blue River, which runs S through the area, and the San Francisco, which cuts across in the S. It includes alpine tundra, forested slopes, deep canyons, lakes, wet meadows, desert scrub.

The Forest has over 800 mi. of trails, most of them in the S portion. Few trails have been developed above the Rim, although construction of a scenic

Rim Trail has often been suggested. Fewer roads crisscross this area, and there are more opportunities for hiking trips of several days. Few of these trails are heavily used. There's not much backpacking, we were told, although some increase has been noticed in the past few years. Forest managers are concerned that the upturn in dispersed recreation may reverse as trails continue to deteriorate for lack of maintenance. Trail washouts caused by storms the previous year had not been repaired.

The high country collects enough winter snow for ski touring and snowmobiling, and these are becoming more popular. At the time of our visit, the Forest was considering a permit application from an entrepreneur who proposed to rent ski equipment and groom trails.

Horse riding is popular, both for hunting and horsepacking. Several outfitters offer services. Forest HQ will supply a list of the authorized outfitters who meet standards, including insurance. Bootleg outfitters also operate.

Wildlife: The diversity of habitats is reflected in diversity of fauna: 242 bird species, 94 mammal, 47 reptile and amphibian, 28 fish. No checklists are available, but the general guides to Arizona fauna should suffice. This is not an area where one expects to see the unusual species that occur near the Mexican border.

FEATURES

Mt. Baldy Wilderness, 7,079 acres. SW of Springerville, the Wilderness projects into the Fort Apache Indian Reservation. The peak of Mt. Baldy, an extinct volcano rising to 11,403 ft., is within the Reservation. Average annual precipitation in the high country is 45 in., half of this falling as snow. Severe thunderstorms are common in July–Aug.

A loop trail of 14 mi. can be used by hikers or horse riders. Trailside camping is permitted, but group size is limited to 5.

The last half-mi. to the top has been legally closed by the Apache Tribe, and trespassers are subject to arrest by tribal police.

Bear Wallow Wilderness, 11,080 acres, about 20 mi. SW of Alpine, bordering the Reservation. Access from US 666 via Forest Road 25. The KP Cienega campground is nearby. The S boundary follows the Mogollon Rim. Elevations 8,000 to 9,000 ft. Bear Wallow Creek cuts across the area from E to W, a broad, rugged canyon with numerous side canyons. Rolling terrain between the side canyons and the Rim. Mixed conifers on N-facing slopes and in canyon bottoms; ponderosa pine on S- and W-facing slopes and on most of the S area; riparian vegetation in the creek bottom. Small stands of Douglas-fir and aspen. A scenic area, attractive for camping, hiking, hunting, fishing. A system trail follows the creek. Visitation is estimated to be 800 to 1,000 visitor-days per year.

Blue Range Primitive Area, 173,762 acres. For backcountry adventures, this is the place to look. The "primitive area" designation is becoming obsolete but is still used. Definition: "administered in the same manner as Wilderness pending studies to determine suitability as a component of the Wilderness System." The area lies between US 666 and the New Mexico border, both N and S of the Rim. Elevations from 5,000 ft. to 9,094 ft. The scenic Blue River cuts through the center. Most drainage is to the Blue River through small canyons. The Forest map shows several trails. *Arizona Trails,* listed below, describes the best of them. We suggest consulting HQ or a Ranger District before undertaking more than a day hike.

Escudilla Mountain Wilderness Area, 5,200 acres, about 15 mi. S of Springerville near the New Mexico border. Access from US 666 and Forest Roads 56 and 275. The central feature is 10,912-ft. Escudilla Peak, third highest in Arizona, a landmark. The area is ringed by steep slopes with a number of talus slides. Most drainage is to the Little Colorado River. There are no perennial streams within the site. Aspen covers 40% of the area, a product of a great fire in 1953. At the top, on the lee side, are spruce-fir stands, covering more than a third of the area. Smaller areas of ponderosa pine and grasslands.

A lookout tower is on top. It was once serviced by a primitive road, but the road is closed and naturalizing. A National Recreation Trail ascends to the top, about a 3-mi. hike from trailhead on FR 56. Trail use is about 1,100 visitor-days per year. Views from the top are the chief attraction.

San Francisco River, 22 river mi. The river enters from New Mexico, crosses the S end of the Forest, then turns S to Clifton. The Blue River joins it midway through the Forest. For about 7 mi. W from the NM border, the river flows in a narrow, steep-walled canyon. There is no access to this section except on the canyon floor. For the next 15 mi., the canyon bottom is wider. The river bed is 200–500 ft. wide, with bordering benches. Access is by Forest Road 212, which comes up the flood plain from Clifton. It can be driven only in the dry season and usually requires 4-wheel drive. It fords the river more than 40 times.

Decades of overgrazing the surrounding area have caused frequent floods, washing away much of the riparian vegetation. Conservationists warn that vehicles are disturbing both avian and aquatic habitats. Wilderness status would bar vehicles, and a 25,560-acre area in NM and AZ was proposed for Wilderness status. It was not included in the Arizona Wilderness Act, and a field task force under the leadership of the Forest Service recommended that the river should not be protected under the Wild and Scenic Rivers Act.

Hiking the river requires frequent wading; horse travel is more popular. Rafting is possible for about one month. Summer swimming is possible in pools. Fishing is poor.

Lakes. The *Recreation Opportunities* pamphlet lists 20 fishing lakes and reservoirs, 6 of them on the Mogollon Plateau W of Springerville, the others within the 20 mi. S of Springerville. Largest is 575-acre Big Lake, SW of Springerville. On the Plateau, largest is 208-acre Chevelon Canyon Lake. Campgrounds are at 4 of the lakes, within a few miles of most others. Elevations range from 6,300 ft. to 9,200 ft. at White Mountain Reservoir. Two smallest lakes are 5 acres each. Campgrounds at or near lakes are often full. *Pintail Lake* is a 300-acre State Waterfowl Habitat Area, 4 1/2 mi. NE of Show Low. Treated sewage effluent from Show Low has been used to create a marsh ecosystem for waterfowl and shorebirds. The Forest made land available and built the dikes and other structures. Construction was completed in 1979. The site has attracted 1,000 to 3,000 wintering ducks and 500 to 1,000 migrating shorebirds, with some nesting pairs, as well as many raptors and perching birds. Resident or transient mammals include rabbit, coyote, fox, javelina, bobcat, mountain lion, bear, mule deer, elk, pronghorn. A path from the parking lot leads to an observation deck. The Arizona Game and Fish Department has plans for an outdoor education building.

INTERPRETATION
Visitor center at Big Lake.

Evening programs, guided hikes, and other naturalist programs have been offered at several campgrounds. Budget cuts are eliminating these in many National Forests.

Nature trails: Mogollon Rim, 2 mi. N of Lakeside. Blue Vista Overlook, on US 666, 33 mi. S of Alpine.

ACTIVITIES
Camping: 34 campgrounds, 773 sites. None are open all year and published opening and closing dates may not be accurate; some campgrounds once open through Oct. now close in Sept.

Hiking, backpacking: Over 800 mi. of trails. Condition of many, we were told, is "on the high side of poor."

Hunting: Deer, elk, pronghorn, bear, lion, javelina, turkey, ducks.

Fishing: Chiefly trout, stocked, in lakes. Some streams also stocked. White Mountain Reservoir is a good fishery in years when snow is plentiful, but sometimes dries up in summer.

Boating: Lakes. *Electric motors only on smaller lakes, 8 hp limit on the larger ones.*

Swimming: Cold water and lack of beaches make lake swimming unsafe.
Ski touring: In the high country. 3-month season.

PUBLICATIONS
Forest map. $1.
Mt. Baldy Wilderness map. $1.
Recreational opportunities pamphlet.
The Rim Lakes. Folder.

REFERENCES
Ganci, Dave. *Hiking the Southwest.* San Francisco: Sierra Club Books, 1983, pp. 113–117.
Mazel, David. *Arizona Trails.* Berkeley, CA: Wilderness Press, 1981, pp. 179–224. (Best available trail guide to the Blue Range Primitive Area.)

HEADQUARTERS: Box 640, Springerville, AZ 85938; (602) 333-4301.

RANGER DISTRICTS: Chevelon R.D., HC-62, Box 100, Winslow, AZ 86047; (602) 289-2471. Heber R.D., Box 168, Overgaard, AZ 85933; (602) 535-4481. Pinedale R.D., Box 778, Snowflake, AZ 85937; (602) 536-7186. Lakeside R.D., Box 488, Lakeside, AZ 85929; (602) 336-2321. Alpine R.D., Box 469, Alpine, AZ 85920; (602) 339-4384. Springerville R.D., Box 640, Springerville, AZ 85938; (602) 333-4372. Clifton R.D., Box 698, Clifton, AZ 85533; (602) 865-2432.

ARAVAIPA CANYON
U.S. Bureau of Land Management
6,670 acres.

> W entrance: From Winkelman, S of Globe, 11 mi. S on SR 77. E on Aravaipa Canyon Rd., well marked; 13 mi. of paved and maintained gravel road. E entrance: From Safford, 15 mi. NW on US 70, then 45 mi. W on Klondyke Rd., graded dirt.

Former Interior Secretary James Watt called it "an outstanding natural area; a gem of the southwestern desert," recommending the canyon for Wilderness status. Senator Goldwater introduced the legislation and spoke at the dedication, calling it "a sparkling gem of the southwestern desert." Almost every natural history magazine has carried an article about Aravaipa, each writer seeking adequate words: "this belle of southern canyons," "incredible scenic beauty and biological treasures."

Few areas are as well protected. Aravaipa's popularity began in the 1950s, and within a decade the 11-mi.-long canyon was showing signs of overuse. BLM declared it a Primitive Area in 1969 and began restricting use in 1973. Today the limits are strict: No more than 50 people can be in the area at one time. Their permits are good for up to 3 days, 2 nights. Reservations can be made up to 6 months in advance; weekends and holidays are quickly booked. Reservations made over one month in advance must be confirmed 15 to 30 days ahead. Annual visitation is now about 2,800.

Any bit of water in the desert is fascinating. Aravaipa Creek is a perennial stream fed by both perennial and intermittent streams, perennial springs, and seeps. The canyon, narrow and twisting, cuts through the Galiuro Mountains from Aravaipa Valley to San Pedro Valley. Elevation at the canyon floor is 3,060 ft. at the E end, 2,640 ft. at the W end. The multicolored canyon walls are up to 1,000 ft. high.

In places the canyon is so narrow hikers must wade, walls rising vertically from the stream edge. More often the canyon floor is wider, a riparian woodland. Even here the hiker may have to cross the stream repeatedly as it meanders. Side canyons offer routes to the rim. In these side canyons, saguaros and other desert flora grow within a few feet of moisture-loving trees and shrubs.

Annual precipitation is about 15 in., with summer and winter rainy seasons. Summer storms are usually short and intense, sometimes producing flash floods that can threaten visitors. A high-water mark has been observed on the canyon walls 39 ft. above normal stream level.

High walls, stream, and vegetation maintain a climate cooler and more humid than that of the surrounding desert. Even so, daily temperature variations are about 40°F. From mid-May to mid-Oct., daily highs commonly exceed 100°. Thus peak visitation is in two seasons: Mar.–May, Oct.–Nov. Winter visitation is moderate, summer light. Summer and winter are the only seasons when one might get in without a reservation made long before.

Plants: The canyon has some of the richest riparian habitat in southern AZ. The riparian community is lushly green, dominated by cottonwood, sycamore, ash, willow, netleaf hackberry, walnut, and mesquite. Above the riparian zone, the desert trees and shrubs include saguaro, palo verde, white-thorn and catclaw acacias, false and honey mesquite, ratany, jojoba. Saguaro and other cacti grow on rocky ledges. Canyon rims have woodland and chaparral species including single-needle pinyon, one-seed juniper, beargrass, Palmer's agave, Palmer's oak, netleaf hackberry, barberry, red-berry buckthorn.

Birds: Checklist of 238 species available. Those of special interest include black and zone-tailed hawks, peregrine falcon, golden eagle. Seasonally common species include pied-billed grebe, mallard, pintail, green-winged teal, ruddy duck, American coot, turkey vulture. Hawks: sharp-shinned, Cooper's, red-tailed, Swainson's, black, northern harrier. American kestrel. Gambel's quail, killdeer; white-winged, mourning, and ground doves; roadrunner, screech and elf owls, poor-will, lesser nighthawk, white-throated swift; black-chinned, Costa's, and broad-billed hummingbirds; belted kingfisher, northern flicker, Gila and ladder-backed woodpeckers, yellow-bellied sapsucker. Flycatchers: western and Cassin's kingbirds; Wied's crested, ash-throated, black and Say's phoebes, western wood-pewee, vermilion, beardless. Swallows: violet-green, rough-winged, barn, cliff. Mexican jay, white-necked raven, bridled titmouse, verdin, white-breasted nuthatch. Wrens: house, Bewick's, cactus, canyon, rock. Mockingbird, curved-billed and crissal thrashers, blue-gray gnatcatcher, ruby-crowned kinglet, phainopepla, loggerhead shrike; Hutton's, Bell's, and warbling vireos. Warblers: Lucy's, yellow, yellow-rumped, Wilson's. Western meadowlark; hooded, Scott's, and northern orioles; western and summer tanagers, cardinal, pyrrhuloxia, house finch, lesser goldfinch, brown and Abert's towhees. Sparrows: lark, black-throated, chipping, Brewer's, white-crowned, Lincoln's. Dark-eyed junco.

Mammals: Checklist available. The caves and ledges of the canyon are habitat for 12 species of bats. Rodents are numerous, species including cliff chipmunk, Yuma antelope squirrel, rock squirrel, valley pocket gopher, Bailey and rock pocket mice, western harvest mouse, cactus mouse, brush mouse, southern grasshopper mouse, Arizona and yellow-nosed cotton rats, whitethroat woodrat. Desert shrew, desert cottontail, blacktail jackrabbit, coyote, gray fox, black bear, ringtail, raccoon, coatimundi, badger; western spotted, striped, and hognose skunks; mountain lion, bobcat, collared peccary, mule and whitetail deer. A herd of 60 to 100 desert bighorn sheep. Most of these species live in the riparian habitat; others come to it for water.

Reptiles and amphibians: Checklist available. Lizards: banded gecko, greater earless, zebra-tailed, collared, long-nosed leopard; Yarrow's, desert, and Sonoran spiny; eastern fence, side-blotched, tree, short-horned, regal horned, Arizona night, Great Plains skink; giant spotted, western, and Chihuahua whiptails; Arizona alligator, Gila monster. Sonoran mud turtle, western box turtle, desert tortoise. Couch's and western spadefoot toads, Colorado river toad, Woodhouse's toad, red-spotted toad, Great Plains toad, canyon treefrog, leopard frog. Snakes: western blind, ringneck, Pima leaf-nosed, coachwhip, Sonoran whipsnake, western patch-nosed, glossy, gopher, common kingsnake, long-nosed, black-necked and checkered garter snakes, western ground, banded sand, Mexican black-headed, lyre, night, Arizona coral. Rattlesnakes: western diamondback, black-tailed, western, Mojave, tiger.

INTERPRETATION: *Information stations* at administrative sites.

ACTIVITIES
Camping: No nearby campground on the W side. On the E, Fourmile Canyon campground in Klondyke.
Hiking, backpacking: The canyon transit can be made in one day, but why would you? Most visitors take two days, allowing time to enjoy the scenery, flora, and fauna. Entrance by permit only. Apply up to 6 months in advance; confirm 15 to 30 days in advance. Stream water must be treated before use. Check for flash flood hazard before entering. For weather information: Aravaipa East, (602) 828-3380; West, (602) 357-7111.
Horse riding: Day use only.

NEARBY
Turkey Creek Canyon; Oak Grove Canyon. Just outside the Aravaipa E entrance is a ranch road up Turkey Creek. Not for sedans; 4-wheel drive, pickup, or hike. Oak Grove Canyon, a tributary, is state land, "as nice as Aravaipa but without the water." Narrow, twisting, much riparian vegetation.
George Whittell Wildlife Preserve, administered by the Defenders of Wildlife, occupies most of the land at both ends of the canyon. It is closed to public access except for the canyon access roads.

No pets are allowed.

PUBLICATIONS
Brochure with map.
Checklists: *Vertebrates of Aravaipa Canyon.*
General information page.

HEADQUARTERS: BLM, Safford District Office, 425 E. 4th St., Safford, AZ 85546; (602) 428-4040.

BOYCE THOMPSON SOUTHWESTERN ARBORETUM
Arizona State Parks Board; University of Arizona; and Boyce Thompson Southwestern Arboretum, Inc.
1,076 acres.

10 mi. E of Florence Jct. on US 60.

Open: 8:00 A.M.–5:30 P.M. daily except Christmas.

This living museum displays more than 1,500 species of desert plants from the United States and other regions, as well as a geological garden and many native birds and mammals. Over 144 bird species and 70 species of mammals, reptiles, and amphibians have been recorded on the grounds.

The Arboretum is within the Tonto National Forest (see entry). Elevation is 2,400 ft. at the Visitor Center, 4,000 ft. at nearby Picket Post Mountain. Annual precipitation here is about 16 in., equally divided between summer and winter.

Visitors can choose short, easy trails or take longer walks into the more rugged terrain. Plants along the trail system are well labeled.

The Arboretum was established in 1927 as a research and education center. It is also a survival center for threatened and endangered species of cacti and succulents. It receives about 70,000 visitors per year.

PUBLICATIONS
Leaflet.
Desert Plants: quarterly journal.

HEADQUARTERS: P.O. Box AB, Superior, AZ 85273; (602) 689-2811.

CHEVELON CREEK WILDLIFE AREA
Arizona Game and Fish Department
668 acres.

Near I-40, 15 mi. E of Winslow.

The Little Colorado River, between Winslow and Holbrook, is an intermittent stream. However, the water table is high, and artesian wells and seeps maintain marshy conditions in some areas, producing food plants attractive to waterfowl. The river's flood plain is a good place to see waterfowl in winter, shorebirds in migration. A diversion dam on Chevelon Creek forms a 120-acre impoundment that usually has 1,000 to 3,000 ducks and a few geese in winter.

CLUFF RANCH WILDLIFE AREA
Arizona Game and Fish Department
440 acres.

From Pima on US 70, 5 mi. S on local roads.

On the E slope of the Graham Mountains at 3,000 ft. elevation. Ash Creek, an intermittent tributary of the Gila River, has a well-developed riparian woodland with cottonwood, willow, ash. Three small ponds totaling 25 acres attract birds and small game.

This is a popular weekend picnicking and fishing spot for local residents. On weekdays it offers good birding.

COCONINO NATIONAL FOREST
U.S. Forest Service
1,835,913 acres; 2,010,749 acres within boundaries.

Surrounds Flagstaff; more than 3/4 of its area S of the city. Crossed by I-40, I-17, US 89, US Alt. 89, and SR 487.

The Coconino is one huge block, almost surrounded by the Kaibab, Prescott, Tonto, and Apache-Sitgreaves National Forests. Most of the Forest is on the Colorado Plateau, with elevations above 6,500 ft. Directly N of Flagstaff are the volcanic San Francisco Mountains, the 4 main peaks including 12,633-ft. Humphreys Peak, highest point in AZ. Lesser peaks are scattered through the N sector. Sunset Crater National Monument is within this sector, Wupatki National Monument on its N boundary (see entries).

S of Flagstaff is a rolling plateau with ponderosa pine forest, meadows, lakes, and scattered peaks, which ends abruptly at the Mogollon Rim, a 200-mi.-long escarpment on which the drop is as much as 2,000 ft. Some of the lowest country, with desert shrub and cactus vegetation, is in the SW, where the boundary is at the Verde River.

Above 7,500 ft., average annual temperature is 42°F and annual precipitation 25–30 in. Between 5,000 and 7,500 ft., average annual temperature is about 50°F and precipitation is between 12 and 25 in. Below 5,000 ft., average temperature is about 60°F and precipitation 10–20 in. Many of the mountains are high enough to intercept moisture, chiefly as winter snow. The Forest has 191 mi. of live streams and 15 small lakes.

The Forest's many attractions and proximity to Flagstaff and Phoenix assure heavy recreational use. Visitation has more than doubled in the past 5 years, to an annual total of more than 3 million visitor-days. Traffic jams are not uncommon in Oak Creek Canyon. Lakes region campgrounds are usually crowded in summer. Quiet places aren't likely to be found on or close to paved roads during the busy season. But the Forest has roadless areas, too. Until 1984 it had only one proclaimed Wilderness, its share of Sycamore Canyon. The Arizona Wilderness Act of 1984 added 8 more, totaling over 8% of the Forest's land area, also adding 2,336 acres to Coconino's part of Sycamore Canyon.

Between these roadless areas are miles of roads, most of them scenic routes: 429 mi. of federal, state, and county roads, 5,129 mi. of Forest Service roads. Almost all the latter are unpaved, and many aren't maintained. Inquire.

Although hiking trails are found throughout the Forest, few of them were planned and built by the Forest Service. Some were traditional Indian pathways and game trails; some were pioneer routes; some have been created more recently by loggers, hunters, and cattle. The best established, 304 miles, have been incorporated in the Forest's numbered system. Many of them have never been improved. Today trail maintenance depends largely on the work of volunteers.

Most of the trails described in the Forest's trail guides are short, less than 4 mi. long. Several are longer, up to 20 mi. Longest is the General Crook Trail along the Mogollon Rim: 53 mi. in the Coconino, 80 more in the Prescott and Apache-Sitgreaves National Forests. Bushwhacking in the canyons cut into the Rim is challenging enough for almost any adventurer.

The Peaks. The San Francisco Peaks are major landmarks in northern Arizona, rising from the dense ponderosa pine forest of the plateau, often to snowy caps. They are now within the Kachina Peaks Wilderness. Four high peaks form a semicircle around an interior valley, the Inner Basin. A chair lift to the ski area on Agassiz Peak serves sightseers in summer. This area has been closed to hiking. Humphreys Peak can be reached by a newly built trail from the Fairfield Snow Bowl Lodge, a round trip of 8 mi. Forest roads encircle the peaks and one leads to the Inner Basin, a spectacular, much-photographed area of aspen groves and meadows. The Basin environment is so fragile that only day hiking is permitted.

C. Hart Merriam developed his concept of "life zones" here in the late 1800s. Six of the seven occur on the slopes. Below 7,000 ft. is a dwarf forest of pinyon pine and juniper. Each higher level is moister and cooler. Next above is the zone of ponderosa pine, then Douglas-fir/white fir, Engelmann spruce/subalpine fir, and bristlecone pine at timber line, above which is alpine tundra.

Volcanic landscape. The N sector is dotted with some 400 volcanoes, of which 200 are cinder cones. Evidence of past volcanism includes beds of cinders and lava caves. The most recent eruptions were at Sunset Crater between A.D. 1064 and 1250. Forest roads cross the area, but deep, loose cinders may require 4-wheel drive.

Forest and lakes. The plateau S of Flagstaff has part of the world's largest ponderosa pine forest, open meadows, numerous lakes, a few perennial streams. It extends to the Mogollon Rim. SR 487 crosses from Flagstaff, passing Upper and Lower Lake Mary, campgrounds, and trailheads, intersecting SR 87 from Winslow. Forest Road 300 follows the edge of the Rim.

Oak Creek Canyon. The Rim turns N on the W side of the Forest. Travelers on US Alt. 89 usually pause at Oak Creek Vista Point before the descent from the Rim into Oak Creek Canyon. The Canyon is the most heavily impacted area in the Forest, and we have provided a separate entry for it.

Below the Rim: Oak Creek is the best known of the canyons that cut down through the Rim toward the Verde River. Sycamore Canyon is a Wilderness shared with the Prescott and Kaibab National Forests. West Clear Creek, Beaver Creek, and Fossil Creek are also scenic, with high cliffs, perennial streams, pools, grottoes, and lush riparian vegetation with cottonwood, sycamore, alder, Arizona walnut, boxelder, ash, ferns, and many wildflowers. At the bottom, these canyons open into desert grassland, and riparian vegetation is replaced by catclaw, acacia, agave, ocotillo, creosote, cholla, and pricklypear.

Oak Creek Canyon opens into redrock country, with magnificent sculptured cliffs, spires, and buttes.

This wide range of elevations provides all-year recreational choices. In summer, visitors come to the plateau as a refuge from the desert heat. We enjoy the plateau most in spring and fall. Skiing, ski touring, and other snow play bring winter visitors to the high country, and this is the time the desert is most attractive. Many residents of northern states spend their winters in communities below the Rim.

Wildlife: The Forest's *Vertebrate Checklist* is one of the best we've seen, noting for each species its relative abundance, seasonality, life zone preference, and special habitat preference (willow thickets, alder trees, cliffs, rodent burrows, etc.). The list is available from the Forest Supervisor's office.

Birds: 306 species recorded. Common or fairly common include eared grebe, Canada goose, mallard, gadwall, pintail, American wigeon, cinnamon teal, northern shoveler, redhead, bufflehead, ruddy duck, turkey vulture, Cooper's and red-tailed hawks, golden eagle, Gambel's quail, wild turkey, American coot, killdeer, long-billed dowitcher, western sandpiper, band-tailed pigeon, mourning dove; flammulated, great horned, and saw-whet owls; poor-will, common and lesser nighthawks, white-throated swift. Broad-tailed and rufous hummingbirds, northern flicker, Lewis' and hairy woodpeckers, vermilion and western flycatchers, black and Say's phoebes, western wood-pewee, horned lark; violet-green, tree, and rough-winged swallows; Steller's, scrub, and pinyon jays; common raven, Clark's nutcracker. Mountain chick-adee, plain titmouse, verdin; white-breasted, pygmy, and red-breasted nut-hatches; brown creeper, house and rock wrens; sage, curve-billed, crissal, and Bendire's thrashers; American robin, hermit thrush, western and mountain bluebirds, Townsend's solitaire, black-tailed gnatcatcher, ruby-crowned king-let, European starling; Hutton's, solitary, and warbling vireos. Warblers: Virginia's, yellow-rumped, black-throated gray, Townsend's, hermit, Grace's, MacGillivray's, red-faced, Wilson's, American redstart. House sparrow, western meadowlark; yellow-headed, red-winged, and Brewer's blackbirds; hooded oriole, brown-headed cowbird, great-tailed grackle; western, hepatic, and summer tanagers; black-headed and blue grosbeaks, lesser goldfinch; green-tailed, rufous-sided, Abert's, and brown towhees; lark bunting. Vesper, chipping, Brewer's, and lark sparrows; dark-eyed and gray-headed juncos.

Mammals: 77 species recorded. Common or fairly common include vagrant and desert shrews. Bats: southwestern, Yuma, cave, long-eared, fringe-tailed, long-legged, California, little brown, and small-footed myotis; silver-haired, western pipistrel, big brown, hoary, western big-eared, pallid, Mexican free-tail. Blacktail jackrabbit, desert cottontail. Abert, red, rock, and golden-mantled squirrels; Harris and whitetail antelope squirrels, cliff and grayneck chipmunks, valley pocket gopher, silky and rock pocket mice, Ord kangaroo rat. Mice: northern grasshopper, harvest, canyon, cactus, deer, brush, pinyon. Arizona, Stephens, and Mexican woodrats; Mexican vole, coyote, gray fox, black bear, ringtail, striped and spotted skunks, elk, mule and whitetail deer, pronghorn.

Reptiles and amphibians: 53 species recorded. Common or fairly common include tiger salamander, western spadefoot. Toads: Woodhouse's, south-western, red-spotted, Great Plains. Chorus frog, Arizona and canyon tree-frogs, leopard frog. Lizards: collared, leopard, lesser earless, greater earless, eastern fence, Clark's spiny, tree, side-blotched, short-horned, desert spiny, Arizona night. Many-lined and Great Plains skinks; plateau, Chihuahua, desert-grassland, and western whiptails. Snakes: narrow-headed and western garter, coachwhip, gopher, common and Sonora mountain kingsnakes, black-tailed rattlesnake, western diamondback, western rattlesnake.

FEATURES

Sycamore Canyon Wilderness, 23,331 acres, plus 32,612 acres in the Prescott and Kaibab NF. One of Arizona's most scenic hiking and backpacking areas. About 15 mi. W of Oak Creek Canyon. The 21-mi.-long canyon has been carved deep into the Colorado Plateau. The widest point is 7 mi. from rim to rim. Deep gorges, high cliffs, spectacular formations of red and white sedimentary rock. Canyon bottoms have riparian vegetation with walnut, sycamore, cottonwood, other broadleafed species. Away from the stream, habitats range from cactus and mesquite at 3,600 ft. elevation in the S portion to Douglas-fir and ponderosa pine at 7,000 ft. on the N rim.

Deer and elk move in and out of the canyon depending on water supply and climate. Often seen: squirrels, chipmunk, rabbit, skunks, fox. Seen occasionally: mountain lion, black bear, javelina, ringtail. Rattlesnakes, centipedes, and scorpions are common.

Access points include trailheads on primitive Forest roads at Sycamore Pass, Turkey Butte, and Red Hill. S entrance access is by Forest Road 131 N of Tuzigoot National Monument. Ask Sedona R.D. about road conditions.

Hiking in summer is not recommended; daytime temperatures often exceed 100°F. Apr.–June and Sept. to mid-Nov. are best. Visitors must carry their own water; the canyon has few springs. Horses require supplemental feed. When we last checked, no commercial outfitter was serving the Wilderness, but inquire.

A small area at the S end of the canyon is closed to overnight camping. This was the only Wilderness in the Coconino until 1984. We were there when the Arizona Wilderness Act added 8 more. Forest HQ had no maps of these areas yet and only limited information for prospective visitors.

Kendrick Mountain Wilderness, 6,510 acres, partly in the Kaibab National Forest. The highest point in the Kaibab NF, rising 3,000 ft. from its base to 10,418 ft. A 4-mi. trail to the top, through ponderosa pine and mixed conifer forest with some open meadows. Trailhead in the Kaibab NF; see entry.

Wet Beaver Wilderness, 6,700 acres. Wet Beaver Creek enters the Verde River near Camp Verde on I-17. It originates on the plateau about 12 mi. E of the Beaver Creek Ranger Station, the primary trailhead, at about 6,200 ft. elevation. It descends through a very steep canyon that gradually opens to the flood plain about 3,000 ft. below. Here, as in nearby canyons, summer daytime temperatures are in the 80s and 90s, nights in the 50s and 60s, winter temperatures about 30 degrees lower. Annual precipitation is about 11 in. on the flood plain, about 13 in. at the headwaters. The wettest months are July–Sept. and Dec.–Jan. May and June are very dry, often causing fire hazard. A Forest campground is near the Ranger Station, where SR 179 crosses the creek. The more accessible part of the area is popular for day hiking, fishing, and picnicking.

Fossil Springs Wilderness, 11,550 acres. Just S of the Mogollon Rim; almost directly N of Strawberry. Outstanding feature is a group of springs discharging a constant 20,000 gallons per minute into Fossil Creek, which once flowed ·through Fossil Creek Canyon. The water is soon diverted by a flume to a power-generating station. Rich riparian woodland. The several side canyons are mostly too steep for hiking in or out. Elevation in the canyon is about 4,400 ft. Access is from the W from the Irving Power Plant. The road beyond the plant is closed, but foot traffic is permitted. Hikers who plan to explore the canyon should allow several days for the outing.

West Clear Creek Wilderness, 13,600 acres. Part of West Clear Creek is shown on the highway map, E of Camp Verde. Clear Creek Campground, near the low end of the creek, is 7 mi. SE of Camp Verde by FH 9 and FR 626. The Wilderness is a strip 1/2 to 2 mi. wide along the canyon, which drops down to the Verde River. Canyon wall is up to 1,000 ft. high. Good fishing. Frequent box canyons require wading or swimming, and should be avoided in stormy weather. The area has been called "some of the most rugged, lonesome country in the state."

Red Rock/Secret Mountain Wilderness, 43,950 acres, is N and NW of Sedona, between Oak Creek Canyon and the Sycamore Canyon Wilderness. The redrock formations include bluffs, outcrops, and canyons. Because of the rough terrain, no trail crosses the area, but trails lead to such destinations as Secret Mountain, Sterling Canyon, Vultee Arch, and Wilson Mountain. It includes the West Fork of Oak Creek and part of the W side of Oak Creek Canyon, making it one of Arizona's most accessible Wildernesses. One rather demanding trail begins at the East Pocket lookout tower on Forest Road 231, dropping down from the Mogollon Rim by switchbacks.

Kachina Peaks Wilderness, 18,200 acres. Directly N of Flagstaff, surrounding the San Francisco Peaks. The Inner Basin has a cherry-stem road access. The area has been well known for its scenic grandeur, attracting hikers, backpackers, hunters, climbers, picnickers, and photographers. Wilderness designation gives the area greater protection, excluding ORVs and other disturbance.

Munds Mountain Wilderness, 18,150 acres. Immediately SE of Sedona, this is another redrock area. Chief features include Horse Mesa, Jacks Canyon, Woods Canyon, part of Rattlesnake Canyon. Best access is from Schnebly Hill Road, with trails to 6,825-ft. Munds Mountain.

Strawberry Crater Wilderness, 10,140 acres. On the Forest boundary, immediately N of FR 545, the road from Sunset Crater National Monument to Wupatki National Monument, at the Painted Desert Vista picnic area. Volcanic cinder and lava flow area. Hot in summer.

Verde River. Although the river approximates the Forest's SW boundary, there are many private inholdings between the actual boundary and the river. Only S of the West Clear Creek confluence does the Forest have much shoreline. Most river access is from the other side of the river. The river can be floated for a few weeks in the spring, but there are no put-in or take-out points on the Forest.

Mormon Lake, about 25 mi. SE of Flagstaff; shown on highway map. When full, it's the largest lake in AZ, covering 2,000 acres, but shallow, with a maximum depth of about 6 ft. When we last stopped there, its area was about 500 acres, and it has been known to dry up completely. It has no inlet or outlet. Few stands of aquatic plants. Waterfowl are attracted when there's enough water: most of the species that visit AZ come here. Nestings have been reported.

Fishing is poor, and the lake is too shallow for fishing or boating. Even so, it's the center of a popular recreation area, with considerable development. A paved road encircles the lake. Two Forest campgrounds are here, as well as inholdings with private homes. E of the highway are the Mormon Lake Cliffs, about 100 ft. high. Trails lead from the campgrounds to Lake Mary and W to Mormon Mountain.

Lakes. The Forest has 15 lakes, most small. Lakes larger than 100 acres include Kinnickinick, Soldier, Long, Blue Ridge Reservoir, Upper Lake Mary, Lower Lake Mary, Ashurst.

INTERPRETATION

The Forest has no visitor center, other than HQ and R.D. offices. No campfire programs, guided walks, other naturalist activities.

Nature trails at Red Mountain and the Mount Elden Environmental Study Area.

ACTIVITIES

Camping: 23 campgrounds; 554 sites. Published seasons range from Apr.–Oct. to June–Aug., but many Forest Service campgrounds have shortened seasons. 10 of the campgrounds are along Oak Creek Canyon, others scattered.

Hiking, backpacking: Long and short trails suitable for any season, though spring and fall are best. July–Aug. thunderstorms are sometimes violent. Flash flood hazards in some canyons.

Hunting: Elk, whitetail and mule deer, pronghorn, black bear, mountain lion, wild turkey, small game.

Fishing: Lakes and streams. Rainbow and German brown trout, northern pike, walleye, catfish, yellow perch, bluegill.

Horsepacking: Forest HQ has a list of outfitters. Many suitable trails.

Boating: Motors permitted on any suitable lake. Ramps at Upper Lake Mary and Stoneham. Motor size restriction at Mormon Lake.

Skiing: Arizona Snow Bowl. Usual season: Thanksgiving to Easter.

Ski touring: Many possibilities, from the San Francisco Peaks to the Rim, on meadows, unplowed roads, etc.

PUBLICATIONS

Forest map. $1.
Recreation guide pamphlet.
Oak Creek Canyon folder.
Sycamore Canyon Wilderness leaflet.
Survival in the Winter Woods. Pamphlet.
Information pages:
    General information.

Vertebrate checklist.
Hiking trails.
Sycamore Canyon Wilderness trail map.
Hiking information; Sedona R.D.
Oak Creek Canyon.
Oak Creek Canyon recreation areas.
Oak Creek Canyon trails.
Mormon Lake trails.
Hiking Trails, Beaver Creek R.D.
San Francisco Peaks summer recreation guide.
Dispersed recreation sites, Beaver Creek R.D.
Recreation opportunities, Mormon Lake R.D.
Mormon Lake crosscountry ski trails.
List of outfitters.
Arizona Snow Bowl. Concession folder.

REFERENCES
Ganci, Dave. *Hiking the Southwest.* San Francisco: Sierra Club Books, 1983, pp. 68–82.
River Runners Guide to the Verde River. Albuquerque, NM: U.S. Forest Service, Southwestern Region, 1984.

HEADQUARTERS: 2323 E. Greenlaw Lane, Flagstaff, AZ 86001; (602) 527-7400.

RANGER DISTRICTS: Beaver Creek R.D., HC 64, Box 240, Rimrock, AZ 86335; (602) 567-4501. Elden R.D., 2519 E. Seventh Ave., Flagstaff, AZ 86001; (602) 527-7470. Flagstaff R.D., 1100 N. Beaver St., Flagstaff, AZ 86001; (602) 779-3311, ext. 1441. Long Valley R.D., P.O. Box 68, Happy Jack, AZ 86024; (602) 774-7289. Mormon Lake R.D., 4825 S. Lake Mary Rd., Flagstaff, AZ 86001; (602) 527-7474. Sedona R.D., P.O. Box 300, Sedona, AZ 86336; (602) 282-4119. Blue Ridge R.D., HC 31, Box 300, Happy Jack, AZ 86024; (602) 477-2255.

FORT APACHE INDIAN RESERVATION
Fort Apache Tribal Council
1,664,972 acres.

S of Show Low. Crossed by US 60, SR 73, SR 260.

The tribe's White Mountain Recreation Enterprise (WMRE) is energetically promoting recreation use of the Reservation. The environment is delightful, above and below the Mogollon Rim, a region of splendid pine forest, 400 mi.

of streams, numerous small lakes. More than 30 developed campgrounds have over 1,000 sites. Fishing and hunting are both said to be excellent. Principal recreation center is Sunrise Resort Park, which has hotel, restaurant, lake, large campground, hiking trails, and ski area.

Any visitor use of the Reservation requires a permit, which can be obtained at the WMRE Game & Fish office or at many tribal stores. Fees for camping, hunting, and fishing are modest. We were told that a small number of trophy elk permits are issued each year—for $7,000 each, which includes guide, outfit, and all other expenses. We were also told there's a three-year waiting list. Other big game species hunted include pronghorn, black bear, mountain lion, and javelina.

HEADQUARTERS: White Mountain Apache Game & Fish Department, P.O. Box 220, Whiteriver, AZ 85941; (602) 338-4385.

GILA BOX; TURTLE MOUNTAIN
U.S. Bureau of Land Management
100,000 acres, including intermingled state and private land.

The highway map shows a roadless area between Safford and Morenci, on both sides of the Gila River. The river can be crossed at Safford or Solomon. BLM advises consulting the Safford office about roads beyond the river.

The area is at the SE end of the Gila Mountains, where the land drops down to the Gila River in a series of ridges and canyons. Principal drainages are Eagle Creek and Bonita Creek, both perennial, both running SE; Turtle Mountain is between them. Elevations are from 3,100 ft. at the Gila River to 6,635 ft. on Turtle Mountain. The area is rugged, colorful. To the NE at Morenci is a huge mine and smelter. Tailings can be seen from some points in the area, and smoke occasionally blows this way.

The area includes two roadless units separated by primitive roads that require 4-wheel drive: Gila Box, 17,831 acres, and Turtle Mountain, 17,422 acres. Access to Eagle Creek is by a mine company road W from Morenci. Much of the land up Eagle Creek is owned by the mining company, which has not objected to public use. Bonita Creek is accessible E from Safford. A 4-wheel-drive road up Bonita Creek crosses the creek repeatedly. Both Eagle Creek and Bonita Creek are excellent birding areas, especially for black and zone-tailed hawks and wintering bald eagles.

The area includes 25 mi. of the Gila River, said to be the last free-flowing section of the Gila in AZ. Also included: 8 mi. of the San Francisco River, 14 mi. of Bonita Creek, 20 mi. of Eagle Creek, and numerous small canyons. The Gila River flows W through a 1,000-ft.-deep colorful canyon. The Gila

Box was studied for Wilderness designation and is eligible for Wild and Scenic River consideration. Opponents included ORV operators, who drive up the canyon during the dry season; motor vehicles are banned from Wildernesses. BLM recommended against Wilderness designation.

The river can be floated in spring, usually Mar.–Apr., sometimes mid-Feb.–late May. A good educational whitewater trip, with only minor rapids. A scenic 2-day trip. Minimum suggested flow is 1,200 cu. ft./sec. measured at the head of the Safford Valley. The rivers are ideal for 12- to 14-ft. rafts, canoes, and kayaks. The river could be hiked in dry weather, but it's usually too hot then; flash floods are a hazard in late summer.

The mouth of Bonita Creek is a popular picnicking and fishing site for local residents, as well as a take-out for float trips.

Plants: Cattle grazing and other influences have eliminated much of the riparian vegetation, which normally includes Fremont cottonwood, Goodding willow, Arizona sycamore, Arizona walnut, velvet ash, netleaf hackberry, mesquite. BLM is planting riparian trees. Above the canyon are grassland, mountain shrub, and desert shrub vegetation types. Common plant species include snakeweed, juniper, evergreen oaks, jojoba, white-thorn, cholla, pricklypear, various grasses.

Wildlife: No bird or mammal lists are available, but the area is an attraction for local birders. Black and zone-tailed hawks often seen. The canyon is a wintering area for bald eagle. Rocky Mountain bighorn sheep have been sighted along Eagle Creek.

NEARBY

See the entry for Gila Lower Box in NM Zone 3, describing a portion of the river just a few miles upstream. Between the two is a narrow 17-mi. strip N of Duncan, AZ, where the river flows between SR 75 and the Southern Pacific Railroad. Land in this strip is mostly private.

ACTIVITIES

Hiking: The Safford-Morenci Trail, 15 mi. long, is an old trade route that crosses Bonita Creek, Turtle Mountain, and ends at Eagle Creek. It is maintained by volunteers. Rugged, much up and down. Fall is the best hiking season.

Fishing: Catfish, in Gila and San Francisco rivers.

HEADQUARTERS: BLM, Safford District Office, 425 E. 4th St., Safford, AZ 85546; (602) 428-4040.

GILA MOUNTAINS
U.S. Bureau of Land Management
60,000 acres.

NE of Geronimo, Fort Thomas, and Pima on US 70. On the border of the

San Carlos Indian Reservation. A good county road, shown on the highway map, is on the N side of the river. Spur roads into the canyons aren't for ordinary cars.

The highway parallels the Gila River. From the river's gently sloping alluvial plain, at about 2,700 ft. elevation, the land rises to about 5,500 ft. on the irregular crests of the Gila Mountains at the Indian Reservation boundary, beyond which is a high plateau. "Escarpment" would be a more accurate description than "mountains."

Most of the relatively flat land near the highway and river is private and developed. Toward the cliffs, the land becomes steep and rugged, with many short canyons and washes. Some of the canyons have permanent streams, a few with fish. Of the total acreage, 31,642 acres applies to two roadless tracts studied for Wilderness designation. High points within these units are 6,340-ft. Gila Peak and 6,444-ft. Hilonsum Peak.

Vegetation ranges from typical desert shrub and grassland to mountain shrub and pinyon-juniper forests at higher elevations, with broadleaf riparian species in the moister canyon bottoms. Botanists studying the Fishhook Canyons area judged the riparian woodlands, grasslands, and an unusual stand of Lowell ash to be in a climax condition and probably the best examples of these communities in the Gila Mountains. The cliffs are prime habitat for raptors.

The area is more suitable for day hiking than backpacking. Most hiking is in canyons. Those of special interest to hikers include Fishhook, Sam, Steer Springs, Dutch Pasture, and the Left Fork of Markham Creek. Upper Fishhook Canyon has some relatively undisturbed grassland demonstrating what the area was like before it was grazed.

Most visitors are local residents who use the area for hunting, ORV activity, etc. Newcomers would do well to visit the BLM office to see detailed maps and get route suggestions.

HEADQUARTERS: BLM, Safford District Office, 425 E. Fourth St., Safford, AZ 85546; (602) 428-4040.

JAVELINA PEAK; SAN SIMON VALLEY
U.S. Bureau of Land Management
50,000 acres.

From Safford, SE on US 70 for 10 mi.; right on Haekel Road through the San Simon Valley. This road fords the San Simon River several times, difficult in high water.

For birders, the approach may be more interesting than the site. About a dozen small ponds have been established along the San Simon River, the largest, Posey Well, about 2 acres, and these attract many waterfowl. Little traffic moves on this road. Ask BLM about numerous side roads, many of which require 4-wheel drive.

Javelina Peak, 5,592 ft., is the highest point in the Whitlock Mountains, an isolated small range between the San Simon and Whitlock valleys. The S end of the Whitlock Mountains is in a Wilderness Study Area. Fine views from the top. The mountains rise abruptly from the valley floor, elevation about 3,250 ft. Several canyons are cut into the range. At the base of the peak is a small area of highly eroded badlands. S of the mountains are about 4,000 acres of heavily vegetated dunes that are used for wintertime ORV activity. Rockhounding opportunities.

HEADQUARTERS: BLM, Safford District Office, 425 E. 4th St., Safford, AZ 85546; (602) 428-4040.

LOST DUTCHMAN STATE PARK
Arizona State Parks
335 acres.

From Apache Jct., 5 mi. NE on SR 88.

A small desert park on the boundary of Tonto National Forest, at the base of the Superstition Mountains. The park adjoins the Tonto National Forest, only a mile from the Superstition Wilderness boundary. This side of the mountains is a steep escarpment rising about 3,000 ft. above the park elevation.

According to the Park leaflet, this is "an ideal base" for hikers and horsemen going into the Wilderness.

The Park is also used as a picnic stop for people on their way to Canyon, Apache, or Roosevelt lakes.

Camping: 35 sites.

HEADQUARTERS: 6109 N. Apache Trail, Apache Junction, AZ 85220; (602) 982-4485.

LYMAN LAKE STATE PARK
Arizona State Parks
360 acres; 1,500 lake acres.

From US 60 just W of Springerville, N 14 mi. on US 180/666.

The lake is irregular in shape, created by a dam built in 1915 for irrigation on the Little Colorado River. At 6,000 ft. elevation, the Park area is flat to gently rolling, with rocky buttes rising several hundred feet on the lake shore. The surrounding area is rolling grazing land.

The hills have a sparse cover of juniper, mixed with plains and desert grasslands. A small herd of bison grazes at Park entrance.

We camped here on a windy, chilly mid-Oct. weekend. We were the only visitors, and the ranger was surprised to see us. Summer is the season. Visitors come for fishing, boating, swimming.

Out of season, the site offers several pleasant short hikes: climbing the buttes, crossing a meadow where spring wildflowers would appear.

ACTIVITIES

Camping: 65 sites, plus 2 boat-access sites. All year.

Fishing: Walleye, northern pike, channel and blue catfish, crappie, and largemouth bass.

Boating: Marina and rentals.

PUBLICATION: Leaflet with map.

HEADQUARTERS: Box 1428, St. Johns, AZ 85936; (602) 337-4441.

MESCAL MOUNTAINS
U.S. Bureau of Land Management/San Carlos Indian Reservation
30,020 acres.

Very difficult access. From Globe, S on SR 77 to Christmas. E on local roads; 4-wheel drive. The area can also be reached from Coolidge Dam on San Carlos Lake. Ask BLM about road conditions. Indian lands are not open to public use. (See entry, San Carlos Lake.)

This country is rough, with about 9 mi. of the isolated, scenic Gila River canyon cutting through the Mescal Mountains. The public land is wedged into the San Carlos Indian Reservation just below the dam. Reservation land is across the river and on the N boundary of the public land, which is about 2 mi. wide.

The canyon is deep, narrow, winding, and mostly inaccessible. It has several attractive side canyons, notably Grapevine and Dick Spring canyons and Mescal Creek. The walls are fractured and steeply tilted rock layers, with sparse desert vegetation on the slopes and shelves between layers, providing many places where a hiker can scramble up or down, but the river is a scrambling rather than a hiking route, and that only when it's dry. The Needle's Eye is a narrow place in the canyon.

Summer temperatures in the canyon are too hot for comfort.

Elevations are from 2,300 ft. where the river leaves the site to 4,300 ft. on the uplands. Vegetation is typical of the Sonoran Desert scrub: saguaro, palo verde, barrel cactus, catclaw acacia, jojoba. Riparian vegetation is dominated by Fremont cottonwood, mesquite, Arizona sycamore, velvet ash, willow, salt cedar. Bald eagle winter in the canyon. Other raptors nest on the cliffs.

This part of the Gila isn't for floating: almost dry when the dam is closed, hazardous when it's open because of overhanging brush, snags, and fences.

HEADQUARTERS: BLM, Safford District Office, 425 E. Fourth St., Safford, AZ 85546; (602) 428-4040.

OAK CREEK CANYON
Coconino National Forest
16 mi.

From Flagstaff, S on US 89A.

The canyon is within the Coconino National Forest, but this concentrated public use area warrants its own entry: more than 2 1/2 million people per year make the transit through the canyon. The surrounding area and trails leading from the canyon are described in the Coconino NF entry.

It has been called one of the most beautiful canyons in the West, and few would disagree, if they can block out the crowds and their litter. Along the road are numerous inholdings with residential and commercial development. The road drops down from tall trees on the Mogollon Rim into semidesert redrock country. Pullouts offer great views from above. Elevation at Lookout Point is 6,500 ft. Below, the road follows Oak Creek, a perennial stream, between 1,200-ft. redrock canyon walls. Almost everyone stops at a bridge where a short trail descends to streamside rock ledges. Many stop at Slide Rock.

By all means visit the canyon, but try to go there mid-week, early or late in the day. If you're camping, try the Cave Spring Campground and hike up into the Oak Creek Canyon Natural Area.

Camping: 6 campgrounds, 173 sites. Season was May–Sept., but it may be shorter now. Inquire.

PUBLICATION: Leaflet.

HEADQUARTERS: Coconino NF, Sedona Ranger District, P.O. Box 300, Sedona, AZ 86336; (602) 282-4119.

PELONCILLO MOUNTAINS
U.S. Bureau of Land Management
25,000 acres, with state and private inholdings.

On the AZ-NM state line. From San Simon on I-10, NE 15 mi. on West Doubtful Canyon road (unmarked) to the mouth of Little Doubtful Canyon. Ask BLM about this and other access roads.

We had too little data for an entry. Our BLM advisor wrote, "You are missing a very choice area," and provided more. An extremely rugged area. The Peloncillos are of volcanic origin. Numerous canyons drain in all directions. Elevations range from 4,000 ft. to 6,401 ft. Little Doubtful Canyon is highly scenic, with an extensive oak forest in the bottom. (There may be locked gates on private land at the mouth of the canyon.) The road in the canyon is in very poor condition. Numerous other short but scenic canyons, including Ward, Indian Springs, Midway, Old Horseshoe, Millsite, and West Doubtful. From the ridge, long-distance views of the San Simon Valley on the W, Lordsburg Playa to the E.

A 12,317-acre roadless area in the most rugged part of the Peloncillos is a Wilderness Study Area. Vegetation includes mesquite, snakeweed, burroweed, turpentine bush, juniper, Emory and Arizona white oaks, creosote, catclaw, whitethorn, agave, and pricklypear. The area has been proposed for reintroduction of desert bighorn sheep. Good deer hunting.

HEADQUARTERS: BLM, Safford District Office, 425 E. Fourth St., Safford, AZ 85546; (602) 428-4040.

PETRIFIED FOREST NATIONAL PARK
National Park Service
93,493 acres.

On both sides of I-40 E of Holbrook.

Open: Daylight hours.

The Park road leaves I-40 at its own exit, going N. First stop is the visitor center. A short loop passes several Painted Desert overlooks. The road then crosses over I-40 and continues through the Park to its S exit near US 180, a 28-mi. journey.

Come here for brilliant colors: those of the petrified wood and those of the sands and clays of the Painted Desert. It has been called the world's best-known and most colorful deposit of petrified wood, from giant logs to heaps of chips. Petrified wood can be found in many places. The Ginkgo Petrified Forest State Park in Washington has a wider range of tree species. Nowhere but here is there such a splendid display.

The N boundary adjoins the Navajo Indian Reservation, and the Painted Desert extends from the Reservation into the N sector of the Park. The colors, spanning the spectrum, are the products of sands and clays containing various minerals. The shades of red, for example, are provided by iron oxides.

About 200 million years ago, this was an extensive flood plain. Great trees were washed here from higher ground, buried in silt, mud, and volcanic ash. Water seeping through this bed gradually replaced wood tissue with silica. In a more recent period of uplift, wind and water erosion removed some of the matrix, exposing thousands of logs and countless fragments in a fascinating desert landscape. More are still buried, along with many animal fossils.

Fractures display a wide range of colors in the petrified wood, many shades of red, yellow, brown, blue, white, gray, and black, less often green. The logs lie in many positions, on pedestals, leaning, horizontal, partially buried, intact, fractured, and in tumbled pieces.

Highest point in the Park is 6,235-ft. Pilot Rock, in the far N. Lowest is 5,350 ft. in the bed of the Puerco River. The landscape is largely badlands, a plateau carved by erosion with many shallow washes and low buttes. At first glance, and in most photographs, one sees little conspicuous vegetation, although there are expanses of grass and desert shrubs. Average annual precipitation is 8 to 9 in., including an average winter snowfall of 10 in.; snow seldom lasts long. Most rain occurs July–Aug. Feb.–June are dry months. Summers are hot, temperatures sometimes reaching 100°F, with cooler nights. Winters are cold, with many subfreezing nights. Spring and fall are pleasant, though often windy.

Plants: Little conspicuous vegetation, but the checklist of seed plants is one of the best we've seen anywhere. Over 300 species are listed, grouped by families, keyed to show flower colors and blooming seasons. Although the blooming of many species is linked to summer rains, a surprising number are listed as blooming in the dry months.

Birds: Checklist of 96 species available, most of them migrants or winter visitors, few resident and common.

Mammals: Checklist of 34 species available. Often or occasionally seen: cottontail, jackrabbit, skunk, coyote, whitetail antelope squirrel, prairie dog, pronghorn. Present but seldom seen: bobcat, badger, porcupine, mule deer. *Reptiles and amphibians:* Checklist of 23 species available. Often or occasionally seen: Lizards: short-horned, lesser earless, eastern fence, sagebrush. Gopher snake, glossy snake, western rattlesnake.

FEATURES

Wilderness areas, 50,260 acres, more than half of the Park. Most of this is in the N sector, beyond the road loop. Another large block is in the S, on the Rio Puerco Ridge, E of the Park road. Trailside camping is the only camping permitted in the Park. Overnight campers must have a wilderness permit. Enthusiasts say any season is a good one for backpacking. Those uncomfortable at 0° or 100°F will prefer spring or fall. Hikers must carry sufficient water. We would want compass and topo map.

Features along the Park road are keyed to the map in the Park leaflet. Highlights, from N entrance to S:

Painted Desert. Visitor center.

Indian ruin. Remains of walls at a site occupied by Anasazi Indians about 600 years ago.

The Tepees. Small peaks.

Blue Mesa. Spur road to parking area. Short trails among petrified logs.

Agate Bridge. The ends of this log are still buried. More than 100 ft. are exposed. A 40-ft. ravine has been carved into the sandstone below.

Jasper Forest Overlook. Looking over great masses of log sections.

Crystal Forest. Before federal protection, collectors and souvenir hunters worked over this area with dynamite and picks.

The Flattops. The road passes through a cleft between two remnants of tableland.

Long Logs and Agate House. The eastern part of Rainbow Forest. Many long logs, only partially exposed. Partially restored pueblo. Self-guiding trail.

Rainbow Forest Museum; Giant Logs. Many large logs; exhibits; lunch room.

Removing even a small bit of petrified wood is a violation of federal law. Specimens gathered outside the Park can be purchased at shops outside the Park.

PUBLICATIONS

Leaflet with map.
Seed plant checklist.
Wildlife checklist.
Hiking in Petrified Forest National Park.
Petrified Forest, a Road Guide.
Weather information; accommodations outside the Park.

REFERENCES
List of publications is available from Petrified Forest Museum Association, P.O. Box 277, Petrified Forest National Park, AZ 86028.
Ash, Sidney R. and David D. May. *Petrified Forest, the Story Behind the Scenery.* Las Vegas, NV: KC Publications, 1969.

HEADQUARTERS: Petrified Forest National Park, AZ 86028; (602) 524-6228.

PICACHO PEAK STATE PARK
Arizona State Parks
3,402 acres.

40 mi. N of Tucson on I-10.

For most visitors, this is an overnight stop between Phoenix and Tucson. The typical visitor is a retired person from California, Texas, or the East who comes in the winter. Few climb the peak. Most hikers are Sunday day-trippers.

The Picacho Mountains are a small range, only 15 mi. long, but they're the only ones nearby. Picacho Peak, 3,382 ft., rises more than 1,500 ft. above the Santa Cruz Flats. From the highway, its upper slopes look like vertical cliffs, and the visitor may be surprised to learn there's a trail to the top. No easy stroll. It's a 20% grade up to the saddle, and beyond are three sections where hikers need the aid of cables. The round trip usually takes 4 to 5 hours. Shortly before our arrival, one visitor announced breathlessly that he'd made it in 48 minutes.

Vegetation on the hillside is sparse, but it includes many giant saguaros.

Lists of plants and birds are being developed at the office. Both were still in early stages when we saw them.

We liked what we saw: a small, attractive natural area, worth stopping for.

INTERPRETATION
Slide programs are presented twice weekly in winter.
Nature trail.
The interpretive program is being revised and expanded.

NEARBY
Across the highway is an area of state-owned land surrounding a 6,400-acre roadless tract of BLM-managed public land that includes 4,508-ft. Newman Peak, highest point in the Picacho Mountains. Palo verde-saguaro is the dominant plant community. A dense stand of saguaro is on the E side of the unit. Vegetation on the high slopes is sparse. The mountain range is rugged,

with escarpments, steep canyons, spires, and sheer rock faces. The principal hiking opportunity is a primitive trail to the top of Newman Peak.

HEADQUARTERS: P.O. Box 275, Picacho, AZ 85241; (602) 466-3183.

SALT RIVER CANYON
Fort Apache and San Carlos Indian Reservations.

On US 60/SR 77, 30 mi. NE of Globe.

One of the most dramatic vistas in Arizona. The highway descends 2,000 ft. by switchbacks to the river bridge, then ascends. Along the way are overlooks and picnic sites. A riverside road leads to falls upstream. Below US 60, the river soon becomes the boundary between the Reservation and the Tonto NF.

SAN CARLOS LAKE
San Carlos Indian Agency
Lake: 23 mi. long, 2 mi. wide.

From Peridot on US 70, S 13 mi. on SR 3.

The lake was formed by Coolidge Dam on the Gila River. The Dam is near the SW boundary of the Reservation. Immediately downstream is the BLM area, Mescal Mountains (see entry), best access to which is through the Reservation.

The Reservation is said to offer some of the state's best hunting and fishing. Permits are required.

HEADQUARTERS: San Carlos Department of Game and Fish, P.O. Box O, San Carlos, AZ 85550; (602) 475-2361, ext. 211.

TABLE TOP MOUNTAIN
U.S. Bureau of Land Management
33,323 acres.

45 mi. S of Phoenix; 20 mi. W of Casa Grande. From the Vekol exit on I-8, 7 mi. W of its intersection with SR 84, turn S. Look for trailhead at intersection 7 mi. S. The mountain is shown on highway map.

A BLM advisor said the trail is hard to find and follow, so a stop at the Phoenix office would be advisable. BLM's file has conflicting evaluations of the site, and it didn't seem to be a good entry. Our advisor disagreed: "One of the most scenic landmarks around, with dense saguaro growth on the south side of the range. Hard hike, but the views from the mountain flat top summit are worth the climb."

Steep, narrow ridges rise from bajadas to the mountain center at 4,356 ft. The 40-acre flat top has a unique high desert grassland proposed for preservation as a Natural Area. In addition to the saguaro area, the slopes have palo verde with mixed cacti and creosote-bursage habitat. The area is considered important habitat for desert bighorn and desert tortoise. Wildlife noted includes quail, various raptors, coyote, javelina.

Several vehicle ways lead to and continue within the site; these have some use by ORVs. Visitor-days are estimated to be about 1,000 per year. From a trailhead at the SW side, a 3-mi. trail goes to the top.

HEADQUARTERS: BLM, Phoenix District Office, 2015 West Deer Valley Rd., Phoenix, AZ 85027; (602) 863-4464.

TONTO NATIONAL FOREST
U.S. Forest Service
2,874,580 acres; 2,969,000 acres within boundaries.

NE of Phoenix. Crossed by US 60, SR's 260, 87, 88, 188, 288.

The Forest, one huge block with only a few inholdings, has a wide range of life zones, from Lower Sonoran Desert to cool pine forests. Lying below the Mogollon Rim, its high country is on the Pinal, Mazatzal, and Sierra Ancha ranges. Its topography includes smaller ranges, some of them quite rugged; isolated peaks, ridges, hills, and buttes; broad river valleys, six large lakes, deep canyons, mesas, basins, and desert plains.

The explosive growth of the Phoenix metropolitan area has had damaging impact on the Tonto. It is now one of the most heavily used National Forests in the nation, receiving over 6 million visitor-days per year. At the same time, curtailed budgets have sharply reduced services to campgrounds and other intensive-use areas. Trail maintenance has almost ceased, except what volunteers do. Some wilderness areas are showing the effects of too many feet. Yet if one avoids the overcrowded places, there are still spectacularly beautiful, quiet regions on the Tonto.

The Forest is generally mountainous, rising from the desert valley in the S and W to the Mogollon Rim. Elevations range from 1,500 to 8,000 ft. The desert region is rolling country with sand washes and occasional mountain outcroppings. The Superstition and Goldfield mountains are within the desert. As the Forest rises above the desert, it becomes an extensive plateau cut by canyons. The Four Peaks are a central geographic feature, rising to 7,657 ft., in what is now a designated Wilderness.

These elevations have produced three major climatic zones. Annual precipitation is about 8 in. in the desert, increasing to about 34 in. on the high slopes. There are two rainy seasons, one in Aug.–Sept., the other in winter. Temperatures range between extremes: a summer high of 115°F in the desert, a winter low of −20° under or along the Mogollon Rim. However, there are opportunities for outdoor recreation in every season. In summer, valley dwellers seek refuge from heat in the high country; in winter, the low and mid-elevations are pleasant. Snow is common at higher elevations, but accumulations aren't dependable enough for a regular winter sports season.

The future of the Tonto is brighter because of the Wilderness Act. Prior to 1984, the Tonto had four Wilderness Areas, totaling 360,000 acres. The Arizona Wilderness Act of 1984 established four new Wildernesses and added acreage to two existing Wildernesses. The total is now 586,000 acres, one-fifth of the entire Forest. These eight areas, in general the least disturbed portions of the Forest, are roadless and now closed to motor vehicles, logging, and most other disturbance. While parts of the Superstition Wilderness are overused, most of the other areas are not, and here the healing processes of nature will be allowed to work.

Plants: Communities range from desert scrub with scattered saguaro cactus through chaparral/pinyon-juniper, up to ponderosa pine and some mixed conifer forest. However, only limited old growth remains and timber harvest is small. Stands are dominated by pole-size trees. Demand for fuelwood has increased.

Riparian areas make up only 1% of the Forest, but their importance is critical. In their natural state, these wetlands are highly productive, add diversity to plant life, and provide water to wildlife. Stream valleys and canyons usually have high scenic value. Many of the Tonto's riparian areas have been heavily impacted by cattle, roads, and recreational activity. Some streambanks are denuded and unstable; stream temperatures are elevated; and wildlife habitat is degraded.

Forest HQ has a checklist of plants, not printed for distribution. Entries for other sites in the Upper Sonoran Desert list typical plant species. The Tonto list seemed most interesting for its flowering plants. Included are carpetweed, spreading dogbane, milkweeds, mahonia, heliotrope, popcorn flower, pricklypear, cardinal flower, bellflower, spider flower, spiderwort, yarrows, asters, thistles, fleabanes, morning glories, geraniums, Rocky Mountain iris, phacelia, beebalm, blazing star, globemallow, four o'clocks, evening primrose, coralroot, prickly poppy, oxalis, gilias, painted trumpet, phlox, eriogonums, spring beauty, columbines, larkspurs, buttercups, ceanothus, cinquefoils, painted cup, toadflax, monkeyflowers, penstemons, speedwells, violets.

Birds: 257 species recorded. HQ has checklist of 126 species, not printed for distribution; it includes no waterfowl or shorebirds. Although we identified no birding "hot spots" comparable to those in southern AZ, birders will find many interesting places in the Tonto. The Forest has several species listed as endangered or threatened, among them bald eagle, peregrine falcon, black and zone-tailed hawks, black-crowned night-heron, osprey, Yuma clapper rail.

Mammals: 78 species recorded. HQ has checklist of 33 species, not printed for distribution.

Reptiles and amphibians: 64 species recorded. HQ has checklist of 28 species, not printed for distribution.

FEATURES

Wilderness maps were not available when we visited in 1984. The Forest map was being revised to include the new Wildernesses and other changes. The new edition was expected to be published by 1986.

Superstition Wilderness, 159,780 acres just E of Apache Junction. A section of the Wilderness boundary is on the Forest boundary. Elevations from about 2,000 ft. on the W to 6,265-ft. at Mound Mountain. In the W, nearly flat desert areas are bordered by steep, often vertical terrain. Land in the E portion is higher and more rolling. The W portion is chiefly Sonoran Desert scrub. Higher country is chiefly chaparral, extensive brush stands that are often dense. A few pockets of ponderosa pine occur at the higher elevations.

It's too hot for summer hiking in the W portion. In the E, at about 4,800 ft. elevations, average daily minimum and maximum temperatures range from 20–55°F in Dec.–Jan. to 55–85° June–Sept.

Portions of the Wilderness are overused, and show it. Of the 12 principal trailheads, Peralta and First Water get 78% of the traffic. Both are on the W side. By contrast, the two least used get only 2%. The booklet listed below under the PUBLICATIONS heading has directions to all trailheads. Within the Wilderness (pre-1984 boundaries) are 180 mi. of system trails, condition ranging from excellent to poor, plus other tracks suitable for hiking. Portions of trails are noted as "difficult to follow," "subject to flooding," and "difficult footing," so it's advisable to ask about current conditions.

The area has no perennial streams, and most springs are used by cattle.

Despite the heavy use, permits are not yet required.

Mazatzal Wilderness, 252,016 acres in the N central portion of the Forest, W of SR 87; most trailheads are reached from SR 87. The area is between the

Verde River and the Tonto Basin. Although this area is popular, visitors are more dispersed than in the Superstition, and many trails are lightly used. Large areas are relatively undisturbed.

Elevations from 2,600 ft. at the SW corner to 7,903 ft. on Mazatzal Peak. The W and N portions are level to rolling, often cut by steep-sided drainages. The central and E portions are steep, rugged, scenic, with deep, nearly inaccessible canyons and sheer escarpments.

Along the Verde River are fine areas of Lower Sonoran Desert scrub, with a variety of cacti, palo verde, ocotillo, and creosote bush. Above the desert scrub and semidesert grasslands is a mountain shrub community, including turbinella oak and manzanita, or, elsewhere, pinyon-juniper. The highest areas have stands of ponderosa pine with small pockets of Douglas-fir. Riparian zones have cottonwood, sycamore, and Arizona cypress. Temperatures are similar to those in the Superstition Wilderness at similar elevations, but much of the hiking country is higher. Snow is common in winter, often restricting travel.

The Wilderness has 240 mi. of system trails, conditions ranging from excellent to poor, plus hikeable tracks. A 28-mi. trail on the W side runs parallel to the Verde River. The Mazatzal Divide Trail, 29 mi., is the major N–S route and is generally well maintained.

Four Peaks Wilderness, 53,500 acres NE of Apache Junction; W of Roosevelt Lake, N of Apache Reservoir. Established as a Wilderness in 1984. It was a popular hiking area, and a trail guide was provided before 1984. At the S end of the Mazatzal Mountains, the Four Peaks are prominent landmarks. Highest is 7,657-ft. Browns Peak. Below the peaks is a complex of ridges and drainages, dropping down to short, deep gorges and bluffs bordering the two reservoirs. Some off-trail travel is feasible at the low elevations, but the steeper, more rugged terrain above requires knowing the trail system.

This terrain has produced interesting plant communities, with striking differences between N-facing and S-facing slopes and juxtaposition of species usually found hundreds of miles apart. The area has one of the highest concentrations of black bear in AZ, so campers should protect their food supply. There are no dependable sources of potable water.

Most trailheads are reached from SR 87. Some access roads require 4-wheel drive. The longest trail is 13 mi.; most are considerably shorter.

Sierra Ancha Wilderness, 20,850 acres on the E side of the Forest, NE of Theodore Roosevelt Lake, E of SR 288, an unpaved road called the Globe-Young Highway. The Wilderness is relatively small, irregular in shape; one neck is only a mile wide. Highest point is 7,733 ft. Aztec Peak, 7,694 ft., is just outside the boundary. Dirt tracks made during the uranium rush of the 1950s are now used as hiking trails. Off-trail hiking is difficult because of dense chaparral and steep-sided canyons. Many cliff dwellings.

Pine Mountain Wilderness, 11,450 acres, plus 8,611 acres in Prescott NF. Small, isolated, a relatively undisturbed forested area, lightly visited. On the Verde Rim, the boundary between the two Forests. High point is 7,621 ft.-Pine

Mountain, reached by trail. Access is on the Prescott NF side, from Dugas, E of I-17 near Cordes Jct. See entry, Prescott NF.

Hellsgate Wilderness, 36,780 acres. Designated a Wilderness in 1984. Not much information was available from Forest HQ that year, but people who had hiked the area were enthusiastic: "Gorgeous . . . challenging . . . wild." Access is from the N by SR 260 and Forest Road 405A to trailhead near the Ponderosa Campground, then on Trail 37. Broken terrain, moderate to steep slopes, long rocky ridges, deep narrow canyons that have water at least part of the year. Highest point is The Butte, 5,842 ft. Before Wilderness designation, visitation was about 1,000 per year.

Salome Wilderness, 18,950 acres. Designated in 1984. W of the Sierra Ancha Wilderness; N of Roosevelt Lake. Highest point is 6,300 ft. on Hopkins Mountain, lowest 2,600 ft. at the lower part of Salome Creek. Access from Forest Road 60. A canyon Wilderness that becomes rougher the further N one goes, culminating at Hell's Hole, an inaccessible area surrounded by high bluffs and dense brush.

Salt River Canyon Wilderness, 32,800 acres. One of the most dramatic vistas in Arizona is the US 60 crossing of Salt River Canyon, between the Fort Apache and San Carlos Indian Reservations, near but not in the Forest. The highway descends 2,000 ft. by switchbacks to the river bridge, then ascends. Along the way are overlooks and picnic sites. A riverside road leads to falls upstream. Below US 60, the river soon becomes the boundary between the Reservation and the Tonto NF. After about 25 mi., it enters the Forest. The 22-mi. segment from here to SR 288 was considered for Wild and Scenic River designation. For most of this distance, the river runs within a steep-walled canyon. The rugged terrain, making land access difficult, has kept this area in natural condition. The riparian areas are habitat for over 200 wildlife species. Until river running became popular, this Wilderness had few visitors. Even now the river segment has only about 5,000 visitors per year, half of them river runners.

Wild and Scenic River designation was recommended in the Forest Service study requested by Congress as the best way to protect natural values. Local interests were opposed. Supporters were shocked when Secretary of Agriculture Block overruled his staff and vetoed protection; he did so chiefly because protecting the natural values would preclude water development projects.

Pinal Mountains, S of Globe. A scenic, rugged area, the Pinal Mountains occupy the SE corner of the Forest. The range is only 10 mi. long, rises to 7,812 ft. at Signal Mountain. Two roads crossing the area are marked "graded," but it's advisable to inquire. The roads lead to several small campgrounds at elevations as high as 7,500 ft. and to several trailheads. The largest campground, with 27 sites, is at Pioneer Pass, elevation 6,100 ft., on the banks of upper Pinal Creek. Campgrounds at these upper elevations are closed by heavy snow in winter, but others at 4,000 ft. remain open. Pine, fir, and aspen stands at high elevations.

Lakes. Six man-made lakes lie E and NE of Phoenix: Horseshoe (2,800 acres) and Bartlett (2,700 acres) on the Verde River; Saguaro (1,280 acres), Canyon (950 acres), Apache (2,600 acres) and the largest, Theodore Roosevelt (17,000 acres) on the Salt River. Theodore Roosevelt Lake was the first large federal reclamation project, completed in 1911. Arizona is said to have the largest per capita boat ownership in the United States (a statement we could not verify), and these are among the popular lakes. Roosevelt, the largest, has the most commercial development. Saguaro, closest to Phoenix, has a busy marina. The Verde River lakes have fewer visitors and less traffic than those on the Salt.

The Salt River lakes are on the Apache Trail, SR 88 NE from Apache Junction. In 1984 the E portion of this road was dirt, not recently bladed. Planned reconstruction of Roosevelt Dam would cut off access to Roosevelt Lake from this direction, but most visitors now use the better road: SR 88 from Globe.

Forest Service campgrounds are on all the lakes. Camping is informal. At Horse Pasture on Roosevelt Lake, more than a hundred RVs were parked at the shore, others back in the trees. Windy Hill has a large paved parking area and a huge ramp. People camp wherever they please. Camping, boating, and fishing are the principal activities. People swim, but this doesn't seem to be popular. Most of the terrain around the lakes is open enough for hiking, but few trails are near the lake shores.

We didn't like Roosevelt Lake well enough to launch our boat. The lake was drawn down 8 to 10 ft. and the shoreline looked raw. It would have felt like cruising in a huge bathtub.

Lower Salt River: Below Saguaro Lake is a 12-mi. section of the river used for tubing in summer. We were told that as many as 20,000 people may float the river this way in one day. We did not go to see it.

Verde River: About 21 mi. of the Verde River were designated an official "Scenic River" by the Arizona Wilderness Act of 1984; an additional 20 mi. were designated a "Wild River." This section, like the Salt River Canyon, is sufficiently rugged to have discouraged development. The meandering river has created a riparian deciduous forest within the Sonoran Desert. Principal species are cottonwood, willow, ash, Arizona oak, hackberry, burrobrush, baccharis, desert willow, mesquite, salt cedar.

Access is difficult by land, often requiring 4-wheel-drive vehicles. Present recreational use is light: camping near the primitive roads, hunting and fishing, floating during spring flows with small rafts or kayaks. Says the Forest Service, "It very definitely is not a river meant for beginners or novices."

NEARBY: *Boyce Thompson Southwestern Arboretum:* 12 mi. E of Florence Jct. on US 60/70. Botanic garden and bird sanctuary. Trails. (See entry.)

INTERPRETATION

The Forest has no visitor center. No campfire programs, guided hikes, other naturalist activities.

Three short nature trails: Desert Vista, Signal Peak, Abert.

ACTIVITIES

Camping: 52 campgrounds, many with undesignated sites. Most were open all year, but better check. Many informal sites.

Hiking, backpacking: Over 800 mi. of trails. Trail maintenance budgets have been severely curtailed, and many trails are in poor condition. Many trail markers have been vandalized. Inquire before any extensive backcountry outing.

Hunting: Mule deer, whitetail deer, javelina, small game.

Fishing: Some trout streams. Lakes: bass, crappie, catfish.

Horse riding: No prohibitions, but some trails are too rocky or steep for horse travel. List of outfitters available.

Swimming: Lakes, some swimming holes in rivers.

Boating: On lakes. Several marinas. Many ramps.

Rafting: Portions of the Salt and Verde rivers are suitable for small rafts or kayaks in spring flows. Many hazards. Inquire.

PUBLICATIONS

Forest map. $1.

Forest leaflet (photocopied).

Wilderness booklets:
  Superstition Wilderness.
  Mazatzal Wilderness.
  Sierra Ancha Wilderness.

Other booklets:
  Four Peaks Trail Guide (now a Wilderness).
  Pinal Mountains Trail and Camping Guide.
  River Runners Guide to the Verde River.
  River Runners Guide; Upper Salt River.

Information pages:
  Existing Native Vertebrate Species.
  General information.

Photocopied flora/fauna lists (several).

REFERENCES

Nelson, D. and S. *Hiker's Guide to the Superstition Mountains.* Glenwood, NM: Tecolote Press, 1978.

Ganci, Dave. *Hiking the Southwest.* San Francisco: Sierra Club Books, 1983, pp. 99–113.

Mazel, David. *Arizona Trails.* Berkeley, CA: Wilderness Press, 1981, pp. 13–83.

HEADQUARTERS: P.O. Box 29070, Phoenix, AZ 85038; (602) 225-5200.

RANGER DISTRICTS: Cave Creek R.D., P.O. Box 768, Carefree, AZ 85377; (602) 488-3441. Globe R.D., Rt. 1, Box 33, Globe, AZ 85501; (602) 425-

7189. Mesa R.D., P.O. Drawer A, 26 N. MacDonald, Mesa, AZ 85201; (602) 261-6446. Payson R.D., 1009 E. Highway 260, Payson, AZ 85541; (602) 474-2269. Pleasant Valley R.D., P.O. Box 268, Young, AZ 85554; (602) 462-3311. Tonto Basin R.D., P.O. Box 647, Roosevelt, AZ 65545; (602) 467-2236.

TONTO NATIONAL MONUMENT
National Park Service
1,120 acres.

From Globe, NW 28 mi. on SR 88.

Open: 8 A.M.–5 P.M. daily. Lower Ruin trail closes at 4 P.M. daily.

Our entries seldom include historical sites, but the main theme here is how the Salado Indians lived in their natural environment. The visitor center exhibits have much to say about native plants. One hikes to the ruins up a desert hillside, with plants identified. The trail takes one into terrain that would otherwise require some scrambling. The bird checklist is applicable to the entire Theodore Roosevelt Lake area. From the visitor center and above one has a splendid view of the lake and surrounding hills.

FEATURES
Visitor center has information, publications, exhibits, film.
Self-guiding trail to the Lower Ruin.
Guided hikes to the Upper Ruin. 3 hrs. Arrangements must be made 2 days in advance (but one can sometimes join a tour at the last minute if the group is small). Tours start at 9 A.M. only.

PUBLICATIONS
Leaflet.
Bird checklist.
Checklist of mammals, reptiles and amphibians.
Self-guiding tour booklet. $0.50.

HEADQUARTERS: P.O. Box 707, Roosevelt, AZ 85545; (602) 467-2241.

TONTO NATURAL BRIDGE
Privately owned

From Payson, 12 mi. NW on SR 87. Left 3 mi. on graded road.

An inholding in the Tonto National Forest. We were told the Arizona State Parks Board has long wanted to acquire the site, but the legislature has not provided funds. The 183-foot travertine arch spans the canyon of Pine Creek, which has deep pools and cataracts. The approach is at the level of the top of the span. To see it properly requires a vantage point, preferably walking down. When we were there a thin stream was falling from the top.

A commercial operation, somewhat primitive, not unpleasantly so.

WALNUT CANYON NATIONAL MONUMENT
National Park Service
2,249 acres.

From Flagstaff, 10 mi. E on I-40.

Open: daily except Christmas Day. Memorial Day–Labor Day: 7 A.M.–7 P.M.; otherwise 8 A.M.–5 P.M.

Two unusual factors caused the Sinagua to choose this canyon about 900 years ago: an abundance of plants for food and fiber and a dependable water supply. The water supply was the result of a thick layer of moisture-retaining volcanic ash deposited about that time, which changed a dry area into rich farmland. That water supply is now supplemented by a dam built in the early 1900s, prior to the establishment of the Monument. Some of the plants found here normally grow only at higher or lower elevations. Black walnut, for example, usually occurs below 5,000 ft., but here it thrives at well over 6,000 where the canyon's shelter and southern exposure give protection and warmth. Douglas-fir usually grows above 8,000 ft. elevation, but here it grows on N-facing slopes, where snowfall provides needed moisture and coolness.

The canyon is about 400 ft. deep. Elevation at the rim is about 6,800 ft. A 3/4-mi. trail descends 185 ft. to the cliff dwellings. Birders will have much use for their binoculars along the trail. A shorter paved trail follows the rim. Off-trail hiking is forbidden.

June–Aug. have the heaviest visitation, Nov.–Feb. the lightest.

Plants: Those the Sinagua used include ponderosa pine, pinyon pine, juniper, Douglas-fir, locust, black walnut, aspen, willow, boxelder, hoptree, hollygrape, serviceberry, elderberry, snowberry, lemonade sumac, mountain-mahogany, cliff rose, currant, saltbush, wild tobacco, Mormon tea, grape, agave, yucca, cacti. List available.

Wildlife: Bird and mammal checklists available.

INTERPRETATION: *Visitor center* has exhibits, literature.

PUBLICATIONS
Park folder with map.
Bird, mammal, and plant checklists.
General information page.
Trail guide. $0.50.

HEADQUARTERS: Walnut Canyon Road, Flagstaff, AZ 86001; (602) 526-3367.

WHITE CANYON
U.S. Bureau of Land Management
6,968 acres.

From Superior on US 60/70, SE about 9 mi. on SR 177. The site lies W of SR 177 between the National Forest boundary and the Gila River.

This site offers attractive opportunities for day hiking from a car camp or a leisurely weekend backpack. The unit is a rugged portion of the Mineral Mountains, with a portion of its outwash plain to the S. Large, hilly mesas are dissected by deep canyons. The rocky terrain displays layering, color, and features sculptured by erosion.

White Canyon descends S into the unit from the Tonto National Forest. About 3 mi. of the canyon are within the unit. The canyon varies from wide to narrow, with 800-ft. vertical walls. The canyon floor includes sandy, rocky, and slickrock sections. The stream is intermittent, but pools remain long after rainfall. Seasonal rains create temporary waterfalls from the rim. Dense growths of willow and shrubs line the canyon. The availability of water and the vegetation attract birds and other wildlife. It is one of the few BLM-managed land areas with both bear and mountain lion.

A striking feature of the site is The Rincon, a large amphitheater towering 600 to 1,000 ft. above the outwash plain.

HEADQUARTERS: BLM, Phoenix District Office, 2015 W. Deer Valley Rd., Phoenix, AZ 85027; (602) 863-4464.

ZONE 5

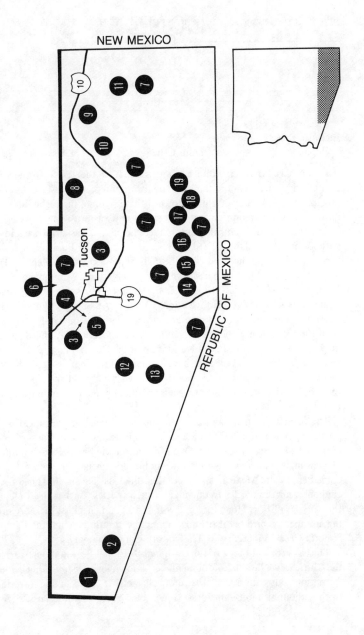

NEW MEXICO

REPUBLIC OF MEXICO

Tucson

ZONE 5

Includes these countries:
Pima   Santa Cruz   Cochise

In southern Arizona, mountain ranges rise from the desert. In the western part of this zone, the mountains are too low to intercept moisture, but annual precipitation increases gradually toward the E: from 4 in. in the far W to 20 in. on the higher mountains of the central and eastern areas.

Tucson is in the central sector. Like Phoenix, it has grown explosively, without coherent plan or heed for resources. But, like Phoenix, it is almost surrounded by public land. On the S is Pima County's splendid Tucson Mountain Park. The two parts of the Saguaro National Monument are E and W of the city. On the N and NE, the suburbs are squeezing against the boundaries of the Coronado National Forest. At Sabino Canyon, visitors must now park outside the gate and proceed on foot or by shuttle bus.

In the western part of the zone, Organ Pipe Cactus National Monument lies between the Cabeza Prieta National Wildlife Refuge and the huge Papago Indian Reservation. These sites have similar natural qualities, and the Monument is more accessible than the others. A visitor should spend several days there before deciding to undertake a more difficult and demanding visit to the Refuge.

The principal central and eastern mountain ranges are occupied by eight separate portions of the Coronado National Forest. Our entry describes each, and each has special features. One of them, in the Santa Rita Mountains S of Tucson, is Madera Canyon, known to birders throughout the world. Many come here to add Mexican species to their life lists. This is only one of several canyons near the border frequented by such species. Birders are welcome in the canyons of Fort Huachuca and will find a good checklist there. A surprising number of birders also know about the tiny but delightful Patagonia-Sonoita Creek Sanctuary of The Nature Conservancy.

The easternmost block of the Coronado National Forest almost surrounds the Chiricahua National Monument, best known for its astonishing geological formations but with many other natural assets. It can be a fine introduction to the adjoining mountain forest, much of it roadless wilderness.

ARIZONA-SONORA DESERT MUSEUM
Private, nonprofit.
100 acres.

14 mi. W of downtown Tucson via Speedway and Gates Pass Rd.

Founded in 1952 by William H. Carr and Arthur N. Pack, both then members of the Pima County Park Committee, which made land available within the Tucson Mountain Park (see entry). Bill Carr had planned and built one of the Nation's first wayside nature museums at Bear Mountain, NY. The Desert Museum has become a model for many others. One Carr himself designed is Ghost Ranch (see entry, NM Zone 1).

The Museum is a botanic garden, zoo, museum, education center, and research institution, in and for the Sonora Desert. From its site on the Tucson Mountains, visitors look out over the Avra Valley to mountain ranges. Wandering the Museum paths, it's impossible to know which plants grew here naturally and which were artfully transplanted from nearby. The Museum has an aviary, but birds of many species frequent the grounds. Years ago we sat one night in a blind near the Director's home and watched deer and javelina come to a water hole.

We first visited the Museum in 1964, a year after two fascinating new watershed exhibits had been completed, one sponsored by the Bureau of Land Management, the other by the Soil Conservation Service. An even earlier exhibit was the tunnel, where visitors' dark-adapted eyes look into the underground dens of kit fox, rattlesnake, and other desert dwellers taking shelter from midday sun.

The Museum continued to grow and innovate, not always in ways that pleased us, especially when the watershed exhibits were neglected and abandoned and the trend seemed to be toward making the Museum a zoo. On our most recent visit, however, we were much impressed by a new earth sciences building and even more by the many lively, well-informed docents giving brief, informal lectures and demonstrations throughout the grounds.

Don't miss it! A day isn't long enough to see it all.

PUBLICATION: Leaflet with map.

ADJACENT
Tucson Mountain Park (see entry).
Saguaro National Monument, Tucson Mountain Unit (see entry).

HEADQUARTERS: P.O. Box 5607, Tucson, AZ 85703; (602) 883-1380.

BABOQUIVARI PEAK
Bureau of Land Management
4,435 acres.

From SR 86 at Three Points, W of Tucson, turn S on SR 286 for about 28 mi. Right turn into Thomas Canyon. Park on State land and hike through the canyon across the ranch.

The Baboquivari Mountains are a N–S range extending 35 mi. from Kitt Peak to the Mexican border. The ridge is the E border of the Papago Indian Reservation. Baboquivari Peak is a massive granite monolith rising to 7,734 ft., over 1,000 ft. above the surrounding mountains, 4,200 ft. above the Altar Valley floor. The peak is known to technical climbers as the only multiday Grade 6, Class 6 climb in AZ. The mountain crest can be hiked.

Some visitors are thought to reach the mountains from the Indian Reservation, presumably having bought permits. From the E, access is across private land through Thomas Canyon. This attractive high desert canyon was purchased by The Nature Conservancy. TNC resold it to a private buyer with conditions intended to preserve the natural qualities of the canyon and provide public pedestrian access to the BLM-managed public land on the E slope of the mountains. No parking or trailhead facilities are available.

On the slopes rising from the valley is a Sonoran Desert community of palo verde, saguaro, ocotillo, and mesquite, blending into chaparral. Higher elevations have Arizona white oak and Mexican pinyon; moister areas have a lusher mix of oaks, pinyon, mountain-mahogany, walnut, and chaparral dense enough to obstruct hikers.

There are no trails above the 4,500-ft. elevation, and the hike to the crest isn't an easy one. The rewards are solitude and splendid vistas. Local hiking and conservation clubs sponsor hikes up Baboquivari. This is a good means of introduction to this rugged area.

HEADQUARTERS: BLM, Phoenix District Office, 2015 W. Deer Valley Rd., Phoenix, AZ 85027; (602) 863-4464.

CABEZA PRIETA NATIONAL WILDLIFE REFUGE
U.S. Fish and Wildlife Service
860,000 acres.

From Gila Bend on I-8, S on SR 85 to Ajo. The visitor contact station is here.

No one visits here casually. Almost all the Refuge is within the Luke Air Force Range. No one may enter without a permit. Permits must be requested 2 to 3 weeks ahead of time so the Refuge office can check flying schedules. When the Range is active, no permits are issued. The applicant must sign a Military Hold Harmless Agreement. Visitors are warned that the area has been a gunnery range since 1941 and has also been a bombing range; unexploded ordnance may be on the ground or just beneath.

Standard two-wheel-drive cars aren't barred, but drivers are warned that low-clearance vehicles may be damaged by brush and rocks and can be trapped in soft, sandy places.

Also, this is one of the hottest, driest deserts in North America. Several thousand tried to cross here on the Camino del Diablo in Gold Rush days. Hundreds died. From then until the 1930s, when prospectors arrived, the region saw few intruders. The prospectors made no strikes and went away.

Despite this, Cabeza Prieta has attractions and enthusiasts. It is one of the last remaining large expanses of Sonoran Desert. The area was made a refuge to preserve desert bighorn sheep. A few remain, perhaps fewer than a hundred, and the Refuge is also home for the endangered Sonoran pronghorn and other rare or endangered species. Although vast expanses are predominantly creosote bush and bursage, it has much of interest to botanists. It has a small, elite following of self-styled "desert rats," outdoorsmen who understand how to survive in these conditions and who enjoy knowing that in the vast backcountry they are unlikely to meet or even see another human. We were told repeatedly that this is one of Edward Abbey's favorite places.

The number of permits issued isn't large, perhaps a hundred in a year, and most of these go to motorists who drive the Camino without venturing far from their vehicles. Vehicles must stay on the few designated roads; permits allow hikers to go into the backcountry, but few do.

Visitors new to the area would do well to go first to the Organ Pipe Cactus National Monument, which adjoins (see entry). Cabeza Prieta has less of the Arizona succulent desert, but some areas have giant saguaro and organ pipe cacti. It has more of the Mexican Sonora Pinacate Lavas, ribbons of black lava that flowed northward among the dunes of the Pinta Sands. Some experience in the Monument is a good preparation for the more demanding conditions of Cabeza Prieta.

Average annual precipitation is about 9 in. in the eastern portion, an almost insignificant 3 in. in the western. Even "desert rats" stay away during the summer.

Birds: Water catchments and wells were dug to provide water for wildlife. These miniature oases now attract birds of many species. 165 species have been recorded, and an annotated checklist is available. Feb.–May and Sept.–Nov. are the best birding seasons.

Mammals: No checklist. Species similar to those occurring in the adjoining

National Monument. Blacktail jackrabbit, desert cottontail, roundtail and antelope ground squirrels, and coyote are the species most often seen. Present but seldom seen include bighorn sheep, pronghorn, mule and whitetail deer, ringtail, bobcat, mountain lion.

INFORMATION: The only visitor contact station is at Ajo. Exhibits, literature.

ACTIVITIES

Camping: No campground; no facilities. Anyone with a permit can camp anywhere.

Hiking, backpacking: The Camino del Diablo is sometimes hiked during the winter months; there's no traffic. Summer hiking anywhere is definitely not advisable.

PUBLICATIONS

Leaflet with map.
Bird checklist.
Amphibian and reptile checklist.
Permit application; hold harmless agreement.

REFERENCE: Ganci, Dave. *Hiking the Southwest.* San Francisco: Sierra Club
    Books, 1983, pp. 151–153.

HEADQUARTERS: Box 418, Ajo, AZ 85321; (602) 387-6483.

CANELO HILLS CIENEGA
Arizona Nature Conservancy
254 acres.

Visitors are asked to call ahead and register on arrival. S of Tucson. From Sonoita at intersection of SRs 82 and 83, S 14.7 mi. on SR 83. Left at turnoff Milepost 16.

Closed Mon.–Tues.

Some say *cienega* is Spanish for "marshland"; others say it means "savannahs dominated by tall grasses with meandering streams in the valley along with numerous springs and wet meadows." Few natural wetlands remain in AZ, and the preservation of those remaining is important. This one has been designated a National Natural Landmark.

The site is within the Coronado National Forest on the E side of the Canelo Hills. At 4,950 ft. elevation, O'Donnell Creek flows in a narrow valley bordered by gently sloping ridges. This is a transition zone between plains grassland and oak woodland. The riparian habitat is dominated by Fremont cottonwood, Goodding willow, and Arizona walnut. Arizona oak appears in the stream forest and, along with Emory oak and alligator-bark juniper, dots the grass-covered slopes.

Other riparian flora include Texas mulberry, arroyo willow, false indigo, golden currant, canyon grape, spike rush, flatsedge, Canada wild rye, spreading dogbane, field mint, black medic, scouring rush, white sweet-clover, pony foot, sideoats grama, and dallis grass.

Among the many plant species dependent on this moist habitat is an orchid discovered here in 1968, the first time the species had been recorded in the United States.

Birds: 170 species recorded. No checklist, but the 48-page *Birds of Fort Huachuca* will serve. (See Fort Huachuca entry.) Notable here are yellow-billed cuckoo, yellow-breasted chat, blue grosbeak, Montezuma quail, Cooper's hawk.

Mammals: Species recorded include striped skunk, raccoon, coyote, bobcat, coatimundi, javelina, whitetail deer.

Fishes: The creek is habitat for several species of endangered fishes.

Camping: A campground is available at Patagonia Lake State Park (see entry).

No pets, camping, hunting, fishing, picnicking, or stepping off the paths.

PUBLICATION: Leaflet.

NEARBY

Mile Hi/Ramsey Canyon Preserve.
Patagonia-Sonoita Creek Preserve.
(See entries.)

HEADQUARTERS: HCR, Box 289; Elgin, AZ 85611; (602) 455-5556.

CATALINA STATE PARK
Arizona State Parks
5,500 acres.

10 mi. N of Tucson on US 89.

An attractive new addition to the State Park system, on the NW slopes of the Santa Catalina Mountains. It happened just in time. Tucson's suburban sprawl has reached the gate. The park seems destined to become an overused city recreation site.

Probably not for a few years. In 1984 the basic facilities were in place, but work was still in progress. On a fine weekday morning, we were the only visitors. From the highway, it's a 2-mi. drive to the trailhead parking, passing campground and picnic area on the way. Foothills are nearby, the mountains not far beyond. The nearer slopes have scattered saguaros and chollas, grasses, shrubs, mesquite. Elevations at the park range from 2,650 to 4,000 ft., with most of the area between 3,000 and 3,200. Two major washes, Sutherland and Canada del Oro, cross the park.

ACTIVITIES

Camping: 50 sites. All year.

Hiking, backpacking: Trailhead parking lot. Within one mi., riparian areas; streams flow most of the year; pools. Signed for Sutherland Trail and Romero Canyon Trail in the Coronado National Forest, Santa Catalina Ranger District. The Pusch Ridge Wilderness isn't far away.

Horse riding: Parking area for horse trailers.

PUBLICATIONS

Leaflet with map.
Bird checklist.
Trail map.

HEADQUARTERS: P.O. Box 36986, Tucson, AZ 85740; (602) 628-5798.

CHIRICAHUA NATIONAL MONUMENT
National Park Service
11,938 acres.

From Willcox, 36 mi. SE on SRs 186 and 181.

Most people come to see the unusual geological formations: thousands of chimneylike columns, many eroded to form balancing rocks. A visitor center is near the entrance. From here a 6-mi. paved road ascends Bonita Canyon to Massai Point, which offers splendid views of the Monument, Sulphur Springs Valley, and San Simon Valley. At the Point are an exhibit building and several trailheads. If you can arrange it, a fine way to see the Monument is to ride up to the Point, then hike down.

Located in the Chiricahua Mountains, the Monument is surrounded on three sides by the Coronado National Forest (see entry). The Chiricahua Wilderness is partially within the Forest, partially within the Monument. Elevations within the Monument range from 5,160 ft. to 7,825 ft. in the upper slopes of Whitetail Canyon. Average annual precipitation is 18 to 20 in., with two rainy seasons, summer and winter. Average annual snowfall is light: 1 to 4 in. Temperatures are moderate. June, the hottest month, has a mean high of 90°F; Jan., a mean low of 29°F.

Plants: Most photographs of the Monument show rocky landscapes, and the Bonita Canyon road offers views of thousands of massive columns. Yet 70% of the Monument area is forested. Vegetation at lower elevations is typically oak woodland, grading through oak-pine woodland to limited areas of ponderosa pine or Douglas-fir on the upper plateaus and N slopes. Prominent tree species include Chihuahua pine, pinyon pine, Arizona cypress, sycamore, several oak varieties.

Birds: Checklist available indicates abundance and seasonality. Seasonally common species include turkey vulture, band-tailed pigeon, white-winged and mourning doves, great horned and elf owls, whip-poor-will, poor-will; black-chinned, broad-tailed, and rufous hummingbirds. Woodpeckers: northern flicker, acorn, yellow-bellied sapsucker, hairy, Strickland's. Flycatchers: ash-throated, olivaceous, gray, dusky, Hammond's. Cassin's kingbird, Say's phoebe, western wood-pewee, Steller's and Mexican jays, common raven, Mexican chickadee, bridled titmouse, bushtit, white-breasted nuthatch, brown creeper; Bewick's, canyon, and rock wrens; American robin, hermit thrush, western bluebird, Townsend's solitaire, ruby-crowned kinglet; Hutton's, solitary, and warbling vireos. Warblers: yellow-rumped, black-throated gray, Grace's, Wilson's, painted redstart. Scott's oriole, western and hepatic tanagers, black-headed grosbeak; rufous-sided, brown, and green-tailed towhees; chipping and rufous-crowned sparrows; dark-eyed, gray-headed, and yellow-eyed juncos.

Mammals: An exceptionally well-annotated checklist says where and when to look for the various species; a "visibility index" estimates the likelihood of seeing them. ("The cliff chipmunk and rock squirrel are very common in the campground. The Chiricahua fox squirrel is often found in canyon bottoms in a pine or cypress tree. The two ground squirrels may be found in low country west of the Monument.") The long list of bat species carries a note that it's difficult to identify them. Other species the visitor might see include blacktail jackrabbit, desert and eastern cottontails, kangaroo rats; brush, cactus, deer, rock, and white-footed mice; Mexican and white-throated woodrats, coyote, gray fox, coatimundi, ringtail, raccoon, striped skunk, javelina, mule and whitetail deer.

Amphibians, turtles, and lizards: Checklist available, also well annotated. Includes spadefoot toads: western, Couch's, plains. True toads: Great Plains, green, southwestern Woodhouse's, red-spotted. Southwestern leopard frog, canyon treefrog. Ornate box turtle. Western banded gecko, Great Plains skink, Arizona alligator lizard; Texas and round-tailed lizards, mountain short-horned lizard. Other lizards: bunch grass, striped plateau, eastern fence, Clark's spiny, Yarrow's spiny; tree lizard, Chihuahua and desert-grassland whiptails, Gila monster, collared lizard.

Snakes: Annotated checklist available. Includes Sonoran mountain king-snake, Huachucan ringed kingsnake, Sonoran blind snake, Sonoran racer, lined coachwhip, red coachwhip, cloudy leaf-nosed snake, Sonoran gopher snake, long-nosed snake, mountain and Big Bend patch-nosed snakes, Mexican and Huachucan black-headed snakes; black-necked, Mexican, and checkered garter snakes; Sonoran lyre snake. Arizona coral snake. Rattlesnakes: massasauga, western diamondback, banded rock, black-tailed, twin-spotted, Mojave, Arizona ridge-nosed.

FEATURES

Sugarloaf Peak, 7,308 ft., is a 1-mi. uphill scenic hike from the Sugarloaf parking area, on one of the many trails built by the Civilian Conservation Corps. One of the highest points in the Monument, with sweeping vistas.

Echo Canyon offers some of the best views of the rock formations. Loop trail from Echo Canyon Trailhead near Massai Point.

Heart of Rocks is a 7-mi. round-trip hike among the formations, including Big Balancing Rock.

Natural Bridge offers a 5-mi. round-trip hike through North Bonita Canyon to a small natural bridge.

Chiricahua Wilderness, 10,290 acres, adjoining Wilderness area in the Coronado NF. Monument literature makes no mention of the Wilderness, and no trails are identified as wilderness routes. The Arizona Wilderness Act of 1984 transferred 850 acres of National Forest land in the Bonita Creek watershed to be added to this Wilderness. Five Research Natural Areas have been established in the Monument. Four of these are on or near the Natural Bridge Trail.

INTERPRETATION

Visitor center has information, exhibits, films. Open daily, 8 A.M.–5 P.M., except Thanksgiving, Christmas, New Year's Day.

Geological exhibit at Massai Point.

Nature trails: Massai Point and Rhyolite Canyon.

Campfire programs: mid-Mar. through Labor Day (approx.).

Guided hikes: mid-Mar. through Memorial Day.

ACTIVITIES

Camping: 26 sites. All year. In late Sept. we saw few other campers. Should this campsite be full, nearby Pinery Canyon in the Coronado National Forest has many informal sites.

Hiking: 17 mi. of trails. Backpacking—trailside camping—is not permitted. However, several trails lead into the National Forest.

Horse riding: Permitted on trails, but no stable or outfitter is nearby.

PUBLICATIONS

Leaflet with map.
Checklists:

Trees and shrubs.
Birds.
Mammals.
Amphibians, turtles, and lizards.
Snakes.
Massai Point trail guide. $0.50.
Rhyolite Canyon Nature Trail Guide. $1.

The park drive has occasionally been closed because of snow, ice, or fallen boulders; closures are usually brief. Flooding caused by heavy summer rains has occasionally blocked access to the park.

HEADQUARTERS: Dos Cabezas Route, Box 6500, Willcox, AZ 85643; (602) 824-3560.

CORONADO NATIONAL FOREST
U.S. Forest Service
1,727,058 acres; 1,853,779 acres within boundaries.

12 widely scattered Divisions are on most of the mountain ranges in SE Arizona. 5 Divisions are N of I-10, others S. Only one Division is W of I-19. No US highway crosses a Division and few state highways cross.

The widely spaced mountain ranges of SE Arizona are not the highest in AZ, but the wide range of elevations, from 3,500 ft. to 10,717, provides great variety and contrast, green slopes rising like islands in the desert.

The Forest contains a great variety of habitats. Most of the arid valleys of SE Arizona are typical of the Chihuahuan Desert, and this community includes the bajadas and foothills of the mountain ranges. The S mountains of the Forest are characteristic of the Mexican Highlands or Sierra Madrean biotic communities. The two large mountain ranges N of I-10 have some affinity with Rocky Mountain flora and fauna, intermixed with species typical of the Madrean. The high country of the Catalinas and Grahams looks much like southern Colorado, while the Patagonias and Huachucas resemble the central Chihuahuan pattern.

The mountains have streams, small lakes, tall trees, countless wildflowers, and the continent's southernmost ski area. The mountains are exceptionally rich in their diversity of flora and fauna. Birders come to the canyons to see species that go no farther north; over 300 species have been recorded in Madera Canyon. Some parts of the Coronado are heavily impacted, far too many people trampling the ground cover, but the Forest has 339,000 acres of roadless Wilderness Areas, and one can always find quiet trails. The network of Forest roads is not extensive, but quiet campsites can be found even on major weekends.

Nogales and Sierra Vista Ranger Districts, 633,780 acres. Four blocks, W, N, and E of Nogales.

The first block, W of I-19, on the Mexican border, is on the Tumacacori Mountains. The only paved road penetrates from I-19 to Pena Blanca Lake, only 50 surface acres but about a mi. long, popular with fishermen. The lake is in handsome, rugged country: steep, irregular hills with many rock outcrops, vegetation mostly grasses and juniper. Lodge, concession. This Ruby-Nogales Road continues past the lake, unpaved, through the town of Ruby and NW to Arivaca; on the way it passes the entrance to Sycamore Canyon in the Pajarita Wilderness (see below). (The Sycamore Canyon Wilderness, surrounding a different Sycamore Canyon, is in the Coconino, Kaibab, and Prescott National Forests.) One Forest campground is at the lake, another 3 mi. closer to I-19. Highest point in this block is 6,440 ft. The lake is at 4,000 ft. The Forest map shows a few trails, but the country is open enough for easy off-trail hiking. Flora of the area include rare species and others seldom seen N of Mexico.

The second, N block, on the Santa Rita Mountains, includes Madera Canyon, reached by a paved road E from Continental on I-19. Mt. Hopkins, 8,585 ft., site of a famous observatory, is a popular hiking destination from the Canyon. A National Recreation Trail goes up 9,450-ft. Mt. Wrightson, at the heart of a 25,260-acre Wilderness proclaimed in 1984. The road from Continental crosses the Santa Rita Experimental Range, a Forest Service research center established in 1903 to study desert grasslands.

The third block is on the Mexican border. Its W half is on the Patagonia Mountains, E of Nogales and S of Patagonia. Highest point is 6,490 ft.; elevations are generally below 5,500. Mining and cattle ranching have been the chief uses here. The area has considerable interest for botanists, notably an undisturbed site SW of Harshaw, at the center of the block. The E half is crossed by SR 83, an all-weather road as far S as Parker Lake. The SE portion is on the Huachuca Mountains. Highest point is 9,466-ft. Miller Peak, in the Miller Peak Wilderness.

The fourth and smallest block, SW of Benson, is on the Whetstone Mountains. No roads cross it; a few primitive roads penetrate side canyons. It has only primitive trails. Highest point is 6,628 ft. Hunting is the principal recreational use. French Joe Canyon is a popular undeveloped camping area.

Santa Catalina Ranger District, 255,708 acres. This R.D. adjoins Tucson and thus has more visitors than other Districts. Its best-known features, both NE of the city, are Sabino Canyon and Mt. Lemmon, highest point in the Santa Catalina Mountains. Pusch Ridge Wilderness borders the N side of the Tucson area. The S portion of the block is on the Rincon Mountains, half surrounding the Rincon Mountain Unit of the Saguaro National Monument (see entry).

Safford Ranger District, 415,132 acres. Four blocks (two large and two smaller), N of Willcox, W of Safford.

No paved road approaches the large western block on the Galiuro Mountains. The closest access is from Bonito on SR 266 W to Sunset. Much of the site is within the Galiuro Wilderness. Peaks over 7,000 ft. Immediately to the N is BLM's Aravaipa Canyon Wilderness (see entry).

The largest of the 4 blocks, nearest to Safford, is on the Pinaleno Mountains, also called the Graham Mountains, highest in the Forest. Mt. Graham rises to 10,720 ft. SR 266, paved here, crosses the S portion of the block. From Swift Trail Junction on US 666 S of Safford, SR 366 is paved part of the way to Riggs Flat Lake. This is a splendidly scenic route, but inquire about road conditions. This block has 5 Forest campgrounds, many informal campsites, a network of trails.

A smaller northern block is on the Santa Teresa Mountains. Highest elevation is 7,150 ft. The Forest map of this block shows a network of trails but no roads, although there are a couple of 4-wheel-drive routes in the N sector.

The smallest of the blocks is on the N end of the Winchester Mountains. The map shows a few mi. of primitive roads, no trails. Highest point is 7,631-ft. Mt. Reiley. A natural area of special interest is Reiley Canyon, an undisturbed riparian forest between 5,500 and 6,250 ft. elevation.

Douglas Ranger District, 422,438 acres. Three blocks. One is on the Dragoon Mountains, W of Sunsites on US 666; principal feature is Cochise Stronghold, favorite summer campsite of the Apache chief and his band.

The largest block is SE of Willcox, on the spectacular Chiricahua Mountains; access from SR 186, SR 181, and US 80. The Chiricahua National Monument is in its N portion. Chiricahua Peak is 9,795 ft. Delightful campsites are along the several scenic creeks: Pinery Canyon, Turkey Creek, Rucker Creek, Cave Creek, with trails into the central Wilderness.

The smallest block, on the Peloncillo Mountains, is largely in NM, reached by county road E from Douglas.

Climate: The weather depends on where you are. When the wind-chill factor is nudging the temperature to zero on one of the higher peaks, it may be a summery 70-plus in the foothills. Average annual precipitation is about 11 in. at low elevations, 35 in. on the high peaks. "One Hour to Canada" was the title of an article in the Arizona-Sonora Desert Museum newsletter, observing that every 1,000 ft. of ascent from the desert is like moving 300 mi. N. The equivalent of a 2,000-mi. journey N can here be enjoyed in an hour's drive. On the way one passes through the life zones of flora and fauna typical of several geographic zones, from cacti to white fir.

Plants: The range of elevations promises a corresponding range of life zones. Ascending Mt. Lemmon, one passes from desert scrub through grassland, shrubland, and oak woodland to conifer forest. As is usually the case, the transitions occur at higher elevations on S slopes than on N slopes. Other factors, including soil type, moisture, wind, and the history of logging and fire, are also influential in shaping plant communities. The transition from zone to zone is seldom abrupt. It's possible to find a saguaro growing beside an oak tree. No description of zones can apply to all the Forest's 12 blocks. The following are typical of what the visitor may see.

Between 3,000 and 4,000 ft. is what many people consider the most interesting desert type, the Upper Sonoran, home of the giant saguaro, together with ocotillo, palo verde, jumping cholla, barrel cactus, white-thorn acacia, and mesquite. Above 4,000 ft., the saguaro is limited by winter frost, and areas of grassland appear, soon to grade into oak woodland. Species here include Emory and Mexican blue oaks, with manzanita, beargrass, Arizona rosewood, some Mexican pinyon, and one-seed juniper.

On Mt. Lemmon and similar mountains, the next zone is likely to be a bit confused, pinyon pine and juniper appearing among the oaks, with Chihuahua pine and a few ponderosa pine. Then, at about 7,000 ft., comes an unmistakable ponderosa pine forest. With higher elevation, Douglas-fir and white fir mingle with the ponderosa, aspen filling gaps caused by fire and blow-downs. Near the top may be a stand of corkbark fir, denizen of the Canadian zone. Also some mountain meadows, maple, Engelmann spruce.

The pattern is somewhat different on the mountains near the Mexican border. The oak woodland includes Emory and Mexican blue oak, with Arizona oak, manzanita, and pinyon pine. Just above, however, is a zone with Apache and Chihuahua pines, silverleaf oak, netleaf oak, and madrone. Next higher come Douglas-fir, white fir, Mexican white pine, and aspen. High in the Chiricahuas are extensive stands of Engelmann spruce.

The vegetation of the canyons, however, is most fascinating to both amateur and professional botanists. More moisture, deeper and richer soils, shelter, and other variables combine to produce a variety of plant communities including many rare species. Upper Carr and Ramsey canyons, for example, in the Huachuca Mountains, produce six species of ferns, three species of orchids, seven lily species, and other flora. By contrast, Goudy Canyon in the Pinaleno Mountains supports a mixed conifer forest between the dry ridges of an isolated desert mountain. Tree species here include white fir, southwestern white pine, Douglas-fir, ponderosa pine, Gambel and silverleaf oaks, and aspen.

Birds: The special habitats of the Coronado are known to birders everywhere, by reputation if not by experience. Many come here each year to add species to their life lists that they could otherwise log only by traveling to Mexico. Probably the best known of the birding hotspots is Madera Canyon, perhaps because it is the most accessible. Others in or adjacent to the Coronado are Ramsey Canyon, Reiley Canyon, Cave Creek, South Fork and East Turkey Creek, Guadalupe Canyon, Aravaipa Canyon. Prominent among the sought-after Mexican species are the coppery-tailed trogon; black, gray, and zone-tailed hawks; Gila woodpecker, rose-throated becard, vermilion flycatcher, phainopepla, Mexican jay, Gould's turkey, several sparrows. Checklists are available for Sabino Canyon and the Chiricahua Mountains. We chose the latter, since it relates species to each of 9 habitat types. Usually we cite only the seasonally abundant or common species. Here we include the fairly common, since these are species many birders seek. The checklist, which notes seasonality, abundance, and habitats, includes mallard, pintail, green-winged and cinnamon teals, American wigeon, northern shoveler; Cooper's, red-tailed and Swainson's hawks; northern harrier, American kestrel, scaled and Gambel's quail, American coot, killdeer, band-tailed pigeon, white-winged and mourning doves, roadrunner. Owls: screech, whiskered, flammulated, great horned, elf. Whip-poor-will, poor-will, lesser nighthawk. Hummingbirds: black-chinned, broad-tailed, rufous, Rivoli's, blue-throated. Coppery-tailed trogon. Woodpeckers: acorn, hairy, ladder-backed, Arizona. Yellow-bellied sapsucker, western and Cassin's kingbirds. Flycatchers: sulphur-bellied, Wied's crested, ash-throated, olivaceous, Hammond's, dusky, western, Coue's. Black and Say's phoebes, western wood-pewee, horned lark. Swallows: violet-green, rough-winged, barn, cliff. Purple martin, Steller's and pinyon jays, common and white-necked ravens, Mexican chickadee, bridled titmouse, verdin, common bushtit, white-breasted and pygmy nuthatches, brown creeper. Wrens: house, brown-throated, Bewick's, cactus, canyon, rock. Mockingbird, curve-billed and crissal thrashers, American robin, hermit thrush, western and mountain bluebirds, Townsend's solitaire, blue-gray gnatcatcher, ruby-crowned kinglet, loggerhead shrike. Vireos: Hutton's, Bell's, solitary, warbling. Warblers: orange-crowned, Virginia's, Lucy's, olive, yellow-rumped, black-throated gray, Townsend's, Grace's, MacGillivray's, red-faced, Wilson's. Painted redstart, eastern and western meadowlarks, red-winged and Brewer's blackbirds; hooded, Scott's, and northern orioles; brown-headed and bronzed cowbirds; western, hepatic, and summer tanagers; cardinal, black-headed and blue grosbeaks, house finch, lesser goldfinch; green-tailed, rufous-sided, and brown towhees; lark bunting. Sparrows: house, savannah, vesper, rufous-crowned, Cassin's, black-throated, chipping, Brewer's, white-crowned, Lincoln's. Dark-eyed, gray-headed, and yellow-eyed juncos; chestnut-collared longspur.

Mammals: No checklist. Noted in various reports: cave myotis, longnose bat, vagrant shrew, longtail vole, kangaroo rat; pocket, deer, and plains harvest mice; grasshopper mouse, Mexican woodrat, pocket gopher, Abert and Arizona gray squirrels; roundtail, Harris, and antelope ground squirrels; Chiricahua fox squirrel, porcupine, jackrabbit, cottontail, ringtail, coatimundi, raccoon, skunks, coyote, gray fox, kit fox, black bear, bobcat, mountain lion, javelina, whitetail deer, mule deer, pronghorn, desert bighorn sheep. HQ reports an occasional Mexican wolf, jaguar.

Reptiles and amphibians: No checklist. Noted in various reports: desert scaly, regal horned, collared, and leopard lizards; skink, Gila monster.

Tarahumara frog (possibly extinct), canyon treefrog. Mud turtle, desert tortoise. Snakes: rat, shovel-nosed, garter, mountain kingsnake, ring-necked. Rattlesnakes: Willard's, Arizona twin-spot, green rock, Arizona black, tiger, ridge-nosed.

FEATURES

Chiricahua Wilderness, 87,700 acres. The original Wilderness of 18,000 acres occupies the crest of the Chiricahua Mountains, with elevations to 9,797 ft. Steep canyons radiate from the summit, several of them well known to birders. The Arizona Wilderness Act of 1984 added 69,700 acres, with 850 acres adjoining in the Chiricahua National Monument.

Several good roads penetrate the block from the E and W to attractive campgrounds at trailheads. Although the Wilderness is readily accessible, the area has some of the roughest country in SE Arizona. Hikers aren't likely to venture far from the established trails.

Most of the area is forested, with good stands of ponderosa pine, Chiricahua pine, Arizona pine, Mexican white pine, Apache pine, Douglas-fir, Engelmann spruce, white fir, aspen, juniper, pinyon, madrone, and oaks. Summers are only moderately hot, winters cold. Average annual precipitation is about 30 in. on the highest slopes. There are some springs and perennial streams, but hikers are advised to carry water.

Galiuro Wilderness, 76,317 acres, including 23,600 acres added in 1984. The Wilderness now occupies most of the block on the Galiuro Mountains. Principal trailheads are on the E, 40 to 57 mi. from Willcox. The mountains are a double range bisected by Rattlesnake and Redfield Canyons. Elevations from 4,000 ft. to 7,671 ft. The area is described as "rough and brushy," rough enough to confine most hiking to the extensive trail network. Vegetation ranges from semidesert grassland through brush, pinyon-juniper, and oak woodland to mixed conifers on the high slopes. The area has no perennial streams but several springs. Visitation is light. Visitors are asked to register at a trailhead registration station.

Pusch Ridge Wilderness, 56,933 acres on the W side of the Santa Catalina Mountains. On the outskirts of Tucson and including the drainage of Sabino Canyon, this is the Forest's most heavily used Wilderness, with many trailheads along the S boundary of the Forest and on the General Hitchcock Road ascending Mount Lemmon. The ridge offers sweeping views of the sprawling city. Elevations from 3,200 ft. to over 8,000 ft. The ridge is often 30°F cooler than the city below. Winter snow cover is usually light. True wilderness qualities are being trampled by too many feet. A herd of about 75 desert bighorns is threatened by disturbance.

The Arizona Wilderness Act of 1984 established 5 new Wildernesses in the Coronado:

Miller Peak Wilderness, 20,190 acres, in the E portion of the Sierra Vista Ranger District, between the Fort Huachuca Military Reservation and the

Mexican border. Forest Roads 48 and 61, SE from Parker Lake, cross the S boundary of the Wilderness. Several trailheads on the W, S, and E. In the NE is Ramsey Canyon, a Nature Conservancy preserve (see entry, Mile-Hi/Ramsey Canyon). Miller Peak is 9,466 ft.

Mt. Wrightson Wilderness, 25,260 ft., on the Santa Rita Mountains. Mt. Wrightson, 9,453 ft., is a popular hiking and backpacking destination from the trailhead in Madera Canyon. Other trailheads include two on the E through Cave Creek and Gardner Canyon. Cave Creek is so named because of nearby caves, the best known being Onyx Cave, a National Natural Landmark. (Another "Cave Creek" is on the E side of the Chiricahua Mountains. It also has caves. See below.) The Santa Ritas are of interest to botanists for the many montane Mexican plants found N of the border only in this region. Birders come to add Mexican species to their life lists.

Rincon Mountain Wilderness, 38,590 acres. Adjoining the roadless area of the Rincon Mountain Unit, Saguaro National Monument (see entry). Access from I-10, on the S, by Forest Road 35. At lower elevations, rolling, rocky hills. At higher elevations, steep hills, rock outcrops, and deep canyons make hiking difficult and horse travel virtually impossible. Four plant associations: desert grassland, chaparral, woodland, riparian.

Santa Teresa Wilderness, 26,780 acres. About 30 mi. W of Safford, between Aravaipa Canyon (see entry) and the San Carlos Apache Indian Reservation. An isolated, rugged mountain range, elevations to 7,481 ft. Access by several Forest roads on the S and W; some may require 4-wheel drive. Terrain and dense vegetation limit travel to trails and jeep tracks.

Adjoining the Santa Teresa Wilderness is the 8,492-acre BLM Black Rock Wilderness Study Area. Present access is by Black Rock Road through the San Carlos Indian Reservation and private land. Past vandalism has caused the San Carlos Apaches to threaten closure. The site is on the steep foothills of the Santa Teresa Mountains. Numerous canyons and washes drain predominantly northward. Elevations from 3,400 ft. to 5,892 ft. on Jackson Mountain. Fine views from the top. Black Rock is a dramatic volcanic plug in the NW of the mountain, steep walls rising 900 ft.

Pajarita Wilderness, 7,420 acres. In the Nogales Ranger District. Chief feature is Sycamore Canyon. Easy access from the Ruby-Nogales road makes the canyon attractive for day hiking. The 7-mi.-long canyon is narrow, twisting, steep-walled, in an area of rolling foothills. Its stream is seasonal, but permanent pools occur. The canyon riparian habitat is noted for its exceptional diversity of plant species. Botanist Leslie N. Goodding called it "a hidden botanical garden." Another called it "one of the most interesting small areas in the United States." Over 660 plant species have been recorded in this small area, 17 unknown elsewhere. The Goodding Research Natural Area was established here in 1970. Grazing was stopped then and natural vegetation began to recover. Sycamore Canyon Trail begins at Hank and Yank Spring, intersects the Border Trail.

OTHER FEATURES

In the Nogales Ranger District:

Madera Canyon. A mountain canyon surrounded by desert. The combination of elevation, moisture, and temperature range, as well as the shape and orientation of the canyon, combine to create habitat conditions for flora and fauna unusual in the United States. 200 bird species have been recorded, many of them rare. The inventory of plants and insects also includes many rare species. Together with the canyon's accessibility, this attracts birders from everywhere.

The paved road ends in a congested area. Years ago the Forest Service allowed summer homes here as well as commercial development. The Bog Springs campground is often full. All this is soon left behind on the trails. Obtain maps and trail information before coming; you won't find them here.

In the Sierra Vista Ranger District:

Parker Lake, 28 mi. S of Sonoita on SR 83, has 130 surface acres. Elevation is 5,400 ft. Fishing and camping; 8 hp motor limit. A trail circles the lake. Considerable shoreline development.

In the Santa Catalina Ranger District:

Mount Lemmon, 9,157 ft., is a handy place for Tucson's 600,000 residents to cool off. The General Hitchcock Highway is a scenic drive to the top. Along the way are overlooks, trailheads, campgrounds, picnic sites, a nature trail. Near the top is a ski area. Cliffs challenge technical climbers.

Sabino Canyon would have been irretrievably damaged had not the Forest Service closed the gate. Urban sprawl was at the Forest boundary. Now cars must be left at the parking area. A shuttle bus carries visitors from the reception area up the canyon. The frequency of buses limits crowds. One can walk, of course. The canyon is still lovely, and it's a fine environmental education site. A bird checklist is available. If you want solitude, look elsewhere.

In the Douglas Ranger District:

Cochise Stronghold, in the Dragoon Mountains W of Sunsites, includes a campground. Above the natural fortress are many observation points. The canyon entrance is narrow, easily defended. Exhibits.

Turkey Creek. Where E-bound SR 181 turns N toward the Chiricahua National Monument, Forest Road 41 continues E along the creek. The Sycamore campground is at Mile 9, at 6,200 ft. elevation, in a forested canyon on the W side of the Chiricahua Mountains. The forest is impressive, big trees: Douglas-fir, ponderosa, alligator juniper, aspen, oaks. The understory is open, good for hiking. Numerous trailheads. The road end is near the Chiricahua Wilderness boundary. Permanent stream in a rock gorge with cascades and small falls. On the third Sunday of Sept., we found this campground deserted.

Rucker Lake is also on the W side of the Chiricahuas, reached by a road E from Elfrida. A small pond, campground, wilderness trailhead. Nature trail from the campground to Vista Point.

Cave Creek, South Fork, is on the E side of the Chiricahua Mountains. From Rodeo, NM, on US 80, a paved road continues past Portal, AZ, up Cave Creek, passing campgrounds and the Southwestern Research Station. From here a dirt road crosses the mountains into Pinery Canyon, emerging near the entrance of Chiricahua National Monument. The gorge is highly scenic, rugged, with pinnacles, overhangs, and cliffs, willow, ash, and walnut growing beside the creek, foliage flaming in autumn. Birders come here hoping to see Bullock's oriole, blue-throated hummingbird, painted redstart, and coppery-tailed trogon, among others.

Pinery Canyon, entered from the W, has a graded gravel road through a quiet scenic area. Many informal campsites in riparian woodland along the creek. 6 mi. in is a sign warning that the next 8 mi. are steep and twisting. In a motor home, we drove slowly, had no difficulties.

INTERPRETATION

The only *visitor center* is at the foot of Sabino Canyon. Exhibits, films, talks, literature. Open 9 A.M.–4:30 P.M. all year; closed Mondays.

Nature trail near the visitor center. Desert plants.

Guided hikes originate at the visitor center. Unscheduled, fall-winter-spring.

ACTIVITIES

Camping: 29 campgrounds, 568 sites. A few all year, others open Feb.–May, close Oct.–Dec.

Hiking, backpacking: 979 mi. of trails. Many are not maintained. Hiking also on little-used or abandoned back roads. In some areas, off-trail hiking is feasible.

Hunting: Deer, pronghorn, javelina, turkey, quail, dove, squirrel, waterfowl.

Fishing: Trout, in a few small lakes and perennial streams. Bass, bluegill, catfish in small lakes and ranch ponds.

Horse riding: On any trails. Forest has no list of outfitters.

Skiing: Mt. Lemmon ski area. Most ranges have too little snow.

PUBLICATIONS

Forest maps, $1 each:

    Nogales and Sierra Vista R.D.'s.

    Santa Catalina and Safford R.D.'s.

    Douglas R.D.

Information pages (Many National Forests are preparing Outdoor Recreation Guides ("ORG's"). The Coronado is ahead of other NF's in this region. The following pages will be included. They have not been reproduced but can be seen at Forest HQ):

    General information (8 pp.).

    Santa Catalina R.D.

Chiricahua Wilderness.
Pusch Ridge Wilderness.
Galiuro Wilderness.
Common mammals of Sabino Canyon.
Santa Catalina Mountains.
Front Range (Santa Catalina R.D.).
North-East Back Country (Santa Catalina R.D.).
Prominent Point (Santa Catalina R.D.).
Seven Cataracts (Santa Catalina R.D.).
Chiva Falls (Santa Catalina R.D.).
Happy Valley (Santa Catalina R.D.).
Central Canyons (Santa Catalina R.D.).
Pusch Peak (Santa Catalina R.D.).
Gibbon Mountain (Santa Catalina R.D.).
La Milagrose and Agua Caliente Canyons (Santa Catalina R.D.).
Lemmon Canyon (Santa Catalina R.D.).
Finger Rock (Santa Catalina R.D.).
San Rafael Valley.
Huachuca Recreation Area (Sierra Vista R.D.).
Middle Canyon (Sierra Vista R.D.).
Miller Peak (Sierra Vista R.D.).
Douglas R.D.
Chiricahua Mountains (Douglas R.D.).
Skeleton Canyon (Douglas R.D.).
Crystal Cave (Douglas R.D.).
Mount Graham (Safford R.D.).
Cochise Stronghold Canyon and campground (Douglas R.D.).
Cave of the Bells (Nogales R.D.).
Sycamore Canyon (Nogales R.D.).
Madera Canyon (Nogales R.D.).
Bird checklist, Sabino Canyon.
Bird checklist, Chiricahua Mountains.

REFERENCES

Mazel, David. *Arizona Trails.* Berkeley, CA: Wilderness Press, 1981, pp. 83–178.

Ganci, Dave. *Hiking the Southwest.* San Francisco: Sierra Club Books, 1983, pp. 117–130.

HEADQUARTERS: Federal Building, 300 W. Congress, Tucson, AZ 85701; (602) 792-6483.

RANGER DISTRICTS: Nogales R.D., 2480 Tucson-Nogales Highway, Nogales, AZ 85621; (602) 281-2296. Sierra Vista R.D., Rural Route 2, Box 1150, Sierra Vista, AZ 85635; (602) 458-0530. Santa Catalina R.D., 2500 N.

Pantano Rd., Tucson, AZ 85715; (602) 296-6245. Safford R.D., P.O. Box 709, Safford, AZ 85548; (602) 428-4150. Douglas R.D., Rural Route 1, Box 228R, Douglas, AZ 85607; (602) 364-3468.

COYOTE MOUNTAINS
U.S. Bureau of Land Management
5,080 acres.

40 mi. SW of Tucson. 2 mi. S of SR 86. 2 mi. E of SR 386, the road to Kitts Peak.

We omitted several attractive BLM sites because they lack legal access. This was one of them. A few weeks later BLM published its draft wilderness recommendations. Coyote Mountains wasn't included, and a BLM advisor wrote, "we were hit with a great public outcry for not recommending this area."

People do come here, several thousand per year, and many are enthusiastic. One called it "the little Yosemite of the Southwest." The advisor urged us to make it an entry, suggesting to readers that they consult the BLM office about access.

Highly scenic, the Coyotes are a detached extension of the Baboquivari Range. Steep, rugged mountains rise from the Altar Valley on the E, nearly a 3,500-ft. change of elevation in 3 mi. Highest point is 6,529 ft. The area includes massive rounded bluffs, sheer cliffs, large open canyons.

From the valley up to about 4,200 ft., vegetation is palo verde-saguaro community with mesquite, ironwood, acacia, cacti. Higher, this merges into chaparral, with manzanita, mahogany, buckthorn, shrub live oak, silktassel. At the highest elevations, Arizona white oak and Mexican pinyon.

The area is prime habitat for deer and bighorn sheep. Both large and small game are said to be abundant.

Visitors come to hike, backpack, hunt, collect rocks, and climb the cliffs. Artists are attracted by the scenery.

The site has several mi. of foot trails.

HEADQUARTERS: BLM, Phoenix District Office, 2015 West Deer Valley Rd., Phoenix, AZ 85027; (602) 863-4464.

DOS CABEZAS MOUNTAINS
U.S. Bureau of Land Management
30,000 acres; some state and private inholdings.

E of Willcox. Shown on highway map. Surrounded by SR 186 and local roads.

The Dos Cabezas Mountains are a NW continuation of the Chiricahuas, between Simon Valley and Sulphur Springs Valley. Base elevation on the SW is about 4,500 ft., on the NE about 4,000 ft. Highest point is 8,363 ft. on the Dos Cabezas Peaks, a prominent local landmark.

Part of this entry is for a 16,671-acre roadless tract around Happy Camp Canyon, reached by a road S from Bowie to a road penetrating the lower end of the canyon, where BLM has a picnic area. This tract has several peaks over 7,000 ft., canyons winding among them. Buckeye and Wood Canyon have traces of old vehicle tracks. Howell Canyon, a tributary of Happy Camp Canyon, has traces of an old road and house foundations from turn-of-the-century mining. Streams in the canyons are intermittent, but enough moisture gathers to support riparian vegetation, including Arizona sycamore, Fremont cottonwood, velvet ash, and Arizona walnut. The upper end of Happy Camp Canyon has groves of sycamore.

Government Peak, 7,587 ft., in the SE portion of the tract, is noted for the granite boulders, balancing rocks, and rock outcrops on its NE slopes, an area some have likened to Cochise Stronghold. Rain produces many small pools and waterfalls.

Upland vegetation is mountain and desert shrub, species including turpentine bush, snakeweed, mountain-mahogany, juniper, oaks, mesquite, grasses, agave, pricklypear. Good deer hunting.

BLM advisors called this a pleasant area for day hiking.

HEADQUARTERS: BLM, Safford District Office, 425 E. 4th St., Safford, AZ 85546; (602) 428-4040.

FORT HUACHUCA
U.S. Army
73,315 acres.

Main gate is on the W side of Sierra Vista; Fry Blvd.

"We always welcome visitors," said the Public Affairs Officer, who sent us a fine packet of data, much of it especially prepared. "Over 40 percent of the Fort could probably be called an outstanding natural area (on the basis of geology, flora, and fauna); however, similar areas with better access occur in southeastern Arizona."

Access isn't difficult. Visitors must have passes, which are issued at the main gate. A map is issued with each pass. The principal roads are well maintained. The Fort has attracted many birders, as well as both amateur and professional botanists.

It adjoins the Coronado National Forest, including its Miller Peak Wilderness, along the Huachuca Mountains. The National Forest map, Sierra Vista Ranger District, shows the Fort in some detail. Elevations range from 4,000 ft. to 8,410 ft. on Huachuca Peak. The mountainous area has three major canyons: Garden, Huachuca, and Blacktail. The land slopes down to the NE into outwash plains.

Plants: The canyons attract the greatest interest. Garden Canyon, about 4 1/3 mi. long, drains to the NE. Elevation is 5,100 ft. at the mouth, rising to 7,750 ft. A paved road leads to the canyon; a dirt road enters it. At the mouth is a desert-grassland zone with scattered agave, cholla, mesquite, and pricklypear. This grades into an oak-manzanita zone, dense stands of mixed shrubs with occasional cacti and juniper. Near the canyon's upper end is a transition to conifer forest. A stream in the canyon is intermittent, but with perennial flow in some areas. Riparian vegetation is dominated by cottonwood, sycamore, Arizona walnut, and bigtooth maple, which produces a brilliant display of fall colors.

About one-third of the site is forested. Forested land generally begins at about 5,000 ft. elevation. Major forest cover types are Upper Sonoran, including mesquite, desert live oak, cottonwood-willow, and pinyon-juniper; and transition, above 6,500 ft., including meadow, aspen, and ponderosa pine. A list of tree species is available. Old-growth Douglas-fir stands are in the Scheelite Canyon watershed, old-growth stands of pinyon pine in the McClure Canyon watershed.

Flowering plants include painted-cup, columbine, sunflower, groundsel, mullein, prickly-poppy, jimsonweed, fleabane, aster, violet, poppy, lupine, rabbitbrush, yarrow, black locust, agave, yucca, sotol.

Birds: 48-page list available, prepared with the aid of the Huachuca Audubon Society, with data from Christmas bird counts back to 1969. Birding spots described are East Range Ponds, Garden Canyon, Scheelite Canyon, Sawmill Canyon, and Huachuca Canyon. Also adjoining Mile Hi/Ramsey Canyon (see entry). Listed are a remarkable 381 species, including 14 species of hummingbirds, coppery-tailed and eared trogons, buff-breasted flycatcher, tropical kingbird, gray hawk.

FEATURES

Garden Canyon Road, Huachuca Canyon Road, and *Canelo Road* are scenic drives to points of interest.

Garden Canyon has 3 primary tributary canyons: *Sawmill Canyon* is in the upper half, branching toward the SE, about 2 1/4 mi. long, elevations from 5,900 to well over 7,750 ft. It has a perennial spring. Vehicles have been excluded to reduce erosion and protect the nesting habitat of the buff-breasted flycatcher. *Scheelite Canyon* is also in the upper half, also branches to the SE, is also about 2 1/4 mi. long. Narrow, rocky, high walls; a sheltered habitat. *McClure Canyon,* about 2 1/2 mi. long, branches toward the NW, begins at 5,500 ft. and climbs to the ridge at 6,750 ft. Its upper half has a perennial spring and a perennial stream.

Huachuca Canyon is on the NW slope of Huachuca Peak. The third recorded U.S. sighting of the Aztec thrush occurred here. Seasonal regulars include trogons and other rarities. Mountain lion are seen occasionally.

INTERPRETATION: *Conservation Education Center,* Bldg. 14444, open Fri., 11 A.M.–5 P.M. Sat.–Sun. 1 P.M.–4 P.M., except holidays.

ACTIVITIES

Camping: 3 campgrounds. No fixed sites. No potable water. Recommended for RVs only. Reservation required: (602) 538-3249.

Hiking, backpacking: 43 mi. of trails, including canyon trails. The Crest Trail extends along the S boundary of the post, connects with trails in the Coronado NF. Backpacking is permitted, but hikers must check with the Post to make sure the area is not closed.

(Hunting, fishing, and horse riding are restricted to Post personnel and other special categories.)

PUBLICATIONS

Map, provided with permit.

Fishing and hunting information.

REFERENCE: McMoran, Charles W. *Trail Guide and Map of the Huachuca Mountains.* Available at local bookstore. $4.95.

HEADQUARTERS: Fort Huachuca, AZ 85613; (602) 538-3249.

THE MILE HI/RAMSEY CANYON PRESERVE
Arizona Nature Conservancy
300 acres.

From Sierra Vista, S 6 mi. on SR 92, then W on Ramsey Canyon Rd. Follow pavement for 4 mi., then cross creek and continue 200 yd. to parking area.

Open: 8 A.M.–5 P.M. Weekday visits are suggested; weekends are crowded.

In 1975, 280 acres was bequeathed to The Nature Conservancy, and shortly thereafter TNC bought the adjoining 20-acre Mile Hi Ranch with 6 housekeeping cabins.

Ramsey Canyon is a heavily wooded, deep, sheltered gorge with a perennial stream and favorable W–E orientation. This combination of factors creates a stable, moist, cool environment unusual in this part of the world, and produces a diverse array of fauna and flora. Five biotic communities are found in the canyon: pine-fir, pine-oak, oak woodland, mesquite grassland, and riparian. The preserve is surrounded on three sides by the Coronado National Forest Miller Peak Wilderness. It is a National Natural Landmark.

Birds: Some species of birds reach their northern limit in the mountains of southeastern Arizona. Such species in Ramsey Canyon include painted redstart, sulphur-bellied flycatcher, hepatic tanager, and such hummingbird species as blue-throated, magnificent, violet-crowned, and broad-billed. Fifteen hummingbirds have been recorded in Ramsey Canyon, including such accidentals as berylline, white-eared, and lucifer. The best birding season is Apr.–Aug. Checklist available.

Mammals: Residents include coatimundi, ringtail, javelina, whitetail deer.

Hiking: A self-guided nature trail follows Ramsey Creek. A longer, steeper hiking trail leads into the National Forest Wilderness Area.

NEARBY
Fort Huachuca (see entry).
Patagonia-Sonoita Creek Sanctuary (see entry).
Coronado National Forest (see entry).
Canelo Hills Cienega (see entry).

Pets are prohibited.
The parking lot is too small for RVs, trailers, buses; call ahead for alternative arrangements.
Reservations are necessary for cabins.

PUBLICATIONS
Cabin brochure.
Bird list.
Nature trail guide.

HEADQUARTERS: The Mile Hi/Ramsey Canyon Preserve, R.R. 1, Box 84, Hereford, AZ 85615; (602) 378-2785.

MULESHOE RANCH
The Nature Conservancy
54,200 acres.

N of Willcox. Adjoining the Coronado National Forest at the S end of the Galiuro Mountains.

Less than 200 people a year visit this site, many of them on field trips organized by the Conservancy. We haven't given specific directions because the stewards want you to write or call a few days in advance; they don't take regular days off and will try to arrange to be there. Don't come in wet weather; the road turns to slick mud.

The Conservancy raised over $1.4 million to establish this site, purchasing 6,300 acres, assuming cooperative management of 22,000 acres of National Forest land, 3,000 acres of BLM land, and 22,900 acres of state land. This encompasses the complete watershed of the upper Redfield Canyon complex, with three pristine perennial streams and spectacular aquatic and riparian communities. Of 30 fish species native to Arizona, 24 are endangered. Five inhabit these desert streams. Elevations range from 3,698 ft. to 7,650 ft. on Dasset Peak. The ranch includes large portions of Hot Springs Canyon and Bass Canyon.

The streams, which flow to the San Pedro River, support a rich riparian community, dominated by sycamore, velvet ash, Fremont cottonwood, Goodding willow, Arizona alder. At higher elevations are mature stands of Arizona cypress and evergreen oak woodlands, with juniper and ponderosa pine.

Birds: No checklist. Best birding season: mid-Apr. to mid-June. Notable species include black, zone-tailed, and gray hawks; golden eagle, peregrine falcon.

Mammals: No checklist. Recorded: bighorn sheep, black bear, mountain lion, bobcat, coatimundi, gray fox, javelina, whitetail and mule deer, coyote.

ADJACENT: The Galiuro Wilderness in the National Forest.

ACTIVITIES
Camping: Permitted in Bass Canyon or Hot Springs Canyon.
Hiking, backpacking: Visitors can hike into the National Forest, about 10 mi. Summer is too hot for much hiking.

HEADQUARTERS: RR 1, Box 1542; Willcox, AZ 85643; (602) 384-2626.

ORGAN PIPE CACTUS NATIONAL MONUMENT
National Park Service
330,240 acres.

On the Mexican border, 140 mi. S of Phoenix via SR 85; 137 mi. W of Tucson via SR 86 and 85.

This huge area lies between the even larger Cabeza Prieta National Wildlife Refuge (see entry) and Papago Indian Reservation. SR 85 enters the Monument just below the town of Why, continues to Lukeville, 27 mi. S, a border crossing. Two graded loop roads are most of the internal road system. The Monument is a destination, well off traveled routes, too far from the cities for a day trip. Visitors camp in the Monument or stay in motels at Ajo, Why, Lukeville, or—across the border—Sonoita.

The park is in the basin and range province. Park elevations range from 1,100 ft. to 4,808 ft. atop Mt. Ajo. It is desert country, valleys and plains between small mountain ranges, receiving less than 9 in. of precipitation per year, almost all of that in midsummer and midwinter. Summer thunderstorms are often violent. Temperatures above 105°F are common in summer, although nights are relatively cool. Spring is the best time for a visit, because the desert may then be in flower. Most visitors come Nov.–Apr.

The area has a few springs and seeps, and wells that were part of a former cattle operation. All are magnets for wildlife. So are the tinajas (water holes).

Plants: Checklist available. Three deserts meet here:

The Arizona Succulent Desert occupies the E half of the park, and this is what most visitors come to see. Here are the stands of organ pipe cactus, for which the park is named, as well as saguaro, pricklypear, chain-fruit and teddybear cholla, agave, ironwood, palo verde, and mesquite, species similar to those found in the Saguaro National Monument (see entry).

The Central Gulf Coast phase of the Sonoran Desert is chiefly in Mexico, extending N from the Gulf of California coast. Some of its unusual plants, chiefly the elephant tree and senita cactus, can be seen in the Senita Basin, at the end of a graded desert road.

The California Microphyll Desert, named for its small-leafed plants, is on the W side of the Park. Most of the vegetation is creosote bush and bursage.

The organ pipe cactus grows in clumps of columnar stems up to 15 ft. high. Large blossoms appear at night, beginning in May, closing the next day. Fruiting follows. Organ pipe and the even larger giant saguaro are closely related to the night-blooming cereus, a small, low-growing plant, inconspicuous except when in flower.

If conditions are right, the flowering annuals burst into bloom between Jan. and Mar. Cacti flower later, most of them May–July.

Birds: Checklist available. Some 275 species have been recorded. The abundant and common species are similar to those occurring at other Sonoran Desert sites, such as Saguaro National Monument. Birders come here chiefly in hopes of seeing some of the rarities. Their best chance is during migrations, and especially following rains. Some of the uncommon (usually seen several times a year) and rare (recorded every several years) species include least, eared, and pied-billed grebes; brown pelican, double-crested cormorant, great blue and green herons, great and snowy egrets, black-crowned night-heron, white-faced ibis, roseate spoonbill, Canada goose. Ducks: mallard, gadwall,

American wigeon, pintail; green-winged, blue-winged, and cinnamon teals; shoveler, redhead, ring-necked duck, lesser scaup, common goldeneye, bufflehead, hooded merganser, ruddy duck. . . . The list is too long to include here, but this gives the flavor of it and explains why many birders head for Quitobaquito, a small oasis on Puerto Blanco Drive. Other good birding spots are Aguajita Spring, Williams Spring, Dripping Spring, and any other wet place, such as Alamo Well.

Mammals: Checklist available. Many of the listed species are nocturnal, and some hibernate in winter. Even diurnal species are most often seen near dawn and dusk. These include various rodents, coyote, javelina, deer, pronghorn.

Reptiles and amphibians: Checklist available. Species listed are mostly the same as those in the Saguaro National Monument entry, except for Ajo Mountain whipsnake, Mexican rosy boa, Organ Pipe shovel-nosed snake. The list includes five species of rattlesnake, and visitors are advised to use a flashlight when walking at night.

FEATURES

Puerto Blanco Drive is a 51-mi. circuit from the Visitor Center. The N leg is one-way westward. The drive circles the Puerto Blanco Mountains and skirts the Mexican border. Spurs to the Quitobaquito oasis and Senita Basin.

Ajo Mountain Drive, 21 mi., is a one-way loop passing the Ajo Mountain canyon trailheads. Impressive stands of organ pipe cactus.

Organ Pipe Wilderness, 313,340 acres, is 95% of the total Monument acreage. All motorized vehicles are excluded. Foot and horse travel only.

In the Ajo Mountains: Alamo Canyon, Estes Canyon, and *Bull Pasture* are unique areas with interesting biota. Bull Pasture has several well-shaded tinajas. Bull Pasture Trail is a route into the high country. Birding is usually good in the canyons. A spur road leads to a small primitive campground at the mouth of Alamo Canyon; backcountry permit required, can be obtained at the visitor center. Large vehicles and trailers are prohibited.

Dripping Springs supplies water year-around to a small cave in the Puerto Blanco Mountains. The water is not recommended for drinking.

ADJACENT: Cabeza Prieta National Wildlife Refuge (see entry).

INTERPRETATION

Visitor center at HQ, 35 mi. S of Ajo on SR 85. Open 8 A.M.–5 P.M.
Walking trails at Desert View, Victoria Mine, Palo Verde. 1.0 to 4.6 mi.
Evening programs and guided walks, Dec.–Mar.

ACTIVITIES

Camping: Main campground, 208 sites. All year. 4-site camp at Alamo Canyon requires a backcountry permit.

Hiking, backpacking: Few hiking trails, but backcountry is open for day-hiking and backpacking. Permits are required for backcountry camping. Hikers should ask a ranger about routes and destinations and tell some responsible person where they're going and when they expect to return. Water must be carried, at least a gallon per day in summer.

Horse riding: Permitted. Special regulations. No stables are nearby and no outfitters serve the area.

Pets are not allowed in backcountry or on scenic trails.

PUBLICATIONS
Leaflet with map.
Checklist of Vascular Plants, 45 pp.
Bird checklist.
Checklist of mammals, amphibians, and reptiles.
Information pages:
   How to Survive Your Visit to Organ Pipe Cactus National Monument.
   Flowering Calendar.
   Backcountry information.
   Alamo Canyon Campground information.
   Mail order publications list.
Monument staff notes that titles change from time to time; a current list, with prices, will be sent on request.

REFERENCES
Ganci, Dave. *Hiking the Southwest.* San Francisco: Sierra Club Books, 1983, pp. 140–145.
Available from Southwest Parks & Monument Association, Organ Pipe Cactus National Monument, Rt. 1, Box 100, Ajo, AZ 85321.
Self-guide booklet, Ajo Mountain Drive. $.25.
Self-guide booklet, Desert View Trail. $.20.
Self-guide booklet, Puerto Blanco Drive. $.25.
Guide to Organ Pipe Cactus National Monument. $1.
Organ Pipe Cactus National Monument. $1.50.

HEADQUARTERS: Route 1, Box 100, Ajo, AZ 85321; (602) 387-6849.

PATAGONIA LAKE STATE PARK
Arizona State Parks
640 acres; 265 acre lake.

From Nogales, 12 mi. NE on SR 82, then 4 mi. on entrance road.

In the Sonoita Valley. The park was planned for intensive use: camping, boating, fishing, swimming, picnicking. The entrance road, a dusty washboard, passes flashy lot sales offices. The area around the lake is divided by steep ravines and side canyons with sparse desert vegetation.

Most visitors come just for the day, so early morning and evening tend to be quiet, especially mid-week. The NE end of the lake, where Sonoita Creek enters, has natural qualities and offers moderately interesting birding.

ACTIVITIES
Camping: 127 sites. All year.
Boating: Ramp. Rentals.

HEADQUARTERS: Box 274, Patagonia, AZ 85624; (602) 287-6965.

PATAGONIA-SONOITA CREEK SANCTUARY
The Nature Conservancy
312 acres.

In Patagonia on SR 82, N on Fourth Ave., W at sign.

This delightful spot attracts birders from far away. The site extends for 1 1/2 mi. along Sonoita Creek, a perennial stream. Vegetation of the narrow flood plain is dominated by huge Fremont cottonwoods and large willows, probably the best example of a type of riparian woodland now extremely rare in AZ. Other floodplain species include Arizona walnut, velvet ash, Texas mulberry. This green strip is bordered by mesquite, catclaw, hackberry, cacti, scattered oaks.

The gravel road leads to several gates. Some are closed when flooding makes it necessary. Newcomers should enter at Gate 2, just beyond which is a bulletin board and shelter with a supply of information pages. A well-maintained trail explores the Sanctuary, looping along an old railroad embankment, then following the creek.

The locale in SE Arizona shares many aspects of the natural history of Mexico.

The site is a National Natural Landmark.

Birds: More than 200 species have been recorded, including many whose prime habitat is Mexico. Birders come to see the gray hawk, beardless flycatcher, rose-throated becard, vermilion flycatcher, Montezuma quail, and the many warbler species on spring and fall migrations.

No camping, picnicking, pets, tape players.

PUBLICATIONS
Leaflet (English and Spanish) with map.
Checklist of birds.

HEADQUARTERS: P.O. Box 815, Patagonia, AZ 85624: (602) 394-2400.

SAGUARO NATIONAL MONUMENT
National Park Service
Rincon Mountain Unit: 62,499 acres; Tucson Mountain Unit: 21,078 acres.

Rincon: E of Tucson via Broadway or 22d St. and Old Spanish Trail.
Tucson: W of Tucson via Speedway and Kinney Rd.

Open daily, 8 A.M. to sunset.

Both sites were set aside to preserve exceptional stands of giant saguaro
cactus.

Tucson Mountain Unit, a day-use area, adjoins Tucson Mountain Park and
the Arizona-Sonora Desert Museum (see entries). It contains a visitor center.
Well-maintained dirt roads lead to hiking and short nature trails, mostly quite
level. Most visits are brief, about an hour.

Rincon Mountain Unit is much larger and more diverse. A visitor center
is near the entrance. Here begins the 8-mi. Cactus Forest Drive through the
saguaro-dominated desert-scrub community. Many pullouts and overlooks
along the way, as well as two picnic areas and two nature trails. Near the
visitor center is a large stand of old giants in decline.

Few visitors venture beyond the scenic drive, but this circles only a small
part of the Monument. The largest part, to the E, is roadless wilderness, to
be entered only on foot or horse. Here the land rises, at times steeply, to
8,666-ft. Mica Mountain.

Summers are hot. May–Sept. daytime averages in the mid-90s, with extremes up to 110°F, especially in June in the saguaro areas. The mountains are
much cooler. Winter daytime highs in the 70s, lows a few degrees below
freezing. This desert has two rainy seasons: summer thunderstorms, gentle
winter rains; average annual precipitation about 11 in. on the desert, 20 in. in
the mountains.

Plants: The saguaro's pleated column may reach a height of 40 or 50 ft.
under favorable conditions, arms branching at about 15 ft. Growth is slow
during the first 10 years of life. The first branch appears when the plant is
about 75 years old and 15–20 ft. tall. Its full height may take 170 years to
attain. The saguaro dominates its part of the desert-scrub biotic community,

its range generally limited to the Sonora Desert E of the Colorado River and S into mainland Sonora, Mexico. It occurs up to about 4,500 ft. elevation.

The saguaro is the northernmost species of the tropical columnar cacti, the organ pipe being a close relative. It is not cold-tolerant. Since 1900, severe freezes have become more common in the Tucson area, killing the youngest and the oldest saguaros in the most exposed sites. Other losses have occurred through illegal collecting and vandalism.

Cacti associated with the saguaro include several cholla species: pencil, Christmas, teddybear, jumping, staghorn, cane. Also pricklypears: purple, spineless, purple-fruited. Also night-blooming cereus, crimson and Fendler hedgehog cacti, common and fishhook pincushion, barrel cactus, cream cactus, Arizona rainbow cactus.

Seeing the desert in bloom is an unforgettable experience, but difficult to arrange. Annuals may blossom any time between Feb. and May, often peaking in early Apr. When, and how massive the display, depends on rainfall, sunlight, and temperatures. Another less-impressive blooming period follows summer rains, usually reaching a peak in Aug.

In the Rincon Wilderness, the saguaro desert-scrub biotic community gives way at about 4,000 ft. elevation to a grassland transition community. Above this, oak-pine woodland gives way to ponderosa pine forest. On the highest N-facing slopes are stands of Douglas-fir and white fir.

Birds: Checklist available. Seasonally abundant or common species include turkey vulture, red-tailed hawk, American kestrel, Gambel's quail, mourning and white-winged doves. Owls: screech, great horned, elf. Whip-poor-will, poor-will, lesser nighthawk, white-throated swift; black-chinned, broad-tailed, and rufous hummingbirds; northern flicker; Gila, acorn, and ladder-backed woodpeckers; western and Cassin's kingbirds. Flycatchers: Wied's crested, ash-throated, Hammond's, dusky, gray, western, Coue's, olive-sided, vermilion, western wood-pewee. Violet-green swallow, purple martin, Steller's and Mexican jays, bridled titmouse, verdin, bushtit. Wrens: house, brown-throated, Bewick's, cactus, canyon, rock. Curve-billed thrasher, American robin, hermit thrush, ruby-crowned kinglet, phainopepla. Vireos: Hutton's, Bell's, solitary, warbling. Warblers: orange-crowned, Virginia's, Lucy's, yellow-rumped, black-throated gray, hermit, Grace's, MacGillivray's, red-faced, Wilson's, painted redstart. Hooded oriole, brown-headed and bronzed cowbirds, western and hepatic tanagers, northern cardinal, black-headed grosbeak, house finch, lesser goldfinch, rufous-sided and brown towhees. Sparrows: lark, rufous-crowned, black-throated, chipping, Brewer's, white-crowned.

Mammals: Checklist of mammals that may occur here. Most are active at night, seldom seen by visitors. Those most often seen include blacktail jackrabbit, desert cottontail, Yuma antelope squirrel, roundtail ground squirrel, coyote, javelina, mule deer.

Amphibians and reptiles: Checklist available. Species a visitor might see include canyon treefrog, leopard frog, Sonora mud turtle. Lizards: greater earless, zebra-tailed, collared, short-horned, regal horned, side-blotched, tree, Clark's spiny, desert spiny, eastern fence, Sonoran spotted whiptail, western whiptail. Snakes: coachwhip, western patch-nosed, gopher, black-necked garter. Rattlesnakes: western diamondback, black-tailed, tiger, western.

ACTIVITIES

Hiking, backpacking: Chiefly in the Rincon Mountain Unit. The Douglas Spring Trail is the principal entrance route, connecting with a 77-mi. trail network. Overnight trips require permits, which can be obtained at the visitor center. Camping is restricted to 6 sites. The highest is Manning Camp, at 8,000 ft. Water may be available but requires treatment.

Horse riding: Horse travel is permitted on most trails. Permits are required for overnight stays, and are rationed.

No pets on trails or in backcountry.

PUBLICATIONS
Leaflet with map.
Checklists:
  Birds.
  Mammals.
  Reptiles and amphibians.
  Cacti.
Information pages:
  Monthly average temperatures.
  The Saguaro Cactus.
  Desert flowering seasons.
  Backcountry travel.
Auto tour guide.

REFERENCE: Ganci, Dave. *Hiking the Southwest.* San Francisco: Sierra Club Books, 1983, pp. 146–149.

ADJACENT: Coronado National Forest (see entry).

HEADQUARTERS: Rt. 8, Box 695, Tucson, AZ 85730; (602) 296-8576.

SAN PEDRO RIVER
Mixed ownerships

E of Sierra Vista.

Birders told us about this area along the San Pedro River between I-10 and the Mexican border. Most land along the river is privately owned.

They said the U.S. Fish and Wildlife Service hopes to acquire some of it. Very dense riparian forest. Four highways cross this section of the river.

TUCSON MOUNTAIN PARK
Pima County Parks and Recreation Department
18,000 acres.

13 mi. from downtown Tucson via Speedway and Gates Pass Road.

Tucson's sprawl is partially confined by a ring of parkland. W of the city, this county park is on the Tucson Mountains, sloping down to the Avra Valley. E of Tucson on I-10, the desert is flat, the creosote-bursage vegetation monotonous. Here the mountains are scenic and fascinating, with a rich assortment of plants, colors changing from season to season. The elevation is about 1,800 ft. generally, extending up another 300–600 ft. in places. This is part of the Sonoran Desert, and this is where many people have fallen in love with the desert.

The park was established in 1929. Since then the damage inflicted by previous overgrazing has been largely repaired by natural processes. From the beginning, the management philosophy has been to protect and preserve natural qualities. We camped here 20 years ago while making a desert film. Tucson has grown enormously since then, but county park staff have resisted "development." In 1959 a misguided U.S. Department of the Interior ordered 7,600 acres opened to mineral exploration. A thousand angry citizens came to a public hearing, and the order was hastily withdrawn.

Our most recent visit was in the third week of Sept. The climate was delightful, the desert lovely, even if not as colorful as it is in spring. Fewer than 10% of the campsites were occupied.

Plants: Giant saguaro cacti dominate the landscape, flowering in May and June, producing red fruits in July. Also prominent are ocotillo, palo verde, rabbitbrush. Chollas: teddybear, jumping, chain-fruited, staghorn, pencil, and cane. Other cacti: pricklypear, Christmas, fishhook, buckhorn, hedgehog. Also catclaw, white-thorn acacia, desert thorn, jojoba, crucifixion bush, four-wing saltbush, brittlebush, limber bush, white ratany, burrobush, burroweed, desert hackberry, Mormon tea, desert ironwood, night-blooming cereus. Wildflowers are seasonally abundant when conditions are right. Spring annuals include fireweed, fiddleneck, locoweed, hairy bowlesia, sand-cress, cryptantha, senecio, devil's claw, cassia, wild mustard, buckwheat, eriophyllum, filaree, desert dandelion, pepperweed, verbena, desert chicory, prickly-poppy, desert marigold, foothill and desert deer vetches, bajada lupine, Mojave desert star, pygmy white daisy, desert zinnia, euphorbia, paperflower, evening primrose, scorpion weed, Indian wheat, brodiaea, globemallow, scalloped-leaf phacelia, delphinium, desert mariposa, penstemon. Summer annuals include trailing allionia, fringed amaranthus, milkvetch, rock hibiscus, fleabane, spinyleaf and narrowleaf asters, datura, sunflower, caltrop.

Birds: Visitor center has a bird list for the Tucson area that we thought surprisingly short. Includes cardinal, bronzed and brown-headed cowbirds; ground, Inca, mourning, and white-winged doves; northern flicker, ash-throated and Wied's crested flycatchers, black-tailed gnatcatcher, great-tailed grackle, Cooper's and red-tailed hawks, American kestrel, black-chinned and Costa's hummingbirds, western kingbird, purple martin, mockingbird, lesser nighthawk, hooded and Scott's orioles; elf, great horned, and screech owls; phainopepla, Say's phoebe, poor-will, pyrrhuloxia, common raven, roadrunner, loggerhead shrike, black-throated and Brewer's sparrows, European starling, white-throated swift, curve-billed thrasher, brown towhee, verdin, turkey vulture, Lucy's warbler, Gila woodpecker; cactus, canyon, and rock wrens. We saw many Gambel's quail.

Mammals: Visitor center has list for the Tucson area. Includes ringtail, coyote, Harris and roundtail ground squirrels, rock squirrel, valley pocket gopher. Hognose, spotted, hooded, and striped skunks. Merriam kangaroo rat, gray fox, badger, mountain lion, bobcat, desert cottontail, blacktail jackrabbit, house and cactus mice; Bailey, desert, and rock pocket mice; whitethroat woodrat, Norway rat, hispid cotton rat, southern grasshopper mouse, mule deer, javelina.

Reptiles and amphibians: Visitor center has list for the Tucson area. Includes Chihuahua and western whiptails, banded gecko, Gila monster. Lizards: zebra-tailed, collared, leopard, lesser earless, greater earless, regal horned, Clark's spiny, desert spiny, tree, side-blotched. Desert tortoise. Toads: Colorado River, desert, red spotted, Couch's spadefoot. Glossy snake, spotted night snake, common kingsnake, western blind snake, Sonora and desert whipsnakes, desert patch-nosed snake, checkered garter snake, lyre snake. Rattlesnakes: western, black-tailed, Mojave, tiger.

INTERPRETATION

Visitor center has exhibits, information. On a shelf are large scrapbooks full of information about the history and natural history of the park. We wish every park had such a record.

Guided hikes and other naturalist programs are offered, but are not regularly scheduled.

ACTIVITIES
Camping: 148 sites. All year.
Hiking: 26 mi. of trails, not well marked, over representative terrain. A 3-mi. trail from the campground to the Arizona-Sonora Desert Museum. Washes are hikable, but watch for flash floods in summer.
Horse riding: Special trails are marked. No corrals, stables, other facilities.

PUBLICATIONS: A number of trail maps are published. County parks and recreation brochure.

ADJACENT
Tucson Mountain Wildlife Area, 100,000 acres, Arizona Game and Fish Department. The area includes Tucson Mountain Park, the Tucson Mountain Unit of Saguaro National Monument, the Arizona-Sonora Desert Museum, and much additional acreage. It was established for wildlife purposes only: to eliminate firearms hunting.
Saguaro National Monument. See entry.
Arizona-Sonora Desert Museum. See entry.

HEADQUARTERS: 1204 West Silverlake Rd., Tucson, AZ 85713; (602) 882-2690.

WILLCOX PLAYA
U.S. Army/U.S. Bureau of Land Management/Arizona Game and Fish Department
37,000 acres.

Just S of Willcox.

Maps usually call the playa Willcox Bombing Range, and much of it is a military reservation. Railroad tracks cross the bombing range. The NW portion, 2,478 acres, has been designated a National Natural Landmark. On the E side is a 555-acre area managed by Game and Fish.

It looks like nothing at all, a featureless dry old lake bed, a vast alkali plain with areas of parched, cracked mud. "Sometimes the only thing you'll see moving is a train," one advisor said. Up close, one sees that some of the perimeter is a wetland, with small areas of shallow standing water, some larger ones with plants typical of alkaline wetlands. The water table is high, within reach of roots. Summer rains puddle, form pools. Freshwater shrimp soon teem, hastening to complete a part of their life cycle before sun bakes the soil again. In winter, water rises to the surface and flows across flat areas and along natural drainages.

Game and Fish has constructed potholes and ponds, dikes and ditches, to make the most of any water that's available. Adjoining acres have been planted with feed crops.

It has become an important migratory bird wintering and staging area. Wintering here are 5,000 to 10,000 ducks, about 8,000 sandhill cranes, 100 Canada geese. Transients include many shorebirds.

NEVADA

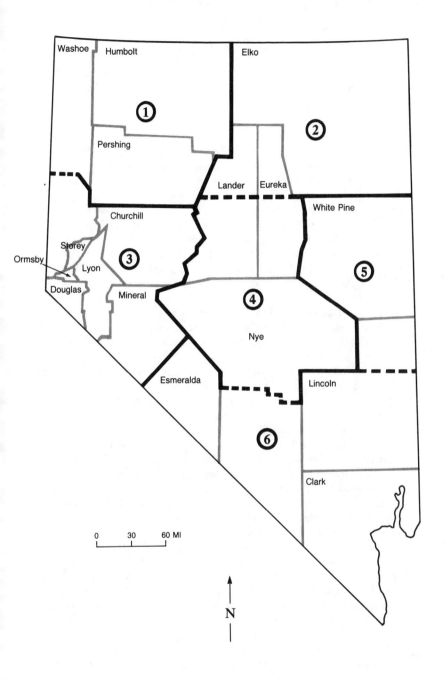

Washoe Humbolt Elko

①

Pershing ②

Lander Eureka

Churchill White Pine

Storey ③ ⑤

Ormsby Lyon

Douglas Mineral ④

Nye

Esmeralda Lincoln

⑥

Clark

0   30   60 MI

N

NEVADA

Seventh largest among the states, Nevada is, next to Alaska, the least known. Two-thirds of its residents live in two metropolitan areas, Reno and Las Vegas, and more than two-thirds of its visitors congregate there. Many of them fly in and out. Of those who drive, most speed along I-80 in the N or I-15 in the S. Three U.S. highways (6, 50, and 95) also cross the state, but except near the cities they are lightly traveled.

Nevada is not on the Grand Tour. It has no National Park, but not because it lacks spectacular features. Nevada's scenery is splendid, and at least four areas have been considered for National Parks, but—according to a U.S. Department of the Interior spokesman—the proposals were shelved because too many Nevadans said they didn't want them.

These park-quality areas are still there, no less splendid because they lack the title. All that's missing are the signposts, visitor centers, campgrounds, flush toilets, and crowds.

Although the state is still sparsely settled, it ranks among the leaders in rate of growth, which worries many Nevadans. A Las Vegas newspaper poll reported that a majority of citizens would like to see growth limited or stopped.

Most of Nevada is government land. Almost 50 million acres (70% of the state) is still undivided public domain, administered by the Bureau of Land Management. Then there are the National Forests, National Wildlife Refuges, and large military reservations. State landholdings are also significant. With so much land publicly owned, why carve out pieces and call them *parks?* As early as 1965, Nevada's Statewide Comprehensive Outdoor Recreation Plan found a shortage of recreation facilities and warned that prime land and water sites would soon be lost if the state did not acquire them.

As in other states, Nevada's popular recreation sites, especially waterside parks, are seasonally crowded. Yet we had no difficulty finding quiet places. In the final phase of our field work, we traveled 6,000 mi., from border to border, camping every night in our vehicle or trailside, and on most nights we were alone. We hiked for many miles in splendid country, rarely meeting other hikers. We sat for hours in an improvised blind beside a pond crowded with migrating waterfowl, and no one came near.

Nevada is predominantly a plateau. In the E, base elevations are from 5,000 to 6,000 ft., in the W, 3,800 to 5,000 ft. Base elevations in the S are generally between 2,000 and 3,000 ft., dropping to the lowest point, 470 ft., at the state's S tip. The state has over 200 mountain ranges, most of them 50–100 mi. long, most of them running N–S. The only significant W–E range is in the NE; this range separates the Great Basin from the Columbia River Basin. Most of Nevada lies within the Great Basin, an enclosed drainage where streams vanish into desert sands.

Nevada is the driest state, thanks to California's mountains, which intercept moisture carried in from the Pacific Ocean. The valleys are arid, receiving as little as 3–4 in. of precipitation annually in the S, 4–8 in. in the high desert of the NE. Precipitation is higher on the mountains, 10–14 in. per year on many ridges, as much as 20 in. on a few of the highest peaks.

It's not all dry. Nevada has seven lakes with more than 10,000 surface acres: Mead, Tahoe, Pyramid, Walker, Mohave, Lahontan, and Rye Patch, and many smaller reservoirs and ponds. In summer, the dry season, reservoirs may be drawn down far enough to impair boating and swimming.

Not only people are attracted by water. In pools left by a recent rain, we saw dozens of waterfowl and shorebirds. Streams rush down from mountain ranges, some of them flowing all year, several offering good fishing. Several valleys have natural wetlands, and more ponds and marshes have been created by state and federal wildlife agencies. All are well patronized by ducks and geese unless withdrawals for irrigation make them dry.

In the NE, summers are short and hot, winters long and cold. Summers are also short and hot in the W, but winters are milder. In the S, summers are long and hot, winters short and mild. When the temperature is over 100°F in a valley, it's likely to be below 85° on the upper slopes.

Snow was several feet deep on the California side of Lake Tahoe when we passed in early April. Snow fell that night between Reno and Carson City, mandating chains or snow tires. A few miles to the E, we saw the last of the snow, except for patches on high peaks.

DRIVING IN NEVADA

The highway map is useful for travel between cities. It doesn't show most of Nevada's roads. Few county roads are shown. The Bureau of Land Management has about 10,000 mi. of roads on the lands it administers. Each National Forest has its road network. Then there are mine, ranch, and power line roads, many of them open to use. None of these appear.

All are clearly shown in the *Nevada Map Atlas* published by the Nevada Department of Transportation, a bound set of 168 black-and-white maps, scale 4 mi. per inch ($12). It's the key to the backcountry. The set is so well organized that pathfinding is simple. We used them constantly and wish every state had such maps. These have much useful detail, but don't depend on them for state route numbers, which were changed after the maps were prepared, or for current road conditions.

A pattern is repeated on almost every map: roads forming a rough oval, stubs penetrating the oval. The oval surrounds a mountain range. The stubs lead into canyons. Most were built to serve mines or ranches, and some still lead to active enterprises. These canyons are the foot and horse routes to the high country.

You should also know about "ways," which aren't mapped. It's often possible to drive across open desert. If repeated use establishes a track, it's a "way"—a route no agency claims or maintains. Some ways are the most-used routes between pairs of towns. Most lead into backcountry.

Before you venture off a main road, consider the special character of Nevada travel. On a paved state highway we saw a sign: "Next gas 102 miles." We drove that distance after sundown and met one vehicle. A CB radio has too little range to be useful here. According to one source, the Highway Patrol has about 12 patrol cars in action during a shift, statewide. On a paved highway, you could be more than 50 mi. from a telephone.

If you *can* telephone, the emergency number is Zenith 1-2000. Information on road conditions can be obtained:

Northern area: (702) 793-1313.

Southern area: (702) 385-0181.

Elko area: (702) 738-8888.

Many Nevadans carry water, bandages, fan belts, tools, food, and even sleeping bags when they venture into backcountry. BLM's pamphlet *Desert Dangers* (see Publications section in this state preface) advises that one vehicle isn't enough; travel in pairs, so one can go for help if the other is disabled. If you have only one, a good rule is to drive in no farther than you're prepared to walk out.

SELECTING SITES FOR ENTRIES

Making selections isn't easy in a state where most of the land is public and undeveloped. It was especially difficult in Nevada, because its over 200 mountain ranges are so similar. We looked for special features. Because Nevada is so dry, the presence of springs or a perennial stream makes a site unusual. We also considered a site's scenic qualities, camping and hiking opportunities, and accessibility. Undoubtedly there are splendid sites we overlooked.

ON FOOT OR HORSEBACK

Nevada's 200-plus mountain ranges are its backcountry. Every range has its drainages, usually a number of deep-cut canyons. Almost always the canyons are the best routes to the ridges, but the canyons themselves are a primary attraction. Some, a minority, have streams that flow all year. Most Nevada streams are intermittent, but many canyons have springs or seeps. The canyons are where moisture gathers, so they have the most vegetation and wildlife.

Backpackers looking for long wilderness trails will find few in Nevada. Some ranges have ridgelines that make reasonable hiking routes, but seldom for as much as 40 mi. Often, however, ridges are rugged, jagged, and exposed. Nevada hikers like to ascend one canyon, descend by another. Innumerable 2- or 3-day trips are possible, and as many opportunities for day hikes, often from a car camp at the end of a stub road.

Hikers can scramble where horses must turn back, so horsemen are well advised to seek route information before mounting.

OUR ZONES

In these guides, we divide states into zones. In drawing zone boundaries we consider physical geography, travel patterns, and the recreation sites. In Nevada, we adopted BLM's six Districts, with minor boundary changes. Too late for us to change, Esmeralda County was transferred from BLM's Las Vegas District to the Battle Mountain District.

Entries usually include headquarters addresses and telephone numbers. This would be needlessly repetitious for BLM sites; the information is in each zone preface.

NEVADA'S VEGETATION

Desert shrub prevails in most lowland areas, up to about 5,500 ft. of elevation. Creosote bush predominates below 4,200 ft., black brush above. Burrobrush and yuccas are common. Others in this association include salt-brush, Mormon tea, brittlebush, bladdersage, snakeweed, skeleton weed, spiny hopsage, and winterfat. Cacti include barrel, pricklypear, beavertail, and cholla.

Sagebrush-grass replaces desert shrub over 5,500 ft. of elevation. Years of overgrazing have degraded what was once good grassland. Sagebrush now predominates.

Pinyon pine and Utah juniper comprise much of the vegetation between 6,000 and 7,300 ft., with black brush and sagebrush in the understory. Other species include cliff rose, Apache plume, mountain-mahogany, green Mormon tea, serviceberry, desert peach, rabbitbrush. In some ranges, ponderosa pine and white fir occur at the upper limits of this life zone.

The subalpine zone occurs on only the highest ranges. A distinctive species here is bristlecone pine, some specimens of which are among the continent's oldest living organisms. This species, often with limber pine, is found between 7,300 and 11,000 ft. of elevation.

A few peaks rise above 11,000 ft. and have an *alpine zone,* above timberline, with low-growing tundra plants that blossom as snow melts.

WILDLIFE

Birding is surprisingly good in Nevada, in part because so much of the state is dry that any bit of water attracts birds. We were astonished the first time we came on a tiny pool of casual water and found it crowded with mallard, pintail, grebe, green-winged and cinnamon teals, and other species. On another occasion, such a pool was inhabited by a dozen madly spinning phalaropes.

If a site could supply a bird checklist, the entry reports most of the seasonally common or abundant species. Some BLM Districts have wildlife lists. We considered including them in zone prefaces and decided a statewide bird guide would be as useful.

The bird checklist for the Las Vegas Division of the Toiyabe National Forest (Zone 6) is arranged by life zones, and it suggests what one is likely to find in similar settings.

Mammal checklists, where available, feature the many species of bats and rodents that are adapted to desert life. The coyote is ubiquitous, as is the blacktail jackrabbit. Desert bighorn sheep inhabit some of the mountain ranges, notably the Sheep Range. The sheep population declined alarmingly because of overgrazing by domestic livestock and diseases transmitted from domestic sheep. Wildlife managers are seeking to reestablish the species. Pronghorn numbers have also declined. Only BLM's Winnemucca District (Zone 1) reported them "common." Mule deer are relatively common wherever they have access to feed and water.

Many species of lizards and snakes are adapted to the desert. BLM's Winnemucca and Las Vegas (Zone 6) Districts have checklists, as do several sites.

GOVERNMENT OFFICES AND PUBLICATIONS

U.S. Bureau of Land Management
Federal Building
300 Booth St.
Reno, NV 89502
(702) 784-5311

BLM manages almost 50,000,000 acres of public land in Nevada, far more than any other agency. Each of BLM's six Nevada Districts once had a Public Lands Guide Map, showing the areas of federal, state, Indian, and private land, as well as the parks, forests, and wildlife areas. We had difficulty assembling a set and were told they were going out of print. Later we saw the first of what seemed to be a new series, called *BLM Recreation Guides*. No date had been set for completion of the series. These maps are not intended to serve as road maps, even for BLM roads.

Each District also had checklists of birds, mammals, reptiles and amphibians, and fishes. Supplies were uncertain.

In every District office we found people who know their areas intimately and were both helpful and friendly.

PUBLICATIONS
BLM Guide to Nevada Campgrounds.
Camping on the Public Lands.
Desert Dangers.

U.S. Forest Service
Intermountain Region
324 25th St.
Ogden, UT 84401
(801) 626-3011

Nevada has two large National Forests: Humboldt and Toiyabe. Each has several scattered Divisions, for which we have separate entries. A small part of the Inyo National Forest projects into Nevada from California.

U.S. Fish and Wildlife Service
Pacific Region
500 NE Multnomah St.
Portland, OR 97232
(503) 231-6121

Nevada has six National Wildlife Refuges (plus two small sites closed to visitors). The Desert refuge is the system's largest S of Alaska, the Sheldon among the largest.

Nevada Department of Transportation
1263 South Stewart St.
Carson City, NV 89712

PUBLICATION: *Nevada Map Atlas.* $12.

Nevada Division of State Parks
Capitol Complex
Carson City, NV 89710
(702) 885-4384

An effort to establish State Parks began in 1935, but it was 20 years before the legislature appropriated money: $40,000 for two years! Why bother? Almost the whole state was open for recreation. But as people found more and more of their special places degraded by litter and filth, they asked for campgrounds, washrooms, launching ramps, and picnic tables. Unique places such as Cathedral Gorge and Valley of Fire demanded protection. So a modest park system has developed. Today the Division administers 21 State Parks with over 150,000 acres of unique scenic areas.

PUBLICATIONS
A Guide to Nevada's State Parks.
Nevada's Trails.

Nevada Department of Wildlife
P.O. Box 10678
Reno, NV 89520
(702) 789-0500

The Department administers a number of large and small Wildlife Management Areas. Like most fish and game departments, Nevada's has been supported by hunting and fishing licenses, and management policies have emphasized game species. The WMA's are open to hikers, birders, and other nonconsumptive users, but there aren't many. We visited most of the WMA's. Few have resident managers. Most are of interest chiefly during bird migrations. The W. E. Kirch WMA in Zone 5 attracts many visitors because of its exceptional bird-watching opportunities.

PUBLICATIONS
Birds of Northwestern Nevada.
Birds of Northeastern Nevada.
Birds of Southern Nevada.

REFERENCES

GENERAL
Two books provide a comprehensive view of Nevada: its history, legends, cities, towns, resorts, and scenery. Both are planned for road travelers. Although quite different, both are excellent.

Toll, David W. *The Compleat Nevada Traveler.* Gold Hill, NV: Gold Hill Publishing, 1981.
Glass, Mary Ellen, and Al Glass. *Touring Nevada.* Reno: University of Nevada Press, 1983.

HIKING, BACKPACKING
Ganci, Dave. *Desert Hiking.* Berkeley, CA: Wilderness Press, 1983.
Hart, John. *Hiking the Great Basin.* San Francisco: Sierra Club Books, 1981.

FLORA AND FAUNA

Ryser, Fred A., Jr. *Birds of the Great Basin.* Reno: University of Nevada Press, 1984.

Lanner, Ronald M. *Trees of the Great Basin.* Reno: University of Nevada Press, 1984.

The Desert Bighorn Sheep of Nevada. Reno: Nevada Department of Wildlife, Biological Bulletin No. 6, 1978.

ZONE 1

1 Sheldon National Wildlife Refuge
2 Pine Forest Range; Blue Lakes
3 Humboldt National Forest, Santa Rosa Division
4 Calico Mountains
5 Black Rock Range
6 Black Rock Desert
7 Jackson Mountains
8 North Fork, Little Humboldt River
9 Twin Peaks
10 Poodle Mountain (Buffalo Hills)
11 Fox Range
12 Rye Patch State Recreation Area
13 Humboldt Wildlife Management Area

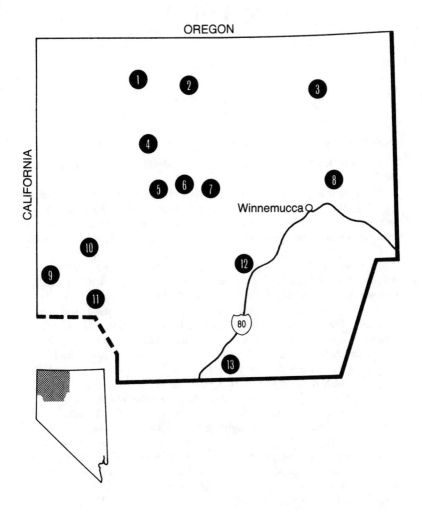

OREGON

CALIFORNIA

1 2 3

4

5 6 7 8

Winnemucca

10
9   12

11   80

13

ZONE 1

Includes these counties:

Washoe   Humboldt   Pershing

Zone 1 is BLM's Winnemucca District. BLM administers 8 million acres of the 10 million in the zone.

The main transportation corridor is I-80, which generally follows the route of the Southern Pacific Railroad. To encourage railroad building, the federal government offered land: alternate sections in a 40-mi.-wide strip along the route. While some changes have occurred, the checkerboard pattern remains: hundreds of 1-mi. squares.

Railroad and highway follow the Humboldt River, a route pioneered by trappers and emigrants. This is the only river that lies entirely within Nevada. It flows generally westward, winding 1,000 miles to achieve 250, too rocky and shallow for navigation, ending not in a sea but in the Humboldt Sink, near Lovelock. NE of Lovelock, the Rye Patch Dam has formed an 11,000-acre reservoir, a popular recreation site. Second largest body of water in the zone is 560-acre Summit Lake, within the Summit Lake Indian Reservation.

Most of the area is high desert and mountains. The lowest elevation is about 4,000 ft., the highest 9,834-ft. Star Peak in the Humboldt Range.

Principal mountain ranges in the N of the zone, from W to E, are the Fox, Granite, Calico, Black Rock, Pine Forest, Jackson, and Santa Rosa. In the S, the Buffalo Hills, Selenite, Nightingale, Truckee, Bluewing, Lava Beds, 7-Troughs, Trinity, Humboldt, East Humboldt, and Tobin. Like most Nevada ranges, they run generally N–S, canted a bit to the NE. Between the ranges are desert valleys. The largest such area is the Black Rock Desert, principal element in a broad system of deserts sweeping NE from N of Pyramid Lake to the Santa Rosa Mountains. The Black Rock Desert includes a huge desert playa, almost totally flat and barren.

At Winnemucca, elevation 4,301 ft., average annual precipitation is about 8 1/2 in. July–Sept. is the dry season. Daily maximum temperatures average about 90°F in July–Aug. but are often higher. Summer isn't a good season for hiking. Night minimums are below freezing from Oct. through Apr., but days are usually pleasant. High mountain slopes receive up to 20 in. of moisture; most winter precipitation is snow.

Plants: Most of the area is in the desert shrub-grass community, mostly northern and salt desert shrub. Some mountain slopes have pinyon-juniper stands. A few of the higher ranges have upper zones of forest-mountain brush. *Birds:* BLM has checklist of 260 species. No indication of abundance or habitat preference. Rare or endangered species include prairie and peregrine falcons, greater sandhill crane. The list includes numerous waterfowl, shorebirds, wading birds. Most of the zone is suitable for ground- and shrub-nesting species, except for the small, scattered groves of aspen, cottonwood, and mountain-mahogany.

Mammals: BLM's list reports 78 species, indicates distribution. Mule deer, pronghorn, and feral burro are common, as are raccoon, porcupine, striped and spotted skunks, pika, rabbit, jackrabbit, marmot, ground squirrels, chipmunk. Mountain lion and bobcat are called "common," though rarely observed. Many bands of wild horses. Often seen: longtail weasel, mink, beaver, badger.

Reptiles and amphibians: 32 species reported. Checklist indicates habitat and distribution. Snakes include 11 nonpoisonous species and Great Basin rattlesnake. Zebra-tailed, collared, northern sagebrush, and side-blotched lizards. Northern desert and pygmy horned lizards common in their habitats, as are several frogs and toads.

Outside the public domain, the largest public site is the 575,000-acre Sheldon National Wildlife Refuge, on the Oregon border. In the Ruby Mountains to the E, also on the border, is the 268,500-acre Ruby Division of the Humboldt National Forest. Many people consider the Ruby Mountains Nevada's most scenic.

The only State Park is Rye Patch State Recreation Area, at the reservoir. This 11,000-acre impoundment is heavily used for fishing, boating, and swimming.

Two Wildlife Management Areas, Humboldt and Fernley, are maintained chiefly for waterfowl.

Upland and big game hunting are the most popular land-based outdoor recreation activities, although game is not abundant.

Winter snow is often sufficient for winter sports. Some visitors enjoy ski touring, snowshoeing, sledding, and snowmobiling. Probably because of the highly developed winter sports areas near Reno, there's no commercial ski area here. Popular areas include the Pine Forest, Santa Rosa, and Sonoma Ranges.

Perhaps because the Sierra Nevada is just to the W and Oregon's Steens Mountain to the N, hiking and backpacking are not major activities here. Except in hunting season, one is unlikely to have much company in backcountry.

BLM has no developed campground in the zone. The Ruby Division of Humboldt National Forest has four. The only state campground is at Rye Patch. One can camp almost anywhere on BLM and National Forest land.

PUBLICATIONS
BLM District map.
BLM checklists of birds, mammals, reptiles and amphibians, fishes.
HEADQUARTERS: BLM, Winnemucca District, 705 E. Fourth St., Winnemucca, NV 89445; (702) 623-3676.

BLACK ROCK DESERT
U.S. Bureau of Land Management
Almost 1,000,000 acres.

N of SR 48 and 49 between Gerlach and Winnemucca.

This huge roadless area is shaped like a lopsided Y: a short stem with unequal arms. The stem, extending S to SR 48/49, is a white playa covering about 116,000 acres, so flat it has only 5 ft. of elevation change in 25 mi. It is almost entirely bare except for small, low-lying mounds or hummocks at its borders, which have a scanty cover of saltbush and greasewood. The bed of silt covering the playa is as much as a mile deep. The high, rugged Jackson Mountains are on the W, the lesser Black Rock Range on the E. Mirages occur. In late afternoon and early morning, the mountains offer a colorful vista.

People drive on the playa in dry months, some following a regular route between Gerlach and Winnemucca, others exploring the interior. Strangers should be wary. The playa is impassable when wet, at times even for hiking. Some wet spots are hazards even in the dry season. People have died when their vehicles were disabled. Day hikes are feasible only in the cooler months. It's no place for backpacking. The playa has been used for landsailing and, like Bonneville Flats in Utah, for seeking land speed records.

The Black Rock Range divides the top of the Y. The western arm is bordered on the W by the Calico Mountains (see entry). It extends N to Soldier Meadows and has low desert shrub vegetation.

The eastern arm follows the course of the Quinn River. It is bounded on the E by the Jackson Mountains (see entry). In summer, the river is dry. For much of the year, any flow is underground. In wet springs, there is sometimes enough water for floating in small inflatables.

Wildlife is generally seen only at the edges of the area.

BLACK ROCK RANGE

U.S. Bureau of Land Management
88,320 acres.

Immediately S of the Summit Lake Indian Reservation. The Black Rock Range divides the two arms of the Black Rock Desert. Access by Soldiers Meadow County Road (HU 217).

Straddles ridges of the Black Rock Range. Elevation from 4,050 ft. to 8,594 ft. The Range is highly irregular, terrain varying from gently rolling to steep and rugged.

Wildlife of the Black Rock Range includes deer, pronghorn, coyote, bobcat, chukar, sage grouse, quail.

The *N portion* is about 7 mi. N–S, 2 to 8 mi. W–E. This portion is dissected by two perennial streams, Soldiers and Colman creeks, which have cut interesting canyons; some riparian vegetation. It also includes 660 acres of the 12,316-acre Lahontan Cutthroat Trout Natural Area. This area, established to conserve a rare fish species, includes Mahogany Creek and its two tributaries: Pole Creek and Summer Camp Creek. Mahogany Creek is the spawning ground for fish migrating upstream from Summit Lake. The lake and 4 mi. of the creek are within the Reservation; 2 mi. are on private land, 6 mi. on public land. In 1976 a 10-mi. fence was built, enclosing 2,410 acres of creek watershed, to exclude livestock. The fenced area demonstrates range recovery from overgrazing.

In the NE sector, higher elevations have aspen-lined, deep, wide drainages; the SE sector has shallow drainages, low buttes. Vegetation is mostly low sagebrush except in drainages.

Camping: Opportunities are best near Colman Creek and Soldiers Creek. These areas also offer the best opportunities for day hiking.

The *S portion* has higher country with deep drainages and rocky outcrops. Pahute Peak (also called "Big Mountain"), 8,594 ft., is in its NW sector. Pahute is nearly flat-topped, with a steep SW-facing slope. Substantially moister than the surrounding deserts, it has two large mountain-mahogany and aspen stands on the E side. Other vegetation is mostly low shrubs. Several springs are in the N sector of this portion, hot springs in the extreme SW.

ACTIVITIES

Camping: Opportunities are said to be good, especially around Pahute Peak, more limited on the W side.

Hiking: Attractive, although access is difficult in some sectors.

Backpacking: Opportunity is chiefly 1- or 2-night trips, chiefly around Pahute Peak.

CALICO MOUNTAINS
U.S. Bureau of Land Management
67,647 acres.

From about 30 mi. NE of Gerlach, the site extends about 19 mi. N to the Summit Lake Indian Reservation. High Rock Lake is shown on highway map but not the best access to the area: well-maintained Soldiers Meadow Rd., HU 217. Inquire at Gerlach.

Includes about 30 mi. of the N–S range. Elevations from 3,950 ft. to 8,491-ft. Donnelly Peak, near the S end. The site is split near its midpoint by private holdings and a road. Both N and S halves are roadless.

N half: About 16 mi. N–S, straddling a ridge of the Calico Mountains. W of the divide, rimrock bluffs drop sharply 700 ft. to the desert floor. High Rock Lake, a 700-acre ephemeral lake, is at the N end of this western strip. It was formed by a landslide that blocked Box Canyon. The acreage E of the divide is split by Box Canyon. The area N of the canyon, about 5 by 5 mi., contains narrow, twisting, colorful Fly Canyon and The Potholes. The larger area S of Box Canyon is a rolling landscape dissected by Cherry Creek, Willow Creek, and Donnelly Creek, sloping down to Black Rock Desert. Elevations from 4,000 to 7,000 ft.

Water is generally scarce, but the S sector has perennial springs, and about 4 1/2 mi. of Donnelly Creek are perennial. At times one can swim, or at least dunk, in the lake and creek. Vegetation is typical desert shrub, sagebrush and saltbush, except for a riparian strip along Donnelly Creek. Wildlife is present but not abundant: a few pronghorn, mule deer, and mountain lion; fair numbers of chukar and sage grouse; a few quail.

The area is interesting to rockhounds: jasper, fire opal, agate, petrified wood.

S half: About 19 mi. N–S, 7 mi. W–E. Straddles the range, which has a high-elevation ridgecrest about 6 mi. long from the N boundary road past Donnelly Peak ("Division Peak" on some maps) to South Donnelly Peak. Donnelly Peak is 8,491 ft., highest point in the site. Dendritic drainages on both sides of the ridge, some of them very wide. On the E side, Petrified Canyon and Mormon Dam Canyon have steep cliffs and colorful ridges. Much of the landscape is colorful; hence the name Calico. Also on the E side is the upper portion of Donnelly Creek, here a perennial stream. About 30 perennial springs in the N and E sectors.

Vegetation is largely big sagebrush and greasewood in lower elevations, thinning out higher up. Large stands of aspen and willow in several of the deeper drainages. Wildlife, not abundant, includes pronghorn, mule deer, mountain lion, kit fox, bobcat. Chukar and sage grouse. Also wild horses.

ACTIVITIES

Camping: Best along Donnelly Creek and near isolated springs in the Donnelly Peak area.

Hiking: The area seems better suited to day hiking than backpacking. Destinations include the lake, Fly Canyon, Donnelly Creek, Box Canyon.

FOX RANGE
U.S. Bureau of Land Management
88,373 acres.

SW of Gerlach. Western Pacific RR on the W; maintenance road provides access. Pyramid Lake Indian Reservation on the S. Local roads from Gerlach and a power line road on the NE boundary.

This scenic roadless area straddles the Fox Range. The site is a triangle about 20 mi. N–S, about 12 mi. at its base, the S end. High point, near the S end, is Pah-Rum Peak, 7,800 ft. The desert floor at about 3,500 ft. slopes gradually up to the 4,500-ft. contour, where mountains rise more steeply. The W side of the range is highly dissected, rugged, with steep canyons and prominent ridges. The dark terrain is interlaced with shades of red and orange. Several narrow, colorful canyons are at the S end. Vegetation mostly sagebrush and juniper.

The E side of the range is smoother, more rolling. It includes several major canyons and drainages. Widely scattered stands of juniper.

Water is scarce. Perennial streams in portions of Rodeo Creek on the E side and in Wild Horse Canyon, which cuts across the SW corner; part of this is a private inholding.

ACTIVITIES

Camping: Limited. Chiefly on E side.

Hiking, backpacking: N area best suited to day hikes. Longer trips can be made in the S, along the ridge to Pah-Rum Peak and in canyons. Best access from the N and E.

Hunting: Pronghorn, deer, sage grouse, chukar, quail.
Horsepacking: Suitable terrain on the E side. Some forage.

HUMBOLDT NATIONAL FOREST, SANTA ROSA DIVISION

U.S. Forest Service
268,493 acres.

From Winnemucca, 22 mi. N on US 95, then right on SR 290. SR 290 crosses the Forest, returning to US 95 36 mi. further N.

This portion of the Forest is 42 mi. N–S, from the OR border. Average width is about 12 mi., narrowing to 6 mi. in the S. The Forest occupies all but the S tip of the Santa Rosa Mountains. The highest sector is in the S, in the loop formed by SR 290 and US 95. A single long, narrow ridge has peaks of 9,728, 9,701, 9,443, 9,515, and 8,663 ft. Terrain in the broader N sector is more complex, from gently rolling plateaus to steep, jagged peaks, canyons. Many springs and intermittent creeks; several streams.

The NE slopes drain to the East Fork of the Quinn River, which flows E, then turns NW, following the N boundary of the Forest to join the South Fork in the NW corner. The South Fork originates in the NW corner of the Forest, flowing NW. A bit further S, the North Fork of the Little Humboldt River is the principal drainage, flowing E. Also from the central area, Martin Creek flows SE. The Santa Rosa Range is one of the prime water-producing areas in northern NV, supplying domestic and irrigation water to the Quinn River and Paradise valleys.

The high peaks of the S portion are primarily granitic extrusions. A lava cap covers the lower slopes and most of the N half of the range. Rhyolite is common in the N, basalt in the S. The drive N on SR 290, following Indian Creek from Paradise Valley toward Hinkey Summit, is scenic, passing lava domes, a natural arch, pillars about 200 ft. tall. The Summit offers sweeping views to the S. Farther along the road, Buckskin Summit offers views to the W. Opposite this summit are the Calico Mountains, on the NE, at the Forest boundary.

The lower slopes are sagebrush rangeland. Riparian vegetation in the deeper canyons and along streams. Quaking aspen, mountain-mahogany, and some limber pine on higher slopes. Throughout the area, an abundant under-story of grasses such as bluebunch wheatgrass, Idaho fescue, and bluegrass makes this prime rangeland.

Birds: No checklist. Chukar and Hungarian partridge abundant along many northern slopes. Sage grouse throughout.

Mammals: Include mule deer, raccoon, badger, mink, beaver, coyote, bobcat, pronghorn, mountain lion.

ACTIVITIES

Camping: One campground with 6 sites, open June–Sept. But camp in any suitable place.

Hiking, backpacking: The Forest map shows well over 100 mi. of numbered trails as well as primitive roads. Check at a Ranger Station for advice on current trail conditions. One of the most scenic trails is along the summit of the southern peaks. Access is up Buffalo Canyon or Rebel Creek on the W, Sugar Creek on the E.

Hunting: Deer, antelope, upland game birds.

Fishing: Rainbow, brown, brook trout.

Ski touring: Tent Mountain is a favored winter sports area.

PUBLICATION: Forest map (Santa Rosa and Humboldt Divisions). $1.

HEADQUARTERS: 976 Mountain City Highway, Elko, NV 89801; (702) 738-5171.

RANGER DISTRICT: Santa Rosa R.D., Winnemucca, NV 89845; (702) 623-5025.

HUMBOLDT WILDLIFE MANAGEMENT AREA
Nevada Department of Wildlife
36,235 acres.

From Reno, NE on I-80 about 80 mi. to Toulon exit. Site is S of the highway.

This is the end of the Humboldt River. The marsh is about 17,000 acres, surrounded by tamarisk and saltgrass. Elevation about 4,000 ft. Construction of the Rye Patch Reservoir upstream reduced the flow of water to the marsh and thus its size, which varies seasonally, and its carrying capacity. It is still an important feeding and resting area for migratory waterfowl, notably Canada goose, pintail, and redhead, as well as a haven for shorebirds.

The site has few visitors except at the opening of the hunting season. No resident personnel. One primitive campground.

JACKSON MOUNTAINS
U.S. Bureau of Land Management
86,668 acres.

Between the Black Rock Desert on the W, Desert Valley on the E. Jackson Creek Rd., N from Sulphur, is on the W boundary, Trout Creek Rd. on the E.

The range is about 40 mi. long, about 12 mi. wide at its midsection, much narrower to the N and S. Most of the mass is above 5,000 ft. elevation. Two roadless areas, divided where Jackson Creek Rd. turns E, straddle about 22 mi. of the range, including the highest country. Private holdings along Trout Creek Rd.

Availability of water attracts many species of wildlife, notably waterfowl. Also chukar, mourning dove, numerous raptors, cottontail, deer, mountain lion.

N portion: The smaller of the two, about 7 mi. N–S. Elevations to 8,425 ft. on Parrot Peak. Deep, rugged canyons descend from the ridge. Principal canyons—Deer Creek, Mary Sloan, Happy Creek, Jackson Creek—have lush riparian vegetation dominated by cottonwood and willow. Most have perennial streams. A few small waterfalls. Vegetation on upper slopes includes juniper, snowberry, gooseberry, wild grape, red-osier dogwood.

The canyons offer the most attractive opportunities for camping and day hiking. Backpacking opportunities are better in the S portion.

S portion: About 15 mi. N–S. Rugged, majestic peaks along the ridge. Highest is 8,910-ft. King Lear Peak. Canyons on the W side are deep, rugged, with rock outcrops and talus slopes, lush riparian vegetation. Higher slopes support juniper, snowberry, gooseberry, wild grape, red-osier dogwood. Terrain on the E side is less dramatic, rolling, with shallower drainages. Springs and creeks in most canyons. King Lear Peak and McGill Canyon are recommended day hiking sites, McGill recommended for camping.

NORTH FORK, LITTLE HUMBOLDT RIVER
U.S. Bureau of Land Management
69,683 acres.

The North Fork originates in the Santa Rosa Range in the Humboldt National Forest, flows SE, then turns SW to join the South Fork about 22 mi. E of the town of Paradise Valley. Access from well-maintained Little Owyhee Rd. (BLM 2003), not shown on highway map.

Gently rolling terrain of sand and sagebrush. The central feature is the river gorge, 14 mi. long, steep-sided, colorful, up to 600 ft. deep, 600–2,700 ft. wide rim to rim. Most of the gorge is highly dissected, with many wide oxbows, caves, basalt spires, precipices, side canyons. Access to the Gorge at Greeley Crossing, on the N end, South Fork ranch road on the S. Riparian plant community includes much willow.

Button Lake, in the NE corner of the site, is a dry lake bed that becomes lush meadow in spring.

Birds: Include great blue heron, turkey vulture, red-tailed and rough-legged hawks, prairie falcon, American kestrel, chukar, sage grouse, great horned owl, mourning dove, belted kingfisher, white-throated swift, violet-green and cliff swallows, northern flicker, black-billed magpie, common crow, American robin, western meadowlark, Brewer's blackbird, northern oriole, sparrows, wrens.

Mammals: Include pronghorn, mule deer, beaver, muskrat, mink, coyote, squirrel, raccoon, bobcat. Caves in the Gorge have bat populations.

ACTIVITIES

Camping: Best opportunities in S portion and at Button Lake.

Hiking and backpacking: Chiefly in the Gorge.

Hunting: Pronghorn, grouse, chukar, California quail, and ring-necked pheasant.

PINE FOREST RANGE; BLUE LAKES
U.S. Bureau of Land Management
25,650 acres.

25 mi. S of Denio. Alder Creek Road, dirt, from Denio to the N boundary of the unit. From SR 140 about 17 mi. S of Denio, about 15 mi. on dirt road to Blue Lakes.

The site straddles a N–S ridge with high, rugged, granitic peaks. Much of the area is over 7,500 ft. elevation, with several peaks over 9,000 ft. Duffer Peak, near the Blue Lakes, is 9,458 ft. The area around the lakes, in the heart of the Range, has high scenic quality: sparkling subalpine lakes, high mountain meadows, "cathedral" peaks. Blue Lake and nearby Leonard Creek Lake attract many campers and fishermen. Because this area is fairly remote—a drive of about 15 mi. over often-rough road—it has few day visitors. About 17,000 acres, including the access road close to the lakes, has been closed to vehicles. Visitors now hike the last 1/2 mi.

The Blue Lakes, elevation 8,500 ft., were formed by glacial moraines, rare in the Great Basin. Topography is generally steep, slopes averaging 60%. Annual precipitation here is 25–30 in., exceptionally high for NV; 60–80% of this falls as snow. Summer daytime temperatures in the 90s. Nights always cool.

Plants: Big sagebrush occurs over most of the range, with low sagebrush at higher elevations, serviceberry and snowberry in moister sites. Predominant grasses are Idaho fescue, bluegrasses, wild rye. Higher elevations have numerous meadows, snow banks, aspen groves in draws, willows along permanent streams, mountain-mahogany. Scattered around Duffer Peak and Blue Lake are about 1,800 acres of whitebark and limber pines, uncommon in this region. Numerous wildflowers include lupine, globemallow, buckwheat, Indian paintbrush.

Wildlife: Relatively abundant and diverse. Large mule deer population. A few pronghorn. Chukar plentiful, sage grouse in fair numbers. Waterfowl and shorebirds visit the lakes. Songbirds include species not often seen in this region, such as pine grosbeak and red crossbill.

ACTIVITIES

Camping: Near the lakes and in open meadows.

Hiking, backpacking: Elevation, availability of water, and terrain make this one of the more attractive areas.

Fishing: Trout in lakes.

Horsepacking: Good access; abundant water and forage.

POODLE MOUNTAIN (BUFFALO HILLS)
U.S. Bureau of Land Management
142,050 acres.

15 mi. NW of Gerlach. SR 447 is on E boundary.

A roughly circular area 18 mi. in diameter, including most of the Buffalo Hills, a basaltic plateau with large, deep canyons radiating generally from the center, descending to desert piedmont. Best foot and horse access is up Poodle Mountain, Jones, and other canyons on the E side. Elevations from 3,850 ft. to 6,958 ft. on Poodle Mountain, near the center of the area.

Desert environment: sparse shrub vegetation with a scattering of juniper on highlands and canyon sides. However, there are over 50 perennial springs, some on private inholdings, and several miles of Buffalo, Jones, and Frog creeks are perennial streams. Water availability is a factor in support of wildlife populations, species including pronghorn, deer, mountain lion, sage grouse, valley quail, and chukar.

ACTIVITIES

Camping: Chiefly from SR 447, in drainage bottoms.

Hiking, backpacking: Opportunities to ascend one canyon, return by another.

Horsepacking: Much of the area is accessible.

RYE PATCH STATE RECREATION AREA
Nevada Division of State Parks
27,680 acres.

From Lovelock, about 22 mi. NE on I-80.

Reservoir formed by damming the Humboldt River. About 11,400 surface acres at full pool. The site is within the broad band of checkerboard land ownership. Most of the private holdings on the lake are on the E shore. The lake is surrounded by low desert hills.

Most development is at the lower end, near the dam. Substantial areas on the upper lake shore are inaccessible by vehicles other than 4-wheel drive. The lake is heavily used for water-based recreation.

ACTIVITIES

Camping: Primitive. No designated sites.

Fishing: Walleye, white bass, crappie, catfish, a few largemouth bass.

Boating: Ramp.

HEADQUARTERS: Capitol Complex, Carson City, NV 89710; (702) 885-4384.

SHELDON NATIONAL WILDLIFE REFUGE
U.S. Fish and Wildlife Service
570,421 acres.

On the OR border. 100 mi. from Winnemucca via US 95 and SR 291.

The refuge was established chiefly for the benefit of pronghorn, but it is now managed for all native wildlife species. While it has no large wetlands, there are enough to attract waterfowl, almost any of the species traveling the flyway. 178 bird species have been recorded. A checklist of all wildlife occurring on the refuge is available. Also maps.

A vast area of rolling hills, flat-topped tablelands, mountains, sharp-breaking rimrock country, and gorges with vertical rock walls. Elevations from 4,000 to 7,300 ft.

Sagebrush rangeland is the almost uniform cover. The region is moister than many parts of NV, receiving about 20 in. of precipitation per year in the higher elevations, mostly as snow. The area has numerous springs, seasonal and perennial streams, and many small reservoirs were developed for wildlife. Range grasses, suppressed by past overgrazing, are now recovering.

From US 140, which crosses the site, one gets a good view of the area. Several unpaved roads are open in good weather, but they should be taken with caution, because there are no regular patrols. For the backpacker and horseman, the entire area is open. Eight roadless portions have been recommended for wilderness status.

When the area became a refuge, the bighorn sheep were gone, mule deer were scarce, pronghorn a scattered few. Sage grouse had been hunted almost to extinction. Deer, pronghorn, and grouse populations are now increasing. Bighorn are present but seldom seen.

Except for hunters, few visitors come this way, and there are no facilities. Spring and early summer are the best times to visit. Snow often closes roads Dec.–May.

ACTIVITIES
Camping: 18 primitive sites.
Hunting: In designated areas; special rules.

PUBLICATIONS
Leaflet with species checklists.
Regulations; hunting map.

HEADQUARTERS: P.O. Box 111, Lakeview, OR 97630; (503) 947-3315.

TWIN PEAKS
U.S. Bureau of Land Management
91,405 acres.

On the CA border W of Gerlach. Bounded by the Home Springs-Painter Flat road on the N; Sand Pass-Gerlach road, Buffalo Meadow Road, Parsnip Creek Road, and Mixie Flat Road on the SE. Immediately W of the Poodle Mountain site (see entry).

Flatlands and low, rolling hills in the NW. Shinn Creek and Smoke Creek are perennial streams. In the E, the terrain is extremely rugged, with numerous canyons, draws, hills, and peaks. The area is above 4,000 ft. elevation, rising to 6,605 ft. at Twin Peaks. The E side descends gradually to Smoke Creek Desert. The Sand Pass-Gerlach road is at the W edge of the Desert. Average annual precipitation is about 8 in.

Attractive features on the E side are Willow Creek, Buffalo Creek, and Chimney Rock Creek, each in a canyon. Predominant vegetation is low sage, juniper, grasses; willow and aspen in some drainages.

HEADQUARTERS: BLM, Susanville District Office, P.O. Box 1090, Susanville, CA 96130; (916) 257-5385.

ZONE 2

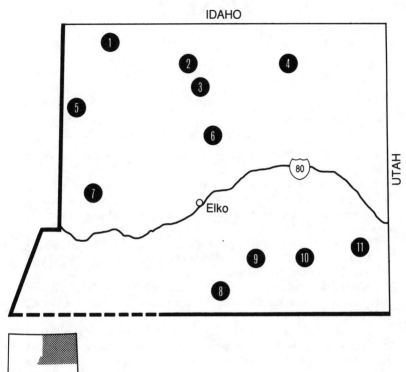

IDAHO

UTAH

80

Elko

1

2

3

4

5

6

7

8

9

10

11

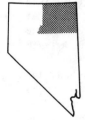

ZONE 2

Includes these counties:

Elko	Lander (N tip)	Eureka (N tip)

Zone 2 is BLM's Elko District. It includes more than 14 million acres, of which 7.5 million are administered by BLM.

The main W–E transportation corridor is I-80. From the W boundary of the zone, it follows the Humboldt River to Elko, then continues E through mountain passes. US 93 in the E portion of the zone is the chief N–S route, crossing I-80 at Wells.

Public and private lands are a checkerboard in a broad, irregularly shaped band across the middle of the zone. Most of the large blocks of public land are N and SE of this checkerboard.

Basin and range topography is typical here, as elsewhere in Nevada. Principal ranges in the N are the Tuscarora and Independence; in the S, the Cortez, Ruby, and Goshute.

This is high country. Elevations vary from about 5,000 ft. in the valleys to over 12,000 ft. on the highest peaks in the Humboldt National Forest. At Elko, elevation 5,060 ft., annual precipitation is just under 10 in. The climate of the zone is semiarid, not as dry as in Zone 1. Some valleys receive less than 8 in. of moisture, some high mountains up to 18 in.

Several streams rising in the N central mountains flow N into Idaho: the Owyhee River and its South Fork, the Bruneau, the Jarbidge, and Salmon Falls Creek. The North Fork of the Humboldt River and Mary's River flow S joining other streams flowing N from the Ruby Mountains to the W-flowing Humboldt River.

At Elko, normal daily maximum temperature is in the 30s and 40s (Fahrenheit) from November through March, in the upper 70s to low 90s in summer. Temperatures are lower on the mountains.

Sagebrush range is the predominant vegetation in the valleys and on the lower slopes. Livestock production is still important, despite depletion of grasses; many cattle and sheep graze on the public land. BLM has seeded thousands of acres to perennial grasses. At higher elevations, pinyon pine and juniper predominate.

The zone has a large population of mule deer. Pronghorn numbers are increasing. Small game includes rabbit, chukar, sage grouse, waterfowl. Some streams have good trout fishing.

Aside from the public domain, the largest public sites are the Humboldt Division of the Humboldt National Forest, in the N central area, and the Ruby Division in the S central. The Ruby Lake National Wildlife Refuge is on the E side of the Ruby Mountains.

Fishing and boating are available on several reservoirs. The largest, Wild Horse, is about 65 miles N of Elko. The zone's only State Park is on this reservoir. Other reservoirs, used chiefly for fishing, are Ruby Lake, Wilson, Crittenden, and Zunino. On the map the Chimney Creek Reservoir looks interesting, but rights to its water are privately owned and it is drawn down considerably each year; also, road access is difficult.

PUBLICATIONS

BLM District map (if available).

Checklists of mammals, reptiles and amphibians.

HEADQUARTERS: BLM, Elko District, P.O. Box 831, Elko, NV 89801; (702) 738-4071.

GOSHUTE MOUNTAINS
U.S. Bureau of Land Management
180,000 acres.

From about 10 mi. W of the UT border at Wendover, extending S about 35 mi. Access by local roads on E side, several of which penetrate the site.

Most of the site, 125,435 acres, is in two adjacent roadless blocks. The W side rises rather steeply from Steptoe Valley, the E side more gradually. Highest peak in the N is 7,994 ft.; in the midsection 8,699 ft. Goshute Peak, about 10 mi. from the S end, is 9,611 ft. The main ridgeline is generally above 7,500 ft. The base of the range is 5 to 6 mi. wide.

The ridgeline is a migration route for thousands of raptors each fall, including goshawk, golden and bald eagles. Fair wildlife population, including wild horses.

The N sector has about 15 canyons, 2 to 4 mi. long. Largest are Morris, West Morris, and Morgan basins; Thirtymile, Johnson, and Erickson canyons. Spring Gulch has a natural arch. Vegetation is fairly dense: grasses and low sagebrush at low elevations, stands of pinyon-juniper with some fir and mountain-mahogany on higher slopes. Several small reservoirs were developed to water stock; these seem to be reverting to a natural condition.

The S sector is more rugged, with many rocky outcrops and sheer rock faces. Several canyons offer good possibilities for hiking and backpacking, notably Lion, Felt Spring, and Ferguson. Several springs are in these canyons, but they are not marked or easy to find.

HUMBOLDT NATIONAL FOREST, HUMBOLDT DIVISION

U.S. Forest Service
763,424 acres.

On the ID border N of Elko. Crossed by SR 225 N from Elko.

This site has the shape of a horizontal boot, toe to the left, pointed S. The main body is 59 mi. W–E, 26 mi. N–S. The toe extends about 25 mi. S and is about 9 mi. wide.

Here at the boundary of the Great Basin the N–S basin and range pattern that prevails over most of NV is much modified. The Independence and Jarbidge Mountains, the two principal ranges, have the N–S orientation, but in a jumble of mountains, valleys, mesas, canyons, and rolling hills. The region is high and cut by shallow and deep drainages, forming intermittent and perennial streams that flow to all points of the compass. While the highest country is in the E, where the Jarbidge Wilderness has 8 peaks over 10,000 ft., peaks over that height also occur in the W. Many over 7,000 and 8,000 ft. are scattered throughout the Division.

Average annual precipitation is about 14 in. at high elevations. While most of this falls as snow in winter, warm season precipitation is about 6 in. The climate is cool. Only about 90 days a year are frost-free on the highest slopes. High trails are usually open by June 15. Snow may fall in early Oct.

The streams and rivers of the Division are headwaters for the North Fork of the Humboldt River, East and South forks of the Owyhee, and the Bruneau. Others contribute to the Salmon Falls River, Mary's River, and Jarbidge River. Wild Horse Reservoir, at the ankle of the boot, has 2,830 surface acres, is only partially within the Forest. A BLM campground, state campground, and Sho-Pai tribal campgrounds are beside the reservoir on SR 225.

Plants: Vegetation is primarily sagebrush and grasses, with associated forbs. Patches of aspen, serviceberry, chokecherry, and other brush occur. Cottonwood and willow along streams. At high elevations, stands of limber pine and subalpine fir.

Birds: No checklist. Mentioned: sage and blue grouse, chukar, mourning dove, various ducks and geese, golden eagle, quail, rough-legged and red-tailed hawks, great horned owl, turkey vulture, songbirds.

Mammals: No checklist. Mentioned: beaver, raccoon, bobcat, mountain lion, mink, muskrat, weasel, porcupine, otter, coyote, cottontail, mule deer, golden-mantled squirrel.

Reptiles and amphibians: Mentioned: Great Basin spadefoot toad, western toad, Pacific tree frog, leopard frog; collared, western fence, sagebrush, side-blotched, and desert horned lizards; western skink, western Great Basin whiptail. Also rubber boa, striped whipsnake, racer, Great Basin gopher snake, wandering garter snake, desert night snake, Great Basin rattlesnake.

FEATURES
Jarbidge Wilderness, 64,667 acres; 28,000-acre addition proposed. One of the most scenic and remote places in NV. A rugged, mountainous region between the Columbia River Plateau and the Great Basin. Habitats range from sagebrush bottoms to rocky peaks with stunted limber pine. The Jarbidge Range has a single crest that maintains an elevation over 9,800 ft. for about 7 mi. The proposed addition includes surrounding canyonlands.

The Forest map shows numbered trails but no contours. A topo is needed for wilderness hiking. Wilderness permits are not required, but those entering are asked to register at trailheads.

ACTIVITIES
Camping: 6 campgrounds, 70 sites. June–Oct.

Hiking, backpacking: Numbered trails and logging roads throughout the Forest. If the Jarbidge Wilderness has more visitors than you prefer—which doesn't happen often—you can find splendid high country elsewhere in the Forest. Year-around hiking is possible at lower elevations.

Hunting: Deer, pronghorn, sage and blue grouse, chukar.

Fishing: Rainbow, German brown, brook trout.

Boating: On Wild Horse Reservoir.

Horse riding: Commercial packers service the Jarbidge. Some private horse use in other areas.

PUBLICATION: Forest map (Santa Rosa and Humboldt Divisions). $1.

HEADQUARTERS: 976 Mountain City Highway, Elko, NV 89801; (702) 738-5171.

RANGER DISTRICTS: Jarbidge R.D., Buhl, ID 83316; (208) 543-4219. Mountain City R.D., Mountain City, NV 89831; (702) 763-6691.

HUMBOLDT NATIONAL FOREST, RUBY DIVISION
U.S. Forest Service
424,472 acres.

SW of Wells. Crossed by SR 229. A principal access route is SR 227 SE from Elko.

The East Humboldt Range, N portion of the Division, extends 25 mi. S from a point near I-80. The range is high, peaks of 11,000 ft. In about half of the area, it is a checkerboard of public and private ownerships. Campgrounds at 13-acre Angel Lake and nearby Angel Creek, near Wells, are the only developed recreation sites in this sector. About 10 numbered trails enter the area from the W side, generally following small drainages, several of them linked by a trail from the N that wanders down the W side of the ridge. Highest point is Hole in the Mountain Peak, 11,276 ft., near the midpoint of the range.

The ridgeline of the Ruby Mountains runs NNE to SSW, the N tip almost meeting the midpoint of the East Humboldt Range; they are separated by Secret Pass and Secret Valley. These mountains, extending about 60 mi., are not the highest in NV, but many visitors consider them the most scenic. Their configuration is the work of glaciers: U-shaped canyons with walls up to 2,000 ft. high, ribbon falls and cascades. Many of the valleys have alpine lakes or tarns.

The N quarter of the Ruby Mountain area is also checkerboarded, but this pattern ends at Lamoille Canyon, which penetrates the range from the NW. This is the principal avenue of visitor activity. Ruby Dome, 11,387 ft., highest point, is about 3 mi. S of the canyon. From this point S is a procession of peaks over 10,000 ft., with the most extensive tundra vegetation in the Great Basin.

A paved Forest road follows the canyon, passing trailheads and campgrounds, into the N end of the Ruby Mountain Scenic Area. The most popular hiking trail, Ruby Crest, runs for 50 mi. from the head of Lamoille Canyon to Harrison Pass, where another Forest road crosses the ridge. Five days is the recommended schedule for this trip, but most backpackers stop at one or more of the high mountain lakes along the way, spend their time there, and turn back.

The Forest map shows many trails leading up drainages and canyons from both the E and W sides, some only short distances, others up and over the ridge. A Forest bulletin, noted below, mentions several of these trails, advising that they cross private land before entering the Forest and owners' permission must be obtained. Ask at a Ranger Station about current trail conditions and whom to ask for such permission.

The Ruby Mountains catch more moisture from passing clouds than lower mountains, about 18 in. per year, most of this as snow. The Ruby Crest Trail is likely to be blocked by snow until about July 1, with snow banks persisting later. Summer thunderstorms are common, often bringing lightning without rain, and hikers are advised to avoid exposed areas, tall trees, and horses when lightning is nearby. Summer days are usually in the 80s, but nights may be frosty.

Plants: Vegetation is generally sparse, sagebrush and grasses on lower slopes. Some dense stands of mountain-mahogany and snowbrush; numerous aspen groves and stands of limber pine. An isolated stand of bristlecone pine, here at the northern limit of its range.

Birds: No checklist. Mentioned: sage grouse, chukar, blue grouse, mourning dove, various ducks and geese, golden eagle, quail, hawks, songbirds.

Mammals: No checklist. Mentioned: mountain lion, bobcat, beaver, mule deer, mountain goat, pika, raccoon, mink, muskrat, weasel, porcupine, otter, coyote, cottontail, golden-mantled squirrel.

Reptiles and amphibians: Mentioned: Great Basin spadefoot and western toads, Pacific tree frog, leopard frog; collared, western fence, sagebrush, sideblotched, and desert horned lizards; western skink, western Great Basin whiptail, rubber boa, striped whipsnake, Great Basin gopher snake, wandering garter snake, desert night snake, Great Basin rattlesnake.

FEATURE: *Ruby Mountains roadless area,* 65,000 acres, proposed for wilderness status. This includes the roadless portion of the Scenic Area.

ACTIVITIES

Camping: 3 campgrounds, 82 sites. Angel Creek and Lake, June–Oct. Thomas Canyon, June–Sept.

Hiking, backpacking: Backcountry permits not yet required. Check with Ranger Station before going far.

Hunting: Deer, upland game birds.

Fishing: Some lakes stocked with brook trout. Others have no fish.

Horse riding: Ask at Ranger Station or HQ about outfitters.

Skiing: Some helicopter skiing Jan.–Mar. We were told of possible ski area development on Tent Mountain.

PUBLICATIONS

Forest map. $1.

Information pages.

REFERENCE: Hart, John. *Hiking the Great Basin.* San Francisco: Sierra Club Books, 1981, pp. 269–291.

HEADQUARTERS: 976 Mountain City Highway, Elko, NV 89801; (702) 738-5171.

RUBY MOUNTAINS RANGER DISTRICT: Wells, NV 89835; (702) 752-3357.

LITTLE HUMBOLDT RIVER

U.S. Bureau of Land Management

96,320 acres.

About 65 mi. NW of Elko. About 4 mi. NW of Midas, a ghost town 4 mi.

W of Willow Creek Reservoir.

The South Fork of the Little Humboldt originates in a low range W of Midas, flows N for a dozen miles, then turns W into Humboldt County where it joins the North Fork (see entry in Zone 1). The highway map shows no roads here, but an unimproved road follows the river above and below the confluence for several miles.

The area has rolling hills, becoming more eroded and canyonlike in the W. The river has cut a steep-walled, winding canyon, with tributaries in side canyons. The canyon floor has some riparian vegetation. 42,213 roadless acres on the N-flowing section have been proposed for wilderness study. Wildlife includes wild horses.

ACTIVITIES

Hiking, backpacking: Chiefly in the canyon. Spectacular scenery, available water, seclusion. In many places, stock and game trails make good hiking routes.

Fishing: Lahontan trout.

NORTH FORK, HUMBOLDT RIVER
U.S. Bureau of Land Management
20,000 acres.

About 35 mi. N of Elko. E of SR 225.

Not to be confused with the North Fork of the Little Humboldt River. This North Fork rises in the Independence Mountains, in the Humboldt Division of the National Forest. It flows SE, then S to join the South Fork. From the Forest boundary to this eastward turn, the river is generally on private land. This entry describes the next dozen miles, after which the river turns S again.

Terrain is generally rolling except for steep banks along the river and Cottonwood Creek. The W portion includes Devil's Gap, where the river flows through a narrow cut between cliffs. Big sagebrush is the dominant vegetation, with some riparian growth.

The area isn't sufficiently large or secluded to invite backpacking, but it offers attractions for day hiking and fishing.

OWYHEE RIVER CANYON

U.S. Bureau of Land Management
29,717 acres, plus 37,783 acres in Idaho.

About 28 mi. W of Owyhee by unimproved roads.

The South Fork of the Owyhee flows NNW into Idaho through a rugged canyon about 45 mi. long, extremely winding. It cuts through desert terrain at about 5,000 ft. elevation. For much of the distance, the canyon walls are precipitous to sheer. Slopes are more gradual in the midsection.

This scenic canyon of the South Fork of the Owyhee River offers opportunities for hiking and backpacking. Travel on the canyon floor is pleasant, though often difficult, following game and stock trails around and over loose volcanic rock.

Rafting the river is said to be feasible Apr.–June. The floatable stretch is about 30 river mi. long, from the Petan Ranch in NV into ID. Class I and II water.

Horse travel in the canyon is not recommended.

ROCK CREEK CANYON

U.S. Bureau of Land Management
24,000 acres.

From Battle Mountain, about 23 mi. N on Izzenhood Rd., then about 8 mi. E on local roads.

This area is generally characterized by low, rolling hills with sagebrush vegetation. Rock Creek has cut a N–S canyon, mostly steep-walled. At the canyon's broadest point, Rock Creek is joined by Antelope Creek, an intermittent stream flowing from the NE. Rock Creek Canyon is about 8 mi. long. Some riparian vegetation, chiefly willow. Its interesting terrain and available water make the canyon attractive to hikers.

Highest point in the area is a 6,153-ft. hill between the two creeks.

RUBY LAKE NATIONAL WILDLIFE REFUGE

U.S. Fish and Wildlife Service
37,632 acres.

From Wells, S 28 mi. on US 93, then SW on SR 229.

An extensive marsh at the foot of the E side of the Ruby Mountains. This and the nearby Franklin Marsh are remnants of an ancient lake that once covered 470 sq. mi. The refuge is a haven for many waterfowl and other birds, for feeding, resting, and nesting. Elevation is about 6,000 ft.

Annual precipitation is about 12 in. The 12,000 acres of wetlands are maintained by collecting and impounding water from some 150 springs at the base of the mountain. The 7,000-acre South Sump, a natural depression, serves as a collection area. Using dikes and ditches, water levels are manipulated to simulate the conditions of natural wetlands.

Marsh vegetation is largely hardstem bulrush. Upland areas have typical desert sagebrush-rabbitbrush cover.

Birding is good at any season. June and July are the months to observe waterfowl and their young. May and Sept.–Oct. are the best seasons for migrants; up to 25,000 ducks and as many coots Sept.–Oct. The riparian habitat along Cave Creek, near HQ, is the best area for passerines.

Visitors are free to walk or drive on most roads and dikes. Boats can be used in some areas, subject to restrictions noted below.

Birds: Almost 200 species use the refuge regularly. One of the densest breeding populations of canvasback in North America. One of the few refuges with nesting greater sandhill crane. Seasonally common or abundant species include eared and pied-billed grebes, great blue heron, snowy egret, black-crowned night-heron, American bittern, trumpeter swan, white-faced ibis, Canada goose, mallard, gadwall, pintail, green-winged and cinnamon teals, American wigeon, northern shoveler, redhead, ring-necked duck, canvasback, lesser scaup, common goldeneye, bufflehead, ruddy duck. Also turkey vulture, red-tailed and rough-legged hawks, northern harrier, sage grouse, American coot, killdeer, long-billed curlew, spotted and solitary sandpipers, willet, lesser yellowlegs, Forster's and black terns, mourning dove, great horned and short-eared owls, common nighthawk, northern flicker, western kingbird, Say's phoebe, willow and dusky flycatchers, horned lark. Also violet-green, tree, bank, rough-winged, barn, and cliff swallows; magpie, common raven, pinyon jay, mountain chickadee, plain titmouse, bushtit, red-breasted nuthatch, marsh wren, robin, Swainson's thrush, mountain bluebird, starling, yellow and yellow-rumped warblers, western meadowlark; yellow-headed, red-winged, and Brewer's blackbirds; brown-headed cowbird, house finch, pine siskin; sage, white-crowned, and song sparrows; dark-eyed junco.

Mammals: Often seen: mule deer, coyote, mountain cottontail, blacktail jackrabbit. Occasionally seen: pronghorn.

Reptiles and amphibians: Often seen: bullsnake, wandering garter snake, Great Basin rattlesnake.

ACTIVITIES

Camping: Not on the Refuge but nearby at BLM's Ruby Marsh Campground, between the Refuge and the National Forest. 35 sites. Apr. 30–Nov. 15.

Hunting: Waterfowl. Limited area and special regulations.

Fishing: Bass, trout. Designated areas and special regulations.

Boating, canoeing: No boats N of Browns Dike. No boats S of Browns Dike, Jan. 1–June 14. Boats without motors or with electric motors, June 15–Dec. 31. Boats with up to 10-hp motors, Aug. 1–Dec. 31. Four launch sites.

PUBLICATIONS

Refuge leaflet.

Bird checklist.

Fishing, boating regulations.

Hunting regulations.

HEADQUARTERS: Ruby Valley, NV 89833; (702) 779-2237.

SALMON FALLS CREEK
U.S. Bureau of Land Management
52,000 acres.

About 50 mi. N of Wells. W of US 93.

North and South forks of Salmon Falls Creek join about 12 mi. W of Contact on US 93. The creek then flows SE, turns NE near the highway, follows it toward Jackpot, and crosses into Idaho. Two roadless areas were considered for wilderness status, one above the confluence, the other at the ID boundary. Beyond the boundary, the creek flows into Salmon Creek Reservoir.

The creek has cut a winding, shallow, but steep-walled canyon across the area. The upstream area is hilly, rugged, rocky, known locally as Bad Lands. Elevation is generally over 6,000 ft., rising to about 8,000 ft. at one point S of the creek, over 7,000 ft. over a large, broad ridge. The area at the border offers a quiet float trip, Class I water, for about 16 mi., as well as hiking and fishing.

Vegetation is sparse except in the canyon, where riparian growth is sometimes so dense a hiker must wade in the stream. Hiking is often on stock and game trails. Campsite can be found in the canyon, but they are not numerous.

ACTIVITIES

Fishing: Rainbow and brown trout.

Canoeing, rafting: Put in at rest area or farther downstream at fish barrier dam; float to reservoir in ID. Class I water.

SPRUCE MOUNTAIN RIDGE
U.S. Bureau of Land Management
67,000 acres.

On the E side of US 93 about 48 mi. S of Wells, extending N.

Spruce Mountain Ridge is about 18 mi. long. It broadens at the S end, forming a U with the Pequop Mountains, which extend NE. Spruce Mountain, near the S end, is the highest point: 10,262 ft. A wintering bald eagle roosting area was recently discovered on the mountain.

From US 93 the land rises gradually to the 7,500-ft. contour, then more steeply. The ridge narrows to the N and drops to about 1,000 ft. above the valley floor. Side canyons are shallow. Vegetation ranges from low sagebrush to pinyon-juniper to a few conifers on Spruce Mountain. About 50 acres of old bristlecone pine.

This is not an outstanding area, but it offers an easy approach from a major highway and fine views of the Ruby Mountains.

WILD HORSE STATE RECREATION AREA
Nevada Division of State Parks
80 acres.

65 mi. N of Elko on SR 225.

A small State Recreation Area on a reservoir that occupies 3,000 acres when full. The reservoir is partially within the Humboldt Division of the Humboldt National Forest. A BLM campground is on the N side. The surrounding area is high, treeless, cold desert.

The SRA is relatively new. Most visitors come to fish. Other water-based activities are increasing. A convenient base for exploring or hunting the area.

ACTIVITIES

Camping: 33 sites. All year.

Fishing: Rainbow trout. Some brown trout and kokanee salmon. Largemouth bass recently introduced. Best months are Jan., May, Sept.–Nov. Ice fishing.

Boating: Ramp planned.

HEADQUARTERS: Elko, NV 89801; (702) Elko operator: toll station North Fork 6493.

ZONE 3

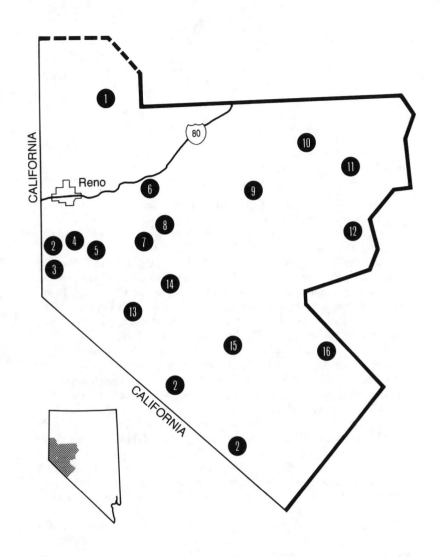

ZONE 3

Includes these counties:

Washoe (S portion)	Churchill	Carson City
Storey	Lyon	
Douglas	Mineral	

Zone 3 is BLM's Carson City District. It includes Carson City, the state capital, Reno, Nevada's portion of Lake Tahoe, and Pyramid Lake. The District includes more than 7 million acres, of which almost 6 million are public domain, administered by BLM.

The zone is partly mountainous, but without the well-defined N–S basin and range pattern seen just to the E. The Virginia Mountains stand between Pyramid Lake and California. The Stillwater Range and Clan Alpine Mountains trend to the NE in the NE sector of the zone, with the Dixie Valley between them. The Wassuk Range is in the S central sector, the Gabbs Valley and Gills ranges in the SE. Elevations range from 3,800 ft. to 11,000 ft.

The zone includes several of the largest water bodies in Nevada: Lake Tahoe, Pyramid Lake, Walker Lake, Lahontan Reservoir, and Washoe Lake. Principal streams are the Truckee River, flowing from Pyramid Lake; Carson River, supplying Lake Lahontan and vanishing into the Carson Sink; and the East and West forks of the Walker River, flowing into Walker Lake.

Much of the western portion of the zone is private land, notably in the corridor from Carson City to Reno. From the NE of the zone, a wide band of checkerboarding marks the railroad route to Reno and California. An Indian reservation surrounds Pyramid Lake. Another large reservation is N of Walker Lake. S of Walker Lake is the U.S. Naval Ammunition Depot, whose bunkers, extending for miles, seem large enough to supply a dozen wars.

Aside from the public domain, the largest public sites are two portions of the Toiyabe National Forest, both extending into Nevada from California.

Annual precipitation ranges from as little as 2 1/2 in. in the Gabbs Valley to as much as 20 in. in the Sierra Nevada foothills. Much of the latter falls as snow, and there are several ski areas.

Exploring Nevada by car offers many visual delights, but few remain around Lake Tahoe. Hotels were built along the shore as early as the 1860s, and subsequent development has been unplanned and unrestrained. The best remaining natural areas lie to the E and SE.

The zone has many scenic drives, most of them off the main routes. An example is the 32 mi. of SR 361 N from US 95 at Luning to Gabbs. The road is good two-lane blacktop with little traffic. From sagebrush flats, it rises to enter a spectacular low range with hills of many shapes: smooth, jagged, rounded, sheer, sculptured in bizarre formations, sometimes capped with rimrock, often topped by spires. Colors include red, gray, tan, purple, yellow, changing with the angle of the sun. One can travel this route to visit Berlin-Ichthyosaur State Park and the Central Nevada Division of the Toiyabe National Forest, both in Zone 4.

Birds: BLM has a checklist of 266 species. Their diversity reflects the diversity of habitats in the zone: from ponderosa pine forest to wetlands to desert playa.

Mammals: BLM's checklist is usefully annotated, describing the habitats where each species can be found.

Reptiles and amphibians: BLM has an annotated checklist.

Fishes: BLM has an annotated checklist.

PUBLICATIONS
Visitor map (if available).
Checklists.

HEADQUARTERS: BLM, Carson City District, 1050 E. William St., Carson City, NV 89701; (702) 882-1631.

ALKALI LAKE WILDLIFE MANAGEMENT AREA
Nevada Department of Wildlife
3,448 acres.

From US 395 where it crosses the CA border SE of Lake Tahoe, take SR 208 about 15 mi. E to Smith. 8 mi. N on local roads.

"Artesia Lake" on some maps. E of the Pine Nut Mountains. We could not include this site in our travel schedule. The Department supplied little information and added nothing when we sent this entry for review. Marshland surrounded by shadscale, maintained for waterfowl. Maps indicate an ephemeral lake of about 3,000 acres, usually dry in summer. Good spring birding. No resident personnel.

HEADQUARTERS: Department of Wildlife, 380 W. B St., Fallon, NV 89406; (702) 423-3171.

CLAN ALPINE MOUNTAINS
U.S. Bureau of Land Management
257,000 acres.

On the E side of Dixie Valley, N of US 50. SR 121 runs N to the town of Dixie Valley. Several unimproved roads lead from SR 121 into canyons on the W flank of the range, including Deep Canyon, Horse Creek, Cow Canyon. On the E, access from US 50 by Bench Creek, Cherry Creek, and War Canyon.

A major N–S range, the ridge over 35 mi. long, base about 12 mi. wide. Highest point is 9,966-ft. Mount Augusta. Vertical relief on the Dixie Valley side is 6,500 ft.

Topography is very dissected, many canyons leading to the ridgetop. Several canyons have perennial streams and springs. Many are highly scenic. Some open, gentle ridges; steep-sided peaks; colorful rock formations.

Several unmaintained roads penetrate canyons. One ascends to within 1 mi. of the top of Mount Augusta, another to near the top of 8,847-ft. Mount Grant.

Most vegetation is pinyon-juniper. Aspen in the higher drainages. Sagebrush throughout. Grass and stunted brush above timberline.

Annual precipitation is 6 to 8 in., most of it as snow in the upper elevations. Ski touring is said to be good, but access to snow areas in winter is difficult, at times nearly impossible.

Wildlife: Includes chukar, sage grouse, golden eagle, prairie falcon, turkey vulture. Also mountain lion, mule deer, coyote, jackrabbit, many bands of wild horses.

Most of this vast roadless area has been recommended for wilderness study. Considered excellent for backpacking. Most of the area is accessible by horse, and feed is adequate.

DAYTON STATE PARK
Nevada Division of State Parks
150 acres.

On US 50, 12 mi. E of Carson City.

A pleasant overnight stop just off the highway, beside the Carson River.

Nearby hills are covered with low sagebrush, scattered pinyon-juniper. Willow and cottonwood along the river. Moderately good birding. Riverside trail.

Camping: 10 sites. All year.

HEADQUARTERS: Nevada Division of State Parks, Capitol Complex, Carson City, NV 89710; (702) 885-4384.

DESATOYA MOUNTAINS
U.S. Bureau of Land Management
51,262 acres.

About 55 mi. E of Fallon at Eastgate.

The mountain mass is about 10 mi. wide. The road crosses the range at Carroll Summit, a pass at 7,452 ft. elevation. This is a good access point. Desatoya Peak, at the S end of the range, is 9,973 ft. elevation. Vertical relief from the valley floor is 4,700 ft.

Highly scenic. Views E to the Toiyabe Range, W to the Stillwater and Clan Alpine ranges, on clear days to the Sierras. The range is sharply dissected by many narrow, steep-walled canyons, some ending in rocky cliffs. On the W side, canyons on the N have intermittent streams. Three on the S have perennial streams. One of these, Big Den, has a 30-ft. waterfall. This canyon is narrow, twisting, with vertical walls and colorful rock spires. Three other drainages have perennial streams.

E of the ridgeline, the terrain is more rolling. There are five perennial streams on this side, other drainages with intermittent streams. All the perennial streams and some others have dense vegetation of aspen, willow, wild rose; many have wildflowers and berries. Stands of pinyon pine and juniper at lower elevations.

Above the canyons, the terrain opens into rolling drainages hemmed in by steep ridges above timberline. Vegetation on the main ridgeline is grasses and scrub. The E side has more of this open terrain than the W.

Terrain, scenery, and availability of water and feed make this one of the best areas in western NV for backcountry travel.

Birds: Most upland species on BLM's District checklist occur here. Noted: golden eagle, prairie falcon, goshawk, turkey vulture, great horned owl, chukar, sage grouse, hummingbirds, other passerines.

Mammals: Mentioned—mountain lion, mule deer, coyote, gray fox, jackrabbit, pika, wild horse. Reintroduction of desert bighorn is being studied.

ACTIVITIES

Camping: Car camping opportunities are limited chiefly by the poor condition of primitive roads penetrating the canyons.

Hiking, backpacking: Good to excellent. Day hiking best on the W side. Backpacking in canyons or along the ridge.

Hunting: Deer, sage grouse, chukar.

Horse riding: Best on the E side and along the ridge.

Ski touring: Snowpack on the ridgeline above 7,500 ft. for 4–5 months in the year. Cross-country skiing opportunities limited by difficult access and frequent sharp winds.

FERNLEY WILDLIFE MANAGEMENT AREA
Nevada Department of Wildlife
13,655 acres.

From Reno, 64 mi. E on I-80. Take second Fernley exit and follow signs.

State HQ supplied little information about this unit, and we did not visit it. At 4,200 ft. elevation, the area is generally flat: marsh and surrounding rangeland. Two ponds totaling 450 acres attract waterfowl in season. Hunting is permitted. Birding could be good outside hunting season. No resident personnel.

FORT CHURCHILL HISTORIC STATE MONUMENT
Nevada Division of State Parks
710 acres.

From Carson City, 35 mi. NE on US 50 to Silver Springs, then 4 mi. S on Alt. US 95.

Built in 1860, the fort was abandoned in 1870. Adobe walls remain. On the Carson River. Flat to rolling alluvial slopes.

Plants: Fremont and eastern cottonwoods along the river, the latter introduced by immigrants. Desert vegetation: sagebrush, shadscale, little greasewood. Flowering plants include globemallow, desert peach, Indian ricegrass, tansy mustard, rabbitbrush.

Birds: The river attracts some waterfowl. Also noted: bluebird, finches, quail, chukar, oriole, swift, woodpeckers.

INTERPRETATION
Visitor center: historical theme.
Nature trail: 1 1/2 mi.

ACTIVITIES
Camping: 20 sites. All year.
Hiking: Beyond site boundaries into nearby hills.
Fishing: Moderate. Carp, catfish, occasional white bass.
Canoeing: During May–June runoff only, to Lahontan Reservoir.

HEADQUARTERS: Silver Springs, NV 89429; (702) 577-2345.

GABBS VALLEY RANGE
U.S. Bureau of Land Management
81,120 acres.

E of Walker Lake. Crossed by SR 361 10 mi. N of Luning, 20 mi. SW of Gabbs.

The zone preface mentioned SR 361 as an outstanding scenic route. The range is on both sides of this highway. The portion to the W has been recommended for wilderness study. Several unmaintained roads penetrate the area.

Highest point is 8,353-ft. Mount Ferguson. Vertical relief from the valley floor is 3,600 ft. Most of the range has rolling to steep slopes. Most drainages are somewhat open and rolling, though some are constricted. Lost Canyon and Red Rock Canyon have perennial water and horse feed. The latter, about 7 mi. NW of SR 361, is penetrated by an unimproved road from Fingerock Wash.

Both foot and horse travel here are easier than in many backcountry sites, but there is less vegetative screening. Scenery and availability of water make this area attractive.

Plants: Mostly greasewood, saltbush, and cheatgrass in the foothills; pinyon-juniper stands on the middle slopes; some willow, aspen, and other riparian vegetation in creek bottoms.

Birds: Mentioned: golden eagle, prairie falcon, chukar.

Mammals: Mule deer, mountain lion, bobcat, wild horse.

LAHONTAN STATE RECREATION AREA
Nevada Division of State Parks
31,322 acres.

18 mi. W of Fallon on US 50.

Damming the Carson River formed a lake almost 9 mi. long with 10,000 surface acres and 70 mi. of shoreline at full pool. Development has been pleasantly limited. A good road crosses the Carson River below the dam and follows the SE lake shore. There is also shore access on the W at Silver Springs. All along the shore are informal camp and picnic sites, some with pit toilets and tables. The lake is surrounded by flat to gently rolling sagebrush shrub land. Low hills to the S.

Boat camping is popular, because of the many secluded coves and islands. Fishing is good. Nearness to Reno, Sparks, and Carson City means crowds on summer and holiday weekends, but we had the place to ourselves in fine weather mid-week in Apr.

HEADQUARTERS: Capitol Complex, Carson City, NV 89710; (702) 885-4384.

LAKE TAHOE NEVADA STATE PARK
Nevada Division of State Parks
13,468 acres.

NE shore of Lake Tahoe, on SR 28.

Three mi. of lake shore plus forested mountains; an area almost 10 mi. long, 6 mi. wide. The principal lakeshore recreation area, Sand Harbor, is usually crowded in summer, filled to capacity by early morning on weekends. Lakeshore parking at the boat launch area is limited to vehicles with boats. Although the backcountry is relatively uncrowded, hikers may have difficulty finding a place to park on summer weekends. (Try Memorial Point for the Hidden Beach trailhead, or Spooner Lake in the S end of the Park.)

The effective size of the Park is increased by several thousand adjoining acres of Toiyabe National Forest land. We noticed discrepancies between Park and Forest maps and were told the U.S. Forest Service has bought additional lands on and near the lake shore. No map of these lands was available, but either Park or Ranger District offices can provide guidance.

Elevations range from 6,229 ft. at the lake to 8,856 ft. inland. Annual precipitation here is 25 to 35 in., June–Aug. is the dry season. The Park includes 381-acre Marlette Lake and 100-acre Spooner Lake, plus the smaller Twin Lakes and Hobart Creek Reservoir, all reached by foot trail.

One long trail runs the length of the Park over forested hills. It has several short spurs and one long spur to the Park's easternmost point. Few people hike this far in a day. The extensive off-trail backcountry is seldom visited except by hunters.

Plants: By 1895 most of the accessible timber had been cut. Some old-growth trees may remain on inaccessible slopes. Some of the new growth is attaining impressive size. Most of the backcountry is covered by coniferous forests, broken by valley meadows. From lake shore to about 7,000 ft., principal tree species are ponderosa, Jeffrey, and sugar pines; white fir, incense cedar, and aspen. This zone grades into red fir forest with a belt of lodgepole pine forest above. Wildflowers include baby blue eyes, peony, pinedrops, snow plant, western bleeding heart, balsam root, blue flax, pussy paws, lupine, columbine, monkeyflower, Indian paintbrush, shooting star.

Birds: Include mallard, common merganser, golden eagle; sharp-shinned, Cooper's, and red-tailed hawks; northern harrier; osprey, American kestrel, sora, killdeer, spotted sandpiper; great horned, pygmy, long-eared, and saw-whet owls; rufous and calliope hummingbirds, northern flicker; Lewis', hairy, downy, and white-headed woodpeckers; western kingbird; willow, Hammond's, dusky, and olive-sided flycatchers; violet-green, tree, bank, rough-winged, and cliff swallows; Steller's and pinyon jays, Clark's nutcracker, mountain chickadee, bushtit, pygmy nuthatch, robin, hermit and Swainson's thrushes, western and mountain bluebirds, golden-crowned and ruby-crowned kinglets. Warblers: yellow, yellow-rumped, hermit, MacGillivray's, Wilson's. Also western tanager, lazuli bunting, pine siskin, dark-eyed junco; white-crowned, fox, and Lincoln's sparrows.

Mammals: Include raccoon, longtail weasel, coyote, mule deer, golden-mantled squirrel, marmot, spotted skunk. Black bear, mountain lion, and bobcat are present, seldom seen.

INTERPRETATION
Guided hikes June–Sept.
Nature trails at Sand Harbor and Spooner Lake.

ACTIVITIES
Hiking, backpacking: 20 mi. of trails. N end trailhead at Hidden Beach, but one must park some distance to the S. S end trailhead at Spooner Lake. N–S trail distance is 16 mi. Two overnight hike-in campgrounds are available. Contact the Park office for reservations.
Hunting: Deer, grouse.
Fishing: Lake. No fishing in Marlette Lake.
Swimming: Supervised, June–Aug.

Boating: Ramps at Sand Harbor and Cave Rock.

Ski touring: 5 mi. of maintained trail at Spooner Lake. Usual season Dec.–Mar. Also moonlight tours during periods of full moon.

PUBLICATION: Leaflet with map.

HEADQUARTERS: P.O. Box 3283, Incline Village, NV 89540; (702) 831-0494.

MASON VALLEY WILDLIFE MANAGEMENT AREA
Nevada Department of Wildlife
12,030 acres.

From US 95 Alt. about 3 1/2 mi. N of Yerington, turn E for 3 mi.

On the main channel of the Walker River, principal water source for the site. The Mason Valley is a moderately settled agricultural and mining area. Ponds and marshes are maintained by dikes, ditches, and other means, to support waterfowl populations.

Site elevation is about 4,300 ft. About 1,700 acres are pond and marsh, with such plant species as hardstem bulrush, cattail, sago pondweed, alkali, bulrush, spikerush, muskgrass, and saltgrass. Other areas include cultivated wildlife feed plots, riparian vegetation, greasewood-saltgrass flats, and areas of buffaloberry and native grasses.

Principal use of the site is by hunters in early fall and winter. Fishing is becoming more popular, spring to fall. Birding is good in the spring.

Birds: Breeding populations of mallard, gadwall, cinnamon teal, redhead, ruddy duck, and pintail. Breeding population of Canada goose. In addition to waterfowl, resident or migratory populations of pheasant, quail, dove, shorebirds, bald eagle, hawks, and songbirds.

Mammals: Noted: deer, coyote, beaver, muskrat, bobcat.

HEADQUARTERS: Lux Lane, Box 1, Yerington, NV 89447; (702) 463-2741.

PYRAMID LAKE
Pyramid Lake Indian Reservation
110,000 acres (lake surface); Reservation is 400,000 acres.

35 mi. NE of Reno via SR 445.

The largest, deepest remnant pool of ancient Lake Lahontan and the largest lake wholly within NV. A blue sea surrounded by high desert hills of gray and pink, unlike the forested setting of Lake Tahoe. The lake is within the Reservation, and tribal permits are required for fishing, boating, and camping. Commercial facilities are at Sutcliffe.

Diversion of water from the Truckee River dropped the lake level by about 60 ft. This wiped out the native cutthroat population, once the basis of a commercial fishery. Pyramid Island was not an island after 1960, until record snowfalls in the Sierras in the years after 1982 raised the lake level by 25 ft.

Most visitors come for boating and fishing, using facilities along SR 446 on the W shore. Fishing, once outstanding, has again improved dramatically. The lake has been called one of the top three trout lakes in America (and by one group as the top trophy lake in the United States).

Most of the lake shore is gently sloping sand, with long stretches of sheer tufa cliffs, piles of tufa rock, and tufa domes. (Tufa is a porous water-deposited rock.)

The Needle Rocks are strange tufa formations rising as much as 300 ft., extending a mile into the lake. When the lake level dropped, some of them became part of the mainland, but they are now islands again. Formerly off-limits to non-Indians because visitors defaced them, they are now open again.

Plants: Juniper on the slopes of surrounding mountains; cottonwood and aspen along the springs in the canyon bottoms. Grasses and wildflowers along the shore.

Birds: Include hawks, eagles, ducks, geese, shorebirds. Many American white pelican.

Mammals: Mule deer, pronghorn, small mammals.

ACTIVITIES

Obtain permits from Paiute office.

Camping: Primitive camping, by permit, on the lake shore. A county campground is at Warrior Point.

Fishing: Tribal permit required; no state license needed.

Boating: Permits at Sutcliffe, a commercial facility; launching at Pelican Point.

The lake is extremely hazardous in windy weather; boaters should keep informed and respond to warnings.

ORVs are prohibited, but horse travel may be authorized. Inquire.

INCLUDES: *Anaho Island National Wildlife Refuge,* 248 acres, is a white pelican nesting colony. The island and adjacent waters for a distance of 500 ft. are closed to the public.

PUBLICATION: Information pages.

REFERENCE: Wheeler, Sessions S. *The Desert Lake: Nevada's Pyramid Lake.* Caldwell, ID: Caxton Press.

HEADQUARTERS: Pyramid Lake Paiute Tribe, P.O. Box 256, Nixon, NV 89424; (702) 574-0140. Or call (702) 673-6335.

RANGER STATION: Sutcliffe R.S., Star Route, Sutcliffe, NV 89510; (702) 476-0132.

STILLWATER RANGE
U.S. Bureau of Land Management
228,430 acres.

On the W side of Dixie Valley. About 30 mi. NE of Fallon. E side access is from Dixie Hot Springs Rd., off US 50, to the mouths of Hare, Mississippi, and White Rock canyons. W side access from Fallon via SR 116 to Stillwater, then NE on Stillwater Rd. to numerous side canyons.

Across Dixie Valley from the Clan Alpine Mountains (see entry). The site is a rough rectangle 33 mi. N–S, 12 mi. wide. Highest point is 8,875-ft. Job's Peak. Vertical relief is 5,400 ft. above Dixie Valley, 5,100 ft. on the Carson Sink side. Lands below the 4,000-ft. contour are relatively flat, rising gently from the boundary roads to the more dissected mountainous terrain, very rough and steep with many cliffs and canyons. The range has a few perennial springs but no significant all-year streams.

Sagebrush and desert shrub dominate the foothills and valley bottoms; pinyon-juniper at mid-elevations; denser in canyons; grasses and stunted brush along the ridges.

Many canyons offer good hiking. In some places, one can hike up one canyon, cross over, and descend by another the same day. Backpacking along the ridge is also feasible, but one must carry water. Sections of the ridge are too rough and rocky for horse travel, but other areas are pleasant and have adequate forage.

Many of the canyons are within oil, gas, and geothermal leases with some current mining and exploration. The BLM office can offer advice on the best access and hiking or riding routes.

Two large portions of the area have been recommended for wilderness study.

STILLWATER WILDLIFE MANAGEMENT AREA AND REFUGE

Nevada Department of Wildlife; U.S. Fish and Wildlife Service
162,000 acres.

From Fallon, 4 mi. E on US 50 to junction with Stillwater Rd., and follow signs.

The Lahontan marshes at the end of the Carson River harbored great numbers of waterfowl until the water was diverted for irrigation in the early 1900s. In 1949 a cooperative state-federal project was undertaken to restore a part of the wetlands. About 21,000 acres of waterfowl habitat have been restored. However, water supply depends on snowmelt from the Sierra Nevada and the demands of irrigation. In some years the marsh is nearly dry.

In years of good water, the area supports peak numbers of 200,000 ducks, 5,000 geese, 5,000 whistling swans. Ducks come through in Mar.–Apr. The fall season begins in Aug.–Sept. when great flights of shorebirds arrive. The fall waterfowl migration peaks in Oct.–Nov.

The land is flat, sparsely vegetated with saltbush, greasewood, other desert shrub. Ten large impoundments have been formed by canals and dikes. Visitors can drive a 24-mi. loop tour or walk through the primary marsh area. However, when the marsh is dry there's not much to be seen; the Refuge manager suggests calling before a visit.

The federal Refuge portion of the area, 24,203 acres, is in the SE sector; it is closed to visitors unless especially authorized.

Birds: Checklist available. Seasonally common or abundant species include eared and western grebes, American white pelican, great blue heron, black-crowned night-heron, common and snowy egrets, white-faced ibis, whistling swan, Canada and snow geese, mallard, gadwall, pintail, green-winged and cinnamon teals, American wigeon, shoveler, redhead, canvasback, bufflehead, ruddy duck, common merganser; red-tailed and rough-legged hawks; northern harrier, kestrel, California quail, Virginia rail, sora, coot, killdeer, long-billed dowitcher, western sandpiper, avocet, black-necked stilt, Wilson's and northern phalaropes, California gull, Forster's tern; barn, great horned, and short-eared owls; northern flicker, western kingbird, horned lark; tree, barn, and cliff swallows; magpie, raven, marsh wren, loggerhead shrike, starling, yellow warbler.

Mammals: No checklist. Blacktail jackrabbit, coyote, a few others.

ACTIVITIES

Camping: Almost anywhere along the road or in parking areas. No facilities; no drinking water.

Hiking: On trails and roads.

Hunting: Waterfowl.

Fishing: Best at Lead or Indian lakes. Catfish, bullhead, largemouth bass.

Swimming: At Likes Lake, 10 mi. W of main marsh.

Boating: Boats sometimes used for hunting in the main marsh area. Very shallow.

PUBLICATIONS

Leaflet with map. (Sometimes available at Hunter Rd. entrance.)
Bird checklist.

HEADQUARTERS: P.O. Box 1236, Fallon, NV 89406; (702) 423-5128. Office is in Fallon.

TOIYABE NATIONAL FOREST, CARSON AND BRIDGEPORT RANGER DISTRICTS

U.S. Forest Service
537,686 acres.

On the CA-NV border, N, E, and SE of Lake Tahoe.

The Toiyabe is the largest National Forest in the Lower 48. The largest acreage is in NV Zone 4. A disjunct portion is in Zone 6 (see entries). This entry describes the Carson and Bridgeport Districts, on the CA border.

The *Carson Ranger District* extends along the eastern front of the Sierra Nevada, straddling the CA-NV border in a strip about 15 mi. wide, 96 mi. long. Of its 325,070 acres, 253,381 acres are in CA and are described in our CA guide. The NV portion consists of patchwork landholdings N of Lake Tahoe and a somewhat more solid block about 5 mi. wide on the E shore of the lake. This portion has several miles of lake frontage, but no indicated campground or other shoreline developments. It surrounds and interlocks with Lake Tahoe Nevada State Park (see entry).

SR 431, the Mt. Rose Highway, follows a winding course NE from the N end of the lake, passing the Tahoe Meadows Snowplay Area, Mt. Rose campground, Mt. Rose Ski Area, and Sky Tavern Ski Area. Elevation of Mt. Rose is 10,778 ft. The ski and snowplay season is generally Nov.–Mar.

From the Ophir Mill historic site on US 395 near Washoe Lake, a 12-mi. scenic hiking trail ascends to the top of Mt. Rose. Near the top, several low-standard trails branch into various tributaries of the Truckee River Canyon.

SR 28 generally follows the E shore of the lake through the District. At about the midpoint, it turns inland for about two mi., passing Spooner Lake and Spooner Summit. At 7,200 to 7,800 ft. elevation, this is a popular ski touring site. One 8-mi. loop from here to Marlette Lake in the State Park can be hiked in other seasons.

Nevada Beach, on the lake near the CA border, was a Forest Service beach and campground when we passed several years ago. It's still there but not listed among the Forest's recreation sites; our guess is that it's now among the sites commercially operated under special use permits.

The *Bridgeport Ranger District* includes 846,475 acres, of which 465,997 are in NV, the rest in CA. The CA portion adjoins Yosemite National Park and includes part of the Hoover Wilderness. It is described in our CA guide. The NV acreage is in two blocks, both on the CA border.

The northern block is crossed by SR 338. Highest point, 10,402 ft., is near the border. Terrain includes the Wellington Hills, foothills of the Sweetwater Mountains, and Grove Hills, peaks and ridges generally in the 7,000–8,500 ft. range. Climate is semiarid; almost all streams are intermittent.

The area is largely roadless and pristine. Recreational use is light, presumably because of the more interesting and less arid country across the border. The Forest map, new in 1984, shows a few trails. The only campground, Desert Creek, is on Risue Road, described as "improved light duty."

The southern block is crossed by SR 359. It adjoins the Inyo National Forest at the CA border. Principal feature is the Excelsior Mountains, described in the Forest map legend as "desolate." On the W side is Alkali Valley and Alkali Lake, a dry lake. The area is largely roadless. The new map shows few trails. No perennial streams; no campgrounds. We drove through on SR 359 and saw nothing that persuaded us to pause.

PUBLICATIONS
   Forest map, Carson R.D. $1.
   Forest map, Bridgeport R.D. $1.

HEADQUARTERS: 1200 Franklin Way, Sparks, NV 89431; (702) 784-5331.

RANGER DISTRICTS: Carson R.D., 136 S. Carson, Carson City, NV 89701; (702) 882-2766. Bridgeport R.D., Bridgeport, CA 93517: (714) 932-7070.

WALKER LAKE
U.S. Bureau of Land Management
38,800 acres (lake surface).

On US 95 N of Hawthorne.

US 95 is a scenic drive along the W shore of the lake. Mt. Grant, 11,239 ft. high, part of the Wassuk Range, towers more than 7,000 ft. above the lake on the W side. The range has 62,000 acres of public land, including wooded canyons that offer pleasant hiking. The lesser Gillis Range is across the lake.

Annual rainfall here is only about 5 in. Winters are mild, summers long and hot.

Diversion of water from the Walker River has caused the lake level to drop about 115 ft. since 1917. The decline continues. Lake water is alkaline.

At Sportsmans Beach, near the highway, BLM has a developed campground. Informal camping elsewhere. The undeveloped E side of the lake can be reached by a graded road from Schurz, on US 95 N of the lake, or from Hawthorne by driving N on SR 839, turning left at Thorne. The E side has miles of sandy beaches.

The S end of the lake is a military reservation.

WASHOE LAKE STATE PARK
Nevada Division of State Parks
3,000 acres.

Off US 395, 7 mi. N of Carson City.

The surface area of this shallow lake is about 5,700 acres, when full. In addition to the State Park, the land area includes the 2,670-acre Scripps Wildlife Management Area on the N.

Washoe Valley, the main traffic corridor between Carson City and Reno, lies between the Carson Range of the Sierra Nevada and the somewhat lower Virginia Range. Most of the lake water drains from the Carson Range. It has high alkalinity and some pollution attributed to nearby grazing.

The lake is an important resting, feeding, and nesting area for duck, coots, and pelicans. Several small islands provide safe nesting sites.

Birds: No list. The wet playa areas E of the dunes are frequented by sandhill crane, great blue heron, white-faced ibis. Noted elsewhere in the park: mountain bluebird, oriole, bunting, yellow-headed blackbird, magpie.

Mammals: No list. Mentioned: ground squirrel, weasel, jackrabbit, coyote, badger, skunk, muskrat, beaver, mule deer.

INTERPRETATION
Nature trail in the dunes and at Headman's Creek.
Guided hikes in summer.

ACTIVITIES

Camping: 25 sites. All year.

Hiking: Two short trails; unlimited bushwhacking.

Hunting: Designated areas, special rules.

Fishing: Catfish, perch, carp, white bass.

Swimming: Unsupervised. Season Apr.–Oct.

Canoeing: Launching ramp. Lake is too shallow for power boats, except when the level is at its highest in spring. Sailing and board sailing with strong afternoon winds.

Horse riding: Hitching posts and water. Horses not permitted in campground, day use area, or on pavement.

Pets not permitted in day-use areas or on the beach.

HEADQUARTERS: 4855 E. Lake Boulevard, Carson City, NV 89701; (702) 885-4319.

ZONE 4

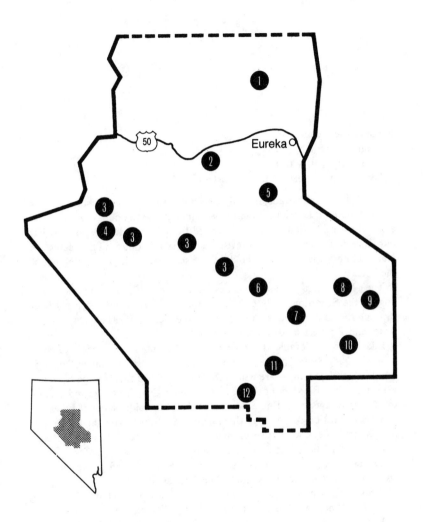

ZONE 4

Includes these counties:
 Lander (except N tip)
 Eureka (except N tip)
 Nye (N portion except for small strip on E)

Zone 4 is central Nevada, the only zone not bordering another state. BLM's Battle Mountain District administers 8 million of the 11.5 million acres in the zone. (Esmeralda County was transferred from BLM's Las Vegas District, our Zone 6, too late for us to revise our zones.) About 3 million acres are National Forest land. Private holdings are scattered, chiefly in the N half of the zone.

The N border of the zone touches I-80. US 50 crosses its middle. US 6 crosses the S portion. Only one paved route, SRs 305 and 376, runs N–S through the zone, which is larger than Connecticut, New Hampshire, Delaware, and Rhode Island combined.

Like most of Nevada, the zone has parallel mountain ranges, running generally N–S. Several of the principal ranges—Paradise, Shoshone, Toiyabe, Toquima, and Monitor—are within the four blocks of the Toiyabe National Forest. In the SE corner of the zone, the Quinn Canyon Range and part of the Grant Range are within a portion of the Humboldt National Forest.

Several short creeks, some of them perennial, drop down from the ranges into the dry valleys, where they disappear. In the N part of the zone, the Reese River and Pine Creek flow to the Humboldt River.

Vegetation is typical of the high desert. Average annual precipitation is about 8 in., less in the valleys, more on the high slopes.

Birds: Checklist of 208 species available. Of the waterfowl and marshland birds listed, most are found in the Railroad Valley wetland (see entry).

Mammals: Checklist of 69 species available, annotated to indicate habitats.

Fishes: Annotated checklist available.

The zone has no large, developed recreation facility on public land. BLM manages the Mill Creek Recreation Site (off SR 305, S of Battle Mountain), a popular fishing and camping site. Entries describe several other BLM sites. The Toiyabe National Forest has 7 small campsites, well away from any main road.

The only State Park, Berlin-Ichthyosaur, is remote, but the route to it is highly scenic. The Lunar Crater Volcanic Field is managed by BLM.

BLM notes "there are thousands of pleasant out-of-the-way spots where one can pitch a tent or park a camper." The zone has some of NV's highest mountains, snowcapped for much of the year. It is not difficult to find a dramatically scenic canyon, with green vegetation bordering a rushing stream, where encountering another hiker or camper is unlikely.

PUBLICATIONS
Recreation Guide. (Map of the BLM District; 1981.)
Checklists: birds, mammals, fishes.
The Pony Express in Nevada.

HEADQUARTERS: BLM, Battle Mountain District, P.O. Box 1420, Battle Mountain, NV 89820; (702) 635-5181.

ANTELOPE RANGE
U.S. Bureau of Land Management
148,300 acres.

From Eureka on US 50, 10 mi. W, then S about 23 mi. on SR 82. Turn E about 5 mi. to the N tip of the unit and the road forming its W boundary.

The Antelope Range ridge is only 1,000 to 2,000 ft. above the valleys to the W and E. Valley floor is about 6,500 ft. elevation. Highest point in the range is Ninemile Peak, 10,104 ft. The area is about 18 mi. N–S. The N end has several perennial streams, mature riparian forests, extensive aspen groves on the plateaulike top. Ninemile Canyon is on the NE boundary. The S portion contains blocky valleys, flat-topped mountains blanketed with pinyon-juniper.

Attractions of the site include untrampled natural meadows, springs, abundant game, aspen forests, opportunity to hike or ride considerable distances at high elevations.

An 87,400-acre roadless portion of this site has been designated a Wilderness Study Area.

BERLIN-ICHTHYOSAUR STATE PARK
Nevada Division of State Parks
1,203 acres.

From SR 361 at Gabbs, E 23 mi. on SR 844. 7 mi. are unpaved but well graded.

This unusual Park is a bit out of the way, but some of Nevada's handsomest scenery is on the route to it. Leaving Gabbs, SR 844 crosses the forested Paradise Range, dips into the sage flats of Ione Valley, then climbs to the Park, on the W slope of the Shoshone Range.

Berlin was a company-owned mining town that prospered 1897–1910. Some old structures remain, now preserved. About 185 million years earlier, this was the shore of a sea, where 60-ft., 35-ton reptiles called *ichthyosaurs* beached and were fossilized. 40 of them were unearthed during excavations in the 1950s. Three are exposed for viewing.

Park elevations are from 6,700 to 7,500 ft. Vegetation is largely pinyon-juniper, with sage and rabbitbrush slopes. About 80 flowering plants have been identified, including Indian paintbrush, prickly poppy, small-leaf globemallow.

Birds: Reported: turkey vulture, chukar, pinyon jay, golden eagle, mourning dove, northern flicker, red-tailed hawk.

Mammals: Common: mule deer, cottontail, jackrabbit, coyote, bobcat, various rodents.

Reptiles and amphibians: Numerous lizards, gopher snake, western rattlesnake.

INTERPRETATION

Fossil House opens May–Aug. at 10 A.M., 2 P.M., 4 P.M. Other months, same hours, but Thurs.–Mon. only.

Interpretive trails: 3 mi., with plaques.

Guided hikes, programs: Occasional, in summer. Inquire.

Camping: 14 sites. All year. During winter, advisable to call the District Office in Fallon for road conditions. (702) 867-3001.

PUBLICATION: Leaflet with map.

HEADQUARTERS: Rt. 1, Box 32, Austin, NV 89310. No telephone.

BLUE EAGLE; GRANT RANGE
U.S. Bureau of Land Management
58,800 acres.

S of Currant on US 6. The site is E of the unpaved road from Currant to Nyala.

The unit lies between two portions of the Humboldt National Forest. Railroad Valley is on the W. A roadless area around Blue Eagle Mountain has been proposed for wilderness status. The unit is about 18 mi. N–S, 7 mi. W–E. Elevations range from 4,800 ft. in the valley to 9,561 ft. on Blue Eagle Peak. High mountains with several deep, narrow, winding canyons, some of them approached or entered by road spurs from the Currant-Nyala road. Steep mountain slopes in the W, gently rolling hills and flat valley floors in the E. Sparse sagebrush at low elevations. Upper slopes have pinyon-juniper, dense in some areas. White fir and bristlecone pine on Blue Eagle Mountain.

ADJACENT

    Humboldt National Forest, Quinn Division (see entry).
    Railroad Valley Wildlife Management Area (see entry).

HICKISON PETROGLYPHS
U.S. Bureau of Land Management

    20 mi. E of Austin on US 50, just W of Hickison Summit. Marked entrance road on N.

Almost all the surrounding land is public domain. Elevation 6,500 ft. A convenient overnight stop with opportunity for open-country hiking. Several examples of Indian rock art. Nearby slopes are moderate to steep. Reddish sandstone cliffs on both sides of trail from parking lot. Mostly sagebrush vegetation. Good grove of juniper at campground.

Camping: 14 sites. All year. No water.

HUMBOLDT NATIONAL FOREST, QUINN DIVISION
U.S. Forest Service
240,000 acres.

    From Warm Springs on US 6, 16 mi. E on SR 375, then 25 mi. NE on

Nyala-Currant Road. 3 mi. beyond Nyala an unimproved road to the SE crosses the site.

Other blocks of Humboldt National Forest land are in Zones 1, 2, and 5. This is the most southern and probably the least visited. Almost the entire area has been proposed for Wilderness status, in two units separated by the midpoint road and excluding strips bordering the several dead-end roads penetrating canyons. The midpoint road is in a pass separating two ranges, the Quinn Canyon and the Grant, both trending NE–SW. Railroad Valley lies to the W, the valley floor at about 5,400 ft. elevation.

Highest point in the Quinn Canyon Range, the S unit, is a bit over 10,000 ft. Several higher peaks are in the Grant Range, topped by 11,298 Troy Peak. Both ranges are penetrated by many canyons on both E and W. The only perennial streams are Cottonwood Creek in the S, Cherry Creek between the units, Troy Creek in the N. Several springs are marked on the map, but they may not be reliable.

Plants: Pinyon-juniper woodland with black sagebrush understory predominates. True and alpine firs are on N exposures at high elevations. Bristlecone pine stands are scattered on high crests.

Wildlife: No checklists. Mentioned are birds of prey: golden eagle, red-tailed hawk, Cooper's hawk, kestrel. Mammals include bats, mice, voles, chipmunk, rock squirrel, longtail weasel, cottontail, blacktail jackrabbit, coyote, bobcat, mountain lion, mule deer, desert bighorn sheep.

ACTIVITIES

Camping: Campground on the midpoint road. 2 sites. June 1–Sept. 30.

Hiking, backpacking: The Forest map shows a number of trails, most beginning at dead-end canyon roads. No indicated ridge trail, but off-trail hiking should be no problem.

ADJACENT

The N portion of the Grant Range is public domain, managed by BLM. See entry, Blue Eagle.

Railroad Valley Wildlife Management Area (see entry).

PUBLICATION: Forest map, Ely Ranger District. $1.

REFERENCE: Hart, John. *Hiking the Great Basin.* San Francisco: Sierra Club Books, 1981, pp. 215–233.

HEADQUARTERS: 976 Mountain City Highway, Elko, NV 89801; (702) 738-5171.

RANGER DISTRICT: Ely R.D., P.O. Box 539, Ely, NV 89301; (702) 289-3031.

KAWICH RANGE
U.S. Bureau of Land Management
55,120 acres.

S by local roads from Warm Springs on US 6. Site is just N of the Bombing and Gunnery Range.

Elevations from 6,040 ft. in Reveille Valley on the E to 9,404 ft. on Kawich Peak. Steep ridges and peaks; long rugged canyons. Several high basins, one with two small perennial lakes. Vegetation is largely dense pinyon-juniper with low-growing sagebrush in the understory. Meadow vegetation around the lakes. Several canyons have perennial streams and limited riparian vegetation. Noteworthy botanical diversity in Longstreet's Canyon on the W side.

The area has been recommended for wilderness study. Other BLM lands adjoin. Scenic value, the streams and lakes, and several informal trails make this little-known site attractive to hikers who prefer solitude.

LUNAR CRATER VOLCANIC FIELD
U.S. Bureau of Land Management
140,000 acres.

On US 6, about 30 mi. NE of Warm Springs.

An extensive, colorful volcanic area in the Pancake Range, mostly on Palisade Mesa. Astronauts trained here, simulating lunar expeditions. Elevations from 5,753 ft. near dry Lunar Lake to 6,570 ft. Average annual rainfall is 4 to 6 in. No all-year water sources are within the area. Vegetation is typical salt desert shrub, with spring wildflower displays in years with good moisture. Birds noted include golden eagle, raven, prairie falcon, hawks. Mammals include antelope ground squirrel, jackrabbit, kit fox, occasional pronghorn.

FEATURES
Lunar Crater, 7 mi. S of US 6. A National Natural Landmark. The crater is 430 ft. deep, 3,800 ft. in diameter.

Easy Chair Crater, 4 mi. SE of the highway. So named because the crater is on the edge of a large cinder cone; from a distance, the imaginative can see the form of a chair.

Black Rock Lava Flow, 2 mi. N of US 6, is the most recent basalt flow in the area, covering more than 1,900 acres.

The Wall, named for its sheer vertical face, is at the E edge of the volcanic field.

The area has a chain of cinder cones 15 mi. long.

ADJACENT: Two adjoining roadless areas have been proposed for wilderness study. *Palisades Mesa,* 99,500 acres, straddles the Pancake Range. It consists of mesas with large boulder outcroppings, lava flows, cinder cones. *The Wall,* 43,300 acres, adjoins on the E, at the W edge of Railroad Valley.

PUBLICATION: Leaflet with map.

MOREY PEAK

U.S. Bureau of Land Management
20,120 acres.

Nearest approach is by local road N from US 6, 21 mi. NE of Warm Springs, through Hot Creek Valley. Road is the E boundary.

A small range, about 12 mi. N–S, up to 6 mi. W–E. Highest point is Morey Peak, 10,246 ft. Mountain is rocky and rugged. Steep canyons penetrate from the W and E. Sixmile Canyon, a long canyon penetrating from the S, has a number of springs, meadow vegetation, an intermittent stream. Several isolated springs elsewhere in the unit. A flat portion of Hot Creek Valley lies on the E side.

Plants: Low sagebrush in the valley; mountain-mahogany, aspen, and pinyon-juniper alternate above. Small stands of bristlecone pine on the peak.

Most of the surrounding area N of US 6 and E of the Toiyabe National Forest is public domain. The Morey Peak area has been designated as a Wilderness Study Area because of its unspoiled natural qualities and isolation.

REFERENCE: Hart, John. *Hiking the Great Basin.* San Francisco: Sierra Club Books, 1981, pp. 189–200.

RAILROAD VALLEY WILDLIFE MANAGEMENT AREA
Nevada Department of Wildlife/U.S. Bureau of Land Management
14,720 acres.

On the S side of US 6, about 10 mi. SW of Currant.

Railroad Valley lies between the Pancake and Grant ranges. An area of
alluvial fans, alkali lake beds, and greasewood flats, at about 4,700 ft. elevation. In 1934, 133,397 acres of public land were set aside as a federal migratory
bird refuge. In 1952 management responsibility was transferred to NV's Department of Wildlife. The refuge has since been reduced to four critical areas,
2 to 4 mi. apart. Management is now a cooperative effort of BLM and the
Department of Wildlife.

Wells, dikes, spillways, and other control measures were built to manage
part of the valley's marsh land and water impoundments.

Birds: More than 100 species use the refuge. Of the 19 waterfowl species,
14 nest in the area. Species include Canada goose, mallard, pintail, green-
winged teal, canvasback, gadwall, wigeon, whistling swan. Shorebirds include
killdeer, sandpipers, avocet, black-necked stilt, phalarope. Also here: grebes,
herons, egrets, white-faced ibis, rails, gulls, terns, swallows, flycatchers, sparrows. Golden eagle, northern harrier, and kestrel also present.

Mammals: Pronghorn, coyote, antelope ground squirrel, water shrew.

Reptiles and amphibians: Side-blotched, western fence, collared, and sagebrush lizards; Great Basin rattlesnake, Great Basin gopher snake.

ACTIVITIES
Hunting and *fishing* attract most visitors. Fishing for largemouth bass and
bluegill at Lockes Pond.

No water or visitor facilities.

PUBLICATION: Leaflet with map.

HEADQUARTERS: Department of Wildlife, Las Vegas District, 4747 Vegas
Drive, Las Vegas, NV 89158; (702) 385-0285.

ROBERTS CREEK MOUNTAINS
U.S. Bureau of Land Management
50,020 acres.

From Eureka, about 11 mi. W on US 50, then about 20 mi. N on local roads
past Roberts Creek Ranch, up Roberts Creek.

The Roberts Creek Mountains offer a wide diversity of terrain, vegetation, and scenery. Almost all the surrounding land is also public domain. In this roadless area, 15,090 acres were recommended for wilderness study. The mountains are a series of rugged peaks forming a broken ridge. Roberts Creek Mountain is 10,133 ft. high. Valleys on either side are about 6,800 ft. Many canyons and valleys surround the ridge, with access from unpaved local roads. The Roberts Thrust Fault is of considerable interest to geologists. Scenic features include several small ponds and a 25-ft. waterfall on Hanson Creek. Roberts Creek is an intermittent stream flowing S.

Plants: Vegetation ranges from sagebrush communities in the valleys to pinyon-juniper on slopes, up to a subalpine herbaceous-sage community with small stands of limber pine.

Relatively gentle topography plus abundant feed and water make this an excellent area for horse travel.

REFERENCE: Hart, John. *Hiking the Great Basin.* San Francisco: Sierra Club Books, 1981, pp. 201–209.

SOUTH REVEILLE RANGE
U.S. Bureau of Land Management
106,200 acres.

SE of Warm Springs; N of the Bombing and Gunnery Range. SR 375 is near the E boundary.

In the central and S portion of the Reveille Range. Elevations from about 5,600 ft. in the valleys to 8,910-ft. Reveille Peak. The roadless area is about 17 mi. N–S, 6 to 13 mi. W–E. Terrain includes flat-bottomed valleys, open rolling hills, flat-topped plateaus, steep-sided mountains, narrow canyons. Sagebrush is dominant below 7,000 ft. elevation, pinyon-juniper above. Wildlife is said to be abundant, which suggests the presence of springs.

TOIYABE NATIONAL FOREST, CENTRAL NEVADA DIVISIONS
U.S. Forest Service
1,942,121 acres.

Several parallel blocks between US 50 and US 6. SR 376 traverses the area, N–S, at about the midpoint.

The Toiyabe is the largest National Forest in the Lower 48, but its parts are widely scattered, some areas as much as 500 mi. apart. Portions are in CA and in NV Zones 3 and 6. About 3/5 of the Forest acreage is here in Zone 4, in the Austin and Tonopah Ranger Districts. This mountainous region of almost 2 million acres is 200 mi. from the nearest city, vast, pristine, remote. Few visitors come here.

The area is in the basin and range province. The Forest land is in five large blocks, two of them joined at their S ends, each block on a mountain range. The ranges are, from W to E: Paradise Range, Shoshone Mountains, Toiyabe Range, Toquima Range, Monitor Range. The valleys between are largely public domain, managed by BLM, with scattered private holdings.

The longest block is on the Monitor Range, about 100 mi. N–S. Shortest is the most western, on the Paradise Range near Gabbs, about 36 mi. The Paradise and Shoshone ranges are crossed by roads near their midpoints, the longer units only by roads near their N or S ends, except for a few unimproved Forest roads. The valley roads are splendidly scenic. SR 376 is paved and well maintained. Each valley has some sort of road, and each offers opportunities to hike up canyons.

These are high, rugged mountains. Valley elevations are generally about 6,000 ft. Many of the mountain peaks are above 10,000 ft., several exceeding 11,000. Highest point is 11,807 ft. Mt. Jefferson in the Toquima Range, followed by 11,775-ft. Arc Dome in the S portion of the Toiyabe Range. Many canyons penetrate the ranges, from E and W, some long, broad, and moderately sloping, others short and steep. Trails go up many of the canyons, often joining near the ridges.

Over 300,000 acres are above the 8,000-ft. contour. This is very rugged terrain: steep slopes, sharp crests, narrow canyons. Above 8,000 ft., annual precipitation is over 15 in.; 90% of it falls as snow between Oct. and May. At the highest elevations, above 11,000 ft., precipitation exceeds 27 in., 95% of it falling as snow.

Because of the heavy snowfall and long winters, these mountains have more perennial streams than most NV ranges, and a number of them have good populations of trout, small but native.

In these mountains are hundreds of miles of trails developed over decades by activities such as mining and prospecting and by sheep and cattle. They are not "system trails," planned and built for recreation. Their use by hikers and backpackers is so small the Forest can't justify expenditures for maintenance. As traditional uses decline, many of these trails are reverting to a natural state.

An exception is the Toiyabe Crest Trail, on the Toiyabe Range, highest and most spectacular of the desert ranges. 72 mi. long, it begins at Groves Lake in Kingston Canyon, about a mile S of the Kingston Guard Station, and follows the ridge S to South Twin River in the Arc Dome Wilderness. Along the way are more than 20 feeder trails providing access from the valleys. This is now a National Recreation Trail.

Plants: Mountain big sagebrush is the chief plant community in the high country. Others are low sagebrush and mountain-mahogany, with quaking aspen and other riparian vegetation in moist canyons. Most of the limber pine that once grew on the mountains has been logged off, and other vegetation changes have been caused by heavy grazing. At lower elevations, pinyon-juniper, with the usual sagebrush community below.

Wildlife: No checklists of wildlife are available. Familiar bird species mentioned include sage grouse, golden eagle, Clark's nutcracker, horned lark, mountain chickadee. Mammals include mule deer, coyote, badger, mountain lion, and desert bighorn sheep, as well as a few introduced beaver.

Most recreation development has been in the Toiyabe Range. Six of the 7 campgrounds are in this range.

FEATURES

Arc Dome roadless area, 94,000 acres, near the S end of the Toiyabe Range, has been proposed for Wilderness study. It includes Arc Dome and 11,353-ft. Toiyabe Dome. Principal drainage is the Reese River, which flows N between the Shoshone and Toiyabe ranges. Columbine Campground, N of the area, and Peavine Campground on the S, are possible trailheads.

ACTIVITIES

Camping: 7 campgrounds. 68 sites. Some May 1–Oct. 15, others June 1–Sept. 15. Six are on fishing streams. Forest map is desirable to find them.

Hiking, backpacking: In addition to the Toiyabe Crest Trail, each of the ranges has hiking and backpacking opportunities. The Forest map shows trails in almost every principal canyon, and sections of associated ridge trails. These trails are not maintained. For more than a casual day hike, consult HQ or a Ranger District for advice on routes and destinations.

Hunting: Deer were rarely seen in the early 1900s. Overgrazing produced a more favorable habitat and populations increased, peaking in the 1950s. Other game species include desert bighorn sheep, elk, blue and mountain quail, chukar, sage grouse.

Horse riding: Consult HQ or Ranger District about trail conditions.

PUBLICATIONS

Forest map. $1.
Travel map. (Shows areas closed to vehicles.)
Information pages.

REFERENCE: Hart, John. *Hiking the Great Basin.* San Francisco: Sierra Club Books, 1981, pp. 144–188.

HEADQUARTERS: 1200 Franklin Way, Sparks, NV 89431; (702) 784-5331.

RANGER DISTRICTS: Tonopah R.D., P.O. Box 989, Tonopah, NV 89049; (702) 482-6286. Austin R.D., Austin, NV 89310; (702) 964-2671.

ZONE 5

1. Goshute Canyon
2. Kern Mountains; Blue Mass Scenic Area
3. Humboldt National Forest, Ely Ranger District
4. Cave Lake State Park
5. Lehman Caves National Monument
6. South Egan Range
7. Mount Grafton
8. Fortification Range
9. W. E. Kirch Wildlife Management Area
10. Parsnip Peak

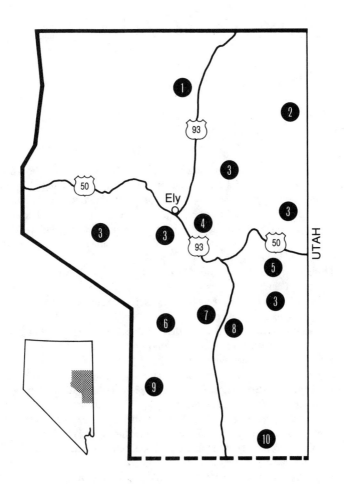

ZONE 5

Includes these counties:
White Pine   Nye (strip on E)   Lincoln (N portion)

Zone 5 is BLM's Ely District, in E central Nevada. It includes about 10 million acres, of which 8 million are public domain, administered by BLM. The District is within the Great Basin, most of it high desert and mountains. Elevations range from about 5,000 ft. in the valleys to 13,061 on Wheeler Peak, second-highest point in NV and the highest mountain wholly within the state. Average annual precipitation is 8 to 12 in., less in some rain-shadowed valleys, over 20 in. on the higher ridges and peaks.

Three major highways cross the zone: US 50 W–E, US 93 N–S, and US 6 SW–NE. They meet at Ely.

BLM has no developed recreation areas in the zone, but who needs them? Our entries describe some of BLM's largest roadless areas, chiefly on mountain ranges. One can usually find a dead-end road leading into a quiet canyon —perhaps one with a perennial stream—camp, and hike for miles up the canyon and along the ridges.

Aside from the public domain, the largest sites are 5 blocks of National Forest land in the Ely Ranger District of the Humboldt National Forest. They include the highest ranges of the zone, the most diverse plant and animal communities, most of the good fishing streams, and several attractive campgrounds. The Snake Division of the Forest includes the Wheeler Peak Scenic Area, which boasts several high cirque lakes, and also includes the Lehman Caves National Monument.

Cave Lake State Recreation Area is in one block of the Forest. Two other State Parks, Spring Valley and Echo Canyon, are within the zone but we put them in Zone 6 because the only access road originates there. (There is an entry in Zone 5 for Spring Valley, but that's a different valley, with no State Park.)

Of the three state Wildlife Management Areas in the zone, W. E. Kirch is by far the most interesting.

The Ruby Lake National Wildlife Refuge is partly within the NW corner of the zone, but most of it is in Zone 2, where the entry appears.

PUBLICATIONS
Public Lands Guide (map).
Welcome to Bristlecone Country.
Species checklists: birds, mammals, amphibians and reptiles, fishes.

HEADQUARTERS: BLM, Ely District, Star Route 5, Box 1, Ely, NV 89301; (702) 289-4865.

CAVE LAKE STATE PARK
Nevada Division of State Parks
1,820 acres.

From Ely, 8 mi. S on US 93, then 6 mi. E on Success Summit Rd.

The Park is within the Schell Creek Division of the Humboldt National Forest, at the foot of the Schell Creek Range. A dam has created a 32-acre impoundment. Park elevation is 7,300 ft. Summers are mild, winters harsh, and snow may block access in winter.

Before the state took over, the pond was a popular local fishing and picnic spot, with no supervision, facilities, or trash collection. The site was unpleasantly fouled and trampled. Under State Park management, conditions are better.

The Park is a convenient base for hiking, hunting, and cross-country skiing in the National Forest.

ACTIVITIES
Camping: 20 sites. All year, road conditions permitting.
Fishing: Rainbow and brown trout. Boats limited to 5 mph, no wake.

PUBLICATION: Leaflet.

HEADQUARTERS: P.O. Box 176, Panaca, NV 89042; (702) 728-4467.

FORTIFICATION RANGE
U.S. Bureau of Land Management
40,000 acres.

From US 93 about 18 mi. S of junction with US 6/50 (2 mi. N of Lake Valley Summit), turn SE at sign "Atlanta." About 15 mi. on local roads to Cottonwood Canyon.

The range is about 20 mi. long, its highest point 8,535 ft. BLM's WSA study rated it "less than outstanding" for recreation, but Cottonwood Canyon is exceptional. A BLM specialist called it "one of the most amazing sights in the Ely District."

Reached from the E side; an unimproved road runs to the mouth. The head of the canyon is a natural amphitheater formed by towering, jagged rock formations ranging in color from white to pink and mauve. Several other canyons, narrow and steep-walled, are on the E side. Riparian vegetation, relatively dense tree cover.

Birds: Include a relatively high raptor population, especially golden eagle. Also ferruginous and Cooper's hawks, prairie falcon, long-eared owl.

Mammals: Include bands of feral goats and wild horses.

GOSHUTE CANYON
U.S. Bureau of Land Management
38,235 acres.

From Ely, 45 mi. N on US 93. W 9 mi. on SR 489. NE on local road, from which spurs lead into canyons. Goshute Creek is about 11 mi. NE.

The site includes part of the Cherry Creek Range and part of Goshute Basin, a large mountain basin. The roadless area is about 14 mi. long, 4 to 5 mi. wide. The mountainous portions are quite rugged, with numerous cliffs and bluffs. Highest point is 10,542-ft. Cherry Creek Peak. Several other peaks are above 9,000 ft. The main ridge trends N–S, with lesser W–E ridges. The mountain base is at about the 6,000-ft. contour. Canyons penetrate the range from both sides. Several canyons have unimproved roads or trails.

The Goshute Canyon Natural Area, 7,650 acres, was designated in 1970, chiefly to protect an endangered fish species that inhabits the creek. The E portion, nearest the road from Cherry Creek, is a narrow canyon. The W portion is the spectacular Goshute Basin, a large bowl rimmed by high mountains, headwaters of Goshute Creek. Limestone crags, springs, stands of aspen, and open meadows make this an attractive camping and hiking area.

Surrounding the canyon is some of the most rugged terrain of the Cherry Creek Range: steep mountains, deep valleys, talus slopes. On the W are rolling hills.

Goshute Cave, at the N end of the site, has 1,500 ft. of passages with common and rare limestone formations.

The mountains are forested with pinyon-juniper, mountain-mahogany, white fir, and aspen. In the central portion of the high country is a large stand of bristlecone pine.

Wildlife includes moderate to high populations of deer, mountain lion, sage grouse, and blue grouse. Bird species also include chukar, great horned owl, golden eagle, Cooper's hawk, prairie falcon, American kestrel. Raptor aeries on cliffs. Other mammals include bobcat, yellow-bellied marmot, wild horse. Elk and pronghorn sightings have been reported.

Hiking opportunities include the open ridgeline, wooded slopes, and heavily wooded draws where hikers would probably be confined to deer trails. Backpacking is said to offer attractive possibilities for those who like challenging terrain.

Recreation visits are estimated to be 1,165 per year, chiefly for hunting and spelunking; all other uses are minor.

HUMBOLDT NATIONAL FOREST, ELY RANGER DISTRICT

U.S. Forest Service
1,071,845 acres.

Five blocks of National Forest land. Ely is roughly the center. The area is crossed by US 50, US 6, and US 93, although these routes run between rather than across blocks.

Other portions of the Humboldt National Forest are in Zones 1, 2, and 4. The units in Zone 5 occupy parallel N–S ranges.

The *White Pine Division,* one of the larger blocks, is about 40 mi. N–S, 15 mi. wide, occupying the White Pine Range. Highest point is 11,513-ft. Currant Mountain, in the S sector. Nearby Duckwater Peak is 11,188 ft.; Mt. Hamilton, in the N, is 10,745 ft. Configuration of the Range is extremely irregular and varied: jagged or rounded peaks, steep or gentle slopes, many canyons, some penetrating far into the Range, with short side canyons. Despite this irregularity, Forest roads and trails enter from the E and W. The Range has numerous springs. Runoff from snow melt is the principal source for many intermittent streams and a few perennial ones, notably White River and Currant Creek, both in the S sector. Three campgrounds are along the White River, one on Currant Creek. Both are good fishing streams. The Forest road N from Currant Creek campground to White River is scenic, passing the base of the steep E face of Duckwater Mountain.

The *Ward Division,* just S of Ely, is the smallest block, about 8 mi. square. It occupies the N part of Ward Mountain. It has one campground.

Next, to the E, is the *Schell Creek Division,* largest of the five. It extends over 53 mi. of the Schell Creek Range. The skyline is dominated by 11,883-ft. North Schell and 11,765-ft. South Schell peaks. Although the range is relatively narrow, it catches enough winter snow to support more than a dozen fishing streams, two-thirds of them on the E side. 7 campgrounds are on or near streams. The Division has many foot trails.

A *scenic route* begins on US 6/50/93 about 7 mi. SE of Ely. Turn E on the road marked "Success Summit." In 6 mi. this comes to the Cave Lake State Recreation Area (see entry), where the route turns N, rejoining US 93 in about 25 mi. Also of interest is Spring Valley, just E of the range, along a road N from US 50 2 mi. E of the Forest boundary. This quiet valley has many dry lakes and intermittent streams. Several primitive roads and trails lead W into the Forest, where some of these streams are perennial and fishable. The lower slopes and valley are important winter deer range. Pronghorn often seen. Most of the land between the road and the Forest boundary is public domain.

The *Mt. Moriah Division,* near the UT border, about 16 mi. N–S, 14 mi. W–E, has a 12,050-ft. peak as its centerpiece. Trails circle and cross the peak. Four fishing streams gather on the slopes.

The *Snake Division* is on the Snake Range, S of Mt. Moriah. This Division is about 25 mi. N–S, about 14 mi. W–E. Within its NE sector is the Lehman Caves National Monument (see entry).

Principal feature of the Division is the 28,000-acre *Wheeler Peak Scenic Area.* Wheeler Peak, at 13,063 ft., is the second highest mountain in NV. Mt. Baker is 12,298 ft.; 4 other peaks in the area are over 11,000 ft. This is a popular scenic area, not a roadless wilderness, but few roads enter it. The principal access is the road from Baker to the National Monument, beyond which a branch follows a circuitous path to the NW, linking several campgrounds. Another branch follows Baker Creek to the SW, just outside the Scenic Area boundaries. A second entrance is from Garrison, UT, SE of Baker, via Forest Road 448, following Snake Creek.

Numerous cirques, several high cirque lakes, and the icefield on Mt. Wheeler are evidences of past glaciation. Earlier geological history can be read in the layered limestone, quartzite, and slate, materials once at the bottom of an inland sea. The E side slopes are gradual. The W drops steeply to Spring Valley (see entry). The area has many limestone caves in addition to those at the National Monument, but these are best left to experienced spelunkers. Lexington Arch, near the Scenic Area, is about 6 stories high.

Plants: The area exhibits almost the full range of plant communities found in NV. Lowest is the Upper Sonoran, characterized by sagebrush and cacti, with pinyon pine and juniper becoming prominent at about 5,000 feet elevation. Next is the transition zone, typified by mountain-mahogany, white fir, and ponderosa pine. In the (next-higher) Canadian zone, one finds Douglas-fir and aspen. Next above is the Hudsonian zone, with limber pine, spruce, and bristlecone pine. Above timberline is the arctic-alpine zone, barren except where soil supports tundra vegetation.

In the high Wheeler Peak Scenic Area, only about 60% of the land is forested. Most of the rest is exposed rock or in the arctic-alpine zone. The forest has many virgin stands. Ancient bristlecone pine forests are on Wheeler Peak and Mount Washington. Isolated specimens of the species are scattered elsewhere.

A plant list for the area includes among the flowering species: sego and tiger lilies, death camas, white bog orchid, columbine, larkspur, buttercup, prickly poppy, tansy mustard, draba, wallflower, stonecrop, cinquefoil, Fremont geranium, ceanothus, violets, blazing star, evening primrose, shooting star, gilia, phlox, phacelia, bluebells, verbena, Indian paintbrush, monkeyflower, penstemon, pussytoes, heartleaf arnica, aster, arrowleaf balsam root, salsify.

Birds: Checklist available for the Wheeler Peak area, which does not include all the habitats in the Ranger District. Seasonally common species include turkey vulture, red-tailed and rough-legged hawks, golden eagle, kestrel, blue and sage grouse, California quail, chukar, mourning dove, great horned owl, common nighthawk, broad-tailed and rufous hummingbirds, northern flicker, yellow-bellied sapsucker, hairy woodpecker, western kingbird, Say's phoebe, olive-sided flycatcher; violet-green, barn, and cliff swallows; Steller's and scrub jays, Clark's nutcracker, raven, common crow, mountain chickadee, common bushtit, dipper, white-breasted nuthatch, brown creeper, house and rock wrens, sage thrasher, robin, hermit and Swainson's thrushes, mountain bluebird, ruby-crowned kinglet, loggerhead shrike, starling, warbling vireo, yellow-rumped and MacGillivray's warblers, yellow-breasted chat, Brewer's blackbird, northern oriole, evening grosbeak, lazuli bunting, Cassin's and house finches, pine siskin, lesser goldfinch, green-tailed and rufous-sided towhees, dark-eyed junco; vesper, chipping, Brewer's, fox, and song sparrows.

Mammals: Checklist is for Wheeler Peak area. Common: hairy-winged myotis, big brown bat, blacktail jackrabbit, cottontail, pygmy rabbit, Townsend ground squirrel, golden-mantled and rock squirrels, least and yellow pine chipmunks, pocket mice, dark kangaroo mouse, kangaroo rat; western harvest, canyon, deer, and pinyon mice; northern pocket gopher, sagebrush vole, bushytail woodrat, shorttail weasel, spotted and striped skunks, coyote, bobcat, mule deer.

Reptiles and amphibians: Checklist is for Wheeler Peak area. Lizards: collared, long-nosed leopard, yellow-backed spiny, Great Basin fence, and northern desert horned. Great Basin spadefoot and Rocky Mountain toads, Pacific tree frog, leopard frog. Snakes: desert striped whipsnake, Great Basin gopher snake, wandering garter snake, desert night snake, Great Basin rattlesnake.

INTERPRETATION

Visitor center at Lehman Caves is jointly operated by National Park Service and Forest Service. Information, exhibits.

Bristlecone Interpretive Trail, 3/4 mi., is a National Recreation Trail.

Early Man Interpretive Trail.

ACTIVITIES

Camping: 14 campgrounds, 150 units. Most open May 15–Oct. 15, 2 open May 1; Wheeler Peak campground not until July 1.

Hiking, backpacking: All Divisions have trails. Those in the Wheeler Peak area have the heaviest use. Schell Division offers what are probably the best opportunities for long-distance mountain travel with water available.

Hunting: Deer, upland game birds.

Fishing: Chiefly in the Schell, Mt. Moriah, and Snake (Wheeler Peak) divisions.

Ski touring: On unplowed Forest roads.

The area has the fewest visitors in the weeks before and after the hunting season. Camping areas are seldom crowded except on the Fourth of July weekend.

PUBLICATIONS
Forest map, Ely Ranger District. $1.
Wheeler Peak Scenic Area map. $1.

REFERENCE: Hart, John. *Hiking the Great Basin.* San Francisco: Sierra Club Books, 1981, pp. 234–268.

HEADQUARTERS: 976 Mountain City Highway, Elko, NV 89801; (702) 738-5171.

RANGER DISTRICT: Ely R.D., P.O. Box 539, Ely, NV 89301; (702) 289-3031.

KERN MOUNTAINS, BLUE MASS SCENIC AREA
U.S. Bureau of Land Management
960 acres.

From US 93, 20 mi. S of Lages, about 33 mi. E on local road to Tippett, then SE about 15 mi. to Blue Mass Canyon.

The Blue Mass Canyon Scenic Area is on the N side of the Kern Range. The mountains here are low. Blue Mass Creek flows through a winding canyon beside an unimproved road. The rugged terrain is noted for a large area of "hoodoo rocks"—large light-colored rocks weathered into grotesque forms. They stand out against the background of pinyon pine. Aspens dot the hillside; patches of seasonal wildflowers. Several side canyons and drainages offer easy hiking routes.

The area is seldom visited except by deer hunters.

KEY PITTMAN WILDLIFE MANAGEMENT AREA
NV Department of Wildlife
1,330 acres.

Near the intersection of US 93, SR 375, SR 318; about 115 mi. N of Las Vegas.

Don't go out of your way to visit, but if you pass this way, pause for a short walk to look around. Two tracts. Parking area for the Nesbitt Lake unit is at the lower end of SR 318, the other entrance just around the corner on SR 375. The Pahranagat National Wildlife Refuge (see entry, Zone 6) is on US 93 about 25 mi. S.

In the Pahranagat Valley, at about 3,800 ft. elevation. Some 400 acres of wetland habitat, 70 acres of agricultural land, surrounded by desert scrub. Nesbitt Lake is about 220 acres, Frenchy Lake 130 acres. Maintained for waterfowl.

Fishing: Bass and catfish in Nesbitt Lake, called excellent Apr.–Aug.

HEADQUARTERS: Hiko, NV 89017; (702) 725-3521.

LEHMAN CAVES NATIONAL MONUMENT
National Park Service
640 acres.

From US 6/50 near the UT border, S 5 mi. on SR 487, then 5 mi. W.

The Monument is within the Humboldt National Forest, Snake Division (see entry), at the edge of the Wheeler Peak Scenic Area. The site is on the E flank of Wheeler Peak, at about 7,000 ft. elevation. Baker and Lehman creeks are on opposite sides of the Monument. Dissolving limestone has created an underground labyrinth of corridors and winding tunnels connecting larger chambers. The gradual seeping of water has formed stalactites, stalagmites, fluted columns, and other formations, many of them colorful.

From Labor Day to Memorial Day, tours are limited to 5 daily, beginning at 9 A.M., the last at 4 P.M. In summer, tours are offered hourly from 8 A.M. to 5 P.M., more often on weekends and holidays. Tours are limited to 30 people and take about 1 1/2 hours.

Visitor center serves both the Monument and the Scenic Area. Open 8 A.M. to 5 P.M. all year.

National Forest campgrounds are nearby.

PUBLICATION: Leaflet with map.

REFERENCE: Halladay, Orlynn J., and Var Lynn Peacock. *The Lehman Caves Story.* Baker, NV: Lehman Caves Natural History Association.

HEADQUARTERS: Baker, NV 89311; (702) 234-7331.

MOUNT GRAFTON
U.S. Bureau of Land Management
73,500 acres.

From US 93, W on local roads near White Pine-Lincoln county line, for E side access. Mount Grafton, shown on highway map, is near the site center.

In the Schell Creek Range, Mount Grafton rises to 10,993 ft. from about 7,000 ft. at its base. Roads and trails used for mining, ranching, and recreation penetrate some canyons of this section of the Schell Creek Range, but none crosses the ridge, and much of the high interior is in natural condition.

Because of its attractiveness, the Mount Grafton Scenic Area was designated by BLM some years ago. The mountain is massive. About 3 mi. of its ridge are above 10,000 ft. elevation. Fine views from the top. Large areas of jagged rock are intermingled with almost pure stands of white fir. Scattered areas of bristlecone pine, some specimens more than 1,500 years old. Subalpine vegetation around the peak. The area is highly rated for hiking, camping, birding, and hunting. Three or four perennial streams. Wildlife includes mountain lion, mule deer, elk, nesting raptors, blue grouse, owls, hummingbirds.

The North Creek Scenic Area is NE of Mount Grafton. Here a steep canyon has a clear, flowing creek, with good opportunities for camping, trout fishing, and rockhounding. The 2 mi. of dense black locust along the creek are unique for this area. Vegetation includes pinyon-juniper on slopes, willow, aspen, grasses, forbs, and many shrubs in the drainage bottom. This area has moderate recreation use.

Best foot access to the Ridge is from Patterson Pass, on local road crossing the range 7 mi. S of Mount Grafton.

PARSNIP PEAK
U.S. Bureau of Land Management
88,175 acres.

NE of Pioche, on US 93. N of Eagle Valley Rd.

This Wilderness Study Area is triangular, its S tip near Pioche, widening to the NE. About 25 mi. long, 4 to 11 mi. wide. Most of the surrounding land is public, and other WSA's lie to the N and E. In the Wilson Creek Range. Parsnip Peak is 8,942 ft. Huge white and pink rock formations weathered into bizarre shapes surround the peak.

The range has several ridges with deep canyons, unlike most other ranges of this area, which have single ridges. Some smooth, open slopes, others with thick stands of pinyon, mountain-mahogany, and some extensive stands of aspen. Ponderosa pines grow among the rock outcrops. A number of springs.

The BLM evaluation rates this site outstanding for natural beauty, and the high country is pristine. It isn't easy to get to it: long grades, thick vegetation, loose rock, places that require scrambling, a moderately difficult hike of about two hours to reach the core area. For those equal to the challenge, these obstacles assure solitude. Indeed, the number of hikers is estimated to be 20 per year.

Wildlife is abundant: deer, bobcat, mountain lion, raptors.

Hunters number less than 300 per year. Hunting is said to be good, but it's a long haul out.

SOUTH EGAN RANGE

U.S. Bureau of Land Management
150,000 acres.

SE of Ely. E of SR 318 from a point near Lund S for about 36 mi.

A large, irregularly shaped range, rising from valleys at about 6,000 ft. elevation. This entry describes two roadless Wilderness Study Areas separated by the Shingle Pass county road.

The mountain base at 7,500 ft. elevation is 2 to 5 mi. broad. Principal peaks are 9,598 ft. and 9,861 ft. The rugged limestone range rises into sheer cliffs along much of the W side, preventing access as far S as Sheep Pass Canyon. The S sector has numerous routes, chiefly primitive and unmaintained. In many places at the highest elevations, there are broad, almost flat tables with scattered timber stands. The slopes on the E side are moderate.

Tree cover is dense in many places, mostly pinyon-juniper with stands of white fir, limber pine, ponderosa pine, and bristlecone pine at higher elevations. Groves of aspen provide displays of fall colors.

The area has an abundance of springs and intermittent springs, but most are fouled by cattle.

Wildlife: Includes red-tailed and ferruginous hawks, prairie falcon, golden eagle, American kestrel, sage grouse, great horned and long-eared owls, turkey vulture, Gambel's quail, mule deer, mountain lion, smaller mammals. The area is said to have an exceptionally high density of prairie falcon nestings.

Access, scenery, and the variety of terrain and vegetation make this an exceptionally good area for hiking, backpacking, hunting, and horse riding, with ample opportunities for solitude. Most visitors are hunters. Angel Cave and other caves attract about 150 spelunkers per year. Cliffs attract a few technical climbers. Hikers and backpackers number less than a dozen per year, horse riders about the same.

W. E. KIRCH WILDLIFE MANAGEMENT AREA
Nevada Department of Wildlife
15,575 acres.

From Ely, 23 mi. SW on US 6, then about 45 mi. S on SR 318.

In the wide, generally flat valley of the White River. Elevation is 5,100 to 5,300 ft. Nearby are small, scattered mountains, one with a peak of 9,861 ft., but the nearest major range is the Grant, about 15 mi. W. The road S from US 6 is paved. When we visited, paving crews were completing the pavement S to US 93.

The White River is intermittent. Construction of dams and dikes has created five reservoirs, including a water storage reservoir, with marsh areas. The site has about 2,000 acres of water and marsh, 2,500 acres of wet meadow, 11,000 acres of rangeland and fallow cropland. Water levels are managed.

The primary objective of the area is support of waterfowl. Up to 9,000 ducks use the area in migrations, and several species nest here. Whistling swans and many shorebirds use the area. Upland game birds are also present, as well as a variety of mammals.

Visitors can see the area by traveling a 16-mi. loop road with several side branches. The primary visitor activity is fishing. Hunting is second, although the site is crowded only on the first day of the hunting season. The small primitive campground is used mostly by hunters and fishermen.

Annual precipitation here averages 8 in., most falling in winter. Summer temperatures often exceed 100°F; winter temperatures occasionally drop below zero.

It's an out-of-the-way place. Soon after we turned S from US 6, a sign warned "102 mi. to the next gas station." But if one is traveling S from Ely, this route isn't much longer than US 93, and wetlands amidst desert are striking. There's good birding here spring, summer, and fall.

Birds: Checklist can be seen at HQ. Major duck species in migration include mallard, pintail, gadwall, cinnamon and green-winged teals, redhead, canvasback, ruddy duck. Nesting: gadwall, cinnamon teal, redhead, ruddy duck. Duck broods begin to appear mid-May and can be observed through the summer. Peak of the duck migration is Oct. or early Nov. Great Basin Canada goose is common, other geese occasional. Whistling swans are common visitors. Coot abundant, up to 10,000 birds. Shorebirds include spotted, least, and western sandpipers; willet, avocet, black-necked stilt, Wilson's phalarope. Wading birds: great blue heron, snowy egret, black-crowned night-heron, American bittern. The breeding population of white-faced ibis is one of only four in NV.

Other common or abundant species include: red-tailed, Swainson's, and rough-legged hawks; northern harrier, golden eagle, prairie falcon, kestrel, ring-billed and Franklin's gulls, Forster's and black terns, mourning dove, great horned and burrowing owls, common and lesser nighthawks, rufous hummingbird, kingfisher, northern flicker, downy woodpecker, western kingbird, ash-throated flycatcher, black and Say's phoebes, western wood-pewee, horned lark; violet-green, tree, rough-winged, barn, and cliff swallows; magpie, raven, pinyon jay, marsh wren, mockingbird, sage thrasher, robin, mountain bluebird, ruby-crowned kinglet, cedar waxwing, loggerhead shrike, starling; yellow, yellow-rumped, and Wilson's warblers; western meadowlark; yellow-headed, red-winged, and Brewer's blackbirds; brown-headed cowbird, western tanager, lazuli bunting, house finch, green-tailed and rufous-sided towhees; savannah, vesper, black-throated, sage, chipping, Brewer's, white-crowned, and song sparrows.

ACTIVITIES

Camping: In a cottonwood grove. 30 graded sites. Water, toilets.

Hunting: Waterfowl.

Fishing: Trout, black bass.

Boating: Boats without motors can be used on the Adams-McGill Reservoir, chiefly for fishing.

PUBLICATION: Map.

HEADQUARTERS: Lund, NV 89317; no telephone.

ZONE 6

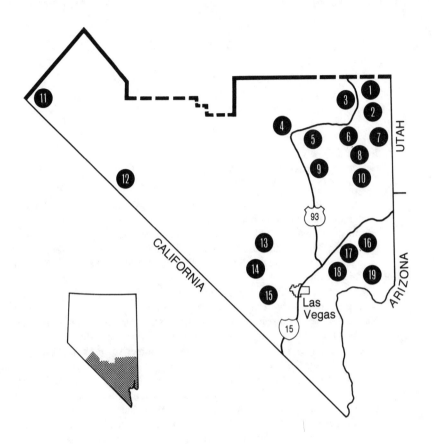

CALIFORNIA

UTAH

ARIZONA

93

Las
Vegas

15

ZONE 6

Includes these counties:
Nye (S portion)	Clark
Lincoln (S portion)	Esmeralda

Zone 6 is BLM's Las Vegas District, southern NV, plus Esmeralda County. It includes about 14.5 million acres, of which 10.3 million are public domain administered by BLM. The Nuclear Testing Site is a major part of the remainder. This site is closed to the public except for the E portion, which is managed as the Desert National Wildlife Range by the U.S. Fish and Wildlife Service.

The zone has both the highest and the lowest points in Nevada. Highest is 13,140-ft. Boundary Peak, on the California border in a section of the Inyo National Forest. Lowest, at 470 ft., is the state's southern tip. The zone includes Lake Mead, Nevada's largest body of water, and the state's driest desert. (Just after we wrote that sentence, a summer storm dumped 4 in. in a day, flooding the town of Overton!)

A portion of the Inyo National Forest projects into Nevada from California. The zone also has a disjunct Ranger District of the Toiyabe National Forest, a 58,000-acre mountainous site just W of Las Vegas.

A corner of Death Valley National Monument extends into Nevada.

By far the most popular outdoor recreation site is the Lake Mead National Recreation Area. As one drives across the desert, it is surprising to see a procession of cars towing boats. People come from afar to boat, water ski, fish, and swim. Recreation centers are often crowded, but Lake Mead and neighboring Lake Mohave are so large that one can find many quiet, isolated places along their shores. Most upland areas are roadless wilderness.

The mountain ranges of this zone are not arranged as neatly parallel as those further N. Nor, on the whole, did they seem as interesting. We did not select as many of them for entries. We won't defend this judgment. The entry for South Pahroc Range shows how an area we overlooked can arouse enthusiasm. No doubt there are many other fascinating backcountry sites few people ever see.

The White River-Pahranagat Valley is a minor waterfowl flyway. Among the state and federal refuges along this route, the State's W. E. Kirch Wildlife Management Area in Zone 5 offers better birding opportunities than any in Zone 6. The Overton refuge at the head of the Overton Arm of Lake Mead probably has good birding at times; most of it was under water when we were there.

The Desert National Wildlife Refuge, maintained for upland game, is huge, and only a small part of it is accessible by automobile. Try it on foot, horseback, or with a 4-wheel-drive vehicle.

Several of Nevada's most interesting State Parks are in Zone 6: the remote, scenic Beaver Dam State Park; the brilliantly colored Valley of Fire; and the dramatic Cathedral Gorge.

PUBLICATIONS
BLM Public Lands Guide. Map.
Species checklists.

HEADQUARTERS: BLM, Las Vegas District, 4765 Vegas Dr., Las Vegas, NV 89108; (702) 385-6403.

BEAVER DAM STATE PARK
Nevada Division of State Parks
2,032 acres.

> From Caliente, 6 mi. N on US 93, then 32 mi. E on a gravel road. Not advisable for trailers.

Close to the UT border. The Park isn't large, but it is surrounded by public domain, including a roadless area recommended for wilderness study. This is one of Nevada's most remote Parks and, many say, the loveliest: high in the mountains, in pine forest, with flowing streams and a small blue reservoir. On the shoreline are some rocky cliffs with pinnacles. Elevations are from 5,100 to 5,500 ft. The Park is usually inaccessible between Nov. 1 and May 1.

Although the Park itself has no high peaks or deep canyons, the terrain is attractively rugged, irregular gullied ravines, small canyons, rocky slopes. Precipitation is 10 to 14 in. per year, most of it in winter.

To the S are the Clover Mountains. On the W and N, the land is flat to gently rolling. Across the border in UT is the Dixie National Forest. Although hunting is not permitted in the Park, opportunities for hunting deer, quail, and chukar are just outside. The surrounding territory offers good opportunities for backpacking and horse travel.

Plants: Pinyon pine and juniper are the principal trees. Sagebrush in the understory. Scrub oak and willow near the creeks. Flowering species include Indian paintbrush, primrose blazing star, sunflower.

Wildlife: No checklists available. Birds noted: belted kingfisher, common nighthawk, hummingbirds, sparrows, owls. Mammals: mule deer, cottontail, blacktail jackrabbit, skunk, coyote, fox, mountain lion.

INTERPRETATION

Campfire programs can be arranged by seasonal ranger.
Scenic trail has tree labels, goes to high overlook.

ACTIVITIES

Camping: 3 campgrounds, one accessible only by pickup truck or 4-wheel-drive vehicle. 52 sites.

Hiking, backpacking: No marked trails outside the park, but they're not needed in this open country.

Fishing: Reservoir and stream. Trout.

The park is 34 mi. from the nearest telephone or gasoline.

HEADQUARTERS: District V, Nevada State Parks, P.O. Box 176, Panaca, NV 89042; (702) 728-4467.

CATHEDRAL GORGE STATE PARK

Nevada Division of State Parks
1,608 acres.

On US 93 just N of Panaca.

Come in the N entrance first, about 2 mi. N of the main entrance. This N approach leads to a splendid observation point overlooking the long, narrow valley. The special nature of the valley is that it has been carved by wind and water from a thick layer of bentonite clay, a soft material that resembles dried mud, in shades of tan and gray. The result is a dramatic array of striking formations: spires, terraces, flutings, domes, fans. From the observation point a stairway leads down to a terrace where one can walk among some of the formations, still well above the valley floor.

The developed area is in the valley. An exceptionally fine nature trail introduces visitors to the desert plants of the region: desert and antelope bitterbrush, rabbitbrush, desert barberry, greasewood, Russian thistle, Mormon tea. Cliffs are 50 to 100 ft. high.

Published descriptions mention caves. We saw none, but we did find several narrow, winding passageways, cuts with vertical walls that almost close overhead. After the first turn, one feels isolated. In places, these passages narrow to slits through which only a child can pass.

Except along the highway, most of the surrounding land is public domain. Elevations in the Park are from 4,700 to 4,900 ft. The land rises gradually to the NW for about 6 mi., then much more steeply up the side of the Highland Range. Highland Peak is 9,395 ft. high.

Annual precipitation in the Park is about 5 in. Summers are dry, winters cold and sometimes snowy. Summer days often reach 95°F but nights are cool. The Park is seldom crowded.

INTERPRETATION: *Campfire programs* and *guided walks* in summer.

Camping: 16 sites. All year. No water Nov.–Mar.

PUBLICATION: Brochure planned.

HEADQUARTERS: P.O. Box 176, Panaca, NV 89042; (702) 728-4467.

CLOVER MOUNTAINS; GRAPEVINE SPRING
U.S. Bureau of Land Management
84,835 acres.

E of SR 317 at Elgin, about 105 mi. NE of Las Vegas. Road access to Cottonwood Canyon between Carp and Elgin. Access to N and E portions by dirt road from Caliente; may need 4-wheel drive.

The Elgin-Carp Road was closed by flooding when we visited, and residents said it often washes out. The site is on the S extension of the Clover Mountains, about 14 mi. N–S, 16 W–E. Rugged peaks, deep twisting canyons, brightly colored scenic rock formations, rolling hills, jagged rock outcrops, steep cliff faces. Cottonwood Canyon, including Pine Creek, in the SW sector, Stokes Flat and Fife Canyon in the N, and Quaking Aspen in the NE, are all good hiking routes. Water is available throughout the area, though it may not be potable because of cattle. Elevations from 3,000 ft. to 7,300 ft.

Vegetation is chiefly pinyon-juniper with stands of ponderosa pine and aspen. Willow and cottonwood in drainages. Prime mule deer area. Many raptors sighted, including peregrine falcon, golden eagle, prairie falcon.

DESERT NATIONAL WILDLIFE RANGE
U.S. Fish and Wildlife Service
1,588,459 acres.

From Las Vegas, 26 mi. NW on US 95. Sign on E side.

Open: 5 A.M.–9 P.M. Overnight by reservation and permit only.

The largest U.S. wildlife refuge outside Alaska, established largely for big-horn sheep, but with many other wildlife species, including 245 bird species. The W half is a gunnery range, closed to visitors. In the E half, all roads are primitive, and use by ordinary passenger cars is "not recommended." A tour route of about 40 mi. cuts across the refuge from the Corn Creek Field Station, the principal entrance, NE to US 93. Call ahead about road conditions.

The Sheep Range runs the length of the public area, N–S. In the S half, the ridge is generally above 8,500 ft. elevation, with peaks of 9,750 and 9,912 ft. In the N half, the ridge drops to about 7,000 ft. The tour route runs between the Las Vegas Range (in the SE corner of the area) and the E side of the Sheep Range. Alamo Road extends from the Field Station to the N boundary, W of the Sheep Range, E of the Desert Range. Off-road vehicle travel is prohibited.

From the Alamo Road, spurs lead off into the Sheep Range, where mountain springs attract bighorn sheep and other wildlife. Here one travels on foot or horseback. To enjoy it fully, one should camp for the night at one of the designated sites. If one hopes to see sheep, the advice is to climb about 3,000 ft. above the valley and find a vantage point.

Visitors are forbidden use of any refuge water source, except in emergency, partly because the limited supply is reserved for wildlife, partly because it's unsafe.

Elevations are from 2,500 ft. to almost 10,000 ft. Annual precipitation ranges from less than 4 in. in the valleys to over 15 in. on higher peaks. The plant communities are typical of the region: creosote bush-saltbush in the open valleys; yucca and Joshua tree; pinyon-juniper on the middle slopes; ponderosa pine and fir; scattered bristlecone pine on the high slopes.

Birds: Checklist available. Small impoundments at the Corn Creek Field Station attract a few migrating waterfowl and shorebirds, but greater numbers and variety can be seen at the adjacent Pahranagat National Wildlife Refuge (see entry). Seasonally common species here include golden eagle, kestrel, Gambel's quail, mourning dove, flammulated owl, poor-will, common and lesser nighthawks, white-throated swift, broad-tailed and rufous humming-birds, yellow-bellied sapsucker, ladder-backed woodpecker; dusky, gray, and western flycatchers, horned lark, violet-green and tree swallows, scrub and pinyon jays, Clark's nutcracker, mountain chickadee, bushtit, white-breasted and pygmy nuthatches, house and rock wrens, mockingbird, robin, hermit thrush, western bluebird, Townsend's solitaire, blue-gray gnatcatcher, water pipit, phainopepla, loggerhead shrike, starling, solitary vireo. Warblers: Virginia's, yellow-rumped, black-throated gray, Grace's, MacGillivray's, and Wilson's. Also western meadowlark; yellow-headed, red-winged, and

Brewer's blackbirds; western tanager, black-headed grosbeak, Cassin's and house finches, pine siskin, green-tailed and rufous-sided towhees, dark-eyed and gray-headed juncos. Sparrows: black-throated, sage, chipping, Brewer's, white-crowned, and fox.

Mammals: Checklist available. Species reported include various bats, cliff chipmunk, blacktail jackrabbit, kit fox, coyote, badger, spotted skunk, bobcat, mountain lion, mule deer, bighorn sheep.

ACTIVITIES
Camping, backpacking, and *horse camping:* All by reservation and permit.
Horse riding: Subject to seasonal restriction except in a designated area at the S end of the Refuge.

PUBLICATIONS
Leaflet with map.
Checklists of birds, mammals, amphibians, and reptiles.

HEADQUARTERS: 1500 N. Decatur Blvd., Las Vegas, NV 89108; (702) 646-3401.

ECHO CANYON STATE RECREATION AREA
Nevada Division of State Parks
920 acres.

14 mi. SE of Pioche via SRs 322 and 86.

When we saw it in 1980, this 65-acre reservoir was new, raw, unattractive. The immediate area around it was scarred and denuded, dust blowing in the wind. The water was low; a state report said the reservoir leaked.

By now the leak may be fixed and the landscape healed. We would still not consider it an entry but for the attractive canyon at the head of the lake. A paved road goes up the canyon between rocky cliffs and talus slopes in shades of red and gray. After a couple of miles, the canyon opens into a broad valley, through which the stream meanders. This is a private ranch. Beyond it, the road crosses a small bridge and enters a forested valley. Our motor home was too heavy for the bridge, but a sheriff's deputy said the road was good all the way to Spring Valley State Park (see entry).

Interpretive programs are offered in summer.

Camping: 34 sites. Apr.–Oct.

HEADQUARTERS: Nevada State Parks, P.O. Box 176, Panaca, NV 89042; (702) 728-4467.

INYO NATIONAL FOREST
U.S. Forest Service
60,654 acres.

On the CA border, SE of US 6. Access roads from US 6 and SR 264.

Most of this Forest, and the best of it, is in California, 1,859,214 acres. Of the NV portion of the Forest, 43,375 acres is in the White Mountains, and 16,919 acres is mostly in the Excelsior Mountains. The White Mountains are high and dry, with colorful canyons descending from Boundary Peak. Boundary Peak, at 13,140 ft., is the highest point in NV, close to the NV-CA line. Mining has been, and still is, extensive.

The Excelsior Mountains have gentler terrain, solitude, and some low-grade springs that serve wild horses and burros as well as domestic cattle. Little mining has occurred here. The roads and trails in both sectors are primitive.

The Forest is fully described in our California guide.

KERSHAW-RYAN STATE PARK
Nevada Division of State Parks
240 acres.

From Caliente on US 93, 3 mi. S on Rainbow Canyon Rd.

In 1985 the Park was closed because of flood damage. No reopening was scheduled.

Except along the highway, the surrounding land is mostly public domain. The Park is a miniature oak forest surrounded by cliffs draped with grapevines. Pools of cool water.

LAKE MEAD NATIONAL RECREATION AREA
National Park Service
1,482,476 acres.

On the AZ border, E of Las Vegas. Visitor center on US 93.

Hoover Dam formed Lake Mead, extending for 115 mi., including 40 mi. into the Grand Canyon of the Colorado River. The lake has a 774-mi. shoreline, surface area of 162,700 acres. To the S, Davis Dam formed Lake Mohave, a narrow reservoir 67 mi. long, from the base of Hoover Dam. Lake Mohave's surface area is 28,200 acres, with a shoreline of 254 mi. The climate is such that fishing, boating, and swimming are pleasant most of the year. As these are two of the largest bodies of water in the Southwest, they attract great numbers of visitors. We camped one night at Echo Bay, a vast development with 166 campsites, a large motel, a marina with every conceivable service, including a fleet of rental houseboats, shops, restaurant, and a surprisingly large residential area, presumably for employees. Certainly not one of our natural areas.

Near any of the developed sites, six on Lake Mead, three on Lake Mohave, boat traffic can be heavy, especially on weekends. But the concentration drops off rapidly with distance, and one who seeks quiet waters can find them. The upland areas, except at the developments, are never crowded. The NRA boundaries enclose an area 8 times the combined areas of the lakes, but even this is not a measure of the open space, since most of the adjoining land is public domain. One can hike for miles with little likelihood of meeting others.

The contrast between land and water is dramatic, since this is one of the most arid regions of the continent, receiving only 3 to 4 in. of precipitation annually. The lowest elevation is 530 ft., below Davis Dam. The surface of Lake Mead, at full pool, can be as high as 1,229 ft. Highest point in the NRA is 7,072-ft. Mt. Dellenbaugh, in Arizona.

The area straddles the Grand Wash Cliffs, the transition between two major geographic provinces. E of the Grand Wash is the Grand Canyon. The exposed rock strata in the Lake Mead area, like those of the Grand Canyon, span nearly the full range of known geologic history.

The surrounding area is seemingly endless desert, much of it flat, some gently rolling or sloping away from scattered mountain ranges. On the N side are the Black Mountains, with 3,069-ft. Pyramid Peak near the shoreline. The more massive Virgin Mountains are E of the Overton Arm of the lake. Most of the land adjoining the NRA here is public domain, managed by BLM, much of it roadless and proposed for Wilderness study. The 30,000-acre Virgin Peak area did not qualify as potential Wilderness because of mining and ranching intrusions, but opportunities for camping, backpacking, hunting, and horse riding are excellent. Virgin Peak is 8,066 ft. A 5,560-acre Natural Area was established here to protect an extreme southern extension of Douglas-fir.

On the S, Lake Mohave is bracketed by the Eldorado and Black Mountains, both long, narrow ranges of no great height.

The best time to explore the uplands is winter and early spring, when daily average temperatures range from the middle 50s to the middle 70s. Summers are described as "fiercely hot," with temperatures up to 120°F. The uplands offer neither shade nor water.

Plants: The arid landscape generally supports sparse growth. The Mohave association includes creosote bush, Joshua tree, burrobrush, many cacti, Spanish dagger, yucca, bursage. At higher levels, some pinyon-juniper forest. Several hundred species of flowering plants occur, many blooming only in years with sufficient spring moisture.

Birds: Checklist available. Seasonally common or abundant species include eared and western grebes, double-crested cormorant, great blue heron, Canada goose, mallard, pintail, green-winged and cinnamon teals, wigeon, shoveler, ruddy duck, common merganser, turkey vulture, red-tailed hawk, kestrel, coot, killdeer; spotted, least, and western sandpipers; avocet, California gull, roadrunner, lesser nighthawk, white-throated swift, northern flicker, western kingbird, ash-throated and dusky flycatchers, Say's phoebe, rough-winged swallow, Steller's jay, verdin, canyon and rock wrens, mockingbird, crissal thrasher, American robin, ruby-crowned kinglet, water pipit, loggerhead shrike, European starling, gray vireo. Warblers: Lucy's, yellow, yellow-rumped, Wilson's, yellow-breasted chat. Also western meadowlark, red-winged and Brewer's blackbirds, northern oriole, brown-headed cowbird, house finch, lesser goldfinch, Abert's towhee; black-throated, sage, chipping, white-crowned, and song sparrows.

Mammals: Desert shrew, California leaf-nosed bat, California myotis, western pipistrel, big brown bat, pallid bat, Mexican freetail bat, blacktail jackrabbit, cottontail, rock squirrel, antelope squirrel, round-tailed ground squirrel, cliff chipmunk, valley pocket gopher, pocket mice, kangaroo rats, various other mice and rats, beaver, muskrat, porcupine, coyote, kit fox, gray fox, ringtail, raccoon, longtail weasel, badger, spotted and striped skunks, mountain lion, bobcat, mule deer, bighorn sheep.

Reptiles and amphibians: Toads include Great Basin spadefoot, Woodhouse's, southwestern, Great Plains, red-spotted. Canyon and Pacific tree frogs, bullfrog, leopard frog, desert tortoise, spiny softshell turtle. Lizards include banded gecko, desert iguana, collared, leopard, chuckwalla, zebra-tailed, desert spiny, western fence, eastern fence, sagebrush, long-tailed brush, tree, side-blotched, short-horned, desert horned, desert night, western whiptail, and Gila monster. Also western blind snake, racer, coachwhip, striped whipsnake, western patch-nosed snake, glossy snake, long-nosed snake, common kingsnake, spotted leaf-nosed snake, western ground snake, western shovel-nosed snake, Sonora lyre snake, night snake; western diamondback, Mojave, speckled, and sidewinder rattlesnakes.

FEATURES

In all, 36 areas totaling 545,645 acres have been proposed for Wilderness designation. The legislation specifies that a Wilderness must be roadless, and many of the proposed units are adjacent, separated only by a road, often an unpaved road. Half of the proposed areas are on Lake Mead and half on Lake Mohave. The average distance from the lake shore to the NRA boundary is about 5 mi. On the upper part of Lake Mead, BLM has proposed Wilderness status for several large tracts of public domain adjoining the NRA, chiefly in the South Virgin Mountains.

Descriptions of all these areas would not serve the reader. Anyone planning more than a short day hike into backcountry should consult a Ranger about destinations, routes, maps, and current conditions.

Many miles of the lake shore are roadless, and the shoreline is irregular, with many quiet coves. Here are countless opportunities for boat camping, with easy access to the isolated backcountry.

Scenic drive: From the Visitor Center, NE on Lakeshore Rd. and Northshore Rd., passing Callville Bay, Echo Bay, and Overton Beach. The Redstone Picnic Area between Callville Bay and Echo Bay presents unusual examples of water- and wind-eroded red sandstone. Just beyond is Valley of Fire State Park (see entry).

INTERPRETATION

Alan Bible Visitor Center is on US 93 W of Hoover Dam. Exhibits, publications, films, botanic garden, nature trail.

Campfire programs fall–spring. Notices posted at campgrounds.

Guided hikes fall and winter. Notices posted.

Lake Mead cruises, daily from Lake Mead Marina.

ACTIVITIES

Camping: 9 campgrounds. 1,200 sites. All year.

Hiking, backpacking: No marked trails, but trails aren't needed in this terrain. Get advice, a topo map. Carry ample water. Don't enter old mine tunnels.

Hunting: Bighorn sheep, mule deer, waterfowl, upland game birds, under state and federal regulations.

Fishing: Largemouth bass, rainbow trout, crappie, silver salmon, channel catfish, bluegill, green sunfish, striped bass. Fishing from a boat requires a license from NV or AZ plus a use stamp from the other state.

Swimming: Lifeguards in summer at Boulder Beach and Katherine. Otherwise, swim at your own risk. Upper Lake Mohave is cold.

Boating: 6 marinas on Lake Mead, 3 on Lake Mohave.

Don't camp in washes, especially when thunderheads are seen; flash floods are common.

Motor vehicles must stay on approved roads; no off-road travel. Approved backcountry roads are marked with yellow arrows. Check with Park Ranger for local conditions.

ADJACENT: In Arizona, Grand Canyon National Park. In 1975, about 440,000 acres were transferred from the Lake Mead NRA and added to the National Park. Not included was the 84,000-acre Shivwitz Plateau, within the loop formed by Lower Granite Gorge.

PUBLICATIONS
Leaflet with map.
Bird, mammal, reptile, and amphibian checklists.

REFERENCES
The Southwest Parks and Monuments Association, 601 Nevada Highway,
Boulder City, NV 89005, has a list of publications on sale. Included:
Trails Illustrated topo map. $4.95.
Auto Tour Guide. $.50.
Cove Map. $.50.
Flowering Plants of Lake Mead. $3.

HEADQUARTERS: 601 Nevada Highway, Boulder City, NV 89005; (702) 293-
4041.

MEADOW VALLEY RANGE AND MORMON MOUNTAINS
U.S. Bureau of Land Management
310,201 acres and 246,812 acres.

W and E of Meadow Valley Wash Road, S of Elgin.

Driving S from Ely to Las Vegas, one comes to Caliente, where US 93 turns
due W for 42 mi. The direct route seems straight S on SR 317, Meadow Valley
Wash Road, but ask about road conditions before proceeding.

The road divides two vast areas. On the W, the Meadow Valley Range is
dominant, a long, thin ridge with rugged limestone peaks and canyons, along
the N and W side. Bunker Hills, on the S side are low, angular, with badland
features. Flat, sloping bajadas fan out to the S and SE, broken by occasional
washes and draws. Vegetation is typical southern Mohave Desert shrub:
creosote bush, small bunchgrasses, yuccas.

About 185,744 acres have been recommended for wilderness study. Best
access is by the Kane Springs Valley Road, shown on the highway map
running SW from Elgin.

The Meadow Valley Wash Road offers the best access to the Mormon
Mountains on the E. Flat, sloping bajadas rise to steep cliffs, canyons, and
peaks. The mountains are so named because the Old Spanish Trail-Mormon
Road came through this area. Typical desert shrub vegetation, with pinyon-
juniper on the slopes, some ponderosa pine above. The site has limestone
caverns of interest to spelunkers. 162,887 acres have been recommended for
wilderness study.

In making our selections from the innumerable public domain tracts in

Nevada, we generally chose those with water, because such sites have the richest flora and fauna. These two vast areas are dry except for a few widely scattered springs. However, we were fascinated by the vastness of the area, its terrain, and its isolation. We enjoyed our short hikes and would like to see more.

REFERENCE: Hart, John. *Hiking the Great Basin.* San Francisco: Sierra Club Books, 1981, pp. 136–142.

MUDDY MOUNTAINS
U.S. Bureau of Land Management
96,170 acres.

S of the Valley of Fire State Park. Generally between SR 169 and SR 167. Access by local roads.

The area lies between the Valley of Fire and Lake Mead. Parts of it have the dramatic qualities of the Valley: brilliant red, orange, and cream sandstone in striking formations. Topography is varied: the mile-high Muddy Mountains are the core area, with jagged peaks and canyons. On the S side are the low, colorful Gale Hills, meeting the shore of Lake Mead. Bitter Spring Valley and White Basin form a bajada sloping E toward Echo Wash. Vegetation is typical Southern Mojave Desert community: low bunchgrass, shrubs, Joshua tree, yucca.

Birding and big game hunting are said to be good. Good chance to observe desert bighorn sheep.

The entire area is accessible to day hikers. The following destinations are popular:

Hidden Valley, Colorock Quarry, and *Wild Sheep Valley,* because of their multicolored, sculptured sandstone formations.

Muddy Peak, 5,432 ft., for a vigorous hike and magnificent views.

Anniversary Narrows, a canyon 1/3-mi. long, only 7 to 15 ft. wide, with walls 400 to 600 ft. high that often overhang the canyon floor. The National Park Service and the Sierra Club regularly schedule day hikes here.

Lowell Wash Basin, almost totally enclosed by the Muddy Mountains on the N, 500-ft. brightly colored cliffs on the W, S, and E.

Bighorn sheep are often seen and sometimes photographed. Rockhounds find jasper, agate, amethyst, opal. Many petroglyphs.

Hiking, backpacking: Hiking season is Sept.–May. Backpacking is limited by lack of water.

REFERENCE: Hart, John. *Hiking the Great Basin.* San Francisco: Sierra Club
   Books, 1981, pp. 129–135.

OVERTON WILDLIFE MANAGEMENT AREA
Nevada Department of Wildlife
17,657 acres.

At Overton on SR 169. NE of Las Vegas.

The area is at the head of the Overton Arm of Lake Mead and adjoins the
Lake Mead National Recreation Area. 9,000 acres of flood-plain riparian
habitat, 8,200 acres of desert rangeland, 250 acres of wetlands, 100 acres of
cropland.

When we visited, the flood plain was flooded. The entrance road had
vanished under water. In waterfowl hunting season, the control booth at the
entrance is presumably manned and the small, primitive campground used.
The busiest time, we were informed, is the goose season. Otherwise the site
has few visitors, perhaps some fishermen.

Since we couldn't get far beyond the entrance, we can't evaluate the site.
The surrounding area is flat and uninteresting. We saw no launching ramp,
and none was reported in the questionnaire we sent. It would not be difficult
to slide a canoe or cartopper into the water, and birding would probably be
good before or after the hunting season.

Birds: Our questionnaire was returned with a long and well-prepared
checklist of 177 bird species on the WMA. The list includes many waterfowl,
shorebirds, and birds of prey, as well as upland species characteristic of the
desert region.

HEADQUARTERS: P.O. Box 406, Overton, NV 89040; (702) 397-2142.

PAHRANAGAT NATIONAL WILDLIFE REFUGE
U.S. Fish and Wildlife Service
5,381 acres.

On US 93 about 6 mi. S of Alamo.

A long, narrow strip on the W side of US 93 in the Pahranagat Valley. Except
beside the highway, most surrounding land is public domain or, to the S, is

in the Desert National Wildlife Range (see entry). The Refuge includes two lakes: Upper Pahranagat, about 1 3/4 mi. long, and Lower Pahranagat, about 1 1/4 mi. long, about 4 1/2 mi. apart.

Most visitors are Las Vegas hunters and fishermen, whose use is seasonal. Other visitors include passing motorists who use the Refuge as a rest stop. When we visited, the Refuge appeared to be closed except for a 1 1/2-mi. road along the E shore of the upper lake. "Area Closed" signs shut off all other roads and paths. A sign prohibiting access to HQ was out of place, we learned. Visitors are urged to visit HQ on arrival, and beyond HQ is a 2 1/2-mi. road open to visitors. The Refuge is relatively new, we were told, and public facilities are in the early development stages. They're likely to stay there while present budget restrictions continue.

Both roads offer good shorebird and waterfowl observation. An Audubon Society sponsors at least two field trips a year here.

Water supply is critical to the Refuge's function. Lake levels fluctuate seasonally, depending on the rate of evaporation and withdrawals by farmers for irrigation. The shore of the upper lake is bordered by cottonwoods. The shore road has numerous turnouts for parking, picnicking, and camping.

Birds: Checklist of 193 species available. Water birds are attracted by the impoundments, ditches, and marshy areas. Some waterfowl spend the winter, unless the ponds freeze over. Some remain through the summer, but peak populations are in the spring and fall migrations. A rookery of great blue heron and double-crested cormorant is at the N end of the Refuge. Open fields attract blackbird, meadowlark, killdeer. The cottonwoods are lively with warblers, finches, and sparrows in spring. Gambel's quail and roadrunner frequent the edges of meadows. Checklist species are much the same as those at the W. E. Kirch Wildlife Management Area a few mi. N (see entry, Zone 5).

In Apr., we saw a few birds on the lake and along the shore. Many more were visible in the closed areas, out of binocular range. We saw much more at the Kirch WMA, but one should not pass this site by without at least a look around.

PUBLICATIONS
Leaflet with map.
Bird checklist (1968—Supply may be limited).

HEADQUARTERS: c/o Desert National Wildlife Range, 1500 N. Decatur Blvd., Las Vegas, NV 89108; (702) 646-3401. Also: P.O. Box 510, Alamo, NV 89001.

QUEER MOUNTAIN; GRAPEVINE MOUNTAINS
U.S. Bureau of Land Management
170,000 acres.

On both sides of SR 267 at the CA border.

SR 267 is the road from Scotty's Junction to Scotty's Castle in Death Valley National Monument. Gold, Cove, and Queer Mountains are on the NW side of the road. Gold Mountain, at 8,160 ft., is the highest point in the range, most of which is between 5,000 and 7,000 ft. elevation. Bonnie Claire Flat lies between this range and the Grapevine Mountains on the SE. These mountains extend into the National Monument, and their highest point, 8,728-ft. Grapevine Peak, is within the Monument. The land slopes E to Sarcobatus Flat.

The area includes many interesting geologic features, including long, narrow canyons, rock strata with bands of white and reddish hues.

The area has no springs or streams, but some E and N slopes are heavily forested, chiefly with pinyon-juniper. Vegetation is mostly desert scrub, with some Joshua trees.

It's not a remarkable area. We note it because many visitors to Death Valley National Monument come this way, and the area adjoins portions of the Monument recommended for Wilderness status.

RED ROCK CANYON RECREATION LANDS
U.S. Bureau of Land Management
62,000 acres.

From Las Vegas, W on SR 159 (Charleston Blvd.).

Throughout its vast domain, BLM does little to promote public recreation. This site is out of character in a most welcome way. The chosen site is so spectacular it has often been used by film companies. E of the highway the land is gently sloping. On the W it rises suddenly 3,000 ft. from the valley floor in dramatic, sheer sandstone cliffs with narrow, deep canyons. The Red Rock escarpment is not as brilliantly colored as the Valley of Fire, but there are enough patches of red to justify the name, as well as bands of white and yellow. The hills are almost bare of vegetation. Some Joshua trees on the valley floor. Along the escarpment are a few pockets of ponderosa pine.

BLM seldom even hangs out a sign to welcome visitors. We know of only three visitor centers elsewhere, and those are simple and unmanned. In 1982 BLM opened here a center fit for a National Park, with dioramas, films, literature, a native plant garden, and attendant naturalists.

Visitors travel a 13-mi. scenic loop that includes the visitor center, picnic sites, pullouts, and trailheads. The site map offers many destinations for short hikes, including White Rock Spring, La Madre Spring, Willow Springs, Lone Pine Springs, Red Rock Summit, Lost Creek Canyon, and more. Brownstone Canyon is noted as a wildlife observation area. Several areas offer technical climbing. Some trails are marked, but hikers head up any promising canyon.

Pine Creek Canyon has a permanent stream that creates a unique microhabitat: dense green vegetation including ferns up to 6 ft. high. It is a designated Natural Area with restricted use.

Most hikers are out just for the day, but there is plenty of backcountry to challenge the backpacker in the cooler months of the year. Most of the land beyond the recreation site is public domain. A ridge in the NW of the site leads into the Toiyabe National Forest (see entry) a short distance away.

INCLUDES: *Spring Mountain Ranch,* 528 acres, Division of State Parks. The state acquired this ranch in 1974. The main ranch house is now a visitor center. Weekend tours of the house and other ranch buildings are available. Day-use area.

Camping: Primitive campground with 15 sites. When we visited, it seemed little used and unmaintained.

PUBLICATIONS
Leaflet with map.
Wildlife checklist.
Spring Mountain Ranch leaflet.

REFERENCE: Hart, John. *Hiking the Great Basin.* San Francisco: Sierra Club Books, 1981, pp. 108–128.

SOUTH PAHROC RANGE
U.S. Bureau of Land Management
28,395 acres.

US 93 crosses Pahroc Summit W of Caliente. The site is S of US 93, W of the summit. Access by local roads.

About 7 mi. N–S, 2 to 4 mi. W–E. The South Pahroc Range has a single ridge rising to about 7,950 ft. elevation. Topography includes cliffs, hills, ridges, saddles, deepcut canyons, washes, drainages, and large boulder fields. The W side has a gradual slope; the upper part of the E side is steeper. Low desert scrub in the valley; pinyon pine, juniper, and scattered white fir stands on the high plateau.

Since we could not, during our field work or our lifetimes, explore all of BLM's 50,000,000 acres in NV, we relied on BLM's wilderness studies and other documents, taped interviews with people who had hiked the areas, and our own samplings. We crossed Pahroc Summit, looked S, and saw nothing remarkable. The BLM staff member who wrote the field reports was enthusiastic:

> . . . fantastic hiking opportunities . . . best backpacking challenge in the Caliente Resource Area. . . . Opportunities for secluded camping are endless . . . island in the sky. . . . Unique rounded rocks, columns, stone faces, balancing rocks and rocks which look like stacked bagels all offer interesting subjects for photography.

Access is said to be easy, on good dirt roads. Twin Springs, on the E side, is a recommended trailhead. The terrain on the E side is rugged, and "challenge" is a code word for hard going. Water isn't mentioned; the only streams shown on the map are intermittent.

Almost all the surrounding land is public domain.

Wildlife: Includes a small mule deer population. Occasional golden eagle, prairie falcon, other raptors.

SPRING VALLEY STATE PARK
Nevada Division of State Parks
1,630 acres.

18 mi. E of Pioche on SR 322. (The Park is in Zone 5, but access is from Zone 6.)

Between the Wilson Creek and White Rock ranges. Includes the southern part of Spring Valley and the canyon leading S to Eagle Valley. A perennial stream has been dammed, forming a 65-acre reservoir. The stream flows through wet meadows. A narrow foothills area ends in steep, rocky slopes with bizarre rock formations. Echo Canyon (see entry), 10 mi. downstream, receives about 8 in. of precipitation a year. Here the average is 12 in.; most of the additional amount falls as snow.

Local residents are the primary users.

TOIYABE NATIONAL FOREST, LAS VEGAS RANGER DISTRICT
U.S. Forest Service
58,039 acres.

From Las Vegas, 15 mi. NW on US 95, then 17 mi. W on SR 157.

Most of the Toiyabe is in Zones 3 and 4, and in CA. This unit is unique, unlike the other R.D.s or its surroundings, a mountain oasis. Although small, it is part of a much larger complex of public recreation lands.

The city of Las Vegas is in hot desert at 2,000 ft. elevation. Within sight of the city is 11,918-ft. Charleston Peak, green, forested, cool, less than an hour away over good roads. Not surprisingly, many people come here, most to take the 9-mi. Deer Creek scenic drive and walk out to the Desert View Overlook (wheelchair access). Many pause to picnic or take short walks. If they return via SR 156 and US 95, it's a 55-mi. outing. Hikers see much more.

Mt. Charleston is the highest point in the Spring Mountain Range, which extends about 50 mi. NW–SE. The mountain is at the range's midpoint. The R.D. includes this peak and 5 others higher than 10,000 ft. It is surrounded by BLM-administered public land. The Spring Mountains entry describes the N portion of the range. 2 mi. SE is the Red Rock Canyon Recreation Lands (see entry). Trails link these areas.

The Forest boundary is at about the 7,000-ft. contour. Topography is generally steep. Most of the area has slopes of 45 degrees or greater. There is almost no flat land, only gentler slopes on canyon bottoms, foothills, and alluvial terraces. The range is penetrated by short, narrow, cliff-rimmed canyons. The two best-known canyons are Kyle, where SR 157 ends at the 7,600-ft. contour, and Lee, where SR 156 ends at 8,700 ft. Both have cliffs with vertical drops of 500 ft.

The two access roads and their scenic connection are the only paved routes in the District. A few short dirt or primitive roads lead to inholdings and summer homes. Two-thirds of the area is roadless, backcountry to be traveled on foot or horseback.

When it's 100°F in Las Vegas, it's 85° or less above the 8,000-ft. elevation here. Average annual precipitation is 4 in. around the city, 11 in. on the Range's lower slopes, 28 in. or more on the peak. Most of this 28 in. falls as winter snow, but summer thunderstorms can bring heavy rains, with flash floods in canyons. As in most desert regions, annual averages mask the extremes of weather. Once 12 to 15 in. of rain fell here in two days. Snow depths of 15 ft. have been recorded, with an overnight fall of 50 in. Dangerous snow avalanches are possible.

Heavy public use has required that the District be managed more and more like a park. At the same time, the range is a vitally important water resource for the arid lands below, and public use must be so managed that this resource is not impaired.

Plants: Approaching the mountains, one is in the desert shrub life zone, characterized by cacti, yucca, and creosote bush. At 5,000 ft. the road enters the pinyon-juniper zone, which includes sagebrush and rabbitbrush. At the Forest boundary, this zone gives way to mountain-mahogany and oakbrush, with scattered ponderosa pine. Higher, the pine stands become thicker and the trees larger. Here the understory has such flowering species as bluebell, snowberry, and penstemon. The pine-fir community extends up to 9,500 ft., including white fir, quaking aspen, and limber pine.

Above 9,000 ft. is the most extensive bristlecone pine stand in the intermountain region, covering over 18,000 acres. Some specimens are thought to be nearly 5,000 years old.

Over 700 plant species have been identified in the Range, 27 of them found nowhere else, 22 others found only in southern NV. The spring wildflower bloom begins in May at the low elevations and continues through July and Aug. on high slopes.

Birds: No published checklist. 137 species identified. In the *pinyon-juniper woodland* and *chaparral* areas, permanent residents include great horned owl, northern flicker, scrub and pinyon jays, mountain chickadee, plain titmouse, common bushtit, Bewick's wren, robin, western bluebird, rufous-sided towhee. Summer brings many more species to this zone, including kestrel, band-tailed pigeon, mourning dove, screech owl, poor-will, common nighthawk, white-throated swift, Costa's hummingbird; ash-throated, dusky, and gray flycatchers; horned lark, white-breasted nuthatch, canyon wren, house finch, green-tailed towhee, rock wren, mockingbird, sage thrasher, blue-gray gnatcatcher, loggerhead shrike, gray vireo, Virginia's and black-throated gray warblers, Scott's and northern orioles, western tanager, black-headed grosbeak, lazuli bunting; black-throated, sage, chipping, Brewer's, and black-chinned sparrows. Many more are recorded as transients.

In the higher *montane forest,* permanent residents include goshawk, golden eagle, hairy woodpecker, Steller's jay, Clark's nutcracker, red crossbill, pygmy nuthatch, Townsend's solitaire, evening grosbeak, Cassin's finch, pine siskin. Summer residents include Cooper's hawk, flammulated and saw-whet owls, broad-tailed hummingbird, Williamson's sapsucker, western wood-pewee, olive-sided flycatcher, violet-green swallow, red-breasted nuthatch, brown creeper, house wren, hermit thrush, western bluebird, ruby-crowned kinglet, solitary and warbling vireos; yellow-rumped, black-throated gray, and Grace's warblers; gray-headed junco. Here too occur numerous transients.

Mammals: Common or abundant species include long-eared myotis; hairy-winged, big brown, red, and hoary bats; cottontail, blacktail jackrabbit; antelope, rock, and golden-mantled squirrels; Panamint and Charleston Mountain chipmunks, southern pocket gopher; canyon, deer, and pinyon mice; packrat, coyote, gray fox, bobcat, mule deer. A few elk, pronghorn, desert bighorn sheep.

Reptiles and amphibians: Few reported, these including western collared, western fence, and sagebrush lizards; striped racer, desert gopher snake.

FEATURES

Charleston Peak can be reached by the 17-mi. National Recreation Trail loop, from Kyle Canyon or Deer Creek.

Mummy Mountain, 11,532 ft., is thought to resemble a giant mummy recumbent on a plateau.

Kyle Canyon has 2 campgrounds, picnic grounds, some commercial facilities.

Cathedral Rock, 3/4 mi. from the Kyle Canyon trailhead, overlooks the canyon. Short trail to a viewpoint.

Deer Creek, on the scenic highway, is one of the few perennial streams. Overlook with wheelchair access.

Lee Canyon has campgrounds, picnic grounds, ski area, snow play area. Limited ski-touring opportunities.

ACTIVITIES

Camping: 5 campgrounds. 325 sites. May–Nov.

Hiking, backpacking: 7 marked trails. Longest is the Las Vegas Divide Trail, not fully completed in 1985, extending N and S from the Forest along the crest of the Spring Mountain Range. 16 mi. have been completed within the Forest. 8 more are planned. When BLM sections are completed, the trail will extend for 50 mi. The S extension will end at Potosi Mountain, crossing BLM's Red Rock Recreation Area. Over 20 mi. of feeder trails. Ask about the current status. Off-trail hiking is feasible in many areas, both within the District and beyond. Check at the Kyle Canyon Ranger Station for trail information and fire conditions. Bring water.

Hunting: Deer, upland small game.

Skiing, ski touring: At Lee Canyon; commercial.

PUBLICATIONS

Las Vegas R.D. map. $1.
Summer/winter travel guide.
Las Vegas/Charleston Mountain Tour Guide.
Mt. Charleston Travel and Vehicle Guide.
Managing Our Heritage.
Mt. Charleston map.

REFERENCE: Hart, John. *Hiking the Great Basin.* San Francisco: Sierra Club Books, 1981, pp. 108–128.

HEADQUARTERS: 1200 Franklin Way, Sparks, NV 89431; (702) 784-5331. Las Vegas R.D.: 500 E. Charleston, Las Vegas, NV 89104; (702) 388-6255. Kyle Ranger Station, on SR 157, is open mid-May to mid-Oct; (702) 388-6551.

VALLEY OF FIRE STATE PARK
Nevada Division of State Parks
46,000 acres.

From Las Vegas, NE 37 mi. on I-15, then E 18 mi. on SR 169.

This dramatically colored and sculptured area was once proposed as a National Monument. Ancient, predominantly red sandstone was uplifted, faulted, then carved by erosive forces into a fantastic array of gullies, pinnacles, columns, caves, and arches. The basic color is brick red, but some layers exhibit shades of yellow, lavender, brown, pink, and gray.

In other parks, notable features are often seen at a distance, from behind guard rails. Here, visitors become involved with the environment. Some rock masses are so riddled with holes as to resemble Swiss cheese. Behind the holes are caves, chambers large enough to admit children, often interconnecting at several levels. As small heads appeared and disappeared in these openings, we talked with parents who could not believe this wonderful play place had not been designed and built for the purpose. Grownups can participate, too, scrambling up ravines, disappearing into passageways and caves.

SR 169 crosses the S portion of the Park, passing many interesting formations. At `midpoint, a Park road goes N to the visitor center and other features.

Lowest point is 1,540 ft. elevation, the highest 3,677 ft. On the E the site adjoins the Lake Mead National Recreation Area near Overton Beach. To the W are the North Muddy Mountains.

At this elevation, the desert is hot and dry. Summer temperatures are usually above 100°F by day, seldom below 85°F at night. Oct.–May is the best time to visit. Easter Week sees the largest crowds.

Plants: Creosote bush community. Flowering species include desert marigold, indigo bush, brittlebush, jimsonweed, broom snakeweed, dune primrose, beavertail cactus. Best blooming season is Mar.–Apr.

Birds: Only a preliminary checklist of 30 species. Noted: loggerhead shrike, roadrunner, red-tailed hawk, rock wren, white-throated swift, gray vireo, raven, black-throated sparrow.

Mammals: Include antelope squirrel, blacktail jackrabbit, cottontail, desert kangaroo rat, deer mouse, desert woodrat, coyote, kit fox, ringtail.

Reptiles and amphibians: Include desert iguana; zebra-tailed, collared, and desert horned lizards; chuckwalla, western whiptail, desert tortoise, Gila monster, banded gecko, sidewinder, gopher snake.

Arthropods: In the fall, tarantulas on mating migration are often seen crossing roads.

INTERPRETATION

Visitor center: Exhibits, information, publications. Open daily 8:30 A.M.–4:30 P.M., except Christmas and New Year's Days.

Mouse's Tank nature trail, 1/2 mi. Plants and petroglyphs.

Guided walks in season.

ACTIVITIES

Camping: 2 campgrounds. 50 sites, including 12 walk-ins.

Hiking: No marked trails, but several washes offer good routes. Ask at visitor center. No trailside camping within the Park.

PUBLICATIONS

Leaflet with map.

Bird checklist.

REFERENCE: *Nevada's Valley of Fire.* Las Vegas, NV: KC Publications, 1979.

HEADQUARTERS: P.O. Box 515, Overton, NV 89040; (702) 394-4088.

INDEX

ABOUT THE AUTHORS

THE PERRYS, long residents of the Washington, DC, area, moved to Winter Haven, Florida, soon after work on these guides began. Their desks overlook a lake well populated with great blue herons, anhingas, egrets, ospreys, gallinules, and wood ducks, a nesting pair of bald eagles, and occasional pelicans, alligators, and otters.

Jane, an economist, came to Washington as a congressman's secretary and thereafter held senior posts in several executive agencies and presidential commissions. John, an industrial management consultant, left that work to spend ten years with the Smithsonian Institution, involved in overseas nature conservation.

They have hiked, backpacked, camped, canoed, and cruised together in all fifty states. They have written more than fourteen books and produced two dozen educational filmstrips, chiefly on natural history and ecology.

Their move to Florida marked a shift from international to local conservation action. They hold various offices in county Sierra Club and Audubon Society groups and the Coalition for the Environment. John is a trustee of the Florida Nature Conservancy.

The guide series keeps them on the road about three months each year, living and working in a motor home, accompanied by Tor II, a black Labrador.